DATE DUE

BRODART   Cat. No. 23-221

D1020039

GAINING ACCESS

American Politics and Political Economy Series

Edited by Benjamin I. Page

John Mark Hansen

GAINING ACCESS

Congress and the Farm Lobby, 1919–1981

The University of Chicago Press

Chicago and London

JOHN MARK HANSEN is assistant professor in the Department of
Political Science and the College, University of Chicago.

The University of Chicago Press, Chicago 60637
The University of Chicago Press, Ltd., London
© 1991 by The University of Chicago
All rights reserved. Published 1991
Printed in the United States of America
00 99 98 97 96 95 94 93 92 91   5 4 3 2 1

ISBN (cloth): 0-226-31554-1
ISBN (paper): 0-226-31556-8

Library of Congress Cataloging-in-Publication Data

Hansen, John Mark.
    Gaining access : Congress and the farm lobby, 1919–1981 / John
Mark Hansen.
        p.   cm.—(American politics and political economy series)
    Includes bibliographical references (p.   ) and index.
    1. Agriculture and state—United States. 2. Lobbying—United
States. I. Title. II. Series: American politics and political
economy.
    HD1765.H36   1991   91-12993
    328.73'078—dc20   CIP

For my parents and grandparents,
who lived it

Contents

Tables

Abbreviations

AAA   Agricultural Adjustment Act
AAA   Agricultural Adjustment Administration
AFBF   American Farm Bureau Federation
BAE   Bureau of Agricultural Economics
CCC   Commodity Credit Corporation
IAA   Illinois Agricultural Association (Illinois Farm Bureau)
MFA   Midcontinent (originally, Missouri) Farmers Association
NCCO   National Conference of Commodity Organizations
NCFC   National Council of Farmer Cooperatives
NCFCMA   National Council of Farmers Cooperative Marketing Associations
NFC   National Farm Coalition
NFO   National Farmers Organization
NFU   National Farmers Union
NPL   Nonpartisan League
NMPF   National Milk Producers Federation
USDA   United States Department of Agriculture

Periodicals

CG   *Country Gentleman*
CQWR   *Congressional Quarterly Weekly Report*
KAL   *Kiplinger Agricultural Letter*
NYT   *New York Times*

PF   *Progressive Farmer*
SF   *Successful Farming*
WDWF *Wayne Darrow's Washington Farmletter*
WF   *Wallaces' Farmer*
WFL   *Washington Farmletter*

Acknowledgments

I am deeply in the debt of many colleagues, who helped to stimulate my interest, refine my ideas and streamline my prose. First, David R. Mayhew, Steven J. Rosenstone, Edward R. Tufte and Stephen Skowronek oversaw the research from its beginnings as a vague idea to its initial completion as a dissertation. Second, Brian Balogh, John F. Padgett and Peter VanDoren pointed out small merits and major flaws that I hope I have addressed to their satisfaction. Third, Christopher H. Achen and the late J. David Greenstone read the entire study and helped me to appreciate its broader significance. Fourth, Gerald N. Rosenberg gave the benefit of his vast experience and wisdom. Finally, David R. Mayhew read every chapter (more than once) and offered comments remarkable for their thoroughness and insight. The generosity of my colleagues improved this book.

I am likewise indebted to institutions and individuals that contributed support and assistance. The Falk Foundation, the Dane G. Hansen Foundation and Yale University gave fellowship support. The Brookings Institution, where I enjoyed a research fellowship, provided a stipend, a home base, a lively set of colleagues and access to all of Washington's resources. Fifteen present and past participants in agricultural policy-making gave freely of their time, interest and information. The Oral History Research Office at Columbia University granted me permission to draw from their oral history interviews, and the Baylor University Institute for Oral History, the Minnesota Historical Society and the Association of Former Members of Congress gave access to their oral history resources through the Library of Congress. Earlier versions of chapter 1, parts of chapter 2 and parts of the Commentary and conclusions appeared in *Studies in American Political Development;* Yale University Press kindly allowed me to use the materials in this book. The

Department of Political Science and the Division of the Social Sciences at the University of Chicago provided time, resources and an unusually stimulating environment. James G. Gimpel and Bartholomew Sparrow assisted capably with the research.

John Tryneski at the University of Chicago Press was a skilled, supportive and persuasive editor.

My wife, Dana Saowalak, bore the spillover burdens of authorship with patience and good cheer.

My parents, Gerald and Joyce Hansen, and my grandparents, John and Sadie Hansen and Bill and Esther Larson, all Kansas farmers, experienced everything I have written about in this book. It is dedicated to them.

Introduction

This book explores the evolution of interest group access in the United States Congress. It identifies and accounts for the initial incorporation of lobbying groups into congressional deliberations; it identifies and accounts for subsequent change.

In doing so, it joins a time-honored debate over interest group influence in Congress, its degree, its nature and its source. One side, represented by Schattschneider, portrays lawmakers at the beck and call of powerful lobbies. The congressional system, he argued, fosters "a free private enterprise in pressure politics" that lavishes favors on the organized and ignores everyone else. Interest groups dominate congressional deliberations.[1]

The other side of the debate, represented by Bauer, Pool and Dexter, sees legislators substantially as free agents. Paradoxically, Dexter countered, the very volume of demands put on Congress limits the influence

1. E. E. Schattschneider, *Politics, pressures and the tariff* (New York: Prentice-Hall, 1935), pp. 30–31; David B. Truman, *The governmental process,* 2d ed. (New York: Alfred A. Knopf, 1971), part 3; Arthur Maass, *Muddy waters* (Cambridge: Harvard University Press, 1951), chaps. 2–3; Earl Latham, *The group basis of politics* (Ithaca: Cornell University Press, 1952); Grant McConnell, *Private power and American democracy* (New York: Alfred A. Knopf, 1966); Theodore J. Lowi, *The end of liberalism,* 2d ed. (New York: W. W. Norton and Co., 1979); Roger H. Davidson, "Breaking up those 'cozy triangles,'" pp. 30–53 in Susan Welch and John G. Peters, eds., *Legislative reform and public policy* (New York: Praeger, 1977). Models of "rent seeking" in economics have a similar cast. See, among others, George J. Stigler, "The theory of economic regulation," *Bell Journal of Economics and Management Science,* 2 (Spring 1971), pp. 3–21; Gary S. Becker, "A theory of competition among pressure groups for political influence," *Quarterly Journal of Economics,* 98 (August 1983), pp. 371–400; Sam Peltzman, "Constituent interest and congressional voting," *Journal of Law and Economics,* 27 (April 1984), pp. 181–210.

1

of pressure groups. Legislators receive far more advice than they can possibly attend, given the other claims on their time, attention and resources. "A congressman's own decisions [therefore] largely determine what pressures will be communicated to him."[2]

The disparity between these two views, between the selective reception of interest group demands and their presumed effectiveness, is the motivating puzzle of the book. How can interest groups be influential in congressional affairs if they simply broker information for their friends?

The key to the solution, I propose, is to adopt Dexter's means to Schattschneider's ends. As Dexter himself argued, "The complexity of the environment that seems to congressmen to rob them of initiative thrusts initiative back on them, for, when the demands on a man's resources clearly exceed his capacity to respond, he *must* select the problems and pressures to which to respond."[3] Limited in time, attention and resources, lawmakers cannot attend to all, but they must attend to some. The decisive stage of interest group influence, therefore, is the choice of the problems and pressures to which to respond. Lobbies achieve influence in Congress to the degree that legislators choose their counsel, to the degree that legislators grant them access.

This study examines that choice. Theoretically, it locates interest group access in lawmakers' strategies for coping with electoral uncertainty. Pressure groups, political parties and other informants offer them information and assistance, all purporting to do them electoral benefit (or at least to do them no harm). Lacking the time and resources to evaluate each situation afresh, however, members of Congress choose the counselors to which they ordinarily attend. Under what conditions, the study asks, will they rely upon interest groups rather than others, whether parties, staff, notables or rival pressure groups? Under what conditions will they make new choices?

Empirically, the study traces the evolution of farm lobby access to deliberations on agricultural price support policy, an arena in which

2. Raymond A. Bauer, Ithiel de Sola Pool and Lewis Anthony Dexter, *American business and public policy*, 2d ed. (Chicago: Aldine-Atherton, 1972), p. 414 and more generally part 5; Arthur Maass, *Congress and the common good* (New York: Basic Books, 1983), chap. 4; Robert A. Bernstein, *Elections, representation, and congressional voting behavior: The myth of constituency control* (Englewood Cliffs, N.J.: Prentice-Hall, 1989). Similar ideas suffuse theories of legislative "shirking" in economics. See, among others, James B. Kau and Paul H. Rubin, *Congressmen, constituents, and contributors* (Boston: Martinus Nijhoff, 1982); Joseph P. Kalt and Mark A. Zupan, "Capture and ideology in the economic theory of politics," *American Economic Review*, 74 (June 1984), pp. 279–300.

3. Bauer, Pool and Dexter, *American business*, p. 414, emphasis Dexter's.

changes in congressional consultation have often been dramatic. Absent in the early 1920s, close working relationships between the farm producer groups and the members of the congressional agriculture committees solidified in the late 1920s and early 1930s, and by World War II the bipartisan "farm bloc" was among the most potent on Capitol Hill. The period after the war, however, brought further change: the injection of partisanship in the Eisenhower and Kennedy years; the declining hegemony of the American Farm Bureau Federation; the rising importance of specialized commodity groups; and the mobilization and politicization of other constituencies, like consumers. Why did these relationships develop, the study asks, when they did and as they did? Why, moreover, did they subsequently change?

Throughout the book, the answers will be found in the varying terms of competition for congressional attention. Informants win access because their offerings, given identifiable political, social and economic circumstances, suit lawmakers' electoral needs better than those offered by their rivals. As the social context of elections changes, representatives choose new advisors, representatives reallocate access.

In sum, this study roots the evolution of interest group access in the decisions of political elites. It does so with explicit attention to the goals of elites. It does so with explicit attention to the political environments of elites. It does so with explicit attention to the alternatives of elites.

The attention to goals, to environments and to alternatives pays dividends. As a theory of evolution, it accounts for the ebbs and flows of interest group access over time in Congress. As a theory of development, it explains the presence and absence of interest group access across arenas in Congress. As a theory of choice from among alternatives, it clarifies the relationship between interest groups, political parties, and other advocates. It elucidates the inherent strengths and limitations of each as representative institutions. Finally, as a theory of elite choice from among alternatives in varying political environments, it pinpoints the source of interest group influence in Congress. Lobbies offer advantages, to be sure, but so do parties, other elites, other lobbies and other advocates. Lobbies gain access when, in the judgment of congressional elites, they represent constituents. They are influential because they determine the kinds of information about constituents that are available to legislators and the kinds of information that are not.

"Access to the legislature," Truman wrote, "is of crucial importance at one time or another to virtually all groups. Some groups are far more successful in this pursuit than others. . . . Some groups achieve highly effective access almost automatically, whereas it is denied to others in spite of their most vigorous efforts."[4] Understanding why some are admitted and why others are denied lies at the heart of my enterprise.

Plan of the Book

This study divides into two parts, each of which examines a significant change in the twentieth-century history of Congress, not only in agriculture.

Part 1 investigates the origins of interest group access. It explores the process by which interest groups succeeded political parties as the most prominent quasi-governmental actors on the congressional landscape.[5] In the theoretical account of chapter 1, accordingly, it creates a stylized competition for access between interest groups on the one hand and political parties and local notables on the other, and it specifies the conditions under which the former best the latter. In addition, it lays out a method for identifying interest group access and evaluating its antecedents. Finally, in the empirical accounts of chapters 2 and 3, it applies and tests the predictions with a detailed analysis of thirty years of political maneuvering over agricultural price support policy. Both chapters characterize the relationships between legislators and interest groups, identify points at which the relationships changed and determine whether changes in fact correlated with fulfillment of theoretical conditions.

Part 2 examines the subsequent evolution of interest group access. It explores the process by which interest group access developed and changed in the period after the New Deal.[6] Chapter 4, therefore, extends and elaborates the theoretical tools of chapter 1, generalizing the

4. Truman, *Governmental process*, p. 321.

5. Grant McConnell, *The decline of agrarian democracy* (Berkeley and Los Angeles: University of California Press, 1953); McConnell, *Private power*, part 1; Robert H. Wiebe, *The search for order* (New York: Hill and Wang, 1967), chaps. 2, 7; Samuel P. Hays, *The response to industrialism* (Chicago: University of Chicago Press, 1957), chap. 3; Richard L. McCormick, "The party period and public policy," *Journal of American History,* 66 (September 1979), pp. 279–98, esp. pp. 295–98; Louis Galambos, "The emerging organizational synthesis in modern American history," *Business History Review,* 44 (Autumn, 1970), pp. 279–90.

6. Hugh Heclo, "Issue networks and the executive establishment," pp. 87–124 in Anthony King, ed., *The new American political system* (Washington: American Enterprise Institute, 1978); Thomas L. Gais, Mark A. Peterson and Jack L. Walker, "Interest groups, iron triangles and representative institutions in American national government," *British Journal of Political Science,* 14 (April 1984), pp. 161–85; Jeffrey M. Berry, "Subgovernments, issue networks, and political conflict," pp. 239–60 in Richard Harris and Sidney Milkis, eds., *Remaking American politics* (Boulder: Westview Press, 1989); Richard F. Fenno, Jr., *Congressmen in committees* (Boston: Little, Brown and Co., 1973), epilogue;

argument to competitions between insider interest groups and other informants, most prominently other interest groups. Chapters 5 and 6 apply and test the predictions against the evolutions of access in agriculture since World War II. Again, they characterize the relationships between lawmakers and lobbies, identify points at which the relationships changed and determine whether changes corresponded with satisfaction of theoretical conditions.

The Commentary and conclusions review the main points of the argument. The chapter applies the theory in other issue arenas, considering the prohibition lobby, the small business lobby and the environmental lobby over time and across space. Drawing from the politics of labor, veterans and foreign affairs, it comments on the nature of the relationship between interest groups and political parties. Finally, expanding upon the themes developed throughout the study, it closes with a reconsideration of the source of interest group influence in the United States Congress.

A Synopsis of the Argument

In broad overview, the argument proceeds as follows. Fundamentally, chapter 1 argues, interest group access results from congressional strategies for dealing with electoral uncertainty. Lawmakers operate in highly uncertain electoral environments. They have an idea of the positions they need to take to gain reelection, but they do not know for sure.

Interest groups offer to help. In exchange for serious consideration of their policy views, they provide political counsel for members of Congress. They provide political intelligence about the preferences of congressional constituents, and they provide political propaganda about the performances of congressional representatives.

Interest groups are not the only congressional informants, however. Political parties, local notables, other interest groups and so forth offer the same types of services to legislators who pay them heed. Thus, lobbying groups are in competition with other informants for the loyalties of members of Congress.

Lawmakers grant interest groups access, then, only when circumstances fulfill two conditions: (1) when interest groups enjoy competitive advantage over their rivals in meeting congressional reelection needs; and (2) when legislators expect the issues and circumstances that established the competitive advantage to recur. Looking back, repre-

---

John T. Tierney, "Subgovernments and issue networks," paper presented at the annual meeting of the American Political Science Association, New Orleans, 1985.

sentatives study recent elections—their own and those of others—for indications of the issue and position advice that performed well and the issue and position advice that performed poorly. That is, they assess competitive advantage. Looking ahead, they evaluate the likelihood that the lessons of elections in the past will continue to apply in the future. That is, they assess recurrence.

Competitive advantage, in short, is an interpretation of the advice that helped legislators most in their past elections. Recurrence is a prediction that the advice will help legislators in their future elections.

In the mid-1920s, the empirical chapters of the study show, the agricultural lobbying groups proved their superiority to political parties in meeting the election needs of midwestern rural legislators. Elections demonstrated the broad popularity of their farm relief program and also demonstrated that advocacy on behalf of farmers allowed lawmakers to escape the factional battles in midwestern Republicanism. In the mid-1920s, moreover, the chronic agricultural depression convinced lawmakers that the popularity of the farm relief issue would not soon subside. In the mid-1920s, accordingly, members of the Agriculture Committee from the Midwest established strong working relationships with the farm groups.

In the early 1930s, likewise, legislators from the rural South created strong consultative ties with the farm lobby. First, the angry agitation for legal limitation of cotton production indicated the urgency and popularity of the measures the farm organizations demanded, securing the farm lobby's competitive advantage. Second, the pessimistic appraisals of the economic prospects of the Cotton Belt persuaded southern lawmakers that the electoral power of the farm relief issue was enduring. In the early thirties, accordingly, members of the Agriculture Committee from the South established close working relationships with the organized representatives of farmers.

The farm lobby's access to the Agriculture Committee continued undiminished for some twenty-five years. On the one hand, the New Deal agricultural adjustment programs institutionalized agrarian demands for government intervention. They institutionalized recurrence. On the other hand, the elections of the thirties and forties consistently ratified the positions of the farm lobby, first in favor of the farm subsidy program and later against the wartime price control program. They supported competitive advantage. The farm lobby's access continued because the underlying conditions did not change.

The conditions for interest group access, however, are general ones, as chapter 4 contends. Political, economic and social change alters the congressional environment, bringing with it new issues, new informants and new electoral uncertainties. Political, economic and social change, therefore, enhances the competitive advantage of some informants and undermines the competitive advantage of others. It induces the recurrence of some issues and circumstances and terminates the recurrence of others. Therefore, generally, lobbying groups gain and forfeit access to congressional deliberations as they win and lose their competitive advantage relative to rival informants and propagandists. They retain and relinquish access as the circumstances underlying their competitive advantage effect and fail to recur.

In the years after World War II, chapters 5 and 6 show, the distribution of access in agriculture changed markedly. In the late fifties, the American Farm Bureau Federation forfeited access to the House Agriculture Committee, first to the Democratic side and later to the Republican side as well. At the insistence of its midwestern affiliates, it committed itself to a controversial price support program, which the Eisenhower administration picked up and adopted as its own. The association with the Republican Party damaged the Federation irreparably. In elections in the late 1950s, farmers discountenanced Republican candidates and with them the Farm Bureau program. Elections, that is, exposed the depletion of its competitive advantage. In the late 1950s, accordingly, lawmakers took back the access of the American Farm Bureau.

Legislators redistributed access, selectively, to other claimants. On the one hand, in the early 1970s they denied access to the organized representatives of consumers. Angered by rapidly rising food prices, urban and suburban voters responded to attacks on the federal farm subsidy program, and congressional consumer advocates sought a place in agricultural policy deliberations. The consumer groups' opportunity, however, was short-lived. Food price inflation soon abated, and the issue died. The consumer lobby failed to gain access in agriculture because the circumstances that created its competitive advantage did not recur.

On the other hand, agricultural policymakers in Congress granted access to agricultural commodity groups. Specialized relative to their competition and consistently supportive of existing farm programs, the commodity groups represented the views of farmer constituents accurately, as elections attested. Collectively, they captured the central position in farm policy once held by the Farm Bureau.

The farm lobby as a whole, however, suffered a marked setback in the sixties, seventies and eighties. As people migrated away from farms, the agricultural organizations represented fewer and fewer constituents, even in the most rural districts. Thus, migration eroded the competitive advantage of every farm organization, and the responsiveness of the Agriculture Committee and the Congress declined.

From this synopsis, the theoretical and empirical aims of the study should be clear. First, the book builds a coherent theoretical account of how members of Congress structure their dealings with policy actors from outside of government—interest groups, political parties and others. Second, it assembles a body of evidence that traces the progress of those relationships and relates their stability and change to congressional evaluations of advantage and recurrence. Uncertainty, interpretation and prediction, it argues, are the behavioral processes by which social change effects political change.

I   THE ORIGINS
OF INTEREST
GROUP ACCESS

1   A Theory of Access

Members of Congress establish close working relationships with policy advocates; those advocates thereby gain access. Their good fortune contrasts with the plight of those denied access. The policy views of advocates with access receive consistent, serious consideration from lawmakers. The policy views of advocates without access do not receive consistent, serious consideration.[1]

Members of Congress grant access to interest groups when two conditions prevail: (1) when lobbying organizations enjoy competitive advantage over other intermediaries from Washington to the district; and (2) when members of Congress expect groups, issues and circumstances to recur.

1. David B. Truman, *The governmental process,* 2d ed. (New York: Alfred A. Knopf, 1971), chap. 9; E. E. Schattschneider, *Politics, pressures and the tariff* (New York: Prentice-Hall, 1935); E. Pendleton Herring, *Group representation before Congress* (Baltimore: Johns Hopkins University Press, 1929). For the style of the analysis, I am indebted to the work of David Mayhew, for its focus on reelection-minded members of Congress; to the work of Richard Fenno, for its attention to the mesh between lawmakers' goals and the constraints of their environments; and to the "new institutionalism" in economics, for its concern with efficient responses to conditions of uncertainty. See David R. Mayhew, *Congress: The electoral connection* (New Haven: Yale University Press, 1974); Richard F. Fenno, Jr., *Congressmen in committees* (Boston: Little, Brown and Co., 1973); Terry M. Moe, "The new economics of organization," *American Journal of Political Science,* 28 (November 1984), pp. 739–77; Oliver E. Williamson, *Markets and hierarchies* (New York: The Free Press, 1975), chap. 2; and Oliver E. Williamson, *The economic institutions of capitalism* (New York: The Free Press, 1985), chaps. 1–3. For a markedly different approach that also begins from the "new institutionalism," see Jonathan Bendor and Terry M. Moe, "Agenda control, committee capture, and the dynamics of institutional politics," *American Political Science Review,* 80 (December 1986), pp. 1187–1207. For a review of other studies, see Keith E. Hamm, "Patterns of influence among committees, agencies, and interest groups," *Legislative Studies Quarterly,* 8 (August 1983), pp. 379–426.

These two conditions are a direct result of congressional strategies for dealing with electoral uncertainty. Say that:

1. Legislators for the most part desire reelection.[2]
2. Lawmakers are uncertain about the issue preferences of their constituents, the salience of issues to their constituents and the effectiveness of various policy options for solving the problems of their constituents.[3]
3. Policy advocates—like parties, interest groups or local elites—offer to mitigate uncertainty by guiding the decisions of representatives. They give lawmakers information about constituent preferences and perceptions, provide technical assistance on policy questions and help to shape constituent evaluations to the members' advantage.[4]
4. The reliability of these informants is not known to representatives without cost.

Finally, say that lawmakers adopt strategies for dealing with uncertainty that work and discard those that do not. At worst, representatives who adopt unsatisfactory strategies select out of Congress; they fail to regain their seats. More optimistically, lawmakers draw lessons from their own campaigns and the campaigns of their colleagues.[5]

Close consultation with interest groups—granting access—is a congressional strategy for dealing with uncertainty. It is a policy of reliance on interest groups for advice and assistance. Lawmakers' attention to interest group cues clearly limits their responsiveness to the demands of others, like parties and local elites, and as long as current counsel is adequate, members of Congress, like most people, prefer to stick with what has worked in the past.[6] Consequently, the establishment of close ties between legislators and lobbies awaits the fulfillment of the two condi-

2. Mayhew, *Congress*, pp. 13–77.

3. John W. Kingdon, *Congressmen's voting decisions*, 2d ed. (New York: Harper and Row, 1981), chaps. 2–8; Richard A. Smith, "Advocacy, interpretation, and influence in the U.S. Congress," *American Political Science Review*, 78 (March 1984), pp. 44–63.

4. Smith, "Advocacy," pp. 44–63; Lewis Anthony Dexter, *How organizations are represented in Washington* (Indianapolis: Bobbs-Merrill, 1969), pp. 65, 130–31; Lester W. Milbrath, *The Washington lobbyists* (Chicago: Rand McNally and Co., 1963), pp. 220–25; Charles L. Clapp, *The congressman: His work as he sees it* (Washington: Brookings Institution, 1963), pp. 188–89.

5. Mayhew, *Congress*, pp. 70–73; Marjorie Randon Hershey, *Running for office: The political education of campaigners* (Chatham, N.J.: Chatham House Publishers, 1984), chaps. 2–5.

6. Mayhew, *Congress*, pp. 67–69; Richard F. Fenno, Jr., *Home style: House members in their districts* (Boston: Little, Brown and Co., 1978), chap. 6; Gary C. Jacobson, *The politics of congressional elections*, 2d ed. (Boston: Little, Brown and Co., 1987), pp. 77–86.

tions listed above. Representatives need indications that interest groups serve their information and propaganda needs better than other informants, that is, they need evidence of lobbies' competitive advantage. Second, legislators need indications that group advantage is sustainable, that is, they need evidence that the issues and circumstances that produced the advantage will recur. Let us consider both in greater detail.

Competitive Advantage

For legislators to prefer the counsel of lobbying groups to the counsel of other informants, interest groups must offer greater advantages or lower costs. This point is surely not surprising. As many others have noted, access rests on "mutual assistance." In exchange for influence on decisions, interest groups provide technical information on policy questions. They gather intelligence on constituents' receptivity to different policy options. They propagandize to create better images for their congressional friends.[7]

But interest groups have no monopoly on these resources. Nearly every outfit in Washington offers "advantages" to legislators who pay them heed. Thus, interest groups are in competition with other informants, and lawmakers must assess when interest groups are superior sources of information and propaganda.[8]

As a simple descriptive matter, of course, lawmakers often do not have to choose between interest groups and other informants. The loose discipline of American political parties and pressure groups allows members of Congress to balance demands at home, even if the sides are irreconcilable in Washington.

Even so, there are two good reasons to construct a theoretical choice. First, the demands that groups, parties and elites make are often enough in genuine conflict, and legislators must decide how to weight them. Analytically, then, the problem is still a problem of choice: lawmakers still must decide whose advice to favor and in what degree. Representatives choose advisers as if they are choosing one or the other.[9]

Second, the stylized competition between interest groups and other

7. See Truman, *Governmental process,* pp. 333–35, among others.
8. Truman, *Governmental process,* pp. 264–70, 321–51; Kingdon, *Voting decisions,* pp. 150–53; Raymond A. Bauer, Ithiel de Sola Pool and Lewis Anthony Dexter, *American business and public policy,* 2d ed. (Chicago: Aldine-Atherton, 1972), chap. 24.
9. See Mayhew, *Congress,* pp. 13–17; Milton Friedman, "The methodology of positive economics," pp. 3–43 in Milton Friedman, *Essays in positive economics* (Chicago: University of Chicago Press, 1953); and Armen A. Alchian, "Uncertainty, evolution, and economic theory," *Journal of Political Economy,* 58 (June 1950), pp. 211–21.

informants has its justification in the problem itself. It forces lawmakers to do theoretically what they in fact do empirically: choose. If representatives could always reconcile the wants of interest groups and others, they would never in any nontrivial sense act contrary to anyone's wishes. Interest group access is important, though, precisely because representatives meet the demands of lobbying groups *at the expense of* political parties, national leaders and perhaps the greater good. What really matters, then, is that lawmakers favor interest groups over others, especially parties. Asking why they do so is the point at which the analysis should begin.[10]

The choice lawmakers face has two main dimensions—efficiency and effectiveness. Interest groups prove superior counsel when they provide information at lower cost than their competitors or when they promote the electoral aims of their clients better than their competitors.

Cost efficiency. Some informants gain an edge by providing information and propaganda more cheaply and efficiently than others. They compete successfully in two ways. First, they reduce lawmakers' out-of-pocket costs by subsidizing intelligence and propaganda. Second, they poll and proselytize constituents more effectively. Two contrasts will make the cases clearer.

First, contrast interest groups and local contacts as conveyors of political intelligence. Networks of local elites are the creations of their clients. Lawmakers invest their own time and resources both to develop the networks initially and to use them subsequently. Interest groups, on the other hand, offer ready-made channels of communication between representatives and constituents. Lobbying groups, rather than legislators, create and maintain the intelligence and propaganda apparatus. Thus, interest groups compete with local notables by subsidizing the costs of communication, through formal organization.

Second, contrast interest groups and political parties as conveyors of political intelligence. Like lobbies and other formal organizations, parties offer ready-made channels of communication. Pressure groups, however, are far more specialized. They offer access to information and propaganda tailored to relatively homogeneous groups of constituents. The more prominent those constituents are numerically, the more attractive members of Congress find such targeting to be. Thus, interest groups compete with political parties by polling and proselytizing constituents more efficiently, through specialization and representation.[11]

10. For a little more expansive treatment of this issue, see Louis Galambos's comments on an earlier version of this chapter, in his "Comment" in *Studies in American Political Development*, 2 (1987), pp. 230–34, and my reply following it.

11. R. Douglas Arnold, *The logic of congressional action* (New Haven: Yale University Press, 1990), pp. 29–30, 64–71.

In sum, lobbying groups enjoy competitive advantage over other counsel when they are formally organized, specialized and representative of more numerous constituents. In serving legislators, they need do no more than avail their existing communications channels to their allies. Groups give politicians an efficient means to come into contact with people who may, depending on their political acumen, be useful in furthering their political ambitions.

Effectiveness. Some informants—especially party organizations—do more for representatives than act as mere conduits for intelligence and propaganda. They potentially mobilize voters. If interest groups are to enjoy competitive advantage over other informants, therefore, their counsel must work better at promoting legislators' reelection aims.

How do lawmakers (and researchers) know when pressure groups do better in promoting electoral goals? Mostly they learn from experience, in elections.

Interest groups, like political parties, offer their adherents electoral assistance. It may be, but it need not be, donations of money, personnel and exposure. When interest groups advise lawmakers on matters of policy, however, they in fact offer electoral assistance of three more subtle types. First, lobbies give their assessments of the issue position preferred by constituents and the intensity with which that position is held. Second, groups proffer an "explanation," or rationale, that they believe will pass muster with constituents, if lawmakers' actions are later challenged. Finally, lobbies give their blessing to an issue position, in effect forfeiting their right to criticize those representatives who support it. In short, pressure groups advise legislators about the likely behavior of voters. Other advocates do so as well.[12]

Elections, therefore, are tests of their predictions, and politicians read their outcomes as soothsayers read cards. "Even though the election result has many of the qualities of a blunt instrument," Hershey observed,

it remains the focal point of the race, and so campaigners try to learn more specific answers from it. Most commonly, they do so by constructing their own explanations of what the voters were trying to say with their ballots. . . . Campaigners have good reason to look for likely interpretations of the election results; if they can derive the most plausible explanation for why they won or lost, and why other candidates similarly situated won or lost, they can better understand how to increase their support with an eye toward the next election.[13]

12. Kingdon, *Voting decisions,* pp. 47–54; Fenno, *Home style,* chap. 5; Smith, "Advocacy," pp. 44–63; Dexter, *Organizations,* pp. 130–31; Arnold, *Logic,* pp. 49–50, 55–56. Even biased information is useful if lawmakers know it is biased. See Randall L. Calvert, "The value of biased information: A rational choice model of political advice," *Journal of Politics,* 47 (May 1985), pp. 530–55.

13. Hershey, *Running for office,* p. 95 and chaps. 2–5; Mayhew, *Congress,* pp. 70–73; Donald R. Matthews, *U.S. senators and their world* (Chapel Hill: University of North

If, after submitting the election to postmortem, they conclude that party regularity has failed them, or colleagues like them, they will more likely turn to other sources of support. If they conclude that lobby advice profited them, or colleagues like them, they will begin to favor interest group counsel over political party counsel.[14]

Most apparently, when lawmakers wish to dissociate from negative party images, they test out new alliances with interest groups. When the economy is sluggish, when the top of the ticket is unpopular and when the policies championed by the party are irksome, politicians de-emphasize their party affiliations and stress interest affiliations, substituting less dangerous identifications for more treacherous ones.[15]

Thus, interest groups enjoy competitive advantage over their rivals when they promote reelection more effectively. Their information and propaganda skills are put to the test in congressional elections, which in the interpretations of official Washington either endorse interest group claims or endorse the claims of alternatives.

Summary. In sum, interest groups enjoy competitive advantage over other informants:

1. When interest groups offer information more cheaply and efficiently. Groups that are organized, specialized and extensive reduce legislators' costs of political intelligence and propaganda.

Carolina Press, 1960), pp. 73–74; Lewis Anthony Dexter, *The sociology and politics of Congress* (Chicago: Rand McNally and Co., 1969), pp. 50–53, 71–75. This construction does not mean that interest groups leave everything to chance, of course. Most importantly, as representatives of identifiable constituencies, they sometimes dissuade challenges to incumbents by declaring themselves satisfied with incumbents' performance or they sometimes encourage opposition by proclaiming themselves disaffected. This reasoning draws from Gary C. Jacobson and Samuel Kernell, *Strategy and choice in congressional elections,* 2d ed. (New Haven: Yale University Press, 1983).

14. The source of these interpretations is beyond the scope of this study, but I will venture a few propositions about the kinds of criteria that influence them. First, politicians employ crude versions of Mill's method of agreement and difference. Common outcomes in constituencies that have characteristics in common raise policies relevant to the common characteristics as causal candidates. Second, politicians seek parsimony. Issues that pertain to characteristics common to greater numbers of outcomes are superior as causal candidates to issues that pertain to characteristics common to smaller numbers of outcomes. Finally, politicians give added weight to "representative" outcomes. Outcomes in constituencies that are more "typical" of a socioeconomic type are more influential in causal attributions than are outcomes in constituencies that are less typical of the type. See Austin Ranney and Willmoore Kendall, *Democracy and the American party system* (New York: Harcourt, Brace and Co., 1956), pp. 340–41; Richard Nisbett and Lee Ross, *Human inference* (Englewood Cliffs, N.J.: Prentice-Hall, 1980), chap. 6; and John Stuart Mill, *A system of logic* (London: Longmans, Green, Reader and Dyer, 1872), chap. 8.

15. Kingdon, *Voting decisions,* pp. 242–61; Anthony Downs, *An economic theory of democracy* (New York: Harper and Row, 1957), chaps. 4, 8.

2. When group advice works better in promoting the reelection goals of members of Congress. Elections that endorse group viewpoints rather than party regularity encourage close working relationships with lobbies.

Under these conditions representatives mitigate their uncertainty about the preferences of constituents, and thereby gain a greater measure of control over their destinies, by consulting with interest groups rather than others. But competitive advantage is useful to lawmakers only if it will carry over into the future. Reliance on interest groups for advice and assistance depends too on whether groups, issues and circumstances persist.

Recurrence

In their dealings with interest groups (and other informants), legislators operate at an acute disadvantage: the political dividends they receive for heeding interest group advice are not immediate. While pressure groups have an instant indication of lawmakers' performance of their end of the bargain, legislators have no immediate information about lobbies' performance of theirs. The value of lobby assistance is unknown to representatives until election day. Thus, members of Congress take advice under conditions of uncertainty. They aim to be on the right side of an issue in the *next* election, but they lack information about what the relevant rewards, the future rewards, will be. A popular and salient stand now is no guarantee of a popular and salient stand later.[16]

Given their disadvantage, when will lawmakers feel confident enough about the future value of pressure group counsel to put their faith in it now? Clearly, only when the future is predictable: when groups, issues and circumstances persist.

The importance of recurrent dealings with advocate groups is apparent enough. It solves one part of the strategic problem. If representatives expect their relationship with a group to recur, they know they may have the chance to retaliate if their ally deserts them. They know, furthermore, that lobbyists know this. Thus, legislators know that expectations of a recurrent relationship will constrain pressure groups from exploiting their immediate advantages. As one lobbyist put it, "I never take a momentary advantage to win a momentary prize. . . . Congress has no place for people who try to pull slick tricks. I have watched persons who operate that way come and go; it eventually boomerangs on all of

16. Arnold, *Logic*, pp. 10–13, 35–37; Bauer, Pool and Dexter, *American business*, p. 452.

them." Members of Congress prefer the counsel of groups only if they expect their dealings to persist.[17]

Expectations of recurrent interaction with interest groups solve only part of the strategic problem, though. Ultimately, lawmakers concern themselves less with the behavior of lobbyists than with the behavior of voters. In advising members of Congress, pressure groups offer predictions about the issues and positions that will be profitable in the next election. Even with the best of intentions, however, lobbying groups might fail legislators if their forecasts are wrong.

Consequently, if lawmakers are to grant access to pressure groups, they must also expect the issues and circumstances that produced their competitive advantage to recur.

The willingness of members of Congress to depend on lobbies depends, at base, on the extent to which competitive advantage now signals competitive advantage in the future. As politicians, legislators have their own workaday theories about the sources of political demands. The advantages that lobbies offer, they know, stem from particular sets of circumstances. Constituent agitation for particular policies and the payoffs from serious consideration of the views of their organized representatives derive from observable stimulants—from acute economic crisis, for example, or from presidential mobilization.[18]

Lawmakers use their theories to assess the probabilities that lobbyists' advice will prove useful in the future: how likely is it that these circumstances will persist and keep this issue important to constituents? If the circumstances seem fleeting, lobbies and constituents stand to lose interest in the issues around which lawmakers have built their accomplishments and campaigns. Lobbies seem unlikely to maintain their superiority in the future, when legislators most need it.[19]

If the circumstances seem recurrent, on the other hand, lawmakers stand to benefit from their attention to the policy concerns of lobbies. The issue remains alive. Consequently, pressure groups still have an incentive to work hard for their friends. Constituents stay primed to re-

17. Milbrath, *Lobbyists*, p. 291 and pp. 286–94; Robert Axelrod, *The evolution of cooperation* (New York: Basic Books, 1984), pp. 126–32; Williamson, *Economic institutions*, chap. 3. Recurrence helps to clarify the importance of a jurisdictional committee system with seniority rights to seats. In contrast to an ad hoc committee system, the committee structure that has evolved in Congress creates a stability of agenda and stability of membership that make recurrent relationships with interest groups more likely.

18. Nisbett and Ross, *Human inference*, chaps. 1, 6 and 9; David E. Price, "Policy making in congressional committees: The impact of 'environmental' factors," *American Political Science Review*, 72 (June 1978), pp. 548–74.

19. Anthony Downs, "Up and down with ecology: The 'issue-attention cycle,'" *Public Interest*, 28 (Summer 1972), pp. 38–50.

spond to appeals. Lobbies seem likely to maintain their superiority in the future.

Before politicians turn to alternative sources of political advice, in sum, they judge the likelihood that the superiority of new sources will continue into the future. Demonstrations of competitive advantage in the last election are simply not by themselves sufficient. Members of Congress do not care about the last election; they care about the next one. Recurrence allows the beneficiaries of interest group advice, legislators, to extrapolate rewards into the future. Said one representative, "You must be as smart in prospect as they [the voters] are in retrospect."[20]

Conclusion

Two circumstances must prevail before close relationships between lawmakers and pressure groups come about: competitive advantage of lobbies over other intermediaries and recurrence of groups, issues and circumstances. When these conditions hold, representatives have minimized uncertainty about their reelection and the reliability of those they depend on for reelection.

And what if the conditions are not met? Simply, the prevailing patterns of access in Congress will not change. Members of Congress, like most people, "are captives of their own pasts. Once they have a clear and well-publicized stance on an issue, they are loath to abandon it even in the face of 'pressure.' They have a share . . . of normal ability to rationalize expedient behavior, but there is a limit to every [lawmaker's] flexibility." Until representatives encounter problems sufficient to modify their evaluations of competitive advantage and recurrence, there is little urgency to innovate.[21]

After a brief explication of my methods, I will put the theory up against the history of interest group access to deliberations over agricultural price support policy. The agriculture committees of the House and Senate have long been known for their close working relationships with the representatives of organized farmers.[22] In agriculture, we see

20. Quoted by Clapp, *Congressman*, p. 178.
21. Matthews, *U.S. senators*, p. 224; Mayhew, *Congress*, pp. 67–69; Kingdon, *Voting decisions*, pp. 274–78.
22. Charles O. Jones, "Representation in Congress: The case of the House Agriculture Committee," *American Political Science Review*, 55 (June 1961), pp. 358–67; Randall B. Ripley and Grace A. Franklin, *Congress, the bureaucracy, and public policy*, rev. ed. (Homewood, Ill.: The Dorsey Press, 1980), p. 94; Grant McConnell, *Private power and American democracy* (New York: Alfred A. Knopf, 1966), chap. 7; Theodore J. Lowi, *The*

interest group access in its purest form. Its evolution, consequently, is especially instructive.

Even more interesting, though, are its subsequent changes. Deliberations over price support policy, bipartisan for over two decades, turned strikingly partisan in the late 1950s and early 1960s, then again turned bipartisan. After a generation as agriculture's leviathan, the American Farm Bureau Federation forfeited its lofty position in the postwar period, losing ground to a variety of more specialized rivals. Agriculture, long thought to be singularly resistant to change, has in fact seen quite important changes.[23] The theory should be able to account for them.

Finally, interest group access to farm policy constitutes a difficult application of the choice theory. Unlike many such ties, the close working relationships between the farm lobby and the agriculture committees did *not* arise because nobody really cared, outside of those most affected. As we shall see, agricultural policy was one of the most pressing political issues of three presidential administrations, and the Republican White House fought the farm lobby tooth and nail. Access in agriculture arose *despite* the contentiousness of the issue.[24]

In broad outline, the story of agricultural price politics goes as follows. The competitive advantage of the farm groups in the Midwest was ambiguous until about 1926, despite the creation of the Farm Bloc in 1921, despite agrarian unrest in the 1922 elections and despite the advent in 1923 of a well-orchestrated pressure campaign for the McNary-Haugen subsidy bill. The 1924 elections, however, indicated that identification with either faction of the Republican Party was quite dangerous, and the 1926 elections were a stunning victory for the farm lobbies. Thus, by 1926 the competitive advantage of organized agriculture in the Midwest was unmistakable.

---

end of liberalism, 2d ed. (New York: W. W. Norton and Co., 1979), chap. 4; Theodore J. Lowi, "How the farmers get what they want," *Reporter*, 21 May 1964, pp. 34–37.

23. Michael S. Lyons and Marcia Whicker Taylor, "Farm politics in transition: The House Agriculture Committee," *Agricultural History*, 55 (April 1981), pp. 128–46; James T. Bonnen, "Observations on the nature of national agricultural policy decision processes, 1946–76," pp. 309–27 in Trudy Huskamp Peterson, ed., *Farmers, bureaucrats, and middlemen* (Washington: Howard University Press, 1980); William P. Browne, *Private interests, public policy, and American agriculture* (Lawrence: University Press of Kansas, 1988).

24. The choice of agriculture was also fortuitous from a research standpoint, due to the topic's abundance of specialized research materials. Because of its size and diversity, the industry supported a large number of publications differentiated by functional audience, by region and by organization. The resources were fairly well indexed in the *Agricultural Index*. Finally, they were unusually accessible, especially in the collection of the National Agricultural Library in Beltsville, Maryland.

Expectations of recurrence originated about the same time. While a severe depression put the issue of price supports on the agenda in 1921, the depression, and hence the issue, was seen as temporary. In 1926, however, agricultural prices again collapsed after a short rally, and midwestern representatives began to see the crisis and the issue as permanent. With both conditions satisfied in the mid-1920s, midwestern Agriculture Committee members strengthened their ties with the agricultural lobbies.

Farm state lawmakers from the South lagged behind, but in the early thirties they too established close working relationships with the national farm lobby. Five years after expectations that the agitation for farm relief would recur came to the Midwest, the same expectations came finally to the South. Unlike those of the Midwest, agricultural markets in the South boomed after the War, and the issue had little urgency until the middle of the decade. In 1926, when a reversal of cotton and tobacco prices put the farm relief issue on the southern agenda, politicians took the reversal as momentary, as indeed it turned out to be. In 1930, however, the onset of the depression devastated the economy of the Cotton Belt, leading southern lawmakers to conclude that agitation for agricultural price supports surely was recurrent.

Likewise, five years after midwestern elections had indicated the competitive advantage of the farm lobby in the Midwest, events indicated their competitive advantage in the South. In 1931, a wave of angry agitation for the legal limitation of crop production swept across the Cotton Belt. The clamor for government intervention to control agricultural production and boost prices demonstrated to rural representatives the great extent of the popularity of the measures the farm groups demanded. Concerned lest the agitation get out of hand, lest the agitation throw out incumbents, southern legislators turned to the farm lobby for its ideas and its blessings. Long irresolute in their commitment to the farm organizations, southern lawmakers reversed themselves in the early 1930s. Assays of competitive advantage and expectations of recurrence won the farm lobby access to members of Congress from the South.

Throughout the 1930s and 1940s, the competitive advantage of the agricultural organizations increased, and expectations that the issue of farm price supports would recur solidified. The New Deal farm programs institutionalized farmer demands for agricultural adjustment, their very success convincing farmers that disaster would follow if ever the programs were terminated. The New Deal farm programs, moreover, helped the Farm Bureau to extend its membership into the South, establishing it as the leading voice of farmers in the South as well as the Midwest. Finally, elections in the Midwest and the South in the 1930s and 1940s consistently ratified the positions of the American Farm Bureau, first in favor of the agricultural adjustment programs, later in opposition to wartime controls on farm prices. Sensible Republicans and Democrats did not even consider trimming the farm program or tightening price controls. Republicans and Democrats who did, did not make it to Congress.

In the 1930s and 1940s, then, interpretations of competitive advantage and expectations of recurrence continued much the same. Consequently, policy interactions on the issue of farm price supports continued much the same. The House Agriculture Committee maintained remarkably close relationships with the farm lobby, especially the American Farm Bureau Federation.

Notes on Method

A systematic examination of interest group access in the United States Congress must come to terms with two central problems of empirical research. The first is measurement. The theory of access invokes three central constructs: interest group access, competitive advantage and recurrence. How might one recognize them empirically? What observable evidence indicates their presence or absence? The second problem is interpretation and causal inference. The theory of access identifies competitive advantage and recurrence as conditions sufficient for interest group access. Are they in fact jointly sufficient? What evidence supports the argument, and what evidence disputes it? What evidence corroborates alternative interpretations, and what evidence contradicts them?

Assessments of interest group access have rarely been self-conscious. Most often, researchers have inferred access from its consequences: lobby group access, they say, brings about public policies that deviate from the desirable. Explanatory theory, however, should not do double duty as measurement theory. In contrast, therefore, I identify access as a kind of congressional behavior—a particular inclination toward interest groups—and specify the observable dimensions of that behavior.

"Access" denotes a close working relationship between members of Congress and privileged outsiders—interest groups, political parties, promoters of causes. In granting access, lawmakers give serious, sustained attention to the policy views of their favored informants. Empirically, therefore, access refers to the status of outside actors in congressional deliberations. It refers, moreover, to the status conferred upon favored outsiders by formal actors, by members of Congress. Lawmakers consider the concerns of some actors legitimate, and they give them respectful hearings. Legislators regard the complaints of others as unwarranted, and they denounce or ignore them.[25]

I gauge the extent of interest group access to the farm policy debates by watching lawmakers and groups interact, most directly in the hearings conducted by the House Agriculture Committee on the major omnibus price support legislation of the post–World War I era. The transcripts of the hearings are the only *consistent* and *comprehensive* record of lawmaker and group interactions over the entire period of time.[26]

The technique makes use of one of the early discoveries of political science: that hearings often are less a forum for gathering information than a ritual for legitimizing decisions. Hearings are a stage show, and lawmakers are keenly aware of their role as actors. They curry the favor of those who are important to them; they feign interest in the testimony of those who can be ignored; and they pummel those they are expected to pummel.

That they do so should come as no surprise to those who have spent time in a witness chair. The favored know their good fortune. "We in the Farmers Union feel like we are a part of the Government," lobbyist Reuben Johnson told a House panel in 1969. "We feel very kindly toward this committee because we feel welcome here. You always listen to our comments, even though you may not act on them." The others sense their exclusion, keenly. "I appeared frequently at committee hearings," grumbled Benjamin Marsh, the head of a leftish prototype of the public interest groups, "but [I] could merely make the record."[27]

Neither should it surprise an academic audience. "Committee members themselves are participants in the struggle of contending groups," Huitt argued, "one phase of which is the public hearing. . . . [At the hearing,] a great deal of information was received from interested groups, which the senators accepted or rejected in accordance with their preconceived notions of the facts." Therefore, he concluded, "the per-

25. Truman, *Governmental process*, chap. 9.

26. In addition, where possible I make use of the other resources that do exist. For the more distant past, the most important sources are biographies and memoirs of public figures (more commonly senators than representatives) and oral histories, especially those interviews conducted by the Columbia Oral History Project. For the more recent past, the more important sources are again oral histories, especially those provided by the Association of Former Members of Congress, and my own interviews with former legislators and lobbyists.

27. *Hearings before the House Agriculture Committee, Subcommittee on Livestock and Grains*, "General farm program and food stamp program," 91st Congress, 1st session, Serial Q, Part 4, 1969, p. 1136; Benjamin C. Marsh, *Lobbyist for the people* (Washington: Public Affairs Press, 1953), p. 166.

ception of the fact situation by public officials might provide a useful index to their group orientations."[28]

In short, lawmakers are on display in congressional hearings, and their reactions to witnesses yield important clues about their relationships with those witnesses. Excluded groups confront hostile questions; irrelevant groups receive no questions; favored groups field softball questions. As patterns of access change, the policy views given serious consideration also change. The behavior of legislators toward particular types of witnesses moves from contentiousness to attentiveness to solicitousness. In each of the chapters, then, I present evidence from the hearings of the status of outside advocates in congressional deliberations.

Next, I turn to estimations of competitive advantage and recurrence. Both assessments hinge on appraisals by representatives and senators.

"Competitive advantage," on the one hand, denotes the superiority of one informant's advice over other informants' advice in promoting the electoral aims of congressional clients. Lawmakers infer competitive advantage from the experiences and outcomes of elections. Accordingly, I canvass representatives' interpretations of the meanings of elections, the issues that proved salient and the positions that proved popular, drawing primarily from the reports in newspapers, periodicals and specialized agricultural journals. Elections satisfy the condition of competitive advantage when legislators conclude that they uphold the predictions of particular informants. Elections leave the condition unfulfilled when legislators conclude that they do not.

"Recurrence," on the other hand, denotes the expected persistence of circumstances that heighten issue salience and stimulate constituent demands. Lawmakers infer the likelihood of recurrence from the nature of those causes. Accordingly, I identify representatives' theories of salience and demand and chart their estimations of the permanence of the causes, drawing again primarily from newspapers, periodicals and farm journals. Circumstances satisfy the condition of recurrence when legislators conclude that they are lasting. Circumstances leave the condition unfulfilled when legislators conclude that they are fleeting.

Finally, I assess the relationship between interest group access, competitive advantage and recurrence. Appropriate to the theory, the test is longitudinal. At each historical juncture, I compare the state of interest

28. Ralph K. Huitt, "The congressional committee: A case study," *American Political Science Review,* 48 (June 1954), pp. 340–65, quotations at pp. 364–65 and p. 364. See also Schattschneider, *The tariff,* p. 39; Herring, *Group representation,* pp. 92–93; and John W. Kingdon, "A House Appropriations subcommittee," *Southwestern Social Science Quarterly,* 47 (June 1966), p. 69.

group access to the degree of satisfaction of the two conditions. The evidence supports the theory to the extent that grants of access and fulfillments of conditions correspond in time.[29]

Temporal correspondence, of course, does not settle the issue of interpretation and causal inference completely. The analysis might be confounded by other causal conditions that occur together with the conditions specified in the theory. By means of various longitudinal and cross-sectional comparisons, however, I address and rule out plausible alternative interpretations of the same sets of historical facts, especially in the chapter conclusions.

Only at the end of the book, though, will the most compelling evidence for the theory be in. The theory of access, I show, explains the achievement of interest group access in agriculture, the denial of interest group access in agriculture, and the forfeit of interest group access in agriculture. Moreover, it explains the patterns of interest group access in other policy arenas, both across space and over time. The theory of access, in short, accounts for a diversity of outcomes that alternatives—systematic and ad hoc—are hard-pressed to match.

In the pages that follow, then, I focus on the dealings of the agricultural interest groups with the congressional agriculture committees. The goal is not a comprehensive history of agricultural price support policy.[30] Rather, it is an analytic history of interest group access in agriculture, at once a more specialized and more generalized objective.

29. See Joseph Cooper and David W. Brady, "Toward a diachronic analysis of Congress," *American Political Science Review,* 75 (December 1981), pp. 988–1006; and J. Morgan Kousser, "Toward 'total political history': A rational-choice program," *Journal of Interdisciplinary History,* 20 (Spring 1990), pp. 521–60. Although the evidence is qualitative, the underlying analytic model is the time-series quasi-experiment. See Thomas D. Cook and Donald T. Campbell, *Quasi-experimentation: Design and analysis issues for field settings* (Boston: Houghton Mifflin Co., 1979), chaps. 2, 5; and Louise H. Kidder, "Qualitative research and quasi-experimental frameworks," pp. 226–56 in Marilynn B. Brewer and Barry E. Collins, eds., *Scientific inquiry and the social sciences* (San Francisco: Jossey-Bass Publishers, 1981).

30. The best overviews are Douglas E. Bowers, Wayne D. Rasmussen and Gladys L. Baker, *History of agricultural price-support and adjustment programs, 1933–84,* Agriculture Information Bulletin No. 485, Economic Research Service, U.S. Department of Agriculture, 1984; Murray R. Benedict, *Farm policies of the United States, 1790–1950* (New York: Twentieth Century Fund, 1953); and Congressional Quarterly, *Farm policy: The politics of soil, surpluses and subsidies* (Washington: Congressional Quarterly Press, 1984), part 2.

2 The Origins of Access in Agriculture, 1919–1932

> New policies create a new politics.
>
> E. E. Schattschneider[1]

By the end of World War I the political potential of farmers had largely come to naught. Compared to industry, agriculture had received few tangible benefits from Congress, despite successive waves of farmer activism in politics. The future looked worse. In 1920, for the first time ever, the Census counted a larger urban than rural population. By 1919, farmers had already lost their greatest advantage, their numerical superiority, but they had little to show for it anyway.[2]

During the 1920s, however, the farmers' political situation began to improve. Congress had traditionally rebuffed agrarian demands for direct intervention in the agricultural marketplace—witness the fate of the subtreasury plan in the 1890s—but during the 1920s it approved price-fixing measures twice. "There is real basis for the statement," wrote one later observer, "that Congress passed more legislation on behalf of agriculture during the period 1920 to 1932 than during its entire previous existence." The reasons were evident. "Congress in recent years," wrote another observer, "has become more and more solicitous of farmer opinion."[3] The modern outlines of agricultural policy mak-

1. E. E. Schattschneider, *Politics, pressures, and the tariff* (New York: Prentice-Hall, 1935), p. 288.

2. For histories of earlier farmers' movements, see John D. Hicks, *The populist revolt* (Minneapolis: University of Minnesota Press, 1931); Theodore Saloutos and John D. Hicks, *Agricultural discontent in the Middle West, 1900–1939* (Madison: University of Wisconsin Press, 1951); Theodore Saloutos, *Farmer movements in the South, 1865–1933* (Berkeley and Los Angeles: University of California Press, 1960).

3. Asher Hobson, "The evolution of farm relief," *American Scholar*, 11 (Autumn 1942), p. 498; Donald C. Blaisdell, *Government and agriculture* (New York: Farrar and Rinehart, 1940), p. 36; Hicks, *Populist revolt*, chap. 7; Grant McConnell, *The decline of agrarian democracy* (Berkeley and Los Angeles: University of California Press, 1953), chaps. 1–7. Cf. James T. Bonnen, "Observations on the nature of national agricultural

ing, then, took shape during the 1920s, as lawmakers opened their deliberations to the farm lobby.

In more than one respect, the chronology is not surprising. In Congress, political parties and their leaders were already enfeebled by the onslaughts of progressivism. The progressives had curtailed the prerogatives of the Speaker and other majority officers of the House. They had fortified, by default, the power of the standing committees. They had starved party organizations of their patronage. Most important, however, as the succeeding pages will show, they had admitted new forces into congressional elections. With the introduction of direct primaries, reformers no longer had to lure voters away from ancestral party attachments. The battle for congressional loyalties, therefore, was met on terms more favorable to interest groups than ever before.[4]

Not until the Great War, moreover, did the farm groups establish a permanent presence in Washington. The Populists' fiasco had convinced farm leaders of the futility of partisan politics, and wartime price controls had underscored the need for a voice in the Capital. Hence, by 1920, four general farm organizations had opened offices there: the Farmers National Council, the National Board of Farm Organizations, the National Grange of Patrons of Husbandry, and the American Farm Bureau Federation.[5]

The Grange and the Farm Bureau by now are familiar, but the others, now defunct, are probably not. The first, the Farmers National Council, was a federation of several regional farm groups and the remnants of the "progressive Grange" movement, six state Granges alienated from the National Grange by its political timidity. The Council's association with the progressive Granges, its designation as Washington spokesman for the National Nonpartisan League (NPL) and its leader's passion for the single tax saddled it with a Washington reputation for radicalism.[6]

---

policy decision processes, 1946–76," pp. 309–27 in Trudy Huskamp Peterson, ed., *Farmers, bureaucrats, and middlemen* (Washington: Howard University Press, 1980).

4. On the congressional reforms, see Nelson W. Polsby, "The institutionalization of the U.S. House of Representatives," *American Political Science Review,* 62 (March 1968), pp. 144–68; and Steven S. Smith and Christopher J. Deering, *Committees in Congress* (Washington: Congressional Quarterly Press, 1984), pp. 18–25. On the factional use of primaries, see Samuel P. Huntington, "The election tactics of the Nonpartisan League," *Mississippi Valley Historical Review,* 36 (March 1950), pp. 613–32; Albert D. Kirwan, *Revolt of the rednecks: Mississippi politics, 1876–1925* (New York: Harper and Row, 1964), esp. chap. 11; and V. O. Key, Jr., *American state politics* (New York: Alfred A. Knopf, 1956), chaps. 4–6.

5. McConnell, *Agrarian democracy,* chaps. 1–6.

6. Alice M. Christensen, "Agricultural pressure and government response in the United States, 1919–1929," Ph.D. dissertation, University of California at Berkeley,

The National Board of Farm Organizations was a more conventional alliance. Its sponsor and patron was the National Farmers Union, whose president, Charles S. Barrett, dreamed of creating "an AFL of agriculture." The Farmers Union, the National Milk Producers Federation and a half dozen minor groups formed the Board in 1917; the Grange, although vigorously recruited, declined to join. In the end, however, the federation was a grand but empty gesture. The Board acted mostly as the lobbying arm of the Farmers Union and the Milk Producers.[7]

The establishment of offices in the Capital was an important step in the development of farm lobby access. Before then, lawmakers seeking to target appeals specifically to farmers had a bewildering 8,600 organizations from which to choose, including 559 in Illinois, 449 in California, 93 in North Dakota, and 2,203 in New York.[8] Working with the farm groups was hardly more efficient than starting from scratch. With the largest of the farm groups based in Washington, however, efficient mouthpieces for congressional communications were finally close at hand.

From the farm lobby's standpoint it was an important step as well. Before World War I, agricultural lobbying in Washington was desultory and casual, occurring only when a crying need arose and when leaders could tear themselves away from their farms. After 1878, for example, "the legislative task [of the Grange] was effectively promoted through the work of an annually-created legislative committee of the National Grange (usually the executive committee)." That committee, according to member T. C. Atkeson,

made a close study of all the bills which dealt with agricultural questions . . . [and] kept in touch with Congress through personal friends in Washington. . . . When any matters in which the farmers were interested were pending before congressional committees, they arranged for a date when we could be heard. Then the members of the committee would go to Washington.

Full-time Washington staffs freed the farm groups from their dependence on the vigilance of friends. Their presence in Washington gave

---

1936, pp. 13–15; J. Clyde Marquis, "The radical minority," *Country Gentleman* (hereafter *CG*), 24 April 1920, p. 26.

7. James H. Shideler, *Farm crisis, 1919–1923* (Berkeley and Los Angeles: University of California Press, 1957), p. 24; Commodore B. Fisher, *The Farmers' Union* (Lexington: University of Kentucky Press, 1920); Edward Wiest, *Agricultural organization in the United States* (Lexington: University of Kentucky Press, 1923); James L. Guth, "The National Board of Farm Organizations," *Agricultural History*, 48 (July 1974), pp. 418–40.

8. J. Clyde Marquis, "Farmers can have what they want," *CG*, 1 November 1919, p. 9.

them the capacity to monitor Congress, with corresponding benefit to their members and leaders. According to one contemporary observer, "national legislation is to the average agricultural citizen something afar off. . . .Hence, he relies for his information upon organizations like the Grange, the Farm Bureau, and similar bodies with representatives at Washington and to a degree acts on their advice."[9]

The Grange, however, was not the one to make the most of its new opportunities. Its move to Washington in 1919 made its legislative director, Atkeson, no more aggressive, and the "lobby acted as a mere clearing house of information and not as a pressure on Congress." In fact, Atkeson had little freedom to be more militant, even had he wanted to be. The Grange had debated the issue of a Washington office for years, often hotly, and the proponents prevailed over the traditionalists only with the argument that an office would keep "unauthorized persons"— probably the progressive Granges—from besmirching the Grange's good name. The move was hardly a mandate for hard-hitting advocacy.[10]

As a political organization, moreover, the Grange suffered an additional handicap: it lacked a broad geographical base. The Grange was the nation's largest farm organization, but its membership was concentrated in the quadrant of the country from Ohio northeast and in the Pacific Northwest. Its predicament was hardly unique, however. The Farmers Union was far more pugnacious, but its membership was just as limited. Once predominantly southern, the inheritor of populism was increasingly confined to the western Great Plains.

The American Farm Bureau Federation, united in 1919 and 317,000 strong, faced none of these problems. Its membership, while concentrated in the Corn Belt, was national, and its rapid growth in a period marked by little upheaval lent it stability and inclined it toward conservatism. The Farm Bureau was also bold. When a 1921 bill to retool the Muscle Shoals dam for production of fertilizer lost on a voice vote, for instance, it asked representatives to report how they had voted to Federation lobbyist Gray Silver. That impertinence caused Silver and president James R. Howard to be hauled up before the House Banking and Currency Committee, where a litany of Farm Bureau crimes was recited. One consequence of the uproar was a change in Federation tactics.

9. Charles M. Gardner, *The Grange* (Washington: National Grange, 1949), p. 93; T. C. Atkeson, "Pioneering in agriculture," *CG*, 14 February 1925, p. 49; Charles Moreau Harger, "Mr. Farmer considers his 'bloc,'" *Independent*, 24 June 1922, p. 541.

10. William G. Carleton, "Gray Silver and the rise of the Farm Bureau," *Current History*, 28 (June 1955), p. 343; T. C. Atkeson, "Pioneering in agriculture," *CG*, 21 February 1925, p. 12; "The Grange on politics," *Hoard's Dairyman*, 6 August 1920, p. 92.

"What will take the place of the lobby?" a *Country Gentleman* reporter asked prophetically. "Contact with the member of Congress through his own people—his constituents. . . . The Washington representative can act as a go-between on occasion. The Farm Bureau Federation has the means to establish this line of communication between Washington and the people at home."[11]

While Silver's methods seem commonplace today, in 1921 they were an innovation. At the time there were interest groups with lots of money but few members and others with members but no money. The Farm Bureau was one of the few with both, and Silver put them to good use.

The technique for exerting political pressure from the grass roots might have been devised earlier . . . but credit for perfecting it goes to [Gray Silver]. At his disposal were district-by-district tabulations of responses to public sentiment polls taken by county farm bureaus at the request of the headquarters in Chicago. . . .If a congressman seemed to be wavering in advance of an important roll call or if someone had the temerity to challenge the Farm Bureau's position, Silver did not hesitate to show him the poll results. In an emergency, he would telegraph directly to state and county offices and know that a flood of wires would pour into his office as evidence that the grass roots were informed and aroused.[12]

The Farm Bureau's pressure did not need to be as blatant as this implies. The efficiency of its political intelligence and propaganda was impressive enough. In 1921, for example, the Federation held hearings on farm distress in counties throughout the farm belt and presented the transcripts to the Joint Commission of Agricultural Inquiry, appointed by Congress to investigate the farm situation. They were marvelous in their extent and detail. "To one acquainted with agricultural conditions," a reporter wrote, "much of the matter contains nothing new. But as human interest documents these county hearings are unique."[13] The constituency resources at the AFBF's disposal were remarkable and unprecedented among agricultural interest groups.

With the farm lobby's move to Washington, then, the stage was set. On the one hand, party leadership was weakened by decades of reform.

11. J. Clyde Marquis, "The Farm Bureau's mistake," *CG*, 7 May 1921, p. 15; *Hearings before the House Banking and Currency Committee*, "Farm organizations," 66th Congress, 3d session, 1921; Robert P. Howard, *James R. Howard and the Farm Bureau* (Ames: Iowa State University Press, 1983), pp. 136ff. Muscle Shoals was the Federation's top legislative priority in 1920.

12. Howard, *James R. Howard*, p. 131; William Johnson, "Charting the Federation's course," *CG*, 24 July 1920, p. 15.

13. Harry R. O'Brien, "The farmers' woes," *Saturday Evening Post*, 22 October 1921, p. 21.

On the other hand, the farm groups were deployed with liaisons from Capital to constituency, channels that legislative allies might use to gather information and distribute propaganda. As the most wealthy, the most extensive and the most committed of the mainline farm groups, the Farm Bureau was the clear kingpin. To leave it at this, however, is to assume that a pivotal change in the relationships of legislators, lobbies and parties followed simply and directly from the fact of the Farm Bureau's organization. It did not. Before the farm lobbies could claim the allegiance of rural lawmakers, legislators needed convincing. They needed to know what the farm organizations could do for them and how they stacked up against the competition, political parties and local elites. Moreover, they needed to know if the advantages were lasting or if they would pass. An extended process of comparison and forecast, that is, had first to play out, before the farm lobby gained access.

Prologue: The Farm Bloc

By the accounts of many, the new, aggressive Farm Bureau was the impetus behind the organization of the bipartisan Farm Bloc, a coalition that looked outwardly like an extraordinary form of interest group access. The Senate Farm Bloc was organized in May 1921, at a meeting of nine senators in Gray Silver's AFBF office. Chaired by Iowa senator William S. Kenyon, a Republican, it claimed up to thirty members at its peak. Its House counterpart, led by Iowa Republican Lester J. Dickinson, was less well organized, and while some accounts put its membership at one hundred or more, the only extant rosters, including J. R. Howard's, list only twenty-eight.[14]

The Bloc did little until late in June of 1921, when Senate leaders tried to adjourn until the House passed a tariff bill. The Senate had not yet acted on any of the twelve measures the Bloc deemed important, and the tariff bill was sure to take precedence once the Senate reconvened. Forewarned by his allies, Silver wired local farm bureaus, and the resulting flurry of protesting telegrams helped to defeat the motion. President

14. Moreover, only four of the twenty-one members of the House Agriculture Committee (plus two future members) were on Farm Bloc rolls, none of them senior. The Senate Bloc, however, listed a majority of the Senate Committee. See "Howard explains agricultural bloc," *American Farm Bureau Federation Weekly News Letter,* 5 January 1922, p. 1; "The agricultural bloc," *Agricultural Review,* January 1922, p. 11; "Farm Bloc," *Bureau Farmer,* January 1931, p. 9; Christensen, "Agricultural pressure," p. 62; Orville M. Kile, *The Farm Bureau through three decades* (Baltimore: Waverly Press, 1948), p. 101n. Throughout the book, I reserve the term "Farm Bloc," capitalized, for the formal body organized in the Sixty-seventh Congress in 1921. I use the term "farm bloc" to refer to the informal alliances of farm state lawmakers in later years.

Harding and the Republican leadership made one more try at adjournment; then they cut a deal. The Bloc agreed to recess once the Senate passed six pending agricultural bills, the most significant of which regulated the packers and the grain exchanges and extended the authority of the War Finance Corporation to make agricultural loans. The compromise got extensive coverage in the press. The Farm Bloc became "the most effective organized force in Congress." "Party leaders and the President himself do not venture a move without consulting it."[15]

The Farm Bloc's successful defiance of party leadership was a dramatic indication of what rural lawmakers and the farm groups could achieve through joint action, and the lesson was not lost on them. For the rest of the decade, re-creation of the Farm Bloc would be the farm lobby's holy grail. But although the Farm Bureau was eager to tell the Farm Bloc story in the most flattering terms possible—later news accounts give Silver a much more prominent role than earlier ones—farm state representatives were reluctant to push things too far. The coalition, after all, had won but a single battle—the adjournment vote—over an opposition it had taken by surprise, and the GOP leadership had supported the passage of the agricultural legislation as part of the deal.[16]

Without any evidence that the Farm Bureau could protect them, rural representatives sought not to invite retaliation from party leaders. Accordingly, the senators and representatives involved, while keen to take credit, went to great pains to minimize the coalition's significance. GOP senator Arthur Capper of Kansas, once described as "the one man in Congress physically able to keep both of his ears on the ground," denied that the Bloc in fact threatened the parties. "We simply try," the senator said, "like a big steering committee, to get cooperation in support of measures of common interest, nobody breaking from his political associations." Thus, the Bloc took no position on the tariff, being careful not to jeopardize its members' standing in their parties. Minnesota congressman Sydney Anderson echoed Capper's assessment. "The thing was too loosely organized and informal for such purposes [as disrupting party leadership]. In fact, its own members didn't consider it a definite organization of any sort." Bloc members compared themselves to the irrigation bloc, the veterans' bloc, and the vaunted "baby" congressmen's (i.e., freshman) bloc.[17]

15. John K. Barnes, "The man who runs the Farm Bloc," *World's Work*, November 1922, p. 52; Theodore M. Knappen, "Farmers in the saddle," *Independent*, 12 November 1921, p. 151.

16. "The farmers' party in Congress," *Literary Digest*, 2 July 1921, p. 14; Alastair Montgomery, "Ferreted facts for farmers," *Successful Farming*, July 1921, p. 8.

17. Stuart O. Blythe, "Progress in Congress," *CG*, March 1926, p. 17; Judson C. Welliver, "The agricultural crisis and the 'Bloc,'" *American Review of Reviews*, February

The Farm Bloc continued its operations in the second session of the Sixty-seventh Congress, but under Capper's leadership—Kenyon had accepted an appointment to the federal bench—it turned into a bipartisan discussion group. It consulted with all the major farm groups, except perhaps the Farmers National Council, and over the next two years it heard from speakers ranging from Agriculture Secretary Henry C. Wallace to Thomas Edison, who, as it turns out, had his own farm plan. After its dramatic victory in 1921, the Bloc accomplished nothing else, and in the Sixty-eighth Congress, in 1923, no one even attempted to reorganize it.[18]

The Farm Bloc, then, was the first indication to agrarian legislators that the farm lobby might be useful for pursuing their policy agendas independent of the parties. From the congressional standpoint, though, there were good reasons why lawmakers did not try to maintain their momentary freedom from the parties. As yet, one condition for interest group access, competitive advantage, was met only ambiguously, and the second, recurrence, was not met at all.

For one thing, representatives did not expect Farm Bloc issues to keep coming up. After the major items on the Farm Bloc's agenda— regulation of packers, grain exchanges, milk distributors and so forth— were passed, "the fighting strength of the group necessarily decreased," and only six months after its great victory, it ran out of things to do. "Both Democratic and Republican Senators who are bloc members said today that there was at present little legislative business which seemed to require the attention of the bloc," the New York Times reported. "Some Republicans believe that some of the strictly 'bloc measures' already have been translated into legislation."[19]

1922, p. 165; Sydney Anderson, "The latest thing in blocs," CG, 31 December 1921, p. 1; Barnes, "The man who runs the Farm Bloc," p. 59; Arthur Capper, The agricultural bloc (New York: Harcourt, Brace & Co., 1922), p. 117; "The Farm Bloc," Literary Digest, 24 December 1921, p. 11. According to more radical senators, there was truth in Capper's protests. Nebraska senator George W. Norris and South Dakota senator Peter Norbeck, both insurgents, regarded the Bloc as a cover for more conservative farm state senators. "It remains to be seen," Norbeck commented wryly about Capper, "how long a man can be a lion in Kansas and a lamb in Washington." See Richard Lowitt, George W. Norris: The persistence of a progressive (Urbana: University of Illinois Press, 1971), pp. 172–74; and Gilbert C. Fite, Peter Norbeck: Prairie statesman (Columbia: University of Missouri Press, 1948), pp. 104–6, quotation at p. 106.

18. Shideler, Farm crisis, pp. 178–79; Capper, Agricultural bloc, p. 146; Homer E. Socolofsky, Arthur Capper: Publisher, politician, and philanthropist (Lawrence: University of Kansas Press, 1962), chap. 14.

19. McConnell, Agrarian democracy, p. 58; "Farm Bloc stays," New York Times (hereafter NYT), 17 February 1922, p. 28; "Congress and the farmer," Wallaces' Farmer (hereafter WF), 2 September 1921, p. 1110.

Doubts that Farm Bloc issues would recur stemmed as well from sanguine appraisals of the farm economy. The agricultural crisis that gave rise to agrarian agitation and the Bloc, nearly everyone thought, would surely be short-lived, even if severe.

Back in 1921 legislators had every reason to be attentive to farmer opinion. Just after the Armistice, the bottom fell out of the grain markets. Wheat prices cascaded from $2.16 a bushel in 1919 to $1.03 in 1921, and corn plunged from $1.51 to 52 cents. More than half a million people left farms in 1921, followed by another million in 1922 and eight hundred thousand in 1923. Clearly, the farm crisis ran deeper than wanderlust at having seen Paris.

While farm depressions were dangerous, however, they were also nothing new. In the 1870s and 1880s, price collapses and bank panics had fomented rural protest, but it had surged and subsided quickly. Thus, the *Times* was inclined to take the Bloc lightly. "It will pass with the depression from which it sprang," the editors forecast, "like the Wheel, the Brothers of Freedom, the Society of Equity, the Farmers Alliance, the Greenbackers and other shadows."[20]

Unsympathetic urban newspaper editors were not the only ones who saw the crisis as fleeting. Before 1925, the depression was widely viewed as the consequence, in Secretary Wallace's words, of "this period of world readjustment" after the War. Wallace had no doubt that "gradually farm prices will be brought into fair relation with other prices," and he and his administration rival, Commerce Secretary Herbert Hoover, predicted shortages rather than surpluses in the future. By 1923, most thought the worst was over. "The pendulum has apparently reached the limit of its swing to the losing side and is coming back," Senator Capper asserted. A "phenomenal rise in agricultural prices [is] likely," another observer agreed.[21]

In the early 1920s, then, there was no hint that agricultural relief was a recurrent problem. The consensus held that the farm crisis would soon be over and with it the need for close attention to rural voices. There was no impulsion, in short, toward close consultation with farm spokesmen. As Representative Anderson diagnosed it, "the farm bloc came into ex-

---

20. "The Farm Bloc," *Literary Digest,* p. 10.

21. "The farmer and his troubles," *Current History,* November 1921, pp. 237, 235; "Doing something for the farmer," *Literary Digest,* 13 October 1923, p. 14; David Friday, "The recovery of agriculture," *American Review of Reviews,* August 1923, p. 182; "Getting the farmer back on his feet," *WF,* 14 December 1923, p. 1671; Herbert C. Hoover, "Some notes on agricultural readjustment and the high cost of living," *Saturday Evening Post,* 10 April 1920, p. 4; Donald L. Winters, *Henry Cantwell Wallace as Secretary of Agriculture, 1921–1924* (Urbana: University of Illinois Press, 1970), p. 71.

istence as an emergency means for handling some of the legislative features of this great and most unusual agricultural emergency. . . . When the cementing force of the group disappeared, the group itself dissolved."[22]

The indications that producer groups might enjoy a competitive advantage over political parties or personal networks were more ambiguous. The 1920 election was a Republican landslide, and while resentment against wartime controls on commodity prices may have been the specific agrarian animus, the rural response did not differ much from that of the rest of the country. In 1920, "a well-defined farm vote had not yet become an object of public alarm."[23]

In 1922, however, the Republicans lost back most of what they had gained in 1920—seventy-six seats in the House and eight in the Senate. On the face of it, farm radicals had engineered a great victory, electing four new senators with impressive agrarian credentials—Lynn J. Frazier in North Dakota, Henrik Shipstead in Minnesota, Smith W. Brookhart in Iowa, and R. B. Howell in Nebraska. Minnesota's Magnus Johnson joined them a year later, prompting *Capper's Weekly* to opine that "Magnus Johnson, Henrik Shipstead, and Brookhart owe their elections more to the ills of the agricultural situation and their extravagant promises to redeem it than anything else."[24]

But Senator Capper's mouthpiece was almost alone in this interpretation. Shortly before the general election, the *Times,* cognizant if not omniscient, foresaw large GOP losses but made no mention of rural discontent, except in Kansas, where Governor Henry J. Allen faced a tax revolt. Another reporter noted that "strenuous efforts have been made to unite the farmers in political action. Conferences have been held and propaganda distributed through every possible channel." But, he added, "the efforts have resulted in no cohesive action. . . . The present campaign and the election will see no organized revolt on the part of the producer . . . except where local conditions affect isolated candidates."[25]

So amorphous was the agrarian unrest, then, that the radical victories in the Midwest seemed each to have its own theme. In Minnesota, where the endorsees of the new Farmer-Labor Party turned out two Republican representatives and one Republican senator, agricultural issues

22. Anderson, "Latest thing," pp. 2, 21.
23. Shideler, *Farm crisis,* p. 30.
24. "Doing something for the farmer," *Literary Digest,* p. 14.
25. "Republicans facing fight to hold House," *NYT,* 7 May 1922, p. II 1; "Apathy of voters clouds election," *NYT,* 5 November 1922, p. 1; Charles Moreau Harger, "Will producers stage a revolt?" *Independent,* 14 October 1922, pp. 199–200.

were most clearly decisive. From there, however, the picture turned cloudy. In Nebraska, the farm crisis touched off a stampede of agrarian candidates, but Republican R. B. Howell capitalized on prohibition and isolationism to defeat Democratic senator Gilbert Hitchcock, a "wet" and a proponent of the League of Nations. In Iowa, Republican Smith Brookhart ignored his opponent and stepped up his attack on the railroad rate guarantees of the Esch-Cummins Act, the handiwork of his Republican rival, senior senator Albert Cummins. In North Dakota, finally, Nonpartisan League Republican Lynn Frazier, removed from the statehouse by recall only a year earlier, had the good fortune to run against stalwart Republican Porter J. McCumber, a twenty-three-year veteran whose mistake was to have put his name, as Finance Committee chairman, on the 1921 Fordney-McCumber Tariff Act.[26]

The 1922 elections, then, were hardly an endorsement of the Farm Bloc or its program, such as it was. In the House, five of the Farm Bloc's twenty Republican members lost their bids for reelection, a proportion no different from that of Republicans generally. As columnist Mark Sullivan wrote in November, "there is no angrier man in the country than the western farmer."[27] His anger, however, was remarkably unfocused.

Rather than a victory for farmers, therefore, the 1922 elections were interpreted as a victory for progressives over the GOP old guard. The *Times,* for example, noted that half the Republican House losses occurred east of Ohio, signifying that the outcome was the result of forces more broad than a farm revolt. It offered the victories of two Republican progressive warhorses, Gifford Pinchot in Pennsylvania's gubernatorial contest and Albert Beveridge in Indiana's senatorial primary, as evi-

26. Chester H. Rowell, "Why the Middle West went radical," *World's Work,* June 1923, pp. 612–22; Chester H. Rowell, "The political cyclone in North Dakota," *World's Work,* July 1923, pp. 265–74; Chester H. Rowell, "La Follette, Shipstead, and the embattled farmers," *World's Work,* August 1923, pp. 408–20; Chester H. Rowell, "Brookhart, Howell, and 'Brother Charlie' Bryan," *World's Work,* September 1923, pp. 478–85; "Panicky Old Guard Senators," *NYT,* 28 May 1922, p. VII 4; "New personalities in the Senate," *NYT,* 12 November 1922, p. IX 1; Frederick C. Luebke, "Political response to agricultural depression in Nebraska, 1922," *Nebraska History,* 47 (March 1966), pp. 15–55; Patrick G. O'Brien, "Senator Robert B. Howell: A midwestern progressive and insurgent during 'normalcy,'" *Emporia State Research Studies,* 19 (December 1970), pp. 6, 13. For more on Brookhart's appeal, see Jerry A. Neprash, *The Brookhart campaigns in Iowa* (New York: Columbia University Press, 1932), and Reinhard H. Luthin, "Smith Wildman Brookhart of Iowa," *Agricultural History,* 25 (October 1951), pp. 187–97. Both Brookhart and Johnson were farmers, and both had long associations with the radical farm groups. The Equity encouraged Johnson to run for office in the 1910s, and the Farmers Union was an early backer of Brookhart. See Magnus Johnson, "The farmer in politics," *CG,* 29 March 1924, p. 1, and Neprash, *Brookhart campaigns,* pp. 32–34.

27. Luebke, "Political response," p. 15.

dence that the stalwarts were on the defensive. Legislators put things in the same terms. The *Country Gentleman* overheard one representative say to another, "It's open season for the fellow who promises most. All of us regulars are up against tough going." Replied the second, "Well, maybe so. . . . But if any son of a gun in my district thinks he can out-promise me this fall, man alive, he will have to lie some."[28]

Agrarian discontent, then, contributed to part, but not the whole, of a progressive revival. In 1923, the "La Follette group" of insurgent Republicans settled into the congressional catbird's seat, displacing the Farm Bloc, and the title of the farmer's best friend passed from the farm lobby's champions to the insurgents. "The farm bloc today," concluded *Country Gentleman*, "is threatened with disruption and political impotence by the very situation it created. . . . Doing something for the farmer has become too much a political asset to be left to the farm organizations." The "radical bloc" had more or less absorbed the agricultural bloc.[29]

Thus, the disinclination of Congress's rural lawmakers to reformulate the Farm Bloc in 1923 had a rational basis. First, the 1922 elections had not shown that the agricultural lobbies could do something for them; for Republicans, the way to avoid defeat in 1922 was not to be a friend of the farmer but to be a progressive. Likewise, the farm groups had not yet come up with an issue—not even as diffuse an issue as farm relief—that would demand consistent congressional attention instead of mere appeasement. What the farm groups needed was an issue that farmers would mobilize around, an issue that would keep them in legislators' consciousness. The equalization fee was that issue.

Courtship: The Early Campaign for the Equalization Fee

Before the advent of the equalization fee, agricultural price-fixing was an issue for radicals, and the mainline farm groups and most of Congress kept it at arm's length. In January 1922, for instance, the House Agriculture Committee took up two proposals for federal price-fixing.

28. "East gave Democrats most gains in House," *NYT*, 15 November 1922, p. 2; Willard M. Kiplinger, "Future of Farm Bloc a Washington riddle," *NYT*, 18 May 1924, p. VII 20; Roy A. Roberts, "Windbags and ostriches," *CG*, 14 October 1922, p. 11.

29. Roy A. Roberts, "Everybody loves the farmer," *CG*, 6 January 1922, p. 13; Clarence Poe, "The world's news," *Progressive Farmer*, Raleigh ed. (hereafter *PF*), 2 December 1922, p. 1011; "Washington dazed by big reversal," *NYT*, 9 November 1922, p. 1; Kiplinger, "Future of Farm Bloc," p. VII 20; Winters, *Wallace*, p. 90; Joan Hoff Wilson, "Herbert Hoover's agricultural policies, 1921–1928," pp. 115–42 in Ellis W. Hawley, ed., *Herbert Hoover as Secretary of Commerce* (Iowa City: University of Iowa Press, 1981), p. 142n.

Both were sponsored by participants in the Farm Bloc—Charles A. Christopherson, a Republican from South Dakota, and James H. Sinclair, an NPL-Republican from North Dakota—but the bills were not Farm Bloc measures. In fact, the Bloc and the farm organizations themselves were deeply split over them.[30]

On the whole, the Agriculture Committee was not very interested in the schemes, although it ultimately reported the Christopherson bill. Except for Sinclair, even the most open-minded committee members voiced their doubts about price-fixing. Wisconsin Republican Edward Voigt worried about the cost; Texas Democrat Marvin Jones worried about the stimulus to production. Nebraska Republican Melvin McLaughlin admitted that he had looked into price-fixing, but he questioned where it stopped. Unlike the Senate Agriculture Committee, which was dominated by western progressives and led by Nebraska senator George W. Norris, the House Committee was not naturally friendly to government intervention.[31]

Neither were the major farm groups. The Farm Bureau, the Grange and the National Board of Farm Organizations stayed clear of the House hearings, but Gray Silver later sent a letter detailing the fallacy of price-fixing. The only farm group leader to appear before the House Committee was Benjamin C. Marsh of the Farmers National Council, which favored the Sinclair bill. Marsh's right to speak for producers was easily dismissed, however. "Where do you vote?" demanded J. N. Tincher, a Kansas Republican. "I voted in New York the last time," Marsh said. Oh, replied Tincher, "Let us talk about that a little." Nobody, not even Sinclair, came to Marsh's defense.[32]

In 1922, then, neither the farm groups nor agrarian lawmakers were ready to advocate intervention in the agricultural marketplace. A year and a half later, though, the farm groups were ready. Nevertheless, their change of heart did not rally lawmakers immediately under their banner. Before close ties with the farm groups made sense, representatives had to discover that the agricultural lobbies offered electoral advantages that were at least the equal of the benefits of party loyalty. Moreover,

30. "Price fixing and the Farm Bloc," *WF*, 3 March 1922, p. 296.

31. *Hearings before the House Agriculture Committee*, "Stabilizing prices of farm products," 67th Congress, 2d session, Serial O, 1922 (hereafter *Hearings*, 1922), pp. 133, 142–44, 25–26. See also *Hearings before the House Agriculture Committee*, "Agricultural relief," 68th Congress, 2d session, Serial CC, 1925 (hereafter *Hearings*, 1925), pp. 302–6. Many on the Senate Committee favored Norris's export financing bill, which Sinclair cosponsored in the House. See Lowitt, *Norris: Persistence of a progressive*, pp. 167–72, 179.

32. *Hearings*, 1922, p. 139; William Johnson, "Can the government save the country," *CG*, 5 May 1923, p. 42.

lawmakers needed assurance that the circumstances that created those advantages would continue into the future. The equalization fee set those forces into motion.

Late in 1921, an Illinois farm equipment manufacturer, George N. Peek, unveiled a farm subsidy scheme that he had concocted along with his lieutenant, Hugh S. Johnson. The plan, which they outlined in a self-published pamphlet entitled "Equality for Agriculture," set the price for the portion of a crop consumed domestically equal to a "ratio price" bearing the same relation to prices of manufactured goods as it had immediately before the war. The plan supported prices by dumping the "exportable surplus" abroad and covered its export losses with an "equalization fee" levied on producers.

Peek tried early to interest the Farm Bureau in the plan, and the second printing of "Equality for Agriculture" bore an encomium to AFBF president J. R. Howard. Neither Howard nor his successor, Oscar Bradfute, was very much interested. Several presidents of state Farm Bureaus were, however, and in January 1924 the Federation's executive committee endorsed the scheme. "I'm ready to go to the mat on the [Peek] bill," Illinois Agricultural Association (IAA) president Sam H. Thompson, the leader of the Farm Bureau's radicals, wrote in March 1924. "They are having a good time down there [in Washington], passing the buck on relief for agriculture. I am going down to find out the situation of this bill."[33]

The other farm organizations were coming around as well. The long-time president of the Farmers Union, C. S. Barrett, was unenthusiastic, but the leaders of midwestern Unions (like John Tromble in Kansas and Milo Reno in Iowa) were so restive that Barrett lacked the political wherewithal to restrain them. Even the Grange, traditionally wary of political activism, swung left in 1923, electing Louis J. Taber to replace Sherman J. Lowell as master. Seen as a compromise candidate between Grange radicals and ultraconservatives, Taber pledged to be "conservative but progressive."[34]

The attraction of Peek's plan to the normally conservative farm groups was partly a matter of timing, partly a matter of presentation, and partly a matter of parentage. First, it was politically well paced. All

33. William Bruce Storm, "An analysis of the Illinois Agricultural Association as a pressure group for farmers," Ph.D. dissertation, University of Chicago, 1950, p. 113; "What is the matter with the export plan?" *WF*, 11 January 1924, p. 47; "Farm relief plan at Washington," *WF*, 18 January 1924, p. 92; Christensen, "Agricultural pressure," p. 149.

34. "National Grange annual meeting," *Hoard's Dairyman*, 7 December 1923, p. 634; "Committee to act on export bill," *WF*, 7 January 1927, p. 6.

the farm lobbies, but especially the Farm Bureau, had been decimated by the agricultural depression. "In a number of states," O'Brien reported in 1923, "the farm bureau is practically on the rocks. . . . In even the strongest Corn Belt states there have been wholesale desertions in county memberships." Between 1921 and 1922, Federation membership posted significant gains in the East, South and West, but its total membership plunged from 466,000 to 363,000, all due to losses in its stronghold, the Midwest. Thus, the Federation desperately needed an issue to excite midwestern farmers—it was about this time that it first applied the adjective "militant" to itself—but more than anything else it needed more prosperous farmers. Five years of chasing after Muscle Shoals had convinced midwestern Farm Bureau leaders that promoting cut-rate fertilizers would neither impassion farmers nor enrich them.[35] In a very real sense, pressing for government action to aid agriculture was a last-ditch bid for self-preservation.[36]

Moreover, of all the farm relief plans—they were legion—Peek's made the "fairest" demands. According to its proponents, the equalization fee discouraged overproduction by cutting the returns to farmers whenever greater proportions of their crop went into exports. The plan was self-financing. Most important, it gave farmers the same "American price" that tariff-protected manufacturers enjoyed, no more and no less.[37]

The plan's sponsors, finally, were far from radical. Peek was a businessman, Johnson was a retired military officer, and both were veterans of the War Industries Board. Further, Peek scored a coup in 1923 when Agriculture Secretary Wallace, alarmed by the Coolidge administration's standpat response to a farm crisis that was fast becoming chronic, decided to move on his own. In September 1923, Wallace presented his endorsement of the Peek plan to Coolidge's cabinet; in October he sent his chief economist, Henry C. Taylor, on a northwest tour to promote

35. On the Muscle Shoals controversy and the Farm Bureau's role in it, see Preston J. Hubbard, *Origins of the TVA* (New York: W. W. Norton and Co., 1961).

36. Harry R. O'Brien, "A million who'll stick," *CG*, 10 March 1923, p. 11; Robert L. Tontz, "Memberships of general farmers' organizations," *Agricultural History*, 38 (July 1964), pp. 143–57; John Mark Hansen, "The political economy of group membership," *American Political Science Review*, 79 (March 1985), pp. 83–88; "Membership paid to the American Farm Bureau Federation," mimeo, American Farm Bureau Federation, 1982, p. 262. Ironically, in the context of 1925, politics was more conducive to the Farm Bureau's organizational maintenance than services. The Federation's ill-fated foray into cooperative marketing had alienated about as many as it had pleased, and it had mired a number of state Farm Bureaus deeply in debt. Politics, therefore, was less contentious than services.

37. Winters, *Wallace*, pp. 259–67.

the plan; and in November he directed Charles J. Brand to prepare a bill, in consultation with Peek. Wallace's endorsement itself lent an aura of respectability. The scion of a family of Iowa newspaper editors and the organizer of the Corn Belt Meat Producers Association, Wallace was highly regarded by midwestern farm group leaders.[38]

In January 1924, Agriculture Committee chairman Gilbert N. Haugen, a Republican from Iowa, introduced Peek's bill into the House. Senate Agriculture Committee chairman George W. Norris had his own bill, so the second-ranking Republican, Charles L. McNary of Oregon, introduced Peek's bill into the Senate. "The McNary-Haugen legislation was not a farm organization bill. It had come from completely outside their ranks, although, from the beginning, the Farm Bureau was most closely associated with the measure."[39]

The House Committee was cowed a bit but not overwhelmed by the new pressure. Proponents and opponents alike exhibited greater independence from the farm groups than they would just a couple years later. The line between the "ins" and the "outs" was not so sharply drawn. And the doubts of both admirers and detractors of the bill reflected concerns about the merits of the bill, not about its organizational support or the representativeness of its backers. Although a number of committee members were eager to assuage the farm groups and their allies, few actively courted them. After all, the agricultural trades opposed the measure. So too did the leadership of both parties.

Haugen's sponsorship of the bill, for instance, indicated no radical streak. Over the years, the up-and-down nature of Iowa Republican politics had reinforced his natural caution. In 1898, Haugen won his first nomination for Congress as a compromise candidate in a deadlocked convention. He was one of the twenty-nine insurgents who cosponsored Norris's revolt against Speaker Cannon, but in the next election the conservatives defected to the Democrats and came within 220 votes of unseating him. Thereafter, Haugen cut his insurgency short and backed Taft rather than Roosevelt in 1912. He was not a member of the Farm

38. Christensen, "Agricultural pressure," p. 145; Winters, *Wallace*, pp. 25–26, 53, 253–64; Rita McDonald and Robert G. Dunbar, "The initiation of the McNary-Haugen movement in Montana and the Pacific Northwest," *Pacific Northwest Quarterly*, 71 (April 1980), pp. 63–71; Keach Johnson, "The Corn Belt Meat Producers' Association of Iowa: Origins of a progressive pressure group," *Annals of Iowa*, 43 (Spring 1976), pp. 242–60.

39. Gilbert C. Fite, *George N. Peek and the fight for farm parity* (Norman: University of Oklahoma Press, 1954), p. 100. In sponsoring the bill, Senator McNary joked to a friend, "I am carrying the wheat man's burden." Roger T. Johnson, "Part-time leader: Senator Charles L. McNary and the McNary-Haugen bill," *Agricultural History*, 54 (October 1980), p. 529; Lowitt, *Norris: Persistence of a progressive*, pp. 179–80, 294–95.

Bloc, and his bill to regulate the meat industry, which became the Packers and Stockyards Act, was embraced by the packers as a lesser evil than Norris's Senate bill.[40]

Haugen's sponsorship of the bill, moreover, was not due to any close ties to Peek or to the Farm Bureau. Peek was a protégé of Democratic financier Bernard Baruch, and Haugen regarded him as a Democratic stalking horse. A. B. Genung, a USDA staff member during Wallace's term, claimed that "McNary from the first had been going along cordially with the Peek group," but he made no mention of Haugen. Of the Iowa delegation, a more logical choice for the bill's sponsor might have been Lester J. Dickinson, "a man easily goaded" because of his scarcely concealed ambition for a Senate seat. Dickinson had chaired the House Farm Bloc, had close ties with the Iowa Farm Bureau, had declared for the Peek plan in 1923, and represented a cash grain district in northwest Iowa that was more fertile ground for conversions to the plan than Haugen's northeastern corn and dairy district.[41]

Dickinson, however, was not the chairman of the committee. Haugen was, and most likely he dropped the bill into the hopper because Wallace asked him. "There is no evidence that Haugen had any part in framing the legislation," says Fite, and "it is doubtful if [he] realized that he had attached his name to a bill that would earn him such a prominent and lasting place in the history of twentieth-century . . . farm policy." Even a cautious man like Haugen, though, found it hard to ignore a ground swell that stood to make him more than an obscure committee chairman. By the time the Committee opened hearings, the plan had won the endorsement of *Wallaces' Farmer*, the most influential farm paper in Iowa, and a number of Iowa county farm bureaus.[42] What's more, the bill had the blessing of Secretary Wallace, making it something of an administration measure, even if Coolidge and Hoover were believed to be

40. Gilbert C. Fite, "Gilbert N. Haugen," pp. 1–14 in John N. Schacht, ed., *Three progressives from Iowa* (Iowa City: Center for the Study of the Recent History of the United States, 1980); Murray R. Benedict, *Farm policies of the United States, 1790–1950* (New York: Twentieth Century Fund, 1953), p. 183n.

41. A. B. Genung, *The agricultural depression following World War I and its political consequences* (Ithaca, N.Y.: Northeast Farm Foundation, 1954), p. 27; Russell Lord, *The Wallaces of Iowa* (Boston: Houghton Mifflin Co., 1947), p. 241; "Wheat, corn, and Capper," *Independent*, 16 January 1926, p. 61; Fite, "Haugen."

42. Fite, "Haugen," p. 8; "The export plan," *WF*, 11 January 1924, p. 44; "What is the matter with the export plan?" *WF*, p. 47. Haugen's predecessor as Agriculture's chairman, Democrat Asbury F. Lever of South Carolina, won lasting renown as the sponsor of the Smith-Lever Act, which created the agricultural extension services. He retired from Congress to a spot on the Farm Loan Board. See J. C. M. (J. Clyde Marquis), "Progress in Congress, *CG*, 23 August 1919, p. 24.

opposed. Not many legislators were in a position where aggressive advocacy would redound so surely in their favor.

Thus, when the hearings commenced Haugen played the cheerleader for the farm organizations backing the bill. When Farm Bureau lobbyist Gray Silver arrived, for example, Haugen led him through the paces:

HAUGEN: The consoling feature about this bill is this: The price is not going to remain down at the ratio price; it is going above.

SILVER: The ratio price is the minimum.

HAUGEN: That is the minimum, and the price, of course, will go beyond that.

SILVER: We trust so.

HAUGEN: . . . The speculators and gamblers will take care of the price then, as they are taking care of it now. In order to gamble they will have to put the price above the ratio price.

Later, the gentleman from Iowa put to use the testimony of witnesses that he had disparaged when they appeared before the Committee only two years earlier.

HAUGEN: Somebody has got to pay the expense.

SILVER: That is right.

HAUGEN: And under the bill the farmers would take care of a part of it [through the equalization fee].

SILVER: Yes.

HAUGEN: The consumer would take the biggest end of it?

SILVER: Yes.

HAUGEN: The consumers, or the representatives of the consumers [the labor unions], say that they will take their share of it. . . . I have been in sympathy with your suggestion [to set the ratio price higher], . . . but I realize that we cannot get it, and I will be satisfied if we accomplish what we accomplish here.

Never mind, as Kentucky Democrat David Kincheloe later pointed out, that the unions had endorsed the Sinclair bill in 1922 and had not yet pronounced on Haugen's bill, and never mind that Haugen had not previously been a great friend of price-fixing.[43] This was Haugen's bid for national recognition, and he needed all the help he could get, especially the help of the Farm Bureau.

With the exception of Haugen, and South Carolina Democrat Hampton P. Fulmer, however, no other members of the committee fell over themselves to curry the farm groups' favor.[44] The proponents of the

43. *Hearings before the House Agriculture Committee,* "McNary-Haugen export bill," 68th Congress, 1st session, Serial E, 1924 (hereafter *Hearings, 1924*), pp. 395, 398, 561; *Hearings, 1922,* pp. 78–86.

44. Fulmer, representative of a cotton district around Columbia, South Carolina, made it clear to opponents that in his view the farm groups were the sole legitimate source

bill—Republicans J. N. Tincher of Kansas and Fred S. Purnell of Indiana, Democrats Thomas L. Rubey of Missouri and Fletcher B. Swank of Oklahoma—were not reluctant to challenge the farm groups or to take into account the interests of groups that opposed farmers. Purnell, for instance, represented a chronically marginal district in western Indiana, a state whose powerful Farm Bureau president, William Settle, was a leader in the McNary-Haugen ranks. Nevertheless, Purnell challenged Silver, albeit cautiously, to consider an opposing point of view.

PURNELL: Will [the bill] . . . wipe out the speculation that now exists?
SILVER: It will tend to do that.
PURNELL: Do you think enough of it will be maintained to be helpful to the market?
SILVER: I am one of those who believe that the market is not maintained by speculation. Consumption is the constant support of the market. . . .
PURNELL: I have the same view, but . . . I am wondering whether or not the operation of the bill would disturb speculation and other features on the market which are generally accepted now as being helpful to it.

Viewed against Haugen's performance, Purnell clearly was not trying to ingratiate himself to the Farm Bureau, although he was smart enough not to push his objections too far.[45]

As in 1922, moreover, proponents were not forbidden to worry about the effects of the bill on traditional agrarian whipping boys. Proponents Sinclair, Rubey, and Swank, for example, joined opponents Kincheloe and Voigt in worrying about how millers would fare under the plan. So great was the Committee's concern for processors that the chairman lost his temper. "I don't understand all this worry about the packers," Haugen thundered. "I think we all agree that the packers can take care of themselves. . . .We need not lose any sleep over [them]."[46]

The trades were not treated so well when they appeared in person.

---

of policy information. "I am curious about this gentleman who made that statement [you just quoted] about the farmers in New England. Did he represent the farmers?" he asked A. P. Husband of the Millers' National Federation. "I think he is . . . the largest dealer of mill feeds in New England and comes into contact daily in his business with farmers," Husband replied. The answer did not satisfy Fulmer. "I might just say that a gentleman here representing farmers from New England tells me they are in a terrible fix out there." "A difference of opinion," Husband claimed. Perhaps, replied Fulmer, laying down his trump card, but "he represents the farmers." *Hearings*, 1924, p. 701.

45. *Hearings*, 1924, p. 402. See also *Hearings*, 1925, pp. 312–17, 345, 392–98, 403–6, 431–35, 443, 471–72, 577–83. In 1924 the main forces behind the Peek bill were the midwestern Farm Bureaus and the northwestern wheat growers cooperatives. See McDonald and Dunbar, "The initiation of the McNary-Haugen movement," pp. 63–71.

46. *Hearings*, 1924, pp. 313, 490, 9–13, 550; *Hearings*, 1922, p. 82.

Haugen confronted the Millers' National Federation with a Federal Trade Commission (FTC) report alleging wartime profiteering in the milling industry. He unearthed another FTC report that detailed abuses by the meat industry. "You know something about the practices of the packers that were pointed out in that report?" he asked Norman Draper, testifying for the Institute of American Meat Packers. "We had an understanding years ago that we would simply forget about that report, . . . but you are bringing it up now. Very well; . . . but you are responsible for it." Haugen's favoritism did not escape the notice of the Committee. Democrat Thomas A. Doyle, who represented Chicago's packinghouse district, finally had enough, and he came to Draper's defense. "You have been mighty agreeable about it, Mr. Chairman, but I do not think you put those same questions, in the same tone, to the proponents of the bill as you have to this gentleman." Aside from Haugen and a few others, notably Tincher and Fulmer, nobody else was really ready to offend the tradesmen—just yet.[47]

In 1924, then, only a few Agriculture Committee members obviously cultivated close relationships with organized agriculture. Caution rather than enthusiasm carried the day as legislators confronting something new looked for accommodation without long-term commitment. The farm groups' turn to price-fixing legislation had not in itself been enough to bring farm state representatives into their camp. The 1924 McNary-Haugen bill died on the House floor, and an attempt to resurrect it in the Senate failed. A 1925 version failed to come to a vote.[48]

Commitment: The Farm Lobby Wins the Midwest

In 1926, though, the McNary-Haugenites came back for a third try, and the landscape was very much changed. The House Committee was as deeply divided as before, perhaps even more so. Instead of one proposal on the docket there now were four: the Peek plan; the administration's farm proposal, sponsored by Kansas Republican J. N. Tincher; a coop-

47. *Hearings*, 1924, pp. 451, 470, 686–91, 156–57. Haugen evidently tended toward pomposity, delivering long-winded speeches with eyes half-closed in enjoyment. "You know, that's a remarkable man, a very remarkable man," Illinois Democrat Henry T. Rainey once told Sam Rayburn, watching Haugen from the well. "He's the only man in the whole world that every time he opens his mouth he subtracts something from the sum total of human knowledge." Later, Rayburn related the story, which may be apocryphal (House Speaker Thomas B. Reed originated the remark), to his Texas colleague, W. R. (Bob) Poage. See the Oral Memoirs of William Robert "Bob" Poage, Baylor University Institute for Oral History, 1985, pp. 53, 762–63.

48. Fite, *Peek*, chap. 5. For an analysis of the votes, see John D. Black, "The McNary-Haugen movement," *American Economic Review,* 18 (September 1928), pp. 408–11.

erative marketing plan, proposed by Kansas senator Charles Curtis, the majority leader, and Louisiana representative James B. Aswell, the Agriculture Committee's ranking Democrat; and the export debenture, the favorite of the Grange, promoted by Illinois Republican Charles Adkins, Texas Democrat Marvin Jones and Michigan Republican John C. Ketcham, the past master of the Michigan Grange.

By 1926, however, the farm lobby had won access to the midwestern members of the Committee, and Agriculture's dealings with the interests assembled were markedly different from the way they had been in 1924. To be sure, the substantive arguments were repeated and addressed, especially by those members who as yet were uncommitted, like Democrat Marvin Jones of Texas and Republican Thomas S. Williams of Illinois. This time, however, the most important points of issue were the fundamental political commitments of Agriculture's members, and even the opponents of the Peek bill recognized it. Thus, for Louisiana's James Aswell, Kentucky's David Kincheloe, New Jersey's Franklin Fort and Kansas's J. N. Tincher, the latter newly defected to the farm lobby's opposition, the major strategic thrust was to discredit the farm representatives who appeared before the panel.

Indeed, the 1926 hearings often had more the character of a credentials fight than a fact-gathering probe. Kincheloe complained, for instance, that the representatives of the Farm Bureau were dodging the real issue. "I want to know what the American farmers think of [the bill]," he told AFBF secretary Frank Evans, "and not the representatives of these organizations." Tincher, likewise, was unimpressed by the proclaimed unity of the Corn Belt Committee, an alliance of Farm Bureaus, Farmers Unions and other organizations from eleven midwestern states. "You may be partially right as to the harmony that exists to-day," he told William Hirth, the Committee's chairman. "But we members of this committee know that it is a joke because we have had them here before. . . .In some seasons of the year everything that the farm bureau wants the farm union is against, and in other seasons of the year the reverse." "I personally doubt," he concluded, "that you are together on this."[49]

The opposition also doubted that the parade of farm group witnesses had anything to do with the true sentiments of farmers. "May I inquire if you honestly believe that one per cent of the American farmers know a continental thing about what is in your bill?" Aswell asked Charles E. Hearst, head of the Iowa Farm Bureau. The farmer, the Louisiana Dem-

49. Hearings before the House Committee on Agriculture, "Agricultural relief," 69th Congress, 1st session, Serial C, 1926 (hereafter Hearings, 1926), pp. 372, 162, 121.

ocrat continued, "has to take what you say on faith, and he has lost considerably that quality of faith in the agitation of politicians. . . . I have letters from Iowa . . . saying that all this trouble in Iowa is largely caused by politicians and salaried agents that have been going around and stirring up these matters."[50]

This time around, however, the friends of the farm organizations were not slow to take up their defense. Michigan's John Ketcham used his examination of Hearst to establish that the Iowa farm leader was a "bona fide" cultivator of Iowa's fine black soil—four hundred acres—and not a "salaried agent." Later, New Jersey's Franklin Fort challenged the right of Farm Bureau president Sam H. Thompson, an Illinois corn farmer, to speak for cattle producers. In response, Illinois Republican Charles Adkins led Thompson through his own biography, all to prove that the AFBF leader was an honest dirt farmer, unselfishly interested in agriculture, and not a full-time malcontent. For good measure, Adkins helped Thompson answer a question posed by Thomas Williams, also of Illinois, who wanted to know why the specialty crops raised in his district did not come under the provisions of the bill. Because land suitable for growing those products was limited, Adkins prompted Thompson, those growers were less at the mercy of processors than corn, wheat and cotton farmers.[51]

In 1926, then, the solicitude the Committee showed to the farm groups was not confined to one or two members, as it was in 1924. With the exception of J. N. Tincher, the representatives from the Midwest, both Republicans and Democrats, shared in it. In discussing the corn provisions of the bill with David Kincheloe, for instance, Farm Bureau lobbyist Chester H. Gray ran into some trouble. Yes, he admitted, the Treasury would have to pay for any export losses that the equalization fee did not cover. But, he insisted, that contingency would not in fact occur. Kincheloe exploded. "We have gone over that a million times," he complained. "I understand your contention is that there is not going to be any loss; but finally, you admit if there is a loss it will come out of the Treasury." At this point, Missouri Democrat Thomas Rubey stepped in on Gray's behalf. "Suppose they make some money out of this corn deal," he asked Kincheloe, "what will they do with the profits?" "I suppose they will reimburse the Treasury," Kincheloe replied, but "I am guessing on that." "He is guessing [too]," argued Rubey. "No,"

50. *Hearings,* 1926, pp. 584–85, p. 161. At this point, Senator Brookhart piped up from the audience, "I presume they referred to me." "I do not know that any of these people knew you at all," Aswell retorted. "They never mentioned you, if they did." *Hearings,* 1926, p. 585.

51. *Hearings,* 1926, pp. 604–5, 781–84.

Kincheloe persisted, "he did not guess at all."[52] Compelling or not, a defense was a defense.

Finally, the special treatment the Committee granted the farm groups did not extend to just anyone. Both sides took great pleasure in demolishing the arguments of unaffiliated farmers who had journeyed to Washington, each with his own panacea. When Edwin McKnight of Medina, New York, brought his, for example, Minnesota Republican August Andresen let him know where he stood.

ANDRESEN: Your plan, as I take it, has received no specific endorsement from any farm organization.

McKNIGHT: No, it has not.

ANDRESEN: What chance do you think your bill has, when it has received no such endorsement from these farm organizations? Do you think we should give the farmer something that he does not advocate himself or give him something that he is not here sponsoring through his personal representatives?

For the midwesterners on the Committee from both parties the important consideration was not that a bill had the support of some farmer, somewhere, but that it had the support of "his personal representatives."[53]

As the decade passed its midpoint, then, the interactions of lawmakers and lobbies changed markedly. From a posture of independence from the farm groups in the early 1920s midwestern legislators moved toward responsiveness in 1926. The turnaround surprised the farm groups as much as anybody. "At the beginning of their [1926] invasion of the capital the farm delegations were taken back by the unexpected manner of their reception," the *Times* reported. "They were welcomed on every hand, . . . told to get together around a table and decide just what it was they wanted." By and large, they did. "The bill reported by the two committees . . . was one which had been practically written by the representatives of the farmers' organizations from the wheat and corn belts and the American Cotton Growers Exchange." The farm lobby won its first measure of access in 1926.[54]

52. *Hearings*, 1926, pp. 707, 825–27.

53. *Hearings*, 1926, pp. 1227, 1349. The degree to which the farm groups controlled the farm relief issue was further illustrated in December 1926, when Haugen balked at some of their proposals. In response, the agricultural organizations "served a virtual ultimatum on him that unless he sponsored their bill it would be offered by Representative Purnell of Indiana, thus minimizing Mr. Haugen's leadership in the contest for government assistance to agriculture." Haugen relented. See "Haugen to sponsor farm bill in House," *NYT*, 20 December 1926, p. 2; "Relief for farmers demanded in House," *NYT*, 16 December 1926, p. 2.

54. "Farmers worried over legislation," *NYT*, 14 March 1926, p. II 1; Christensen, "Agricultural pressure," p. 219.

The Committee's orientation changed because conditions had changed. Much had happened in the two years between 1924 and 1926. Electoral outcomes had indicated that alliances with the farm groups were becoming more advantageous. Furthermore, the economic prognosis had worsened, bringing with it expectations that demands for farm price stabilization indeed would recur.

Back in 1924, it had looked as if the agitation for the McNary-Haugen bill might be over and done with. Grain prices had risen dramatically. Wheat jumped from 93 cents in 1923 to $1.25 the next year, and corn went from 81 cents to $1.06. Political optimism rose with the grain markets. Republican vice-presidential nominee Charles G. Dawes predicted a revival of the European market and greater domestic buying power, both of which would help farmers out of their doldrums. Democratic presidential candidate John W. Davis agreed. As A. B. Genung observed, "it was hoped and believed in Washington [in 1924] that the worst part of the actual depression was over."[55]

That optimism made even the strongest supporters of the McNary-Haugen plan a little hesitant to push it as aggressively as the farm groups desired. "I am in sympathy with some movement of this kind," Nebraska Republican Melvin McLaughlin told Silver in 1924, "but I am wondering a little bit whether we are making sufficient progress in the normal way so that we might be able to get through and be better off, in two or three years from now, than by bolstering ourselves up in some artificial manner that may not be economical." The consequence of optimism, then, was temporization. Even its supporters regarded the 1924 McNary-Haugen bill "as an 'emergency measure,'" and late in 1924 Senator McNary stated that he would not press the bill in the next session, so confident was he that the emergency was over. "With his prestige and influence in the Senate enhanced by his own overwhelming reelection," Johnson wrote, "McNary was reluctant to risk his standing with a futile fight for a farm bill that the president and party leadership opposed, and that no longer seemed so politically and economically urgent. In the fall of 1924 farm prices were rising, and this clearly took the edge off the agricultural emergency."[56] Thus, the improvement of the farm economy in 1924 only confirmed that farm relief was not an

---

55. Genung, *Agricultural depression*, p. 36; Stuart O. Blythe, "'Brass tacks,'" *CG*, 11 October 1924, p. 6; E. V. Wilcox, "The farmer and Democracy," *CG*, 11 October 1924, p. 7.

56. *Hearings*, 1924, p. 403; Eric Englund, "The dilemma of the Corn Belt," *World's Work*, November 1926, p. 44; Johnson, "Part-time leader," p. 531; "Differ on farm bill," *NYT*, 15 November 1924, p. 2; Steve Neal, *McNary of Oregon: A political biography* (Portland: Western Imprints, 1985), chap. 11. The Illinois Agricultural Association's lob-

issue that would long have much salience. Legislators foresaw no recurrence.

Expectations reversed, however, as the market reversed in 1925. Corn lost 36 cents a bushel in 1925; later that year wheat followed its plunge. This downturn, following a modest upturn following a four-year depression, was enough to make even optimists wonder whether the farm crisis really was temporary. For many years, the economic prophets had held out the hope that a rebuilt, prosperous Europe would restore American agriculture to solvency. The large world crops in 1925 and 1926 betrayed that hope. "I do not think that [the agricultural situation] is in the process of working itself out, of curing itself," economist E. G. Nourse concluded at the end of 1925. "I still believe that the situation is with us and that it is idle for American agriculture to expect a return of prosperity because of the rehabilitation of the world market on which we depended to a considerable extent." Others agreed. "The easy, automatic European food market of the pre-war days has gone forever," wrote Henry A. Wallace, the son of the late agriculture secretary. Unfortunately, added University of Wisconsin economist B. H. Hibbard, "we shall have surpluses of agricultural products for many years to come."[57]

The gloom was not limited to agricultural economists. "The causes of this [depression] are permanent," argued Iowa senator Smith Brookhart, and "the condition itself is permanent." Consequently, Farm Bureau president Sam Thompson concluded, "farm relief is no longer considered an emergency matter."[58] The 1926 version of the Peek plan established a permanent export corporation rather than limiting its life to a few years, as earlier bills had specified. With the farm economy in a lasting state of torpor, legislators were going to have to deal with this issue for a long time to come.

If momentarily improved conditions could not kill the issue, moreover, it certainly was not going to die of neglect. In 1924 nobody could tell if the farm lobby's enthusiasm for subsidies would outlast the fading agricultural depression. In fact, many in Washington suspected that the Farm Bureau hierarchy was pursuing the McNary-Haugen legislation

byist, Chester C. Davis, recalled things similarly: in 1924, "I really thought I was through on this thing." Reminiscences of Chester C. Davis, Columbia Oral History Collection, 1953, p. 167.

57. E. G. Nourse, "The agricultural outlook," *Rural America*, December 1925, p. 5; H. A. Wallace, "Three roads to better times," *WF*, 23 July 1926, p. 988; B. H. Hibbard, "What about the surplus?" *PF*, 3 April 1926, p. 438.

58. Smith W. Brookhart, "The plight of the farmer," *Nation*, 7 April 1926, p. 367; "Farmers to stress relief," *NYT*, 5 December 1926, p. 15.

only to placate its restless midwesterners. "In 1924," recalled Chester C. Davis, the lobbyist for the Illinois Farm Bureau, "we didn't have the American Farm Bureau with us." Within a month of the burial of the 1924 Peek bill, however, farm leaders met in St. Paul, where they vowed to carry on the fight. They created the American Council of Agriculture, with Peek at its head, to coordinate the efforts of the various protagonists.[59]

By 1926, therefore, the probability was high that the issue of farm relief would not soon lose its salience, especially in the Middle West. That fact did not escape the notice of House Committee members. In 1926, Ohio Republican Charles J. Thompson reviewed the Farm Bloc's many victories with Sam Thompson. "I want to say in defense of this committee that we have been trying to help the farmer," he told the Farm Bureau leader. "We have passed all this legislation, and yet we find that the farmer is still here, still knocking at our doors." Thanking him politely, Thompson assured him that their presence nevertheless would continue: "Even if you pass this legislation I would not want to promise that we would not be back here again." In that case, the representative from Ohio continued, "you are always welcome to come before this committee. We like to meet around this table and thrash out these problems."[60] As soon as they expected the farm relief issue to recur, as they did in 1926, lawmakers were eager to cooperate with the farm lobby.

By 1926, the competitive advantage of the farm lobby was evident as well. The appeal of the Peek plan in farm regions surprised even veteran lawmakers. Five-term representative David Kincheloe, for example, expressed bafflement at the idea that such a new proposal could so quickly gain such a wide following. "How can these organizations throughout the United States have any intelligent conception of the content of these bills?" he inquired of Charles Holman of the National Board of Farm Organizations. "By what method is it gotten to them?"[61] In 1924, the

59. Davis reminiscenses, p. 183; H. A. Wallace, "Re-forming the battle lines," *WF*, 18 July 1924, p. 985; William Hirth, "American Council of Agriculture," *WF*, 20 June 1924, p. 897; Christensen, "Agricultural pressure," p. 151.

60. *Hearings*, 1926, p. 835–36.

61. *Hearings*, 1924, p. 418. The Minnesota Farm Bureau conducted a straw poll in March 1924 and placed it in the record. By its count, 17,773 Minnesota farmers favored the equalization fee and only 102 opposed it. "Referendum so one sided that count is growing monotonous," its telegram concluded. What is remarkable is not the lopsidedness of the tally—the bias of the poll is obvious—but the ability of the Minnesota Farm Bureau to contact nearly 18,000 farmers so quickly. See *Hearings*, 1924, p. 740. For the reaction of Minnesota representatives to the movement, see Jon M. Wefald, "Congressman Knud Wefald: A Minnesota voice for farm parity," *Minnesota History*, 38 (December 1962), pp. 177–85.

efficiency of the farm lobby's political intelligence was a revelation to the Agriculture Committee.

The awareness of the farm lobby's electoral potential was elevated, moreover, when the farm organizations decided to play hardball. Believing that internal dissension had damaged their effectiveness in 1924, the Peek forces spun out three new organizations over the next eighteen months: the American Council of Agriculture and the Corn Belt Committee, both of which have been mentioned already, and the Committee of Twenty-two, an organization of businessmen sympathetic to McNary-Haugenism. The coalitions themselves were largely of symbolic importance; the American Council of Agriculture and the Corn Belt Committee relied heavily on their member organizations, especially the Farm Bureau, for their political punch. Years later, Sam Thompson recalled the Corn Belt Committee as a mixed blessing, noting that an effective lobbying effort required both an experienced Washington staff and "thorough local organization." "The Committee lacked this machinery," he both complained and boasted, "or rather, it depended on the machinery of member Farm Bureaus and other affiliated groups."[62]

To be sure, such self-congratulation had to be taken with a grain of salt, but it had an important grain of truth even so. If anything, the Farm Bureau turned even more militant than the Peek lobbies. In October 1924, for example, its *Weekly News Letter,* sent to all county farm bureaus, printed the voting records of members of Congress on bills the AFBF considered important. The Federation's Washington office had kept the tallies for years, but it had released them before only in response to inquiries from Farm Bureau members, to avoid the appearance of partisanship. Their dissemination was unlikely to strike immediate fear in the hearts of Corn Belt representatives, but it was a dramatic indication of the Federation's serious intention to win the farm relief fight. In December 1924, at its annual meeting, Farm Bureau delegates endorsed

62. Sam H. Thompson, "The battle for equality," *Bureau Farmer,* September 1929, p. 8; "Corn growers plan fight in capital," *NYT,* 29 January 1926, p. 9. Senator Capper concurred in Thompson's assessment. "The Farm Bloc, the National Grange, and other farm organizations were in that [McNary-Haugen] fight too," he recalled in 1940, "but it was the Farm Bureau that really provided the national leadership. It mobilized farm sentiment back of the program." Arthur Capper, "A look backward at the 20's," *Nation's Agriculture,* January 1940, p. 32. As peripheral as the Committee of Twenty-two was, it may have been the group that called the Iowa congressional delegation on the carpet in their meeting at Des Moines in January 1926. Representatives Aswell and Kincheloe both made gleeful reference to the "spanking" of the Iowa delegation, and the Iowa representatives appeared together only at that meeting. See *Hearings,* 1926, pp. 48, 236, 254; and Christensen, "Agricultural pressure," p. 187.

the McNary-Haugen bill, ratifying the decision the executive committee had reached eleven months earlier.[63]

Meeting the next year in Chicago, the Farm Bureau turned its 1925 convention into "the Sarajevo of the farm revolt." The keynoter was Calvin Coolidge, and the president was anything but conciliatory. He declared that the agricultural depression was over, and he condemned attempts at price-fixing. As Genung drolly put it, "it remained for Coolidge to kick over such small edifice of tolerance in the West as [Agriculture Secretary William] Jardine had been able to build up." The Federation's reaction to the president's message was swift and bold. Illinois Agricultural Association president Sam H. Thompson made an angry speech denouncing Coolidge, and the Illinois, Indiana and Iowa delegations nominated Thompson for Federation president. After three ballots, the Midwest and South coalesced behind the "rough-and-ready dirt farmer," purging the conservative incumbent Oscar Bradfute, an Ohio cattle breeder invariably described as "the farmer who looks like a banker."[64]

The Farm Bureau's rebuke of President Coolidge raised quite a few eyebrows. "Among a substantial number of men here," wrote the Washington correspondent for *Wallaces' Farmer,* "the Farm Bureau has been looked upon as a 'me too' organization for the administration." No longer. The Federation's revolt, he continued, put midwestern lawmakers on notice, powerfully enough to unite them on the Peek plan and, possibly, to re-create the Farm Bloc. The implications of the revolt, in fact, extended beyond states where the Bureau was well organized. "The Farm Bureau is largely a corn belt organization," the *Agricultural Review* noted. "But it has suddenly become the rallying point for numerous people in many other states who approve of the action at Chicago, but who would not otherwise affiliate or work with it. The Federation is now recognized champion and leader of the Government Export Corporation movement."[65]

At the opening of the Sixty-ninth Congress in 1925, then, it was clear that the farm groups meant business. Whether they could back up their

63. "What he saw in the Washington, D.C., office of the A.F.B.F.," *American Farm Bureau Federation Weekly News Letter,* 9 October 1924, p. 1; Donald R. Murphy, "Farm Bureau backs export plan," *WF,* 19 December 1924, p. 1633.

64. George Fort Milton, "The revolt of the Western farmer," *Independent,* 22 May 1926, p. 597; Genung, *Agricultural depression,* p. 38; H. A. Wallace, "Farm Bureau votes for export plan," *WF,* 18 December 1925, p. 1665; Kile, *Farm Bureau,* p. 53.

65. "Farm bloc may reorganize in Congress," *WF,* 25 December 1925, p. 1696; (W. I. Drummond), "That Farm Bureau upheaval," *Agricultural Review,* January 1926, p. 2.

words with action, however, was still a question. Early in 1924, for instance, political analysts had made dire forecasts of the prospects for opponents of farm relief. "Wherever I have gone," wrote a *Country Gentleman* correspondent, "the McNary-Haugen bill has overshadowed mere candidates. . . . If it fails to pass, votes are going to be affected." Agrarian discontent augured well, insiders thought, for the presidential candidacy of Wisconsin senator Robert M. La Follette.[66]

In 1924, however, the farm revolt was not to be. Coolidge won the Republican nomination easily, posting primary victories over Robert La Follette and Hiram Johnson in such farm states as Illinois and Nebraska—even in fickle North Dakota. Come November, La Follette's candidacy on a Progressive ticket fell far short of expectations as he carried only his home state. In Minnesota, Republican regular Thomas Schall turned out Farmer-Labor senator Magnus Johnson. In Iowa, Senator Smith Brookhart, the darling of the agrarian radicals, needed a handful of disputed votes to hold off conservative Democrat Daniel F. Steck, the open choice of many of Iowa's regular Republicans. In the House of Representatives, finally, enough conservatives won their elections to restore effective control to the regulars. The explanation seemed plain enough. "A rise in the price of wheat in the summer of 1924 was enough to send millions of malcontents back to the Republican party." In the 1924 elections, the Ku Klux Klan was a bigger factor than farm radicals.[67]

In its larger picture, however, 1924 was not as much a defeat for the farm lobby as a draw. Although cooperation with the farm groups had not been decisive, it did not seem to have hurt. Out of the 161 lawmakers who voted for the McNary-Haugen bill in 1924, 129 returned to the House. Of the rest, the retirees and the losers, half yielded to candidates who also pledged their support. In the twenty-two states west of the Mississippi River, the McNary-Haugenites lost only six representatives and two senators. Perhaps these numbers did not justify the claim that "this was a mandate to the good and faithful servants of agriculture to continue their efforts." Nevertheless, they did indicate the popular ap-

66. Stuart O. Blythe, "Who do the farmers want for President?" *CG*, 7 June 1924, p. 33; Elmer Davis, "Power of La Follette group still doubtful," *NYT*, 24 February 1924, p. VIII 10; "La Follette hurries back to Washington," *NYT*, 31 May 1924, p. 9.

67. "Bitter fight ahead on farmers' bill," *NYT*, 30 March 1924, p. IX 6; "Republicans regain grip on Congress," *NYT*, 6 November 1924, p. 1; "The latest edition of the farmers' revolt," *New Republic*, 13 January 1925, p. 205; Harry R. O'Brien, "Why the Northwest went for Coolidge," *CG*, 27 December 1924, p. 16; "Victories by Klan feature election," *NYT*, 6 November 1924, p. 1. Early in 1926, Democrats and conservative Republicans combined to deny Brookhart his seat, citing irregularities in the balloting. Steck became the first Democratic senator from Iowa since before the Civil War.

peal of farm relief, even in a year in which the political tides were running against it.[68]

Such was the interpretation of Gilbert Haugen, for instance. He typically took 60 percent of the vote in his northeastern Iowa district, but in 1924 he won more than 70 percent for only the second time in his fourteen-term career. Consequently, when a reporter informed him of Senator McNary's disinclination to reactivate their bill, "Mr. Haugen declared . . . that in his campaign for re-election he had promised his support to farm relief legislation, and that he would continue to work to that end." In Missouri, likewise, Democratic representative Thomas Rubey invoked the lessons of his 1924 election to justify his strong support of farm relief in 1926. "I had a gentleman running against me in the last campaign who made [the McNary-Haugen bill] the issue," he recalled. "I live in a district that is very close, and yet, in that campaign, after fighting it out all over the district, I received the largest majority I ever received"—in a Republican year, no less—"so I am not afraid of the McNary-Haugen bill."[69]

Equally important to the perception of the farm groups' competitive advantage, however, was the destruction of La Follette's Progressive Party, the last third party of any significance to make a serious bid for the farm vote. Angry regulars in Minnesota had gotten rid of one agrarian radical, Magnus Johnson, and disgruntled stalwarts in Iowa had nearly gotten rid of another, Smith Brookhart, even at the expense of the loss of the seat to a Democrat. In January 1925, moreover, the resurgent Republican leadership punished Senators La Follette, Brookhart, Ladd and Frazier (and several House progressives) for their apostasy, stripping them of their seniority. In the Midwest, therefore, the message of 1924 was loud and clear: in the long term, insurgency was almost as dangerous as regularity. Consequently, a more specific brand of dissent, alliances with the farm groups, held wide appeal. As Noyes observed, the division in the ranks of midwestern Republicanism had "left room for much independence of action." In 1922, the progressives had taken over the Farm Bloc; after 1924, the new farm bloc annexed them in turn.[70]

If midwestern lawmakers had any doubts about the growing advan-

68. C. Reinold Noyes, "The restoration of the Republican Party," *North American Review*, March 1925, p. 419.

69. "Differ on farm bill," *NYT*, p. 2; *Hearings*, 1926, pp. 1010–11.

70. Noyes, "Restoration," p. 417; Stuart O. Blythe, "When is a Republican not a Republican?" *CG*, 13 June 1925, p. 19; Erik Olssen, "The progressive group in Congress, 1922–1929," *Historian*, 42 (February 1980), pp. 253–54; Clarence A. Berdahl, "Some notes on party membership in Congress, II," *American Political Science Review*, 43 (June 1949), pp. 492–97. The stimulus that intraparty strife gave to close relationships with

tages of farm lobby alliances, the 1926 elections surely dispelled them. The new year had barely begun, but already party stalwarts were in danger. "Politicians know that the issue raised in the West, namely a government subsidy to the farmers in handling the export problem, has all the ear-marks of an effective campaign weapon," wrote a wire service reporter. "And the time is opportune because . . . the aspirants for Congressional nominations are looking around for an opportunity to oppose the men who hold seats in the Congress. This invariably has the effect of turning otherwise regular Republicans into insurgents."[71]

One early convert was Iowa senator Albert Cummins, facing another GOP primary against Smith Brookhart, whom the Senate had just denied his seat. In December 1925, Cummins informed Coolidge that it would not be possible to win renomination in Iowa without backing the McNary-Haugen bill, and a few weeks later he announced that he had always been in favor of the principle of the plan, a statement damaging by the fact that he had had to make it. Cummins and Indiana senator James E. Watson, both administration regulars, suddenly became ardent McNary-Haugenites. Watson led the Senate floor fight for the bill. Cummins denounced Treasury Secretary Andrew Mellon for his letter attacking the bill. Watson made it, but barely. Cummins did not, and neither did standpat incumbents Robert N. Stanfield in Oregon (defeated by Frederick Steiwer) and William B. McKinley in Illinois (defeated by Frank L. Smith) and Irvine Lenroot in Wisconsin, who held his ground on the farm relief issue but lost to La Follette protégé John J. Blaine. In all, 1926 spelled defeat for six farm state senators, four of them casualties of GOP primaries.[72]

---

pressure groups was nowhere better illustrated than in the career of William Lemke. Lemke began his political career as an attorney for North Dakota's Nonpartisan League (NPL), and he was elected attorney general on its ticket. In the late 1910s, however, the conservative faction of the North Dakota Republican Party, which called itself the Independent Voters Association (IVA), reasserted itself, and the NPL branch of the party split further into factions favoring and opposing Governor William Langer. By the early 1920s, Lemke was without a political future. Although still tied closely to the NPL, he lost his grip on it after being recalled from the office of attorney general in 1921. In the late 1920s, he turned to the North Dakota Farmers Union for help. The Union hired him as a speaker, and after his first election to Congress in 1932 the National Farmers Union bought him radio time to promote his farm credit bill. (It became the Lemke-Frazier Act.) Because of his advocacy for farmers, Lemke became so popular that neither the NPL nor the IVA dared not to endorse him, and North Dakota voters elected him time and again—he served until 1950—while both NPL endorsees (like James Sinclair) and IVA endorsees (like Thomas Hall) went down to defeat. See Eugene C. Blackorby, *Prairie rebel* (Lincoln: University of Nebraska Press, 1963).

71. "Mutterings of rebellion on the farm," *Literary Digest*, 16 January 1926, p. 6.

72. In November, GOP senator Richard P. Ernst fell to Democratic representative Alben W. Barkley in Kentucky, and Republican senator John W. Harreld lost to Democratic

House elections told the same story. Reporters found extreme resentment against the Coolidge administration's farm policy in Iowa, Illinois and Indiana and labeled it a factor in six other states. Looking over the results of the primary season, they judged seven states likely to send complete delegations to Congress pledged to the equalization fee. For the farm lobby, even the particulars looked good. Agriculture Secretary William Jardine's campaign swing across Kansas, Senator Curtis told Coolidge, "did the party no good," and he advised the president not to send the secretary (and former president of Kansas State College) back to Kansas again. Although a supporter of the Peek bill, Nebraska Republican Melvin McLaughlin fought for his political life (unsuccessfully) against progressive Democrat John N. Norton, a former Nebraska Farm Bureau president "who is preaching farm relief with capital F's and R's." In Iowa, finally, Gilbert Haugen himself battled rumors that he was in trouble, not because of his views but because "he did not work half as hard as he should have to get his bill passed." "In Iowa," the *Times* concluded, "it is not a question of whether a man is for or against farm relief, but a question of how far he is willing to go."[73]

---

congressman Elmer Thomas in Oklahoma. "Administration to deal with surplus," *WF*, 1 January 1926, p. 10; "All-Iowa meeting backs export plan," *WF*, 8 January 1926, p. 35; Stuart O. Blythe, "The Midwest has a bone to pick," *CG*, September 1926, p. 12; "Senate debates farm relief bill," *WF*, 25 June 1926, p. 894; "Brookhart wins Senate nomination, defeating Cummins," *NYT*, 8 June 1926, p. 1; "Iowa primary awakens Senate," *WF*, 18 June 1926, p. 872; "Stanfield defeat, third in series, jolts Old Guard," *NYT*, 23 May 1926, p. 1; Alfred Holman, "Oregon expects a Republican sweep," *NYT*, 6 June 1926, p. II 2. Cummins, who died shortly after the primary, had one of the more ill-starred Senate careers of the time. He was first elected in 1908 as a progressive foe of the railroads. He gradually grew more conservative, however, and while chairman of the Interstate Commerce Committee in the 66th Congress he sponsored the Esch-Cummins Act, which returned the railroads to private management after the war. One section of the bill guaranteed the roads very profitable returns, and that damned Cummins forever in the eyes of the radical agrarians. In 1924, a coalition of progressives led by Robert M. La Follette stripped him of his committee chairmanship. Republican regulars, however, refused to give the post to La Follette, who was next in line. After a long deadlock, they joined with Democrats to appoint Ellison D. (Cotton Ed) Smith, a South Carolina Democrat. To my knowledge, Smith was the only member of the minority party to chair a standing committee of the Senate in the twentieth century. See Davis, "Power of La Follette group still doubtful," p. VIII 10; Clarence A. Berdahl, "Some notes on party membership in Congress, I," *American Political Science Review*, 43 (April 1949), p. 320; and Lowitt, *Norris: Persistence of a progressive*, pp. 223–25, 384–86.

73. Charles Frederick Williams, "William M. Jardine and the development of Republican farm policy," Ph.D. dissertation, University of Oklahoma, 1970, p. 175; "Democrats expect Nebraska victory," *NYT*, 14 October 1926, p. 4; "Haugen in danger of defeat in Iowa," *NYT*, 12 October 1926, p. 3; Blythe, "The Midwest has a bone to pick," p. 12; "Corn Belt revolt stirs Republicans," *NYT*, 16 August 1926, p. 4; "Oklahoma," *NYT*, 3 November 1926, p. 4.

The farm organizations' maneuvers in these elections appear remarkably subtle. If the farm groups deployed money or manpower, the practice was not extensive enough or unusual enough for anyone to comment on it. Rather, the farm lobby's most potent weapon was to encourage or discourage challenges to incumbent lawmakers by voicing their displeasure or satisfaction with their performance. For example, the announcement of farm leaders in 1926 that "they will . . . campaign vigorously against congressional candidates who do not take a decided stand in favor of equality for agriculture" was a virtual solicitation of ambitious politicians. The prospect of a disaffected constituency brought attractive candidates out of the woodwork. As one reporter commented, "the crowd-complex is exemplified by the political movement of the agricultural population. Fluent speakers, radical utterances in farm papers, exploitation of individual losses combine to furnish fuel for the politician, who is not slow to capitalize any symptoms of unrest."[74]

In 1926, in sum, the conditions for interest group access to congressional deliberations were finally satisfied. The elections of 1924 and (especially) 1926 demonstrated the efficacy of the farm groups' appeals. The developments of the farm economy in 1925 and 1926 demonstrated the durability of those appeals—the agitation would not die and the salience would not fade. The farm groups enjoyed competitive advantage over party regularity, and that advantage was believed to be recurrent. In 1926, the McNary-Haugen bill came to a vote in both houses. In 1927, in lame-duck session, the McNary-Haugen bill passed both houses.[75] The farm lobby had made support for its program, for the McNary-Haugen proposal, the litmus test of farm relief.[76] The farm lobby had won its access.

These conclusions, however, did not hold true for two sets of legisla-

---

74. Blythe, "The Midwest has a bone to pick," p. 128; Charles Moreau Harger, "The political clouds out West," *Independent*, 1 September 1923, p. 82. The farm groups also helped dissuade challengers by expressing public appreciation for the efforts of their friends. See The Observer, "Taking the temperature of public opinion," *Bureau Farmer*, February 1927, p. 7; (Chester H. Gray), "Our Washington letter," *Bureau Farmer*, December 1927, p. 11; The Observer, "The 'greatest' annual meeting," *Bureau Farmer*, January 1928, p. 4; John P. Wallace, "What is going on in Washington," *WF*, 22 January 1926, p. 112; John P. Wallace, "What is happening at the nation's capital," *WF*, 1 March 1929, p. 356.

75. The McNary-Haugen bill passed again in 1928. President Coolidge vetoed it both times. See Fite, *Peek*, chaps. 10–12; and Black, "McNary-Haugen movement," pp. 408–11.

76. Arnold calls these policies "politically compelling." See R. Douglas Arnold, *The logic of congressional action* (New Haven: Yale University Press, 1990), pp. 77–78.

tors. The first set, as I will discuss shortly, was southerners. The second set, a set of one, was Jasper Napoleon Tincher, the Republican from the Seventh District of Kansas. In 1926, almost every other midwestern representative moved closer to the farm groups. Tincher, though, moved away, and his reasons for doing so tell us lots about the opposing motivations of his colleagues.

"Poley" Tincher was a huge man—he weighed about three hundred pounds. He was flamboyant, grandiloquent and popular. First elected in 1918, he was closely associated with Senator Capper, his cosponsor of the Grain Futures Act. In 1926, though, Tincher decided not to run for reelection, citing the financial sacrifices of public office.[77] He did an about-face on the McNary-Haugen bill, converting from its strongest champion to its greatest detractor.

Tincher explained that the farm organizations had made the bill unacceptable by deferring the equalization fee on corn and cotton, subverting their principles to expedience. Why the principles would suddenly outweigh the prospective benefit to his district in Kansas, a major wheat producer, is not immediately clear. A tantalizing hypothesis, however, is that Tincher's career was tied to the Republican Party and there his first loyalties lay. After deciding not to seek another term, he "grabbed the publicity, the prominence, and such measure of approval as there may be, for introducing [the Coolidge administration's bill]." That approval was important, because Tincher was a party man. In 1924, the *Times* confirmed his stature in the Republican Party, reporting his preference for Nicholas Longworth in the House Speaker's contest. That fall, he barnstormed the country with Kentucky congressman Alben Barkley, debating the parties' presidential platforms. In 1928, he won the honor of nominating Senator Curtis for president. Finally, in 1926, just before his retirement, he became chairman of the House Republican Steering Committee, a post that gave him broad influence over the agenda of the House.[78] Poley Tincher went his own way on farm relief, in short, because the Republican Party had more to offer him than any farm group. Party leadership was his choice, and regularity was its price.

His defection earned him the lasting hatred of the farm lobby. Kansas

77. *Hearings*, 1926, pp. 1276–77; Nellie Snyder Yost, *Medicine Lodge* (Chicago: Swallow Press, 1970), pp. 135, 137–38. Before his election to Congress, Tincher claimed a small bit of notoriety by representing David Nation in his divorce suit against his wife, Carry A. Nation, the hatchet-bearing prohibition crusader.

78. "Fake farm relief," *WF*, 23 April 1926, p. 628; *Hearings*, 1926, p. 1273; "J. N. Tincher, debated Barkley in 1924," *NYT*, 7 November 1951, p. 29; "Threaten to bar farm relief at all costs," *NYT*, 9 May 1926, p. 15; "Wants Longworth in chair," *NYT*, 20 December 1924, p. 17; Yost, *Medicine Lodge*, pp. 135–36. See also *Hearings*, 1925, pp. 468–69.

Farm Bureau president Ralph Snyder mounted such bitter attacks that Tincher threatened to organize a putsch in the Kansas Farm Bureau. In 1927, debate grew so heated that Tincher came to blows with another Kansas heavyweight, 275-pound representative James G. Strong, a McNary-Haugen supporter. When *Wallaces' Farmer* reproduced a Farm Bureau map of the 1926 House vote, finally, it made a point of identifying Tincher's district, a solitary "nay" in a sea of "ayes." In the end, however, the farm groups succeeded, one could say. Tincher's successor was Clifford R. Hope, who from beginning to end was a champion of farm price supports. Significantly, as Ralph Snyder recalled, "Poly stayed at home thereafter."[79]

In 1926, then, the farm lobby won access to the midwestern members of the Agriculture Committee. But it had taken rather more "persuasion" than the theory might imply. It had taken the longest farm depression in American history to convince agrarian lawmakers that intervention to maintain commodity prices was a recurrent issue. And it had taken electoral bludgeoning about the heads of Republican representatives to convince them of the farm groups' competitive advantage. The choice midwesterners made, perhaps, was the only choice they could have made.

Still, a real choice had been made. The events of 1926 convinced lawmakers that the presence of the farm groups would be profitable and lasting. In 1921 an insistent new force in agricultural politics and a severe economic crisis had added up to a Farm Bloc that had triumphed, then quickly collapsed. In 1924 an insistent new force armed with a popular new issue had generated interest but not solicitude. Only in 1926, when an insistent new force with a popular new issue joined up with proof of the farm lobby's competitive advantage and proof of the issue's staying power did lawmakers fall into line.

And why did it take so much? The answer, I think, is that the parties forced the issue. Farm relief policy was not lodged in some backwater, away from the care and scrutiny of party and president. It was the major annoyance of the Harding, Coolidge and (later) Hoover presidencies, and each administration put forth its own alternatives to head off the

79. Ralph Snyder, *We Kansas farmers* (Topeka: F. M. Steves and Sons, 1953[?]), p. 39; *Hearings*, 1926, pp. 1277–78; "Senate debates farm relief plan," *WF*, 4 June 1926, p. 820; Yost, *Medicine Lodge*, pp. 138–39. According to Forsythe, Hope initially disappointed the Kansas Farm Bureau by telling them that he could not support the McNary-Haugen bill because he did not think it would work. Whatever his misgivings, though, Hope prudently kept them to himself and voted for the equalization fee both in Committee and on the floor. See James L. Forsythe, "Clifford Hope of Kansas: Practical congressman and agrarian idealist," *Agricultural History*, 51 (April 1977), pp. 407–9; "Farm relief wins in House committee," *NYT*, 27 March 1928, p. 1.

more radical farm lobby proposals. The farm groups triumphed because the parties lacked not the power to contain them but the will to channel them, a point I will develop in the Commentary and conclusions. In the South, we shall see presently, the choice was cast less starkly.

The South Responds: Debentures, Allotments and Political Necessities

As of 1926, the forces that motivated alliances with the farm groups in the Midwest barely registered in the South.[80] On the Committee and on the floor, southern attitudes toward the farm lobby ranged widely. At one extreme, Agriculture's most junior Democrat, Hampton P. Fulmer of South Carolina, was a champion of the radical farm groups' perspective. At the other extreme, the Committee's two ranking Democrats, James B. Aswell of Louisiana and David H. Kincheloe of Kentucky, were the farm lobby's most dedicated antagonists. In between, Committee veterans Marvin Jones of Texas and Fletcher B. Swank of Oklahoma, both Democrats, were sympathetic to the farm groups' program but noncommittal to its sponsors.

The great variety of southern responses in the midtwenties had three sources, each of which defeated demonstrations of the farm lobby's competitive advantage and forestalled recurrence of the farm relief issue.

The first, quite simply, was the relative health of southern agriculture. Unlike corn and wheat, cotton and tobacco thrived after World War I, as traditional European markets reopened. In 1923, cotton sold for 28 cents a pound, and tobacco sold for 20 cents, roughly twice their historical averages. "While the agricultural readjustment will be somewhat slow and somewhat irregular," the southern journal *Progressive Farmer* concluded in 1924, comparing cotton to western crops, "we cannot doubt but that it is inevitable."[81] Agricultural price stabilization was not a recurrent issue in the South; in fact, it was not really an issue at all.

Second, the region's resolute devotion to the Democratic Party—and the clubby conduct of its Democratic primaries—limited the opportunities for farm group influence in its elections. Most southern Democratic parties harbored agrarian and bourbon factions, and appeals to farmers were routine, but the economic issues that animated the

---

80. Based on additional research, this section differs significantly from an earlier published version, "Choosing sides: The creation of an agricultural policy network in Congress, 1919–1932," *Studies in American Political Development*, 2 (1987), pp. 218–27.

81. "Better times ahead for farmers," *PF*, 5 July 1924, p. 778.

cleavage in the 1890s were secondary, by the 1920s, to the moral issues of prohibition and Ku Klux Klan "Americanism." Absent specifically agricultural unrest, there was little the farm lobby could offer to entice southern lawmakers away from their customary allegiances to the Democracy or to their friends and neighbors. The midwestern agrarians who tried to create an alliance with cotton growers, accordingly, were frustrated by southern Democratic complacency. "The corn belt, in common with the other farming sections, needs representatives who are primarily representatives of agriculture and only secondarily Republicans or Democrats," *Wallaces' Farmer* editor Donald R. Murphy explained. "The corn belt probably is better equipped this way than any other section. The South in its farming territory seems to be particularly handicapped by too many professional Democrats."[82]

Finally, the farm lobby's biggest problem in Dixie was the poor organization of its southern branches. Both the Grange and the Farmers Union had their origins in the South, but by the 1920s, the Grange had no affiliates in any of the eleven Confederate states and the Farmers Union hung on mostly in southwestern wheat states, chiefly in Oklahoma. At one time or another during the decade, twelve of the fourteen states of the American Farm Bureau's southern region had dues-paying affiliates. The only robust organization among them, however, was Alabama's, where membership represented one-third to one-half of the twenty- to thirty-thousand-member Farm Bureau enrollment of the entire region. Outside of Alabama and Oklahoma, and a little bit of Texas, the national farm groups were barely established in the South.[83]

82. Donald R. Murphy, "The Corn Belt's next move," *New Republic*, 28 July 1926, p. 275; Anne O'Hare McCormick, "The South: A fabric of cotton," *New York Times Magazine*, 1 June 1930, p. 1; V. O. Key, Jr., *Southern politics in state and nation* (New York: Alfred A. Knopf, 1949), part 1; Julius Turner, "Primary elections as the alternative to party competition in 'safe' districts," *Journal of Politics*, 15 (May 1953), pp. 197–210; David Chalmers, "The Ku Klux Klan in the politics of the 1920s," *Mississippi Quarterly*, 18 (Fall 1965), pp. 234–47; Charles C. Alexander, *The Ku Klux Klan in the Southwest* (Lexington: University of Kentucky Press, 1965); Norman D. Brown, *Hood, bonnet, and little brown jug* (College Station: Texas A&M University Press, 1984); James Benson Sellers, *The prohibition movement in Alabama* (Chapel Hill: University of North Carolina Press, 1943), chap. 10; Jeanne Bozzell McCarty, *The struggle for sobriety* (El Paso: Texas Western Press, 1980).

83. Fisher, *Farmers' Union*, p. 16; Wilson Gee and Edward Allison Terry, *The cotton cooperatives in the Southeast* (New York: D. Appleton-Century Co., 1933), p. 38; Wiest, *Agricultural organization*, p. 398; Theodore Saloutos, *Farmer movements*, chap. 2; "Membership paid to the American Farm Bureau Federation," pp. 250–51; Theodore Saloutos, "The Alabama Farm Bureau Federation," *Alabama Review*, 13 (July 1960), pp. 185–98. Because of the Farmers Union presence, Oklahoma's response to the farm lobby resembled the responses of its northern neighbors more than its southern neighbors. See

The early 1920s, then, offered southern members of Congress a great deal of freedom in their dealings with the farm lobby. The conditions of the period permitted little role for the agricultural pressure groups, and individual attitudes toward them varied widely. The farm groups promised no competitive advantage; the farm relief issue was not recurrent; and the loose discipline of southern electoral competition allowed lawmakers considerable flexibility. In 1926, in short, access for the farm lobby did not have the same force of necessity in the South as it had in the Middle West.

In the late 1920s, however, change began to overtake the South, at first marginally. Its instruments were the state cotton cooperatives, the most significant southern farm organizations in the early 1920s. Organized with the assistance of California cooperative promoter Aaron Sapiro and the state agricultural extension services, their hallmark was the "iron-clad" contract, a five-year agreement that obligated co-op members to deliver their production to the pool. The cooperatives paid growers a cash advance equal to whatever they could borrow against the value of the crop; they paid the balance after marketing the cotton. Established between 1921 and 1923, the cooperatives quickly flourished, and by 1924 they controlled a quarter of the cotton crop in some states, although less than 5 percent in others.[84]

Eric Manheimer, "The public career of Elmer Thomas," Ph.D. dissertation, University of Oklahoma, 1952, pp. 34–57; and Philip A. Grant, Jr., " 'Save the farmer': Oklahoma congressmen and farm relief legislation, 1924–1928," *Chronicles of Oklahoma*, 64 (Summer 1986), pp. 75–87.

84. Gee and Terry, *Cotton cooperatives,* chap. 2; Grace H. Larsen and Henry E. Erdman, "Aaron Sapiro: Genius of farm co-operative promotion," *Mississippi Valley Historical Review,* 49 (September 1962), pp. 242–68; William Johnson, "Cotton cooperatives at the crossroads," *CG,* 6 December 1924, p. 16; *Hearings before the House Agriculture Committee,* "Agricultural relief," 70th Congress, 1st session, Serial E (hereafter, *Hearings,* 1928), p. 261. Sapiro also helped organize tobacco cooperatives. Within a year of its founding the Burley Tobacco Growers Cooperative Association had enlisted 75 percent of the burley growers. See John K. Barnes, "An even break for the farmer," *World's Work,* October 1922, pp. 612–22; Clarence Poe, "Talking about cooperative marketing," *PF,* 7 July 1923, p. 683; William E. Ellis, "Robert Worth Bingham and the crisis of cooperative marketing in the twenties," *Agricultural History,* 56 (January 1982), pp. 99–116; and Carl C. Erwin, "The Dark Tobacco Growers Cooperative Association, 1922–1926," *Business History Review,* 40 (Winter 1966), pp. 403–31. The southern extension services' advancement of the cotton cooperatives is one reason why farm bureaus were slow getting started in the South. The exception was Alabama, where the extension service decided to promote the Alabama Farm Bureau instead of an incipient cotton growers association. Cotton co-ops in Alabama, Texas, Mississippi and Louisiana were Farm Bureau affiliates. See Gee and Terry, *Cotton cooperatives,* pp. 58–60; and Robert Hargrove Montgomery, *The cooperative pattern in cotton* (New York: Macmillan Co., 1929), pp. 76–77.

Until 1926, the cotton cooperatives showed little interest in legislative farm relief. With a strong cotton market, a proposal to tax growers to sell more cheaply abroad was not very enticing, and the "Sapiro coops" as a group, federated into the National Council of Farmers Cooperative Marketing Associations (NCFCMA), were implacably hostile to Peek's legislation, one provision of which would establish a government export corporation to compete with them. Fully satisfied with the situation, the cotton cooperatives did not even bother to respond to the early, halfhearted overtures of the national farm groups.[85]

In 1926, however, their interest in the Peek plan quickened when cotton prices skidded from 20 cents to 13 cents a pound. The market's sudden plunge awakened the cotton cooperatives to the limitations of purely private price-fixing and to the advantages of public authority. Furthermore, their interest was encouraged, to Sapiro's displeasure, by National Council secretary Walton Peteet, a Texan and formerly the head of the American Farm Bureau's cooperative marketing division. At Peteet's instigation, the American Cotton Growers Exchange conducted hasty negotiations with the Peek forces, winning a three-year deferral of the imposition of the equalization fee on cotton. In April 1926 the cotton cooperatives swung behind the bill.[86]

The cotton industry's conversion to the Peek plan had two distinct effects on the relationships of southern lawmakers to the farm lobby.

On the one hand, it kindled such sympathy as already existed in the South into genuine support. In the Agriculture Committee, the sigh of relief was almost audible when C. L. Stealey, manager of the Oklahoma Cotton Growers Association, came before the Committee to announce the alliance. Marvin Jones of Texas, who had voted for the 1924 McNary-Haugen bill, was pleased that the cotton growers had finally added their consent. F. B. Swank of Oklahoma could hardly contain his excitement. "You have made as clear, logical, and intelligent a statement as was ever made before this committee," he told Stealey. "I get a chance to vote for him, you understand," replied Stealey, to laughter. They understood.[87]

In the House and the Senate, the support of the cotton cooperatives, supplemented in 1927 by the endorsement of the tobacco cooperatives, herded southerners into the McNary-Haugen coalition in numbers suf-

85. "Federation of co-operatives meets," WF, 16 January 1925, p. 72; Larsen and Erdman, "Aaron Sapiro"; James L. Guth, "The National Cooperative Council and farm relief, 1929–1942," Agricultural History, 51 (April 1977), pp. 442–43.

86. Benedict, Farm policies, pp. 223–24; Christensen, "Agricultural pressure," pp. 203–10; "Cotton men join with Corn Belt," WF, 16 April 1926, p. 592; "Rumpus over farm plan," NYT, 23 April 1926, p. 4; Fite, Peek, chap. 10.

87. Hearings, 1926, pp. 1080, 1074–78.

ficient to pass the bill in 1927 and again in 1928. The pact between the Corn Belt and the Cotton Belt won the farm lobby the votes it had previously lacked.[88]

On the other hand, it brought the farm organizations no more access than they had enjoyed before. In the Committee, the breach between midwestern and southern attitudes toward the farm lobby was as wide as ever. As we have seen, the midwestern members of the Agriculture Committee had already reached an understanding with the agricultural organizations: they would go as far as necessary to secure farm relief, as long as the farm organizations did their part. By 1928, the bargain was explicit:

FRED S. PURNELL (R., Ind.): If some of us decide to follow the views of the farm organizations, as we have done here for a number of years, and take responsibility for sending a bill down to the President which we know now will be vetoed, and rely upon your judgment and the farmers get no legislation, then you take responsibility for our action.

CHESTER H. GRAY (American Farm Bureau Federation): We are not shirking that responsibility.

PURNELL: I say it is a two-edged sword. If we do what we think is right and it does not agree with what you think is right, then we are responsible, but if we follow your judgment and are wrong, that is your responsibility.

GRAY: That is a very gentlemanly and very exact way of stating it, I believe.[89]

A good fraction of the Committee's southerners, however, were still unwilling to play the farm lobby's game:

JAMES B. ASWELL (D., La.): Mr. Chairman, I want to ask a question. If this committee should fail to keep in exact step with Chester Gray, would the committee be abolished by reason of that fact?

DAVID H. KINCHELOE (D., Ky.): . . . So far as I am concerned, when

---

88. Fite, *Peek*, chaps. 11–12; Black, "McNary-Haugen movement," pp. 408–11; "South holds fate of M'Nary measure," *NYT*, 27 November 1926, p. 5; "Haugen bill strong," *WF*, 11 February 1927, p. 210; H. A. Wallace, "How the farm bill went through," *WF*, 25 February 1927, p. 301. For accounts of the motivations behind the southern turnarounds, see Escal Franklin Duke, "The political career of Morris Sheppard, 1875–1941," Ph.D. dissertation, University of Texas, 1958, p. 358; Martha H. Swain, *Pat Harrison: The New Deal years* (Jackson: University Press of Mississippi, 1978), p. 14; Robert Dean Pope, "Senatorial baron: The long political career of Kenneth D. McKellar," Ph.D. dissertation, Yale University, 1976, pp. 155–57.

89. *Hearings,* 1928, pp. 43–44, pp. 18, 28, 37–38, 46–47, 57, 61, 332, 425–26. A comparison with Purnell's reaction to similar farm lobby demands in 1925 shows the degree to which midwestern relations with the farm lobby had changed. In 1925, Purnell and other midwesterners were obviously irritated that the farm groups continued to push the McNary-Haugen bill, despite Coolidge's landslide the November before. *Hearings,* 1925, pp. 432–33, 493–95.

anybody begins to try to browbeat this committee it does not take well with me, and Mr. Gray does not get anywhere with me, as a member of this committee, by any threat.

Throughout the 1928 hearings on the McNary-Haugen bill, southern lawmakers led the attacks on the farm groups again, even when southern witnesses presented the farm lobby's views. Congressional defenders of beleaguered cotton organizers, such as they were, hailed from the Middle West. Despite the addition of the cotton and tobacco growers' support, the farm lobby's access to the southern members of the Committee was no broader in the late twenties than it was in years earlier.[90]

Even among the farm lobby's southern sympathizers, moreover, the farm organizations' definition of the farm relief issue was no more authoritative after the corn and cotton alliance than before it. Conscious of the need for a response to the agricultural depression, southern lawmakers turned not to the relief plan of the Peek lobby, the equalization fee, but to the relief plan of the National Grange, the export debenture. In the late 1920s and early 1930s, the debenture's most prominent promoters in Congress were two Texans, Representative Marvin Jones and Senator Tom Connally, and its most loyal adherents were southerners.[91] As written into several bills, the debenture program earmarked a percentage of tariff revenues for the payment of bounties ("debentures") to exporters of agricultural products. For southern Democrats, it had several attractions. It promoted exports of cotton, half of which was shipped abroad already. It financed the program out of the proceeds of the hated tariff, thereby avoiding an unpopular new tax on producers, the equalization fee. Finally, and most importantly, it symbolized the attentiveness of southern congressional delegations to the economic predicament of southern farmers.[92]

90. *Hearings*, 1928, p. 206, pp. 23–28, 32–34, 96–97, 112–13, 147, 195, 201–2, 222–26, 236–40, 256–63, 288–89, 462, 471–90, 659–61. The same southern independence held true on the floor. "Senate passes McNary–Haugen bill," *WF*, 18 February 1927, p. 245; "More support for Haugen bill," *WF*, 10 February 1928, p. 212; "Consistent southern Democrats," *NYT*, 5 May 1928, p. 16. See also Philip A. Grant, Jr., "Southern congressmen and agriculture, 1921–1932," *Agricultural History*, 53 (January 1979), pp. 339–46.

91. The debenture's adoption by southern legislators had nothing to do with granger agitation in southern states. The first grange in Texas, although organized in Jones's Panhandle district, was not established until 1931. Pressure politics was not the Grange's style in any event. "Grange invasion of the Southland gets a good foothold in Texas," *National Grange Monthly*, June 1931, p. 5; *Hearings*, 1928, p. 306; Fred Brenckman, "Defending the interests of the farmer," *National Grange Monthly*, September 1929, p. 10.

92. Joseph Stancliffe Davis, *The farm export debenture plan* (Stanford: Food Research Institute, 1929); Irvin M. May, Jr., *Marvin Jones: The public life of an agrarian advocate*

To the farm groups' dismay, however, the export debenture also diverted southern lawmakers from the farm relief fight, as the Peek lobby, at least, had defined it. "While the export debenture plan undoubtedly had a number of things to commend it," midwestern editor Henry A. Wallace groused, "no friend of the farmer should have brought it in at this time."[93]

Despite the addition of the cotton and tobacco growers' endorsements, in sum, southern support for the farm lobby was as irresolute in the late 1920s as it was in the early 1920s. To be sure, the alliance added votes to the farm organizations' column, but it did not overcome the resistance of its southern opponents or the independence of its southern sympathizers. The alliance of corn and cotton won the farm lobby no more access in the South than it had before.

The reasons were clear. In the South, the problems that had incapacitated the farm organizations in the early 1920s persisted into the late 1920s. The farm organizations remained unable to demonstrate their competitive advantage over southern politics as usual, and the farm economy continued to counteract judgments of the farm relief issue's recurrence. Fundamentally, nothing had changed.

First, the farm relief issue was a recurrent part of the southern political agenda only ambiguously. In the late twenties, the dominant perceptions of the nature of the cotton depression still could not sustain a belief in the relief issue's permanence, despite the cooperatives' attempts to induce it. On the one hand, North Carolina senator Furnifold M. Simmons wrote, "cotton surpluses are temporary, not permanent in nature." On the other hand, he continued, "the cotton industry is perennially subject to the danger of overproduction." Even if that were true, however, it implied that this crisis was no different from any earlier crisis, and farmers and legislators had managed to live through them just fine. In 1927, as if to confirm the lack of recurrence, cotton prices rose to their precrisis level, and the clamor for farm relief quieted.[94]

(College Station: Texas A&M University Press, 1980), chap. 5; Grant, "Southern congressmen," pp. 347–49; *Hearings*, 1928, pp. 324–32; Marvin Jones, "Advantages of the export debenture plan," *National Grange Monthly*, April 1928, p. 7; Tom Connally, "What export debenture really means," *National Grange Monthly*, January 1931, p. 4. In the two instances in which the debenture came to a vote, as amendments to the Agricultural Marketing Act in 1929 and to the Smoot-Hawley tariff bill in 1929 and 1930, southerners supported it in droves: 85 percent southern approval in the House, 98 percent approval in the Senate. Fred Brenckman, "The story of the export debenture plan," *National Grange Monthly*, June 1930, p. 3; Richard V. Oulahan, "Democrats make debentures issue," *NYT*, 5 May 1929, p. 1.

93. Wallace, "How the farm bill went through," p. 301.

94. F. M. Simmons, "Cotton and the McNary-Haugen bill," *CG*, August 1927, p. 12; "News farmers want to know," *PF*, 7 August 1926, p. 834.

In the late 1920s, likewise, the farm groups were no closer to competitive advantage than they had ever been before. In the South, candidates for Congress raised the equalization fee issue only rarely, and when they did, the issue was seldom decisive. Tom Connally of Texas, for instance, encountered two opponents who assailed his resistance to the McNary-Haugen bill, once in his 1926 bid for reelection to the House and once in his 1928 bid for election to the Senate. In both races, the issue was more an irritant than an impediment.[95]

The farm lobby's alliance with the cotton and tobacco cooperatives, moreover, gained it little true leverage. The cooperatives were unconvincing apostles of farm relief, as southern opponents of farm relief were quick to point out. When B. W. Kilgore, president of the American Cotton Growers Exchange, testified before the Agriculture Committee in 1928, for example, Louisiana's James B. Aswell was prepared for an ambush:

ASWELL: You made a statement that your cotton exchange demands the equalization fee or nothing, in substance?

KILGORE: You remember just how I answered.

ASWELL: I remember what you said. What part of the cotton producers do you claim that your exchange represents right now?

KILGORE: At its best it represented 10 per cent of them.

ASWELL: May I interrupt you to read the report of the Department of Agriculture, prepared at my request. . . . I would like the committee to get this [reading]: "The average of the United States"—that is, the cotton sections— "1921 and 1922, handled by the cooperatives was 5.3 per cent; 1922 and 1923, it was 7.4 per cent; 1924–25 it was 8 per cent; and 1925–26 it was 9.1 per cent." That is the highest?

KILGORE: That is the highest.

ASWELL: That was not 10 per cent. . . . I want the committee to note, if they will, that the American Cotton Exchange does not represent the cotton growers of the South.

In short, the cooperatives' political handicaps were obvious—they did not represent many farmers—and they only worsened. In 1927, beset

---

95. Tom Connally, *My name is Tom Connally* (New York: Thomas Y. Crowell Co., 1954), pp. 113, 127; Irvin S. Taubkin, "Texas takes steps to aid cotton men," *NYT,* 19 August 1928, p. II 8; "Connally beats Mayfield in Texas primary," *NYT,* 27 August 1928, p. 3. See also Daniel W. Hollis, "Cole L. Blease and the senatorial campaign of 1924," *Proceedings of the South Carolina Historical Association,* 1978, pp. 53–68; T. Harry Williams, *Huey Long* (New York: Alfred A. Knopf, 1969), p. 468; Virginia Van der Veer Hamilton, *Hugo Black: The Alabama years* (Baton Rouge: Louisiana State University Press, 1972), chap. 6; Pope, "Senatorial baron," pp. 180–86; "Robinson opens campaign," *NYT,* 27 July 1930, p. 2; "South Carolina to vote tomorrow," *NYT,* 25 August 1930, p. 2.

by a weak cotton market and the simultaneous expiration of the first ironclad contracts, the Alabama Farm Bureau Cotton Association lost over half its members. It was lucky; the Georgia, South Carolina and North Carolina Cotton Growers' Associations lost nearly 90 percent of theirs. "It is not unlikely," *Progressive Farmer* concluded, "that the whole national program of farm legislation has been seriously crippled and delayed, if not destroyed, because of the failure of Southern farmers to stand solidly with Western farmers in organizations demanding [farm] relief."[96]

In the late 1920s, then, farm lobby access in the South was no more extensive or intensive than it was a few years earlier, despite the advent of southern farm relief pressures. The weak sense of the issue's recurrence and the inability of the farm lobby to demonstrate its competitive advantage left southern lawmakers a wide range of options. The representatives of the South, even if sympathetic, refused to adopt the farm organizations' perspectives as their own.

In the early 1930s, however, reorientation occurred. In the throes of the Great Depression, southern perceptions of issue permanence and interest group advantage changed dramatically. The global depression of 1929 retrenched European export markets, and cotton and tobacco prices marched steadily downward. Cotton fell from 17 cents in 1929 to 10 cents in 1930 to less than 6 cents in 1931. Tobacco dropped from 18 cents to 13 cents to barely 8 cents. By the opening of the Seventy-second Congress in 1931, the leading cash crops of the South earned less than half what they had two years before.

The desperate condition of the southern agricultural economy in the early thirties completely reoriented perceptions of the farm relief issue.

First, the terrifying collapse of the southern agricultural economy transformed a weak sense of the recurrence of demands for farm relief into a strong sense. "In the case of cotton and tobacco," *Progressive Farmer* admitted in 1931, "what confronts us is not just an emergency that will pass in one year, two years, or even five years. . . . No, on the contrary, we are faced with a lasting, permanent, here-to-stay change in conditions."[97]

Second, and importantly, the collapse of the cotton economy prompted a reevaluation of the farm lobby's competitive advantage. The depression devastated every class of cotton producer, from planter to yeoman to tenant to cropper, and it touched off agitation for farm relief

96. *Hearings*, 1928, pp. 259–60; "A farmers' organization in every neighborhood," *PF*, 24 September 1927, p. 976; Gee and Terry, *Cotton cooperatives*, p. 154.

97. "We must change not for a year but for a lifetime," *PF*, 1–14 October 1931, p. 618.

in the South on a scale unequaled since the Populist upheaval of the
1890s. Amid growers' calls for some sort of acreage control, Louisiana
governor Huey P. Long proposed a cotton holiday, a state-enforced ban
on cotton production in 1932. Within days, a special session of the
Louisiana legislature passed it unanimously; within weeks, a special
session of the South Carolina legislature also approved it. Met by conservative opposition in Texas, the largest cotton state by far, the
"drop-a-crop" proposal lost its momentum, but the agitation did not.
Confronted with protests and mass meetings, a special session of the
Texas state legislature voted down the cotton holiday bill, then voted
up a 70 percent cut in cotton acreage. In all, five southern states—
Louisiana, South Carolina, Texas, Arkansas and Mississippi—enacted
cotton control legislation in 1931.[98]

Southern senators and representatives took a healthy interest in the
proceedings. When state officials gathered at a 1931 conference to consider holiday legislation, Eugene Talmadge observed, "United States
senators and congressmen . . . were as thick as flies around a hash
joint." Their concern was only prudent. For the first time in their
careers, southern members of Congress were behind the eight ball on
agricultural issues. Organized or not, legions of cotton farmers spoiled
for farm relief—any farm relief—and scores of governors and state legislators, who had promoted aid to cotton, stood by, ready in case incumbents faltered. The crop control movement was a direct, undisputed
threat to the tenure of southern congressmen in office.[99]

98. Robert E. Snyder, *Cotton crisis* (Chapel Hill: University of North Carolina Press,
1984); Renwick C. Kennedy, "Six cent cotton; a southern tragedy," *New Republic*, 16
December 1931, pp. 129–30; Irvin S. Taubkin, "East Texas in arms over oil production,"
NYT, 5 April 1931, p. III 5; "Says 5 more states will set cotton curb," *NYT*, 8 September
1931, p. 44; "Texas House rejects Long's cotton plan," *NYT*, 12 September 1931, p. 2;
"Cotton parley votes for 50% acreage cut," *NYT*, 24 November 1931, p. 43. During the
cotton crisis of 1926, conferences entertained similar proposals, but the agitation was not
as widespread. Moreover, the impetus was from agricultural lenders rather than growers,
and the solutions offered were more often private (cotton pools) than legislative. See
George Milton Fort, "Can cotton be controlled by law?" *Independent*, 6 November 1926,
p. 531; "Baruch advises holding cotton crop," *NYT*, 11 October 1926, p. 10; "For cotton
relief by holding crop," *NYT*, 14 October 1926, p. 27; "Finance Alabama cotton," *NYT*,
26 October 1926, p. 39; "Demand Texas cotton cut," *NYT*, 27 October 1926, p. 16;
"South acts quickly to hold its cotton," *NYT*, 2 November 1926, p. 43; "Would regulate
cotton acreage by law," *NYT*, 17 February 1927, p. 11.

99. Snyder, *Cotton crisis*, p. 40, p. 52; "Wants Board to buy cotton at 12 cents," *NYT*,
19 August 1931, p. 4; "Hoover transmits new cotton plan," *NYT*, 24 August 1931, p. 9;
"Discuss purchase of cotton by Board," *NYT*, 29 August 1931, p. 3; "Robinson asks cut in
cotton acreage," *NYT*, 5 September 1931, p. 23.

In the early 1930s, then, the farm relief high ground suddenly became the most important electoral resource in the rural South, and by virtue of its historic leadership of the farm relief movement, the equalization fee lobby controlled it. With the pressures building at home, southern Democrats, newly installed in the congressional leadership after an absence of twelve years, needed a farm program, and the farm organizations were ready to help.

Sensing the direction of the partisan winds, the American Farm Bureau Federation named Alabama cotton planter Edward A. O'Neal to succeed AFBF president Sam H. Thompson, a Hoover appointee to the Federal Farm Board. The grandson of one Alabama governor and the nephew of another, O'Neal operated a cotton plantation overlooking Muscle Shoals. He became Federation vice president in 1923, after two years at the Alabama Farm Bureau's helm, and in 1925, the delivery of his bloc of southern votes swung the Federation's presidency to Sam Thompson. Symbolically, the 1925 election consummated the Farm Bureau's "marriage of corn and cotton," although that alliance was more poetic than substantial. The Corn Belt continued to dominate the Farm Bureau, but O'Neal had too many useful qualities for the Federation to pass him over in 1931. As a Democrat, a southerner and a cotton farmer, with a vast network of contacts throughout the cotton states, O'Neal was a spokesman for southern farmers in Congress, a propagandist for southern legislators back home.[100]

Under O'Neal's stewardship, the Farm Bureau moved gradually away from the Peek plan and gradually toward a farm relief proposal more in line with southern needs. In May 1932, it agreed to lobby alongside the Grange and the Farmers Union on behalf of almost any farm relief program, be it the equalization fee, the export debenture or the domestic allotment. As the presidential campaign swung into high gear, however, the prospects for the fee and the debenture dimmed. In a speech in Topeka in September 1932, Franklin D. Roosevelt lent his endorsement to the domestic allotment plan, and with his landslide victory two months later, the Farm Bureau yielded to pragmatism. In December 1932, Farm Bureau leaders gave the allotment plan their private approval, and in January 1933, O'Neal made the endorsement public. "The equalization fee and the debenture . . . have not lost their attraction," Chester Gray

100. Theodore Saloutos, "Edward A. O'Neal," *Current History,* 28 (June 1955), pp. 356–61; Saloutos, "Alabama Farm Bureau," pp. 189–90; Kile, *Farm Bureau,* p. 134; Christiana McFadyen Campbell, *The Farm Bureau and the New Deal* (Urbana: University of Illinois Press, 1962), pp. 37–38, 42, 58–60; P. O. Davis, *One man: Edward Asbury O'Neal III of Alabama* (Auburn: Alabama Polytechnic Institute, 1945).

assured Farm Bureau members, "but temporarily they have been laid aside for consideration of the farm allotment plan."[101]

The domestic allotment fit the political needs of southern Democrats quite well. It was, in a sense, the only farm relief plan that was politically tested in the South. It called for direct cash payments to farmers, financed by a tax on processors, in exchange for limitations on plantings. It was conceived by William J. Spillman in the Bureau of Agricultural Economics in the mid-1920s, and it was originally applied, to wheat, by Montana State College economist M. L. Wilson. Southern legislators, however, found the allotment plan particularly attractive. "The [cotton control] legislation passed by Louisiana, Texas, and South Carolina in the Fall and Winter of 1931–32," a 1934 study noted, "indicated the South's demand for some form of acreage control." Indeed, contemporaries affirmed, in 1931, "after the failure of all other plans, we believe that three out of four cotton farmers would vote for the regulation of cotton acreage by law." Unlike the fee and the debenture, then, the domestic allotment plan was something of a known quantity in the South. The popularity of acreage control had already been assessed and found acceptable.[102]

In the early thirties, therefore, the conditions for lobbying access to southern members of Congress were fulfilled. Agitation for farm relief was widespread and dangerous, and given the condition of the farm economy, the agitation was not soon to end. The farm organizations

101. Chester H. Gray, "Jobs for the special session," *Bureau Farmer*, April 1933, p. 3; James A. Hagerty, "Roosevelt maps farm relief program, pledges tariff aid in Topeka speech," *NYT*, 15 September 1932, p. 1; William D. Rowley, *M. L. Wilson and the campaign for the domestic allotment* (Lincoln: University of Nebraska Press, 1970), chaps. 7–8; Campbell, *Farm Bureau*, pp. 50–57; Reminiscences of Milburn L. Wilson, Columbia Oral History Collection, 1956, pp. 614–57; "News of the Farm Bureau," *Bureau Farmer*, February 1932, p. 8; Edward A. O'Neal, "Prevent revolution," *Bureau Farmer*, March 1933, p. 3; Richard S. Kirkendall, *Social scientists and farm politics in the age of Roosevelt* (Ames: Iowa State University Press, 1982), chap. 2. The Farm Bureau was the only national farm organization to muster much enthusiasm for the allotment plan. Firebrand Farmers Union president John A. Simpson detested acreage control; moderate Grange master L. J. Taber was typically noncommittal. See Rowley, *M. L. Wilson*, pp. 187–88; Gilbert C. Fite, "John A. Simpson: The Southwest's militant farm leader," *Mississippi Valley Historical Review* 35 (March 1949), pp. 563–84.

102. Charles S. Johnson, Edwin R. Embree and W. W. Alexander, *The collapse of cotton tenancy* (Chapel Hill: University of North Carolina Press, 1935), p. 48; "The cotton surplus problem," *PF*, 15–30 September 1931, p. 586; Donald R. Murphy, "Can we control production?" *WF*, 16 April 1932, p. 219; "'Domestic allotment' farm relief," *PF*, January 1933, p. 3; Louis H. Cook, "Domestic allotment," *CG*, February 1933, pp. 10–11; Rowley, *M. L. Wilson*, chap. 8; Wilson reminiscences, p. 742.

were positioned to defuse it, headed by a sympathetic leader and willing to accommodate southern desires with policies more in line with southern needs. True, the competitive advantage of the farm organizations was not yet proven in elections, as it was and continued to be in the Midwest.[103] Rather, it was proven in agitation. The campaign for a cotton holiday in the South indicated grass roots support for the idea of acreage control, an idea the Farm Bureau hastily and obligingly adopted as its own. As the representative of a demonstrably popular program of acreage control and price support, made all the more credible by the leadership of O'Neal, the Farm Bureau dispensed indulgences against charges of indifference and neglect, the most likely weapons of challengers to southern incumbents.

In the early 1930s, therefore, the farm lobby's hopes for access in the South were finally met. Southern lawmakers opened the Seventy-second Congress in 1932 in an anxious mood, and their courtship of the farm lobby commenced. As the first order of business, the House Agriculture Committee, newly under Democratic control, met for a day of hearings solely to hear the views of the Farm Bureau, the Grange and the Farmers Union, the first time it had extended them the courtesy of an unshared forum. The southerners were impatient for answers. "I want to say this, as one member of Congress," Georgia Democrat William W. Larsen told Farmers Union president John A. Simpson.

I am willing to follow out any program that you gentlemen, the leaders of the great farm organizations, will outline in something besides resolutions. Bring in a plan or the bill that you want us to pass. . . . Do you not think that if the leaders of these great agricultural organizations in the country—you have some fine organizations—would get together and instead of passing resolutions, instead of making beautiful speeches . . . draft a bill, and guarantee to the Agricultural Committee that if the bill were enacted into law that you would stand by and abide by its results, the committee would recommend and the Congress would

103. On the continuing effectiveness of the farm relief issue in midwestern elections, see L. C. Speers, "Farm bill veto opens the 1928 battle," *NYT,* 6 March 1927, p. IX 1; Roland M. Jones, "Western corn belt tastes prosperity," *NYT,* 31 July 1927, p. II 9; "Howell in lead in Nebraska," *NYT,* 11 April 1928, p. 2; "Smith Iowa victory spurs Hoover foes to push farm issue," *NYT,* 9 April 1928, p. 1; Richard V. Oulahan, "Election issues press to front," *NYT,* 20 July 1930, p. III 8; "Wheat prices loom as campaign issue," *NYT,* 21 July 1930, p. 5; Walter M. Harrison, "Oklahoma's Moses has new tax plan," *NYT,* 3 August 1930, p. III 5; "Nebraska," *NYT,* 2 November 1930, p. II 2; Richard V. Oulahan, "Republicans lose grip on Congress," *NYT,* 6 November 1930, p. 2; "Kansas governorship becomes doubtful," *NYT,* 6 November 1930, p. 5; Patrick G. O'Brien, "William H. McMaster: An agrarian dissenter during 'normalcy,'" *Emporia State Research Studies,* 20 (June 1972), p. 39.

pass it. Do you not think that we would be willing to follow you in the matter? I think I will if the farm organizations agree on it.[104]

The understanding that southerners reached with the farm groups was a simple one. In essence, they promised to support whatever the agricultural organizations wanted, but only if the farm lobby would stand by it, that is, only if the farm groups would defend them before voters if the program proved unpopular. The 1932 farm relief hearings, consequently, turned on assays of the farm groups' resolve, led by the Committee's new Democratic chairman, Marvin Jones of Texas:

> JONES: Are we to regard this [bill] as a getting together of the farm groups?
> CHESTER GRAY (American Farm Bureau Federation): Yes; indeed.
> JONES: You have gotten together by taking all the plans and offering all of them?
> GRAY: Yes; that is indeed true. . . .
> JONES: You have the equalization fee plan, the debenture plan, and the allotment plan in this bill. If the committee should see fit to eliminate the debenture plan and the equalization plan and take the allotment plan alone, would you be willing to support that?
> GRAY: We will stand by it, or any similar actions.
> JONES: If the committee should see fit to eliminate the allotment plan and the equalization fee and take the debenture plan, would you fellows all get behind it and let the other plans go?
> GRAY: Yes, sir; that is the understanding.
> JONES: If the committee should see fit to eliminate the debenture plan and the allotment plan and sponsor the equalization fee plan, then all of you agree that you will abandon the other plans and follow the arrangement?
> GRAY: That is the understanding.[105]

The understanding reached, the Agriculture Committee hearings of December 1932, called to consider Jones's domestic allotment bill, went off without a hitch. The farm organizations, assured of a friendly reception, sent only a handful of witnesses, and O'Neal waived most of the time they were allocated. The basic point, after all, was already estab-

104. *Hearings before the House Agriculture Committee*, "Program of the national farm organizations," 72d Congress, 1st session, Serial A, 1932 (hereafter *Hearings*, "Farm organizations' program," 1932), pp. 28–29.

105. *Hearings before the House Agriculture Committee*, "Farm marketing program," 72d Congress, 1st session, Serial E, 1932 (hereafter *Hearings*, "Marketing program," 1932), p. 163, pp. 27–28, 76–77, 95, 166–71. See also Marvin Jones, "The second ten years," *Nation's Agriculture*, January 1940, p. 13. As if to test the farm groups' consistency, others on the Committee, particularly Republicans, asked them to repeat their precise positions on the Agricultural Marketing Act and queried whether they still stood by them even after the Federal Farm Board's failures. See, e.g., *Hearings*, "Farm organizations' program," 1932, pp. 32–33.

lished. "Does this general program have the unanimous indorsement of the farm representatives?" Jones asked Frederic P. Lee, the Washington attorney retained by the Farm Bureau to draft the bill. "It has the unanimous indorsement of all the farm representatives present," Lee confirmed.[106]

By the dawn of the New Deal, then, the agricultural interest groups had won access to members of Congress from the Middle West *and* from the South. "The farm lobby," a veteran Washington reporter observed, in December 1932, "is the most powerful single-industry lobby in Washington." In 1933, the House Agriculture Committee received the draft of the Agricultural Adjustment Act and reported it in just four days, with neither hearings nor amendments.[107] In a little more than a decade, farmers had taken a policy domain open to producers, suppliers, processors and even consumers and made it their exclusive province.

Conclusion

The origins of interest group access in agriculture trace to the 1920s. Two features of the chronology stand out. First, rural legislators maintained their independence from the farm groups for years after the advent of farm relief pressures. Second, lawmakers from the Middle West developed cooperative relationships with the agriculture lobby years before lawmakers from the South.

The chronology has major implications: it helps to rule out plausibly competing explanations. First, members of Congress did not simply take the farm lobby at its word from word one. The existence of the farm organizations, their placement in Washington and their adoption of a

106. *Hearings before the House Agriculture Committee*, "Agricultural adjustment program," 72d Congress, 2d session, Serial M, 1932, p. 16, pp. 17, 265; May, *Marvin Jones*, pp. 90, 100–102; Van L. Perkins, *Crisis in agriculture* (Berkeley and Los Angeles: University of California Press, 1969), pp. 32–33; "Farm bill drafted along allotment lines," *NYT*, 14 December 1932, p. 17; "Farm parity bill reported to House," *NYT*, 4 January 1933, p. 1; "Farm bill planned in simplified form," *NYT*, 3 February 1933, p. 2. The hearings on the Jones bill, held after the 1932 elections, gave evidence that midwestern lame ducks (that is, every midwestern Republican except Clifford Hope) resented the farm lobby's turn to the allotment plan. Hearings held prior to the election, however, demonstrated continued farm lobby access to Agriculture's midwesterners. See pp. 19–20, 90–91, 101, 148–52, 204; and compare *Hearings*, "Marketing program," 1932, pp. 23–25, 68, 80–81, 84, 93, 170–74. On Hope and the domestic allotment, see Forsythe, "Clifford Hope," pp. 409–11; Rowley, *M. L. Wilson*, pp. 137–42, 153.

107. *Kiplinger Agricultural Letter* No. 96, 31 December 1932; George Hoffman, "Executive-legislative relations in the first AAA," Ph.D. dissertation, University of Chicago, 1961, chaps. 2–3; Perkins, *Crisis*, chaps. 3–4.

farm relief program were insufficient reasons for access. Lawmakers did not automatically recognize the right and ability of the farm lobby to speak for farmers. Had they done so, access would have been immediate. Instead, access was delayed.

Second, members of Congress did not simply "get used to" the farm lobby. The appearance and reappearance of the farm organizations before the Agriculture Committee and the iteration and reiteration of their farm relief demands were insufficient reasons for access. Lawmakers did not open up to the farm lobby simply because they got to know it better. Had they done so, access to midwestern and southern members would have been simultaneous. Instead, access was dissynchronous.

The argument offered in chapter 1 accounts for both features. First, farm lobby access to rural legislators was delayed because fulfillment of the conditions for access was delayed. Before 1926, lawmakers had limited evidence that the farm organizations' aid in elections measured up to their parties'. Before 1926, likewise, they believed that the farm relief issue would not recur. Antagonizing others to satisfy the farm lobby's demands made no sense as long as its ability and future commitment to protect its partisans was unknown. Before 1926, then, members of Congress avoided reliance on the farm groups.

After 1926, the story changed. Higher prices for farm commodities were the difference between success and failure for millions of farmers, and in the 1924 and 1926 elections midwestern lawmakers learned that advocacy of the farm lobby's subsidy plan insulated them from party competition and internecine Republican bickering. Likewise, 1926 revealed that the farm crisis would not abate. The farm groups—and farm voters—were unlikely to abandon their friends in the future. In the late 1920s, then, midwestern lawmakers grew to rely on the agricultural producer groups for advice and assistance.

Second, farm lobby access to rural legislators was dissynchronous because fulfillment of the conditions for access was dissynchronous. In contrast to the Middle West, the health of the agricultural economy in the South persisted into the early 1930s, forestalling recurrence of agrarian demands for farm relief. Likewise in contrast, the farm lobby's weakness in the South continued into the early 1930s, delaying the display of its competitive advantage.

In the early 1930s, however, conditions changed. Southern agriculture lay prostrate before the worldwide depression; southern demands for farm relief grew in extent and in force; forecasts of the future turned pessimistic. Lured by an escape from recurrent challenges on farm issues, southern representatives turned to the farm lobby for advice and assistance. In the South, as in the Midwest, the farm lobby won access only after it had shown its competitive advantage, only after its issue had proven recurrent.

Members of Congress, in sum, withheld access from the agricultural interest groups until they could see that their advice was correct. The farm groups needed to show that they really spoke for farmers—they needed elections or agitation that endorsed the program they had put before Congress. Likewise, the farm groups needed to show that they would continue to speak for farmers—they needed conditions that preserved the salience of the program they had put before Congress.

By the dawn of the New Deal, they had shown both. The farm lobby's access in Congress was complete.

3   The Maintenance of Access
in Agriculture,
1933–1947

> Regardless of the outcome of the elections the farmer
> is still the "pampered pet of politicians," and will get
> all that he can grab during the next four years at
> least.
> *Kiplinger Agricultural Letter* (1936)[1]

On 12 May 1933, President Franklin D. Roosevelt approved the Agricultural Adjustment Act, the capstone of the farm lobby's ten-year battle for farm relief. The new statute directed the secretary of agriculture to raise agricultural prices and granted him broad powers to fulfill his mandate. First, it authorized application of the voluntary domestic allotment plan to seven "basic" commodities. It allowed the secretary to collect a tax from agricultural processors and to use the proceeds to recompense farmers who cut back their production of corn, cotton, hogs, milk, rice, tobacco or wheat. Second, the act permitted negotiation of marketing agreements between the growers and processors of any agricultural commodity. It authorized the secretary to mediate the terms of marketing contracts and to enforce them (if need be) by licensing firms in the industry. Whether through production allotments, marketing agreements or combinations thereof, the Agricultural Adjustment Act prescribed parity prices for the commodities farmers produced.[2]

To administer the government's new responsibilities, the Agricultural

1. *Kiplinger Agricultural Letter* (hereafter *KAL*) No. 201, 3 October 1936.
2. "Parity" was an index of the purchasing power of one unit of an agricultural commodity. It represented the price needed to give a bushel of corn or a pound of cotton (or whatever) the same buying power as it had in the period 1909 to 1914. For a discussion, see Robert L. Tontz, "Origin of the base period concept of parity: A significant value judgment in agricultural history," *Agricultural History*, 32 (January 1958), pp. 3–13. For a quick introduction to farm program terminology, see Marvin Duncan and C. Edward Harshbarger, "A primer on agricultural policy," *Federal Reserve Bank of Kansas City Monthly Review* (September–October 1977), pp. 3–10. For a good summary of the provisions of the Agricultural Adjustment Act and succeeding statutes, see Douglas E. Bowers, Wayne D. Rasmussen and Gladys L. Baker, *History of agricultural price support and adjustment programs, 1933–84*, Agriculture Information Bulletin No. 485, Economic Research Service, U.S. Department of Agriculture, 1984.

Adjustment Act created a new agency within the Department of Agriculture (USDA), the Agricultural Adjustment Administration (AAA). Roosevelt reached deep into the farm relief lobby to staff it. As agriculture secretary, the president chose Henry Agard Wallace, the developer of hybrid seed corn, the editor of *Wallaces' Farmer,* the promoter of farm relief, and the son of Henry Cantwell Wallace, Warren Harding's agriculture secretary. Roosevelt named George N. Peek to the top post at Triple A.[3]

In conception and in fact, the Agricultural Adjustment Act was the fruit of the farm lobby's decade-long labor for "equality for agriculture." Sponsored by South Carolina Democrat Hampton P. Fulmer, it sailed through the House of Representatives in a matter of days. In the Senate, it encountered resistance only from its friends; agrarian radicals, who objected that the bill did not go far enough, proposed amendments to remonetize silver and to substitute "cost of production" for "parity" as the bill's prime objective; the former passed and the latter failed. With or without changes, however, the legislation gave the agricultural organizations, especially the Farm Bureau, nearly all they had asked for. "The sole aim and object of this act," Peek affirmed in his first Triple A press release, "is to raise farm prices. . . . This is just what farmers through their organizations have been demanding for a dozen years."[4]

3. In addition, Wallace chose Chester C. Davis, a veteran lobbyist for the Illinois Agricultural Association, to direct the AAA's Production Division, and he named M. L. Wilson, the domestic allotment publicist, to head the Wheat Section. Theodore Saloutos, *The American farmer and the New Deal* (Ames: Iowa State University Press, 1982), chap. 4; Gilbert C. Fite, *George N. Peek and the fight for farm parity* (Norman: University of Oklahoma Press, 1954), pp. 248–55; Van L. Perkins, *Crisis in agriculture: The Agricultural Adjustment Administration and the New Deal, 1933* (Berkeley and Los Angeles: University of California Press, 1969), chap. 5; Russell Lord, *The Wallaces of Iowa* (Boston: Houghton Mifflin Co., 1947), chaps. 9–10; Reminiscences of Milburn L. Wilson, Columbia Oral History Collection, 1956, p. 1080; Reminiscences of Chester C. Davis, Columbia Oral History Collection, 1953, p. 281; Louis H. Cook, "Domestic allotment," *Country Gentleman* (hereafter *CG*), February 1933, p. 11; Henry A. Wallace, "Fight for higher prices," *Wallaces' Farmer* (hereafter *WF*), 7 January 1933, p. 3.

4. George N. Peek (with Samuel Crowther), *Why quit our own* (New York: D. Van Nostrand Co., 1936), p. 20; John L. Shover, "Populism in the nineteen-thirties: The battle for the AAA," *Agricultural History,* 39 (January 1965), pp. 17–24; Perkins, *Crisis in agriculture,* chaps. 3–4; George C. Hoffman, "Executive-legislative relations in the first AAA," Ph.D. dissertation, University of Chicago, 1961, chaps. 3 and 5; Arthur M. Schlesinger, Jr., *The coming of the New Deal* (Boston: Houghton Mifflin Co., 1958), chaps. 2–3; Christiana McFadyen Campbell, *The Farm Bureau and the New Deal* (Urbana: University of Illinois Press, 1962), chap. 4; "What the farm bill will do," *WF,* 15 April 1933, p. 163; "Congressional domestic allotment plan," *Hoard's Dairyman,* 10 March 1933, p. 105; "No prosperity without acreage control," *Progressive Farmer* (here-

For the farm lobby, then, the Hundred Days was a historic triumph. Congress was responsive; the administration was sympathetic; the federal farm program was favorable. The farm lobby's privileged access to members of Congress, hard won just years before, paid handsome dividends.

Reinforcement: Agriculture in the New Deal

For the duration of the New Deal, the dividends continued, the access endured. The pattern of consultation consolidated in the early 1930s held force throughout the decade, in all three of its aspects.

First, New Deal legislators indulged the farm organizations with solicitude and respect. They were so permissive, in fact, that the leaders of the USDA routinely exploited the farm lobby's access to expedite their legislation and to shield their more controversial proposals from congressional attack. Prior to introduction, Agriculture Secretary Henry Wallace deliberately sought the approval of farm organization leaders for each of the major New Deal farm law proposals—the Agricultural Adjustment Act of 1933, the Agricultural Adjustment Act Amendments of 1935, the Soil Conservation and Domestic Allotment Act of 1936 and the Agricultural Adjustment Act of 1938. The 1938 legislation, for instance, emerged from a conference of farm lobby leaders called by Wallace and dominated by the Farm Bureau. The proposal, however, hewed closely to the outlines of the "ever-normal granary," Wallace's controversial mix of mandatory nonrecourse loans and strict production quotas. "Although the Department of Agriculture carefully dodged all hint of parenthood," *Business Week* observed, "that bill differed in only a few respects from the legislation advocated by all the Triple A spokesmen for some months." The farm lobby's access to Congress made it a useful tool for the Democratic USDA.[5]

after *PF*), May 1933, p. 3; "The New Deal for you," *Bureau Farmer*, June 1933, p. 3; Louis H. Cook, "Powers of the farm bill," *CG*, August 1933, p. 14; *Kiplinger Washington Letter*, "Industry control postscript No. 24," 11 November 1933; *KAL* No. 120, 7 October 1933, No. 121, 21 October 1933; H. C. Taylor, "National policies affecting country life," *Rural America*, October 1933, p. 4; "One year old," *Bureau Farmer*, April 1934, pp. 3, 12. In assembling the list of "basic" commodities, moreover, Congress deferred to the wishes of each industry, adding milk and omitting cattle on the recommendation of the producer groups. In 1934, the Jones-Connally Act made rye, flax, barley, grain sorghum, peanuts and cattle basic commodities, and the Jones-Costigan Act added sugarcane and sugar beets. For an analysis of the patterns of inclusion and exclusion, see Bruce L. Gardner, "Causes of U.S. farm commodity programs," *Journal of Political Economy*, 95 (April 1987), pp. 290–310.

5. "The farm market today—and tomorrow," *Business Week*, 4 September 1937, p. 43; Campbell, *Farm Bureau*, chaps. 4 and 7; Michael W. Schuyler, "The politics of

As Washington insiders expected, the congressional reception for the farm organizations was recurringly compassionate and friendly. The House Agriculture Committee acknowledged their leadership, sometimes formally. In 1937, for instance, Committee chairman Marvin Jones more or less turned over the management of the hearings to Farm Bureau president Edward A. O'Neal, frequently asking him to call the next witness. Likewise, the Committee consistently sought out the farm lobby's advice. In his exchange with Farm Bureau attorney Frederic P. Lee, for example, Illinois Democrat Scott W. Lucas underscored the weight of the Farm Bureau's opinion:

LUCAS: I am curious to know whether or not these gentlemen believe that this excess marketing penalty, as provided in section 11, is absolutely essential to the complete efficacy of the bill?

LEE: In the judgment of the farm leaders that have been preparing this measure, it is necessary.

LUCAS: Was there any protest among farm leaders who prepared this measure, or was that unanimously supported?

LEE: I will yield on that question to Mr. O'Neal. However, as I recall it personally, there was among those farm leaders who prepared this measure, so far as I know, unanimous agreement on it. . . .

O'NEAL: I would just amend that just a little bit to say that the Grange and the Farmers Union people, when we had our original conference with the Secretary, wanted to sign a document protesting to certain phases of that. Now, they have not reported . . . on these features of the bill.

LUCAS: So far as the Farm Bureau Federation is concerned, my statement is correct?

O'NEAL: You are right on the Farm Bureau; yes.[6]

To be sure, the farm lobby's access to Congress had its limits, as the USDA learned. In 1937, it proposed a program of mandatory non-

---

change: The battle for the Agricultural Adjustment Act of 1938," *Prologue*, 15 (Fall 1983), pp. 166–69; "National agricultural conference is organized," *American Farm Bureau Federation Weekly Newsletter*, 23 January 1934, pp. 1–2; *KAL* No. 207, 26 December 1936; A Washington Reporter, "A new adjustment pattern," *Nation's Agriculture*, February 1936, p. 4; "New AAA introduced by farm leaders," *American Farm Bureau Federation Weekly Newsletter*, 25 May 1937, p. 1; *KAL* No. 212, 20 February 1937; *KAL* No. 217, 1 May 1937; *KAL* No. 218, 15 May 1937; Stanley High, "Will it be Wallace?" *Saturday Evening Post*, 3 July 1937, p. 85; Paul W. Ward, "The AAA puts on false whiskers," *Nation*, 22 January 1936, p. 94.

6. *Hearings before the House Agriculture Committee*, "General farm legislation," 75th Congress, 1st session, Serial C, 1937 (hereafter *Hearings*, 1937), p. 51 and pp. 1, 55, 86, 93, 95, 110, 135, 20, 91–92, 149; *Hearings before the House Agriculture Committee*, "Amendments to the Agricultural Adjustment Act," 74th Congress, 1st session, Serial E, 1935 (hereafter *Hearings*, 1935), pp. 155, 220, 236–37, 307–8; "Illinois farmers back AAA," *WF*, 11 February 1939, p. 74.

recourse loans and strict production quotas on five basic commodities—cotton, corn, wheat, tobacco and rice. The legislation guaranteed U.S. Treasury payments and Commodity Credit Corporation (CCC) loans to growers who observed their quotas. Moreover, whenever commodity prices fell below the value of their loans, it allowed farmers to redeem them by forfeiting their crops to the CCC (hence, for the government, they were "nonrecourse" loans).

To many House Committee members, the legislation was unattractive: its controls were too rigid and its costs were too high. Despite its putative Farm Bureau sponsorship, four high-ranking Committee Democrats refused to sponsor it, and the chairman, Marvin Jones, prepared a more moderate alternative. Even the supporters of the bill, moreover, cautioned the farm lobby that it could push things too far. After voicing his support, for example, Colorado Democrat Fred Cummings qualified it with a warning:

CUMMINGS: I am in favor of this legislation and am thoroughly convinced that we need some program of production control throughout the United States, but the question in my mind is whether or not the farmers who are getting a pretty good return for their efforts are going to be satisfied if we put some kind of control program now. They will say that they have made money in the last six months, and we put on this legislation to control their production, and they will not only resent it in the cotton section but the wheat and other commodities. . . .

J. R. MITCHELL (D., Tenn.): In other words, they would throw this whole group out.

CUMMINGS: Not only that, but the principle which we have been fighting for would go along with the members of Congress, and the work that has been done, building up this program, would go with it. And the question is, Do you want us to go ahead, or should we await further developments?

Like most of his colleagues, Cummings was eager to hear the farm lobby out, but he wanted to be sure that it knew of the stakes.[7]

In the House Agriculture Committee, access did not bring unques-

7. *Hearings*, 1937, pp. 108, 103–5, 174–77; T.R.B., "Washington notes," *New Republic*, 24 November 1937, p. 73; Schuyler, "The politics of change," pp. 165–78; Donald R. McCoy, "George S. McGill of Kansas and the Agricultural Adjustment Act of 1938," *Historian*, 45 (February 1983), pp. 189–92; *KAL* No. 221, 26 June 1937; *KAL* No. 222, 10 July 1937; "Another farm bill is drawn up," *WF*, 31 July 1937, p. 555; *KAL* No. 229, 16 October 1937; "House passes new farm bill," *WF*, 18 December 1937, pp. 936–37; Thomas H. Coode, "Tennessee congressmen and the New Deal, 1933–1938," *West Tennessee Historical Society Papers*, 31 (October 1977), pp. 140–42. Jones's independence traumatized the Farm Bureau and the USDA. The Farm Bureau organized a protest in his Panhandle district, and *Wallaces' Farmer*, virtually a USDA house organ in the 1930s, printed a thinly fictionalized conversation between "Jones," "a fellow in Con-

tioning obedience. Rather, it brought a commitment to hear the farm lobby's case, to debate the alternatives, and *jointly* to determine the course of American price support policy. "One of the fine things about the twenty years during which this organization has operated," Marvin Jones told the Farm Bureau's 1939 convention, "is that we have learned to go into a huddle for our signals, and then like a football team, fight the common enemy."[8] The sense of alliance, the sense of common cause, was typical. Whatever the differences on particular pieces of legislation, in the 1930s, as before, the farm lobby's interest was foremost.

On farm policy questions, secondly, Congress set partisanship aside. Despite the adjustment program's Democratic paternity, farm state Republicans regarded AAA and its advocates with benevolence. Many GOP veterans, in fact, considered it the offspring of the cherished McNary-Haugen bills, as to a degree it was. Just as the Peek plan received Democratic support, ranking Republican Clifford Hope commented, "Now, under a Democratic administration, farm measures bear a Democratic label but receive the support of farm-minded members, Republican and Democratic alike."[9]

The Republican members of the Agriculture Committee, therefore, were far from uncooperative. In their dealings with the farm lobby, they were often inclined to even greater generosity than their Democratic counterparts. "I do not think there is any member on this committee who is not willing to give the farmer the same advantages that have been given to industry under the operation of the [National Recovery Administration] codes, and I, personally, will go as far as I can to see that agriculture gets those advantages," Minnesota Republican August H. Andresen told Grange master Louis J. Taber in 1935. "I, personally, would favor the fixing of price for the farmer, the price at which the commodity would be sold. That might be a little radical, but I feel it is important to take far-reaching steps to help the farmer." Support for the farm organizations' position, then, cut consistently across party lines. "Congress is fundamentally pro-AAA," the Kiplinger service noted in 1935.

---

gress" who opposed the bill, and "Smith," a farm organization man who supported it. Farm Bureau vice president Earl C. Smith was the reputed author of the 1937 proposal. See Irvin M. May, Jr., *Marvin Jones: The public life of an agrarian advocate* (College Station: Texas A&M University Press, 1980), pp. 150–66; Marvin Jones, *Marvin Jones memoirs,* ed. Joseph M. Ray (El Paso: Texas Western Press, 1973), pp. 73, 134; "Still agin it," *WF,* 20 November 1937, p. 854; *KAL* No. 220, 12 June 1937; Campbell, *Farm Bureau,* pp. 111–15.

8. Marvin Jones, "The second ten years," *Nation's Agriculture,* January 1940, p. 13.

9. Clifford R. Hope, "Congress from the inside," *Nation's Agriculture,* February 1936, p. 13.

"Republicans and Democrats are in general agreement that the administration's farm program has been more successful than any other. Congressmen with farmer constituents want certain phases of AAA kept."[10]

Finally, Congress treated the agricultural trades with antagonism and scorn. In 1935, for instance, the House Agriculture Committee took up the Triple A's proposals for amendments to the Agricultural Adjustment Act. Designed chiefly to facilitate the marketing agreements program, the amendments granted the secretary even greater powers to inspect and license agricultural processors, and representatives of the trades trooped before the Committee to protest. They encountered a solid wall of hostility. The ranking members of both parties, Marvin Jones of Texas and Clifford Hope of Kansas, launched a vituperative attack on General Mills vice president Sydney Anderson, whose distinguished service as a GOP member of the House from Minnesota (1911–1925) had included the direction of the Joint Commission of Agricultural Inquiry.

H O P E : Is it not true that the processors and the distributors of agricultural products . . . have suffered less during the depression than other lines of industry?

A N D E R S O N : I presume that is true. . . .

H O P E : And yet during most of that period the farmer has been practically down and out. . . .

A N D E R S O N : Unfortunately; yes.

H O P E : Do you not believe that it would be better for the processors and the farmers and the country in general if there could be some equalization of that burden . . . by which the processor would have cooperated with the farmer in distributing his products to see that he got a fair price for them?

A N D E R S O N : I think he has done that.

H O P E : Well, in what way? He has not sacrificed his profit at all; he still has his business, and the farmer has lost it.

In truth, the Agriculture Committee had the same misgivings about the amendments as the trades, and it raised them with AAA administrator Chester C. Davis. It had little tolerance, however, for those whose habitual warnings of disaster stood in the way of more aid for farmers. "When the fortune teller has been so wrong in his former predictions," Jones told a lobbyist for the meat industry, "we cannot be criticized if we say that he might miss it again when he tells us what will happen."[11]

10. *Hearings,* 1935, p. 153; *KAL* No. 167, 13 July 1935; "Congressman Hope promises support," *American Farm Bureau Federation Weekly Newsletter,* 2 October 1934, p. 1; *Hearings,* 1935, pp. 55, 235.

11. *Hearings,* 1935, pp. 120, 254, 108–22, 203–8, 244–56, 19–87. The Committee's worries about the effect of the proposed amendments on agricultural cooperatives

The interests of agricultural processors, then, were far from the Committee's concern. As Kiplinger politely phrased it, the "attitude of both congressional agricultural committees appears to be unfriendly to the trades. This is a standard phenomenon which the trades seem to overlook year after year."[12]

During the New Deal years, in sum, the Agriculture Committee's pattern of consultation reproduced the early thirties. It paid minimal attention to the trades, and it professed minimal loyalty to party. Instead, it pledged allegiance to farm producers and abided by their organized representatives.[13] The close working relationships between the House Agriculture Committee and the farm lobby continued.[14]

The stability of the farm organizations' access in the 1930s derived from two factors. First, beliefs in the recurrent potency of the farm relief issue were reinforced by the very artificiality of the farm program. Second, beliefs in the farm lobby's competitive advantage were reinforced by the results of congressional elections, even when Democratic candidates lost them. The farm organizations' access persisted because the conditions that established it persisted.

First, during the New Deal, the circumstances that caused the issue of farm relief to recur did not change. The Agricultural Adjustment Act treated the symptoms but not the cause of the agricultural depression, and the rural community was convinced that hard times were imminent if the Triple A were terminated. "In my observation," Henry Wallace

---

and the wisdom of granting greater power to liberal reformers in the USDA delayed passage of the amendments for over a year. "Fight for your program," *Bureau Farmer,* June 1934, p. 6; "A.F.B.F. battles middlemen who would kill program," *American Farm Bureau Federation Weekly Newsletter,* 15 May 1934, p. 1; *KAL* No. 131, 24 February 1934; *KAL* No. 138, 2 June 1934; *KAL* No. 148, 20 October 1934; *KAL* No. 156, 9 February 1935; *KAL* No. 162, 4 May 1935.

12. *KAL* No. 158, 9 March 1935.

13. The agrarians' constituency, moreover, was primarily large commercial farmers rather than smallholders, tenants or sharecroppers (although each chamber had its friends of small farmers, most prominently Texas representative Marvin Jones and Alabama senator John H. Bankhead II, both Democrats). The well-documented Farm Bureau attack on the New Deal program for tenants and croppers, the Farm Security Administration, proceeded legislatively through channels other than the agriculture committees. See David E. Conrad, *The forgotten farmers: The story of sharecroppers in the New Deal* (Urbana: University of Illinois Press, 1965); and Sidney Baldwin, *Poverty and politics: The rise and decline of the Farm Security Administration* (Chapel Hill: University of North Carolina Press, 1968).

14. There were exceptions, but they were few. Illinois Democrat Harry P. Beam, who represented Chicago's packinghouse district, and Texas Democrat Richard Kleberg, whose family controlled the gigantic King Ranch, were generally more sympathetic to agricultural processors, especially the packers. See, e.g., *Hearings, 1935,* pp. 40–51.

told the Committee in 1937, "the farm group has reached the conclusion that as a group it will not abandon the concept of parity price and parity income, no matter what the present situation may be. They will continue to fight for it." "I thoroughly agree with you on that," Marvin Jones responded.[15]

Wallace spoke with the benefit of hindsight; such prophecies had proven true before. In January 1936, the Supreme Court had ruled the Agricultural Adjustment Act unconstitutional, and the prospect that farmers might never receive another government check had stampeded Congress into action. It passed the Soil Conservation and Domestic Allotment Act within eight weeks—in less time, that is, than it had taken to pass the original. "When [the National Recovery Administration] was abolished," *Congressional Digest* observed,

there was no demand from any source for its revival. . . . With the agricultural interests, however, the conditions were decidedly different. . . . Whereas business quickly forgot about NRA, organized agriculture came to the front promptly with a demand for the continuation of the government farm subsidy.

Constituent demand for agricultural price supports, members of Congress concluded, would certainly continue.[16]

Second, elections in the 1930s consistently underscored the farm lobby's competitive advantage. The Farm Bureau's prominence in the passage and administration of the Agricultural Adjustment Act enabled it to stabilize and expand its membership, especially in the South, where in the late 1930s membership increased tenfold, to more than one hundred thousand.[17] In the minds of voters and politicians alike, the close association between the farm organizations and the Triple A program turned farm state elections into tests of their mandate, and the supporters of government aid to agriculture won many more than they lost.

In the South, the Farm Bureau benefited from the obvious popularity

15. *Hearings*, 1937, p. 182; *Hearings*, 1935, pp. 95–96.
16. "The new soil conservation act—substitute for A.A.A.," *Congressional Digest*, March 1936, p. 68; A Washington Reporter, "A new adjustment pattern," *Nation's Agriculture*, February 1936, p. 4; "Seething vacuum of the AAA," *Literary Digest*, 18 January 1936, pp. 5–6; Morton Taylor, "The Middle West answers the Court," *New Republic*, 26 February 1936, p. 71.
17. Farm Bureau recruitment was most successful in Alabama, North Carolina and Georgia, although membership increased handsomely in Arkansas and Mississippi as well. Texas was a perennial disappointment. "Membership paid to the American Farm Bureau Federation," mimeo, American Farm Bureau Federation, 1982; Campbell, *Farm Bureau*, chap. 6; Gladys Baker, *The county agent* (Chicago: University of Chicago Press, 1939), pp. 141–43; John Mark Hansen, "The political economy of group membership," *American Political Science Review*, 79 (March 1985), pp. 86–87.

of the New Deal program. In 1935, 94 percent of the nation's cotton growers participated in it, and referenda on subsequent compulsory programs registered majorities of four to one on up. Understandably, southern New Dealers rushed to embrace it, to favorable effect. In 1936, for example, Georgia senator Richard B. Russell buried his primary challenger, Governor Eugene Talmadge, with one simple issue: the New Deal, especially farm relief. "The farmers are awake to the fact that my opponent is promising them nothing except to cut off their checks," Russell told rural Georgians, "while I stand for larger benefit checks." For southern New Dealers, the Farm Bureau's relief program was electoral bedrock.[18]

In the face of the Triple A's appeal, even the most steadfast southern conservatives pulled their punches on farm issues. South Carolina senator Ellison D. (Cotton Ed) Smith, the chairman of the Senate Agriculture Committee, opposed every aspect of the New Deal, including the original AAA, but he soon made one exception. "He decided to compromise by holding hearings in agricultural regions [in 1937] to learn what the 'one-gallus farmer' really wanted. He discovered to his horror that they

18. William Anderson, *The wild man from Sugar Creek: The political career of Eugene Talmadge* (Baton Rouge: Louisiana State University Press, 1975), p. 164; Howard N. Mead, "Russell vs. Talmadge: Southern politics and the New Deal," *Georgia Historical Quarterly*, 65 (Spring 1981), p. 37; Karen Kalmar Kelly, "Richard B. Russell: Democrat from Georgia," Ph.D. dissertation, University of North Carolina, 1979, pp. 214–22, 258–78; Roy E. Fossett, "The impact of the New Deal on Georgia politics, 1933–1941," Ph.D. dissertation, University of Florida, 1960, pp. 88–90, 164–77; Edwin G. Nourse, Joseph S. Davis and John D. Black, *Three years of the Agricultural Adjustment Administration* (Washington: Brookings Institution, 1937), pp. 64, 137, 273–74; Henry I. Richards, *Cotton and the AAA* (Washington: Brookings Institution, 1936), chap. 10; Robert E. Martin, "The referendum process in the agricultural adjustment programs of the United States," *Agricultural History*, 25 (January 1951), pp. 34–47; "Split on farm marketing quotas," *Business Week*, 17 December 1938, p. 18. Russell was so close to Farm Bureau president Edward O'Neal, one account holds, that O'Neal asked him to name the Georgia Farm Bureau's president when it was organized in 1939. Interview with Roger Fleming, December 1986. On other southern New Dealers, see Frank Freidel, *F.D.R. and the South* (Baton Rouge: Louisiana State University Press, 1965), p. 63; Virginia Van der Veer Hamilton, *Hugo Black: The Alabama years* (Baton Rouge: Louisiana State University Press, 1972), pp. 238–39; Virginia Van der Veer Hamilton, *Lister Hill: Statesman from the South* (Chapel Hill: University of North Carolina Press, 1987), chap. 4; Chester M. Morgan, *Redneck liberal: Theodore G. Bilbo and the New Deal* (Baton Rouge: Louisiana State University Press, 1985), chap. 9; Walter L. Hixson, "The 1938 Kentucky Senate election," *Register of the Kentucky Historical Society*, 80 (Summer 1982), p. 327; J. B. Shannon, "Alben W. Barkley: 'Reservoir of energy,'" pp. 240–56 in J. T. Salter, ed., *Public men in and out of office* (Chapel Hill: University of North Carolina Press, 1946), p. 240; Orville M. Kile, *The Farm Bureau through three decades* (Baltimore: Waverly Press, 1948), pp. 213, 241–42, 248, 280, 288, 319–20; "After 20 years—VICTORY," *Nation's Agriculture*, June 1941, p. 1.

wanted crop control. 'I didn't feel so good when I went in there,' he said after one meeting, 'but now I'm sick.' Ailing or not, he promptly rammed a crop-control bill through his committee." Thereafter, Smith confined himself to periodic expressions of irritation and turned over de facto leadership of the committee to a more sympathetic colleague, Alabama's "Parity John" Bankhead. Under the pressure of possible primary challenges from more liberal candidates, Dixieland conservatives abandoned opposition to the adjustment program and occasionally jumped out in front. On this one issue, the popularity of the Farm Bureau program turned southern reactionaries into fellow travelers.[19]

In the Middle West, likewise, rural lawmakers who opposed organized agriculture, already a scarce breed, were pushed even further toward extinction. Senator Lester J. Dickinson of Iowa and Senator Thomas P. Gore of Oklahoma were two prominent examples. Dickinson, a Republican, was a one-time leader of the Farm Bloc. Gore, a Democrat, was a one-time Wilsonian progressive. With its love of intervention and its free-spending ways, however, the New Deal was more than either could take; both opposed the New Deal and its agricultural adjustment program, loudly and belligerently. Their constituents responded. In 1936, Dickinson and Gore succumbed to ardent New Dealers. In Iowa's general election, Dickinson fell to Governor Clyde Herring. In Oklahoma's four-way Democratic primary, Gore ran last. Farm voters squared accounts with saviors who forsook them.[20]

19. Robert McCormick, "He's for cotton," *Collier's,* 23 April 1938, p. 48; Leonard Neil Plummer, "Ellison Durant Smith: 'A politician from the Old South,'" pp. 344–54 in J. T. Salter, ed., *Public men in and out of office* (Chapel Hill: University of North Carolina Press, 1946), pp. 350–51; Daniel W. Hollis, "'Cotton Ed Smith'—Showman or statesman?" *South Carolina Historical Magazine,* 71 (October 1970), p. 248; *KAL* No. 409, 29 July 1944; *KAL* No. 458, 15 June 1946; T.R.B., "Washington notes," *New Republic,* 20 October 1937, p. 300. On other southern conservatives, see Luther Harmon Zeigler, Jr., "Senator Walter George's 1938 campaign," *Georgia Historical Quarterly,* 43 (December 1959), pp. 333–52; Anthony J. Badger, *Prosperity road: The New Deal, tobacco, and North Carolina* (Chapel Hill: University of North Carolina Press, 1980), pp. 81–90; John Robert Moore, *Senator Josiah William Bailey of North Carolina* (Durham: Duke University Press, 1968), chaps. 6–7; "Potato control," *Time,* 9 September 1935, pp. 16–17; "Potato debate," *Business Week,* 12 October 1935, pp. 18–19; "Secretary Wallace's 'hot potato,'" *Literary Digest,* 12 October 1935, pp. 6–7. The most prominent exceptions were Virginia senators Carter Glass and Harry F. Byrd. For the reasons, see Robert F. Hunter, "The AAA between neighbors: Virginia, North Carolina, and the New Deal farm program," *Journal of Southern History,* 44 (November 1978), pp. 537–70.

20. "Farmers unite to back AAA," *WF,* 25 May 1935, p. 327; "AAA Act passes Senate," *WF,* 3 August 1935, p. 443; "Congress acts on new farm bill," *WF,* 29 February 1936, p. 167; "Dickinson's record on farm exports," *WF,* 25 April 1936, p. 320; "Landon takes Dickinson's farm program," *WF,* 24 October 1936, p. 728; "If farmers reward their enemies," *WF,* 24 October 1936, pp. 729–30; Monroe Lee Billington, *Thomas P. Gore:*

What did the farm organizations actually do in these elections? In terms of pressures, as traditionally conceived, they did precious little. The farm groups may have contributed money; they may have contributed manpower; but if they did, they did so silently.[21] Rather, their involvement was more subtle. Above all, the farm organizations brokered information to incumbents, to challengers and to voters. First, acting as barometers of farm opinion, they indicated the strength or futility of opposition candidacies. On behalf of Missouri representative Clarence Cannon, for example, Edward A. O'Neal convened a meeting of "big mules" and told them, "If you know what's good for you, you'll support Clarence." Second, acting as observers of Washington behavior, they indicated the wisdom or folly of voters' possible choices. Early in the New Deal, for instance, the farm groups cautioned farmers to distinguish carefully between Democratic liberals who supported Triple A and Democratic conservatives who opposed it, between McNary-Haugenite Republicans who backed Triple A and stalwart Republicans who fought it. To their members, that is, the farm organizations signaled their assessments of candidates' performance. To the candidates, they signaled the leanings of constituents. They both predicted and shaped the choices and behavior of voters.[22]

With election results like these, therefore, in the South and in the Midwest, the farm lobby benefited enormously from its identification with the New Deal farm program. Be they Republicans or Democrats, rural representatives could not easily oppose the farm organizations' platform, even if it also happened to be the New Dealers'. Consequently, the terms of partisan competition changed, but to the farm lobby's advantage. If farm state Republicans could not offer something else to farmers, they could certainly offer more.

From the very beginning of the adjustment programs, farmers had tolerated production control largely because they prized the associated

The blind senator from Oklahoma (Lawrence: University of Kansas Press, 1967), pp. 163-77; Royden J. Dangerfield and Richard H. Flynn, "Voter motivation in the 1936 Oklahoma Democratic primary," Southwestern Social Science Quarterly, 17 (September 1936), pp. 97–105.

21. Accounts sometimes hint at substantial involvement, but the specifics are never clear. See V. O. Key, Jr., Southern politics in state and nation (New York: Alfred A. Knopf, 1949), pp. 55-56, 100, 155, 192n; David R. Mayhew, Placing parties in American politics (Princeton: Princeton University Press, 1986), p. 166.

22. Fleming interview; "Fight for your own," Bureau Farmer, October 1934, p. 6; "Where do your candidates for Congress stand?" WF, 27 October 1934, p. 609; John H. Fenton, Politics in the border states (New Orleans: Hauser Press, 1957), pp. 143–45. See also Richard Lowitt, George W. Norris: The triumph of a progressive, 1933–1944 (Urbana: University of Illinois Press, 1978), chap. 13; Campbell, Farm Bureau, pp. 109–10.

payments. In the late 1930s, accordingly, Republicans pledged to do the New Deal one better: to maintain payments but impose less onerous restrictions. In 1938, for example, GOP candidates fanned agrarian resentment against the strict new production controls of the 1938 Agricultural Adjustment Act, forcing Democrats who supported it onto the defensive. "In some districts of the middle western states," one agricultural journal observed, "candidates for congressional nominations are making their campaign in opposition to the crop-control program. And it is said they are receiving strong farmer support." Come November, Republicans swept the farm belt. In Kansas, former GOP governor Clyde M. Reed racked up huge majorities in western wheat counties on his way to defeating Senator George S. McGill, the 1938 AAA's sponsor. In Ohio and Wisconsin, Republicans took back two more Senate seats from Democratic New Dealers. Throughout the Corn Belt, the GOP reclaimed at least a dozen House seats.[23]

From a farm policy standpoint, however, the distinction between Republicans and Democrats was a slight one. To its beneficiaries and its victims, the 1938 backlash against the New Deal was not a repudiation of the farm subsidy program but a complaint about its inadequacy. Overall, Democrats suffered the consequences of a deepening farm recession, but in most cases, rural voters selected candidates pledged to uphold the farm program, not to dismantle it. Despite the Republican tide, Democratic senator Guy M. Gillette spoiled Lester J. Dickinson's bid for a comeback in Iowa, and Democratic representative Scott W. Lucas, who "headed [the] cornbelt fight for mandatory loans," captured a Senate seat in Illinois. Moreover, despite farmers' gripes about the new Triple A, Kansas congressman Clifford R. Hope and Iowa congressman Fred C. Gilchrist, its GOP defenders, won reelection handily, Hope in the very counties where Senator McGill had run most poorly. Finally, despite the agitation of the AAA issue, Senator Clyde M. Reed refused to reopen the farm relief question. Eastern Republicans may have taken the GOP resurgence as permission to scrap Triple A, but farm state Republi-

23. "Washington adjusting self after adjournment of Congress," *National Butter and Cheese Journal*, 10 July 1938, p. 36; Gilbert C. Fite, "Farmer opinion and the Agricultural Adjustment Act, 1933," *Mississippi Valley Historical Review*, 48 (March 1962), p. 673; McCoy, "George S. McGill," pp. 199–204; *KAL* No. 243, 30 April 1938; *KAL* No. 244, 14 May 1938; *KAL* No. 245, 28 May 1938; Milton Plesur, "The Republican congressional comeback of 1938," *Review of Politics*, 24 (October 1962), pp. 548–49; James T. Patterson, *Congressional conservatism and the New Deal: The growth of the conservative coalition in Congress, 1933–1939* (Lexington: University of Kentucky Press, 1967), pp. 268–69 and chap. 8. The outcry put the Farm Bureau on the defensive, too. "Certain Farm Bureau officials are now beginning to regret the Bureau ballyhoo which claimed credit for the AAA of 1938," Kiplinger reported. *KAL* No. 247, 25 June 1938.

cans wanted nothing of it. "As far as I am able," Hope told the Kansas Farmers Union, "I am going to try to keep the Republican party committed to a sound, sympathetic agricultural policy, but if the party does not see fit to go along that line, I will simply have to part company with it, as far as that issue is concerned."[24]

In the farm regions of the country, in sum, the elections of the thirties endorsed the farm relief program of organized agriculture. The popularity of agricultural adjustment, amply demonstrated, warded politicians away from opposition to it. North or South, Republican or Democrat, the New Deal farm programs were politically compelling.[25]

The New Deal, consequently, preserved the access of the farm lobby to the deliberations of the congressional agriculture committees. The continuing advantage of the farm lobby and the continuing salience of

24. "House passes new farm bill," *WF,* 18 December 1937, pp. 936–37; James L. Forsythe, "Clifford Hope of Kansas: Practical congressman and agrarian idealist," *Agricultural History,* 51 (April 1977), p. 419; "Election affects farm program," *WF,* 19 November 1938, p. 781; *Kiplinger Washington Letter,* 12 November 1938; "Many in congressional 'dairy bloc' eliminated by election," *National Butter and Cheese Journal,* 25 November 1938, p. 26; "Farm bill passes Congress," *WF,* 26 February 1938, p. 152; "Pope-McGill bill is farm hope," *WF,* 20 November 1937, p. 853; Jerry Harrington, "Senator Guy Gillette foils the execution committee," *Palimpsest,* 62 (November/December 1981), pp. 170–80; Francis W. Schruben, *Kansas in turmoil, 1930–1936* (Columbia: University of Missouri Press, 1969), pp. 19–27, 147; Edward L. Schapsmeier and Frederick H. Schapsmeier, "Scott W. Lucas of Havana: His rise and fall as majority leader in the United States Senate," *Journal of the Illinois State Historical Society,* 70 (November 1977), pp. 304–5; Eric Manheimer, "The public career of Elmer Thomas," Ph.D. dissertation, University of Oklahoma, 1952, pp. 134–41; Iwan Morgan, "Factional conflict in Indiana politics during the later New Deal years, 1936–1940," *Indiana Magazine of History,* 79 (March 1983), pp. 37–38, 48, 52, 54; J. L. Sayre, "Gerald P. Nye: 'Essentially negative,'" pp. 127–46 in J. T. Salter, ed., *Public men in and out of office* (Chapel Hill: University of North Carolina Press, 1946), p. 139. See also *KAL* No. 193, 13 June 1936; *KAL* No. 200, 19 September 1936; *KAL* No. 287, 9 December 1939; "Digging bait for farm vote," *WF,* 30 December 1939, p. 798; "Illinois Republican leaders about-face," *American Farm Bureau Federation Weekly Newsletter,* 2 October 1934, p. 1. In other areas, particularly the upper Midwest, Republicans ignored the AAA and instead took aim at the administration's reciprocal trade program. In Wisconsin, aware that his opponent's attempts to amend the 1938 AAA on behalf of dairy farmers made it difficult to capitalize on the farm issue, Republican challenger Reid F. Murray decided instead to dramatize the dairy industry's objections to reciprocal trade. Murray purchased a Canadian dairy calf, named it "Reciprocity," and carted it around to campaign appearances. He swamped Progressive House incumbent Gerald Boileau. Interview with Hyde Murray, December 1986; Interview with Melvin R. Laird, Association of Former Members of Congress Oral History Project, 1979, p. 10; Arthur W. Schatz, "The Reciprocal Trade Agreements Program and the 'farm vote,' 1934–1940," *Agricultural History,* 46 (October 1972), pp. 498–514.

25. R. Douglas Arnold, *The logic of congressional action* (New Haven: Yale University Press, 1990), pp. 77–78.

farm relief reinforced the pattern of bipartisan solicitude for the farm organizations and bipartisan hostility toward the trades that had prevailed since the early 1930s. First, the popularity of agricultural adjustment silenced southern stalwarts, fortified southern liberals and overwhelmed midwestern conservatives. It transformed a partisan tug-of-war into a partisan bidding war. Second, the very artificiality of the commodity subsidy programs prevented a lasting solution to the economic troubles of agriculture, insuring that demand for the farm lobby's program would not soon abate. Competitive advantage plus recurrence equaled access.

Reinforcement: Agriculture in War and Peace

Outwardly, the conduct and context of agricultural policy-making changed tremendously during World War II. In rural areas as elsewhere, the Great Depression lifted, the New Deal withered and the Republican Party revived. When the House Agriculture Committee met to write a new postwar farm law in 1947, it convened in a climate of prosperity, under Republican control.

The Committee's actions, however, belied any changes; in its orientations it resembled its immediate past.

First, the Agriculture Committee of the Eightieth Congress shunned partisanship. Despite the first Republican leadership in sixteen years, and despite newfound GOP optimism for control of the White House, the prospects for a major overhaul of farm policy were exceedingly slim. "Odds are," Wayne Darrow predicted in an election postmortem, "the bi-partisan farm bloc will succeed in holding its own on the general policy of broad aid to agriculture." Rural Republicans and rural Democrats thought basically alike, as the farm lobby well recognized. "It delights my heart," Edward A. O'Neal told the Committee, "to see that when there is a great issue that has to do with agriculture there is a combination between the two parties."[26]

Second, the Committee confirmed its allegiance to organized agriculture. In advance of its regular hearings, GOP leaders set aside a day to hear the Farm Bureau's thoughts on the whole of farm policy, the first time the Committee had ever extended such a courtesy to a single, pri-

26. *Wayne Darrow's Washington Farmletter* (hereafter *WDWF*) No. 165, 9 November 1946; *Hearings before the House Agriculture Committee*, "Long-range agricultural policy," 80th Congress, 1st session, 1947 (hereafter *Hearings, 1947*), p. 66. "There has been basic agreement between Democrats and Republicans on most of the basic farm issues," Kiplinger noted. "They have voted much the same." *KAL* No. 467, 19 October 1946.

vate organization. The meeting, as it turned out, was a stormy one; Farm Bureau policy was in a state of transition, and O'Neal was in no position to give guarantees. Nevertheless, the Committee treated Federation officials with its customary enthusiasm and respect. Georgia Democrat Stephen Pace, for instance, closed his argument with a plea for assistance:

PACE: You think the farmers of this nation are entitled to parity for their products?

O'NEAL: Yes, sir.

PACE: Then what can be the objection to following it, at least on the basis of 90 percent of parity or a comparable price?

O'NEAL: Well, it is a very complicated thing. . . .

PACE: Do you mean to tell me that you do not approve of a permanent support at 90 percent of parity of farm prices? . . .

O'NEAL: No, we haven't taken any action. We have been studying it to see how it works out. We have insisted for 2 years. That is pretty good; [Farm Bureau leaders] are insisting on keeping it.

PACE: I am asking you to help us [preserve the Farm Bureau's commitment to price supports at parity].

O'NEAL: I will, provided you do some other things that I am going to ask you.

As in 1937, therefore, the Committee's dispute with the Farm Bureau was a disagreement among friends. "I would not think that there is any particular difference between your organization and the House Committee on Agriculture or, I might even say, the Congress on the program you recommend," Mississippi Democrat Thomas Abernethy assured O'Neal. "We appreciate what you have done."[27]

In 1947, in short, farm lobby access to the House Agriculture Committee still was matter-of-fact. "Congress will listen to farm organizations," Kiplinger noted, "then act."[28]

Finally, the Committee lavished its affection on agricultural producers and spurned everyone else. At its regular hearings on long-range price support policy, it treated the handful of tradesmen who dared to show up to a morning of bipartisan business-bashing. Ranking Demo-

27. *Hearings before the House Agriculture Committee*, "Farm program of the American Farm Bureau Federation," 80th Congress, 1st session, 1947 (hereafter *Hearings*, "Farm Bureau program," 1947), pp. 11–12, 7. The Committee closed its hearings on long-range farm policy in 1948 by setting aside another day to hear the Farm Bureau and its new president, Allan B. Kline of Iowa. Traditionally, only secretaries of agriculture received such special attention. See *Hearings before the House Agriculture Committee*, "Farm program of the American Farm Bureau Federation," 80th Congress, 2d session, 1948.

28. *KAL* No. 468, 2 November 1946. See also Walter W. Wilcox, *The farmer in the Second World War* (Ames: Iowa State College Press, 1947), chap. 22.

crat John W. Flannagan's demolition of R. C. Woodworth, from the National Grain Trade Council, was typical:

> FLANNAGAN: You represent the class that takes a toll off the farmer's products when they are sold. . . . But glancing over your prepared statement you seem to pay little, if any, attention to the price the farmer is going to receive. . . . How would you protect the farmer?
>
> WOODWORTH: We have tried to make some suggestions here, Mr. Flannagan, which we think will be helpful.
>
> FLANNAGAN: Just point out a suggestion that would protect the farmer in any way in his price.
>
> WOODWORTH: I think a combination of many of these things will protect him somewhat in his price.
>
> FLANNAGAN: Name them. I have read your statement but I cannot recall any.

In 1947 as before, the sole aim and object of agricultural price support policy was to "protect the farmer." Viewpoints that conflicted were summarily dismissed.[29]

Thus, the Committee's standard mode of operation—its ecumenical respect for the farm lobby, its ecumenical contempt for the trades— continued through the war and bided after. So did the conditions that created and sustained it.

First, farm price support policy remained a primary issue throughout the countryside. Under the stimulus of the war and under the protection of the government, American agriculture lately had flourished. The war's end, however, rekindled agrarian fears of a depression as severe as the last one, itself the unwanted effect of an armistice.

Farm politicians knew the danger well. "In light of our past experience," Missouri Democrat Orville Zimmerman asked, "do you think we should have available machinery at all times to stabilize the price of farm commodities?" "We certainly feel we should keep that machinery intact," Illinois Agricultural Association (IAA) president Charles B. Shuman replied. "We have problems in agriculture which are very similar, I am sure, to the conditions we had in the past, and we certainly want to keep the machinery that we have set up." Even in affluence, the price support issue recurred.[30]

---

29. *Hearings,* 1947, pp. 273, 275–77, 273–88, 573–85. Labor was no more a favorite: see pp. 597–619. Again, there were but a few exceptions. Pennsylvania Republican Chester H. Gross showed greater interest in the views of food processors than in the views of the Farm Bureau, but he was isolated completely. "Mr. Chairman," he protested to Clifford R. Hope, "I think the members on this side of the committee [the Republicans] ought to have a chance to ask a few questions about some of these matters that the other side [the Democrats] has been developing." See *Hearings,* 1947, pp. 585, 66–67, 283–84.

30. *Hearings,* "Farm Bureau program," 1947, p. 5. See also Richard Wilson, "The farmer's Washington," *Successful Farming,* December 1944, p. 29; "Keeping tabs on

Second, the evidence of the farm lobby's competitive advantage was all the more convincing. Organizationally, wartime prosperity bolstered the ranks of all the farm organizations, in particular the Farm Bureau. The Federation's membership topped a million in 1946, a 150 percent increase over 1940.

Politically, moreover, congressional elections underscored the authority of the farm organizations, in particular, again, the Farm Bureau. The war put a long moratorium on agricultural legislation, and from 1938 until 1947, the Agriculture Committee did no business on price supports. The farm organizations, however, found plenty to do. To the delight of inflation-hungry farmers, the O'Neal-rallied farm bloc staunchly resisted Roosevelt's price control program, and in the 1942 midterm elections, the Republicans reaped the windfall. The GOP deposed fifty Democratic representatives and eight Democratic senators, among them Michigan senator Prentiss M. Brown, who led the administration's efforts to hold the line on farm prices. "When the 78th Congress convened" in 1943, *Business Week* reported, "members from the major farm states were convinced that their political future depended upon aggressive action to get higher prices for farm commodities."[31]

The farm lobby's muscle registered in Congress. "It is no exaggeration to attribute to O'Neal the power to control a majority of votes in both the House and the Senate," the *New Republic*'s T.R.B. lamented, "even though he and his lobby represent the interests of a small minority

---

Washington," *Nation's Agriculture*, February 1944, p. 12; *Washington Farmletter*, 29 July 1944; *Washington Farmletter*, 19 August 1944; *KAL* No. 409, 29 July 1944; Allen J. Matusow, *Farm policies and politics in the Truman years* (Cambridge: Harvard University Press, 1967), pp. 120–24.

31. "Farm bloc gets its revenge," *Business Week*, 6 March 1943, p. 17; "The nation: 'God forbid . . . such disunity,'" *Time*, 5 October 1942, pp. 19–21; "Congress, led by farm bloc, takes the offensive," *Business Week*, 20 February 1943, p. 43; Helen Fuller, "Inflation's family tree," *New Republic*, 20 December 1943, pp. 875–78; "The Farm Bureau," *Fortune*, June 1944, p. 156; Arthur Moore, "Earl Smith: Farmers' boss," *Atlantic*, January 1945, pp. 85–90; Lowitt, *Norris: Triumph of a progressive*, pp. 420–30; Harl A. Dalstrom, "The defeat of George W. Norris in 1942," *Nebraska History*, 59 (Summer 1978), pp. 231–58; Iwan Morgan, "The 1942 mid-term elections in Illinois," *Journal of the Illinois State Historical Society*, 76 (Summer 1983), pp. 123–25; Willard M. Kiplinger, *Washington is like that* (New York: Harper and Brothers Publishers, 1942), p. 178; Dean Albertson, *Roosevelt's farmer: Claude R. Wickard in the New Deal* (New York: Columbia University Press, 1955), chaps. 11–17; Wesley McCune, *The farm bloc* (Garden City, N.Y.: Doubleday, Doran and Co., 1943); Roland Young, *Congressional politics in the Second World War* (New York: Columbia University Press, 1956), chap. 4. In part because of the farm bloc's efforts, farmers did quite nicely during World War II. Farm prices increased twice as fast as wages between 1939 and 1945, according to USDA economist Walter Wilcox. The net incomes of cotton farmers increased by 109 to 190 percent; of Corn Belt farmers, 186 to 205 percent; and of southern plains wheat farmers, an astonishing 778 to 1,102 percent. Wilcox, *Second World War*, pp. 250–53.

of well-to-do farmers."[32] Exaggerated or not, the reputation did not hurt.

Thus, the farm lobby's competitive advantage over other informants was as firmly established after the war as it ever was before. The farm relief issue was as salient as it ever was before. The farm lobby spoke truth for farmers; by all indications it would continue to do so.

Accordingly, the farm lobby ended World War II in exactly its position prior to the war: at the peak of its influence in Congress. "I know you will agree with me that the responsibility lies in your farm bureau, with your knowledge and grasp of agricultural affairs all over the country, to keep us informed to the extent that we will make better Representatives and be better able to take more accurate positions in the country," New York Republican Edwin A. Hall told Ed O'Neal. "We will be delighted to do that," O'Neal assured him. "We certainly have a very vital interest in that."[33]

Conclusion

The most remarkable feature of this chapter is the continuity, the inertia. Through almost two decades, through liberal ascendancy and conservative revival, the farm lobby's access was a constant. On issues of agricultural policy, Democrats and Republicans, southerners and midwesterners, harkened to the views of the American Farm Bureau.

In the 1930s and 1940s, responsiveness to organized agriculture became the "natural" or "normal" orientation of rural representatives in Congress. Having years ago taken true headings, the veterans charted a course of long standing, and the newcomers apprenticed to the direction of their mentors. In the 1930s and 1940s, lawmakers gave access to the farm lobby routinely, without giving it much thought.

The routine, however, was not the motive. Like most routines, interest group access had the power of experience and anticipation behind it. Beginning in the twenties, lawmakers discovered the farm lobby's superior information and propaganda. Beginning in the twenties, likewise, representatives expected its prepotency to stay. By the thirties, only the old-timers remembered the original conflicts, but all the others saw the lessons perpetually reinforced. Access persisted because the conditions that caused it persisted.

In the thirties and forties, first of all, the recurrence of the farm relief issue continued. Far from ending the demands for farm subsidies, New

32. T.R.B., "The farm bloc," *New Republic*, 25 January 1943, p. 118.
33. *Hearings*, "Farm Bureau program," 1947, p. 28.

Deal agricultural policy actually institutionalized them. As legislators well knew, producers of the basic commodities owed the security of their livelihoods to the adjustment program, and they believed—correctly—that to terminate it would precipitate an economic and political disaster. Of necessity, therefore, the farm price support issue was a recurrent issue.

In the thirties and forties, second of all, the competitive advantage of the farm relief lobby continued. The popularity of the agricultural adjustment program, coupled with the support of the farm organizations, translated almost any rural discontent into an electoral endorsement of whatever the Farm Bureau wanted, which was higher prices. In the early 1930s, farm belt Democrats rode into office on a wave of agrarian gratitude for Roosevelt's relief and resentment against Hoover's depression. In the early 1940s, farm belt Republicans bounced back on the strength of agrarian annoyance, first with Roosevelt's recession and later with Roosevelt's price controls. Thus, farmers' propensity to reward the president's party for economic success and to punish it for economic failure played to the advantage of the farm lobby. Whatever the conditions, candidates pledged to improve them, whatever their party. No matter who won, the farm lobby won: it claimed that farmers wanted more; invariably they did. Elections consistently ratified the positions of organized agriculture.[34]

In the 1930s and 1940s, as a consequence, lawmakers stayed the course they had set on the eve of the New Deal. The farm lobby's access in Congress held at its peak.

34. See the "politicians' theory of economics and elections," in Edward R. Tufte, *Political control of the economy* (Princeton: Princeton University Press, 1978), pp. 5–9.

II   THE EVOLUTION
            OF INTEREST
            GROUP ACCESS

4   A Theory of Access:

Amplifications

and Extensions

Lawmakers grant access to interest groups because the electoral information and propaganda the groups offer suit their electoral needs better
than the services that other informants offer, given the political, social
and economic circumstances of the time. Looking back, politicians
study recent elections for indications of whose issues and positions sell
well and whose issues and positions sell poorly. Looking ahead, they
distinguish fleeting influences on elections from lasting ones. They
adopt the advice and information of interest groups (1) when they judge
that lobbies enjoy competitive advantage over other informants in meeting their electoral needs, and (2) when they expect the issues and circumstances that established the lobbies' competitive advantage to recur.

During the 1920s, members of Congress from the Middle West and
the South turned away from traditional cue givers, from political parties
and from local informants. For their political advice, they turned instead to the agricultural interest groups, particularly the American
Farm Bureau Federation. In the late twenties and early thirties, elections
revealed the electoral power of the ideas the farm lobby promoted, and
the consistently debilitated state of the agricultural economy guaranteed permanence to the issue's agitation. In the late twenties and early
thirties, accordingly, the elected representatives of agricultural constituencies granted access to the organizational envoys of midwestern and
southern farmers. They turned serious consideration toward the farm
lobby's views.

Congressional preferences for the farm lobby's counsel continued
into the thirties and forties. Absent information that conditions had
changed, absent indications that competitive advantage had eroded or
recurrence had concluded, members of Congress preserved the arrangements that had served them so well in the past.

The protraction of congressional relationships with lobbying organizations is not, however, preordained. "Depending on the circumstances . . . , some groups will enjoy comparatively effective access, and others will find difficulty in securing even perfunctory treatment," David B. Truman wrote. "As conditions change, as some of these influences become more and others less potent, the fortunes of group claims upon the legislature will rise or decline."[1]

The circumstances that create competitive advantage and the circumstances that guarantee recurrence, that is, are subject to changes as the economic, social and political milieu evolves. Economic development, industrialization, population growth and migration vitalize new issues and retire old ones, mobilize new interests and quiet old ones, endow new political resources and drain old ones. Societal change, therefore, alters the environment—both in Washington and at home—in which members of Congress work. It creates new issues, new informants and—most important—new electoral uncertainties.[2]

Economic, social and political change, therefore, enhances the competitive advantage of some informants and undermines the advantage of others. It induces the recurrence of some circumstances and terminates the recurrence of others.

Theoretically, then, change resembles creation. Members of Congress lack full information about the preferences of their constituents, doubly so when political, economic and social change alters voters' preferences. As constituencies change, legislators refashion their working relationships with outside informants in order to take advantage of better options for meeting their needs for effective political intelligence. Whether interest groups compete with parties or with each other makes little theoretical difference. The question is fundamentally the same: under what conditions do lawmakers rely on some sources of information, propaganda and assistance rather than others?

---

1. David B. Truman, *The governmental process*, 2d ed. (New York: Alfred A. Knopf, 1971), p. 350 and pp. 437–38. See also Richard F. Fenno, Jr., *Congressmen in committees* (Boston: Little, Brown and Co., 1973), especially the epilogue.

2. Their genesis is well beyond the scope of this book; I will therefore take their appearances for granted. For these issues theorized, see, among others, Truman, *Governmental process*, chap. 2; Mancur Olson, Jr., *The logic of collective action* (Cambridge: Harvard University Press, 1971), chap. 6; Robert H. Salisbury, "An exchange theory of interest groups," *Midwest Journal of Political Science*, 13 (February 1969), pp. 1–32; Jack L. Walker, "The origins and maintenance of interest groups in America," *American Political Science Review*, 77 (June 1983), pp. 390–406; Anthony Downs, "Up and down with ecology: The 'issue-attention cycle,'" *Public Interest*, 28 (Summer 1972), pp. 38–50; Jack L. Walker, "Setting the agenda in the U.S. Senate," *British Journal of Political Science*, 7 (October 1977), pp. 423–45; John W. Kingdon, *Agendas, alternatives, and public policies* (Boston: Little, Brown and Co., 1984).

This chapter, consequently, reprises the theoretical argument of chapter 1, elaborating aspects of the theory that are important to understanding postwar agricultural policy-making, the subject of the next two chapters. The argument should look very familiar. First, lobbying groups gain and forfeit access to congressional deliberations as they win and lose their competitive advantage relative to other political informants. Second, lobbying groups retain and relinquish access as the circumstances underlying their competitive advantage effect and fail to recur.

Taking each condition in turn, let us examine the evolution of access more fully.

Competitive Advantage

For members of Congress, the most valuable information outlines the effects of various issues and alternatives on their constituents. Such information helps to offset their chronic uncertainty about their prospects for reelection. Lawmakers receive political advice from any number of informants, from political parties, from local acquaintances and from scores of lobbying organizations. The quantity of advice that they actually can heed, however, is closely limited by their time, by their resources and by the indivisible quality of their votes.

Accordingly, political advisers are in competition for legislators' attention. Their access, their chance to be taken seriously, depends upon their ability to convince lawmakers that theirs is consistently the best argument for representatives in their districts. Informants prove their advantage over their competitors in one of two ways. First, they provide information and propaganda more efficiently than their rivals. Second, they promote the electoral aims of their congressional clients more effectively than their competitors.

Cost efficiency. Lobbying organizations offer members of Congress the benefits of ready-made channels of communication to distinct, differentiated groups of constituents. For friendly lawmakers, they provide information tailored to the particular needs and concerns of prominent publics in the district. For friendly lawmakers, they disseminate flattering performance reports to attentive and appreciative electors.

Under most conditions, more specialized interest groups perform the tasks of information and propaganda more efficiently than their less specialized counterparts. For dovetailing reasons, they offer a closer fit between the particular services they provide and the particular services lawmakers need. First, they provide more specific services. The specialized lobbies offer information and propaganda that are undiluted by the intraorganizational compromises made necessary by more inclusive organization. Representing fewer viewpoints, they communicate the particular interests of their members more coherently. Second, they meet lawmakers' more specific needs. The interests composing particular states or congressional districts are typically more homogeneous than the interests composing an entire industry or an entire nation, and legislators represent states and congressional districts rather than industries and nations. Thus, the more specialized information and propaganda that narrowly drawn lobbies provide speak more directly to the more specialized constituency needs of members of Congress.[3]

Specialized lobbies provide advice more efficiently than their more general rivals. They establish competitive advantage over umbrella groups in much the same way as the umbrella groups establish competitive advantage over political parties: by representing the narrower interests of constituents more efficiently.[4]

Effectiveness. In exchange for serious consideration of their policy views, informants give members of Congress their predictions about the electoral consequences of acting on them. They assess the extent of dis-

3. Truman, *Governmental process,* pp. 167–87, 297–301, 385–86; Grant McConnell, *Private power and American democracy* (New York: Alfred A. Knopf, 1966), chap. 4; James Q. Wilson, *Political organizations* (New York: Basic Books, 1973), pp. 308–15; Robert H. Salisbury, "Interest representation: The dominance of institutions," *American Political Science Review,* 78 (March 1984), pp. 64–76. Bauer, Pool and Dexter dissent, for reasons that are not clear. Raymond A. Bauer, Ithiel de Sola Pool and Lewis Anthony Dexter, *American business and public policy,* 2d ed. (Chicago: Aldine-Atherton, 1972), chap. 22.

4. The argument also has an important implication for the assessment of the role of congressional staffs. The vast expansion of the legislative bureaucracy in the 1960s and 1970s—before World War II, House members typically employed two staffers and senators six; by 1980, representatives averaged seventeen staffers and senators seventy-five— gave lawmakers another alternative to the information and counsel of interest groups and other advocates. In contrast to outside informants, in-house staffers were both loyal and specialized: they owed their livelihoods to particular legislators, and they provided information and propaganda tailored to particular constituencies. According to Fiorina, the new staffers allowed lawmakers to do small favors for constituents by intervening on their behalf in Washington's labyrinthine bureaucracies, thus enabling lawmakers more easily to maintain themselves in office. (See Morris P. Fiorina, *Congress: Keystone of the Washington establishment* [New Haven: Yale University Press, 1977].) Put in the language of this study, caseworkers gave legislators the opportunity to propagandize on their own behalf. The new staffers, however, also helped to monitor district opinion. Their frequent contact with constituents and their problems put them in a position to determine what was on voters' minds, providing members of Congress with better constituency information at no direct cost. The provision of subsidized alternatives likely undermined the access of competing informants, like interest groups and parties, to congressional deliberations. Personal staff equipped lawmakers with made-to-order information and propaganda that they lacked decades ago, loosening dependence on sources outside congressional control. (Unfortunately, as of now, I lack the evidence needed to take the point beyond conjecture.)

trict support for the position, the depth of that support and the extent of the opposition.

Lawmakers test informants' predictions in elections. Sometimes, the conclusions they draw corroborate the information allies have passed to them. Elections substantiate informants' competitive advantage.

Other times, however, elections cast doubt on informants' advice. They indicate that issues are less salient than informants had claimed. They show that positions are more conflictual than informants had claimed. They demonstrate that the preferences of constituents are different from what informants had claimed.

First, lawmakers seek to be on the right side of issues about which their constituents care deeply.[5] Thus, the value of political advice about an issue appreciates as salience increases and diminishes as salience decreases. In turn, salience increases and decreases as the economic and social interests of constituents change or as the content of the agenda changes. Either way, informants gain or lose competitive advantage relative to their rivals. Their message gains or loses its urgency relative to the other messages to which members of Congress could attend, issues of lesser or greater importance to greater numbers of constituents. Patterns of access change, then, as issue salience changes. Representatives of more salient viewpoints gain access; representatives of less salient viewpoints lose access.

Second, lawmakers attempt to identify with issues on which the district is in agreement and to avoid issues on which the district is in conflict.[6] When issues become conflictual, legislators look for allies who help them to straddle the divisions, that is, they look for less controversial appeals around which to build their campaigns. Patterns of access change, then, as the contentiousness of issues changes. Representatives of more consensual viewpoints gain access; representatives of more conflictual viewpoints lose access.

Finally, lawmakers attempt to be on the right side of important issues. Occasionally, however, the advice of certain informants proves incorrect, judging from the outcomes of elections. National organizations embrace policy positions that particular localities cannot accept, and candidates offer local voters the choice, perhaps advisedly but often un-

5. John W. Kingdon, *Congressmen's voting decisions,* 2d ed. (New York: Harper and Row, 1981), pp. 43–45, 248–50; David E. Price, "Policy making in congressional committees: The impact of 'environmental' factors," *American Political Science Review,* 72 (June 1978), pp. 560–71.

6. Price, "Policy making," pp. 569–72; Kingdon, *Voting decisions,* pp. 243–50; James L. Sundquist, *Dynamics of the party system,* rev. ed. (Washington: Brookings Institution, 1983), pp. 306–8.

wittingly or unwillingly. Given the options, voters make their decisions, and legislators draw lessons from them. Patterns of access change, then, as elections prove informants right or wrong. Representatives whose viewpoints elections endorse maintain access; representatives whose viewpoints elections contradict lose access.

Summary. Informants lose competitive advantage relative to other informants:

1. When rival groups deliver better information at lower cost. Groups that are specialized reduce legislators' costs of political intelligence and propaganda.
2. When elections prove the inferiority of their assistance and advice. Diminished issue salience, greater issue conflict and decreased reliability of customary sources of information and propaganda prompt lawmakers to turn to rival sources of electoral advice.

Under these conditions, greater uncertainty about the information and assistance legislators need to do their work undermines the confidence they place in their informants. Their informants' access suffers.

Recurrence

When lawmakers grant access to informants, they make an investment in the issues and positions conveyed by those informants, in that they devote their limited time and resources to those issues and positions rather than to others. The return, they hope, is reelection, but they can never be sure. After all, the most important elections are the next ones, and politics gives no guarantees that positions and strategies that worked the last time will work equally well the next time.[7]

The importance of pending elections, and the ambiguity and uncertainty that surround them, puts a sizable premium on predictability. Before they invest in the issues and positions of particular informants, representatives need assurances that the investment will pay off a year or two down the line. In short, they require indications that the competitive advantage of their advisers will continue into the future, that is, they re-

7. Richard F. Fenno, Jr., *Home style: House members in their districts* (Boston: Little, Brown and Co., 1978), pp. 10–18; David R. Mayhew, *Congress: The electoral connection* (New Haven: Yale University Press, 1974), pp. 47–49; Thomas E. Mann, *Unsafe at any margin: Interpreting congressional elections* (Washington: American Enterprise Institute, 1978); R. Douglas Arnold, *The logic of congressional action* (New Haven: Yale University Press, 1990), pp. 10–13, 35–37.

quire indications that the circumstances that created the competitive advantage of their advisers will recur.

If circumstances do not recur, legislators hazard that constituents will no longer respond to their efforts and that informants will no longer promote their efforts, attentions having turned in other directions. If circumstances recur, however, legislators can be reasonably certain that constituents will continue to respond to their efforts and that informants will continue to promote their efforts.

Expectations of recurrence, or its lack, derive from the workaday theories about the sources of political demands that politicians use to order their world. Economic and social distress, presidential initiatives and sustained media coverage all increase the attention that constituents pay to particular issues.[8] In the judgment of political observers, these stimulants of political action and attention might be enduring or they might be passing.

Members of Congress grant access to informants that enjoy competitive advantage based on issues of chronic importance to voters. Interests that depend upon bread-and-butter issues to sustain their agitation and organization more easily create impressions of their agendas' recurrence. Conversely, they deny access to informants that enjoy competitive advantage based on issues of passing importance to voters. Interests that depend upon a sense of crisis to sustain their agitation and organization, that is to say, most groups with purposive orientations, only with great difficulty create judgments of their agendas' recurrence.[9] With ample justification, lawmakers expect bread-and-butter interests to stay on the scene; they expect crisis interests to pass soon from the scene.

Before politicians grant access to new informants, in sum, they judge the probability that their superiority will continue into the future. Competitive advantage, as demonstrated in prior elections, is not by itself sufficient. Members of Congress care little about prior elections; they care a lot about the next one.

8. Price, "Policy making," pp. 571–72; Shanto Iyengar and Donald R. Kinder, *News that matters: Television and American opinion* (Chicago: University of Chicago Press, 1987); Lutz Erbring, Edie N. Goldenberg and Arthur H. Miller, "Front-page news and real world cues: A new look at agenda setting by the media," *American Journal of Political Science,* 24 (February 1980), pp. 16–49; Roy L. Behr and Shanto Iyengar, "Television news, real-world cues, and changes in the public agenda," *Public Opinion Quarterly,* 49 (Spring 1985), pp. 38–57.

9. Anthony Downs, "Up and down with ecology: The 'issue-attention cycle,' " *Public Interest,* 28 (Summer 1972), pp. 38–50; Wilson, *Political organizations,* pp. 45–51. See also John E. Chubb, *Interest groups and the bureaucracy* (Stanford: Stanford University Press, 1983), pp. 28–45.

Conclusion

Political, economic and social change introduces new interests and new issues, and therefore new uncertainties, into legislators' electoral environments. In light of these developments, lawmakers reevaluate the informants to which they grant access.

Members of Congress alter their customary patterns of consultation only when events fulfill two conditions. First, new informants must prove their competitive advantage over old informants. Elections must demonstrate that their information and propaganda more accurately reflect the salient preferences of constituents. Second, the circumstances that made the competitive advantage of new informants possible must recur. Politicians must discern a persistent basis for interest mobilization and attention.

In short, interest groups provide information and propaganda that mitigate lawmakers' uncertainty about their fates in elections, but they are not alone in the provision. Interest groups compete with political parties, with local notables and with other interest groups. Political, economic and social change structures the terms of the competition.

During World War II, the political influence of the farm lobby reached its apex. In sheer reputation for power, the agricultural organizations reigned alongside the business lobbies and the labor unions as the "Big Three" of American politics. "Predictions in politics are always hazardous," Dayton D. McKean wrote in 1949, "but it does seem probable that agricultural interests over the next few years will get most of what they want."[10]

The farm lobby's fearsome reputation had basis in fact: it got results. After a decade of agitation, organized farmers won the Agricultural Adjustment Act, and Washington's generosity toward farmers increased steadily. In 1941 and 1942, the congressional farm bloc pushed farm subsidies up to unheard-of levels, pledging farmers 90 percent of parity for their crops for the duration of the war and for two more years after. "As matters now stand," Fortune commented in 1944, "few things in politics are as certain as [Farm Bureau president] Ed O'Neal's ability to get votes. . . . On the floor of the House of Representatives the Farm Bu-

10. Dayton David McKean, Party and pressure politics (Boston: Houghton Mifflin Co., 1949), p. 460; V. O. Key, Politics, parties and pressure groups (New York: Thomas Y. Crowell, 1942), part 1; David B. Truman, The governmental process, 2d ed. (New York: Alfred A. Knopf, 1971), chap. 11; Kenneth G. Crawford, The pressure boys (New York: Julian Messner, 1939), p. 6; Willard M. Kiplinger, Washington is like that (New York: Harper and Bros. Publishers, 1942), p. 178; Stuart Chase, Democracy under pressure (New York: Twentieth Century Fund, 1945), chaps. 2, 9.

reau can pass or stop any *farm* measure on which it makes a determined fight."[11]

After World War II, however, the farm lobby got fewer and fewer— but more and more impressive—results. On the one hand, its political benefits eroded. From the late forties to the late seventies, federal price guarantees for the major political commodities dropped (in real dollars) by roughly one-third; from the late fifties to the late seventies, agricultural adjustment expenditures fell from over 5 percent of federal outlays to less than 1 percent; and from the late fifties to the early seventies, the average support payments received by farmers diminished (in real dollars) by almost one-half.

On the other hand, in an increasingly inhospitable political environment, the farm lobby saved the agricultural adjustment policies from extinction. From the late forties to the late seventies, the farm population shrank from 15 percent of the polity to barely 3, but the farm lobby repulsed all attempts to phase the farm program out. Today, none of the farm organizations, not even the American Farm Bureau, ranks among the major players in American politics. Given what they have to work with, however, the farm lobbies collectively rank among the most successful.

The farm lobby's failures and its successes track its failures and its successes in gaining access in Congress, four aspects of which will be the subject of the next two chapters. First, in the fifties and sixties, the writers of farm policy removed the American Farm Bureau Federation from its preeminent position in agricultural politics; second, in the sixties and seventies, they installed the commodity organizations collectively in its place. Third, in the sixties and seventies, the writers of farm policy less and less paid their heed to the farm lobby's counsel; fourth, in the seventies and eighties, they scarcely at all paid their heed to the consumer lobby's advice.[12] In short, Congress reallocated access within the farm lobby, Congress restricted access for the farm lobby, but Congress denied access to the consumer lobby.

In the fifties, sixties and seventies, then, access changed, and the changes are theoretically explicable. The argument runs as follows.

11. "The Farm Bureau," *Fortune,* June 1944, p. 196 (emphasis in original).

12. See James T. Bonnen, "Observations on the nature of national agricultural policy decision processes, 1946–76," pp. 309–27 in Trudy Huskamp Peterson, ed., *Farmers, bureaucrats, and middlemen* (Washington: Howard University Press, 1980); William P. Browne, "Policy and interests: Instability and change in a classic issue subsystem," pp. 182–201 in Allan J. Cigler and Burdett A. Loomis, eds., *Interest group politics,* 2d ed. (Washington: Congressional Quarterly Press, 1986); Harold D. Guither, *The food lobbyists* (Lexington, Mass.: Lexington Books, 1980).

In the late 1950s, chapter 5 shows, the intramural dispute over flexible price supports called the competitive advantage of the American Farm Bureau Federation into question. In 1947, the Federation elected conservative midwestern leadership and endorsed a policy of lower, more flexible farm price supports, both over the objections of the southern Farm Bureaus. The 1948 elections, however, returned Harry Truman to the White House, restored Democratic control in Congress and raised doubts about the accuracy of the Farm Bureau's counsel, as Democrats directed attacks on GOP farm policy and won surprising gains in midwestern districts. Intrigued by the possibilities of a farmer-labor alliance, Agriculture Secretary Charles F. Brannan mounted a challenge to the Farm Bureau's policy leadership, advancing the innovative Brannan Plan in 1949. The Farm Bureau weathered the Democrats' challenge. In 1950, Congress and farm voters decisively rejected the Brannan plan.

The elections of the late 1950s, however, steadily eroded the Farm Bureau's competitive advantage. Early in the Eisenhower administration, the Federation's national leadership forged an alliance with Agriculture Secretary Ezra Taft Benson. Their partnership convulsed the farm bloc and divided it into warring partisan camps. More important, it linked evaluations of the Farm Bureau's competitive advantage to the performance of Republican Party candidates. The association seriously damaged the Farm Bureau's reputation for electoral influence: from 1953 through 1960, Eisenhower's farm policy met rejection in midwestern congressional contests.

The result was erosion of the Farm Bureau's access to deliberations over agricultural price support policy. Beginning in the late 1950s, lawmakers from rural districts, first Democrats and then Republicans, became increasingly willing to disregard the views of the American Farm Bureau. In contrast with their earlier behavior, they disagreed openly and unapologetically with the Farm Bureau leadership. They revoked the privileges of first hearing and special attention that the Farm Bureau had once enjoyed. Convinced by elections that the Farm Bureau's information and propaganda had failed them, agrarian lawmakers restricted the access of the American Farm Bureau.

Concurrently, the fifties, sixties and seventies produced a variety of alternative sources of information and advice, but in a context that was very, very different. Rapid migration from farms to towns and cities sapped agrarian voting strength in Congress, and urban representatives asserted themselves increasingly in the affairs of American agriculture.

Chapter 6 identifies the consequences for access in agriculture. It draws a contrast between the fates of two competing interests, both of which sought access to agricultural policy deliberations in the 1950s, 1960s and 1970s.

In the early 1970s, angered by skyrocketing food prices, urban and suburban voters responded to attacks on federal farm policy, and for the first time, congressional consumer advocates sought a place in agricultural price support debates. The consumer movement's inroad, however, was short-lived. Food price inflation soon abated, and the effectiveness of the issue died. The consumer lobby failed to win access in agriculture because the circumstances that created the salience of its issue did not recur.

In the early 1960s, in contrast, the agricultural commodity organizations secured access to agricultural price support deliberations. Ideologically uncommitted and pledged to the maintenance of existing farm programs, the commodity groups represented the preferences of American farmers, as members of Congress read them. Specialized relative to their competition, the general farm organizations, they more coherently represented the views of the more specialized agricultural communities. Collectively, the agricultural commodity organizations captured the central position once held in farm policy debates by the American Farm Bureau.

For the farm lobby as a whole, however, the setbacks of the sixties and seventies contrasted unfavorably with the triumphs of the thirties and forties. As people migrated away from farms, the agricultural organizations represented fewer and fewer voters, even in the most rural congressional constituencies. Thus, migration eroded the competitive advantage of every element of the farm lobby, and the responsiveness of Congress to agricultural interests declined. Within the congressional farm bloc, legislators pressed ahead when necessary with policies disliked or even opposed by the whole of the farm lobby, an occurrence that was unthinkable a generation before. Within congressional farm bill coalitions, rural representatives cut deals with nonagricultural interests (especially food stamp interests), a necessity that was unimaginable a generation before.

From the forties through the seventies, in short, social and economic changes worked to the advantage of some elements of the farm lobby and to the disadvantage of all. The American Farm Bureau Federation lost its competitive advantage relative to its competitors in agriculture; thus, its access narrowed against the access of the commodity organizations. As the representatives of dwindling numbers of farmers, however, the farm organizations fought defensive battles to preserve programs whose day was quickly passing.

5 The Erosion of Access in Agriculture, 1948–1981

> The big game is the party game because in the last
> analysis *there is no political substitute for victory in
> an election.* . . . A wise political leader chooses the
> arena in which he makes his bid for power.
>
> E. E. Schattschneider[1]

In the fifties and sixties, the farm lobby's access in Congress underwent historic changes, changes that rival those of the twenties and thirties in their scope and importance. In the thirties and forties, the American Farm Bureau Federation was a major player in national politics and the preeminent player in agricultural affairs. In the fifties and sixties, however, the Farm Bureau forfeited a substantial part of its claim on the attention of Congress, as it and the Farmers Union allied themselves more closely with the Republican and Democratic parties, respectively.

The debate over postwar agricultural price support policy set these changes in motion.

Cracks in the Edifice: Flexible Price Supports and the 1948 Election

In 1947, with World War II ended, the need to overhaul the farm program was the most open secret in Washington. The farm bloc's crowning wartime achievement, the Steagall Amendment of 1941 (as amended), required the government to support six "basic commodities" and fourteen "Steagall commodities" at 90 percent of parity for the duration of the war, plus two years after.[2]

The Steagall guarantees presented Washington with an acute political problem. On the one hand, financially the government could not af-

1. E. E. Schattschneider, *The semisovereign people: A realist's view of democracy in America* (Hinsdale, Ill.: Dryden Press, 1975), p. 57 (emphasis in original).

2. Murray R. Benedict, *Farm policies of the United States, 1790-1950* (New York: Twentieth Century Fund, 1953), pp. 415–16; Walter W. Wilcox, *The farmer in the Second World War* (Ames: Iowa State College Press, 1947), pp. 243–46. The basic commodities were corn, cotton, peanuts, rice, tobacco and wheat.

ford to extend them any longer. With slackening peacetime demand, extension promised to saddle the Treasury with huge obligations and to burden the market with mammoth surpluses. On the other hand, politically the government equally could not afford to let them lapse. Absent new legislation, the farm program reverted to the terms of the 1938 Agricultural Adjustment Act, to its relatively strict production controls and its relatively stingy price supports, now a hard sell in the farm belt after five years of prosperity. As the Darrow newsletter summarized it, "the furrowing of official brows is most intense about the two-year period during which Congress has promised price supports on certain crops at 90 percent of parity. But farm program thinkers in both parties look beyond that period to some system of keeping farm income at financially—and politically—satisfactory levels. The Government has a bear by the tail and can't let go."[3]

As a way out of the dilemma, the Truman administration proposed a compromise. In October 1947, after months of study and consultation with farm organization leaders, Agriculture Secretary Clinton P. Anderson unveiled a long-range farm plan that neatly split the difference between the Steagall Amendment of 1941 and the Agricultural Adjustment Act of 1938. First, it recommended a system of mandatory price supports for the basic commodities and discretionary price supports for others. Second, it proposed to vary the price support level from 60 to 90 percent of parity, in inverse proportion to supply, in emulation of market signals. In political terms, the administration rejected the "high and rigid" price supports of the Steagall Amendment in favor of the "flexible" price supports of the Triple A; at the same time, it ratcheted price floors closer to the 90 percent standard of the Steagall legislation than to the 52 to 75 percent interval of the Triple A.[4]

The Truman proposal was closely in agreement with the thinking of the new leadership of the American Farm Bureau. In December 1947, at the Federation's annual convention, delegates chose vice president Allan B. Kline to succeed Edward A. O'Neal, who retired after sixteen years as Farm Bureau president.

In both his manner and his outlook, Kline was a distinct contrast to his predecessor. O'Neal was an Alabama cotton planter, an impulsive and convivial southern gentleman. Since 1933, under O'Neal's leader-

3. *Washington Farmletter,* 2 September 1944.

4. Angus McDonald, "Anderson's program," *New Republic,* 10 November 1947, pp. 30–31; Benedict, *Farm policies,* pp. 472–73; *Kiplinger Agricultural Letter* (hereafter *KAL*) No. 493, 18 October 1947; *KAL* No. 497, 13 December 1947; *KAL* No. 516, 21 August 1948; *Wayne Darrow's Washington Farmletter* (hereafter *WDWF*) No. 212, 4 October 1947, No. 233, 28 February 1948.

ship, the Farm Bureau's alliance of corn and cotton had stood on the twin pillars of price support and production control, tenets that O'Neal and his vice president, Earl C. Smith of Illinois, had vigorously defended.[5]

Kline, on the other hand, was an Iowa hog producer, a thoughtful and deliberate prairie yeoman. Like many other Corn Belt farmers, he had chafed under New Deal production restrictions. Demand for pork and beef, he and his allies reasoned, was very sensitive to cost, and Corn Belt farmers lost more in sales than they gained in price. In the 1940s, bit by bit, Kline's thinking found its sanctuary in the midwestern Farm Bureaus; Kline himself assumed the leadership of the Iowa Farm Bureau in the wake of a rebellion against the incumbent, Francis Johnson, a man "long suspected . . . of being too faithful a disciple of Earl Smith."'By the end of the war, midwestern Farm Bureau leaders feared that a continuation of high and rigid farm supports would price the Corn Belt out of the market, and they rallied back of flexible farm supports. In 1947, Farm Bureau delegates endorsed both Kline and his program; they resolved in favor of variable price supports at 60 to 90 percent of parity.[6]

Within the American Farm Bureau, however, the elevation of Kline and the embrace of flexible price supports were not universally acclaimed. In the South and on the Plains, growers of cotton and wheat found the farm program's improvement in price well worth its sacrifice in volume, because demand for those two crops was relatively insensitive to their cost.[7] Consequently, they judged flexible price supports a

5. Arthur Moore, "Earl Smith: Farmers' boss," *Atlantic*, January 1945, pp. 85–90; "The Farm Bureau," *Fortune*, June 1944, pp. 156ff.; Orville M. Kile, *The Farm Bureau through three decades* (Baltimore: Waverly Press, 1948), pp. 327–428.

6. "The Farm Bureau," *Fortune*, p. 159; "Kline heads Farm Bureau," *Wallaces' Farmer* (hereafter *WF*), 4 December 1943, p. 735; Katharine and Henry F. Pringle, "The Farm Bureau's fighting man," *Country Gentleman*, December 1949, p. 22; "Farm lobby strength," *Congressional Quarterly Log for Editors*, 19 November 1948, p. 869; *WDWF* No. 222, 13 December 1947; Victor L. Albjerg, "Allan Blair Kline: The Farm Bureau, 1955," *Current History*, 28 (June 1955), pp. 362–68; D. B. Groves and Kenneth Thatcher, *The first fifty: History of Farm Bureau in Iowa* (Lake Mills, Ia.: Graphic Publishing Co., 1968), pp. 115–29. Kline's most important protégé was Illinois Agricultural Association president Charles B. Shuman, successor to Earl C. Smith. See John J. Lacey, *Farm Bureau in Illinois: History of Illinois Farm Bureau* (Bloomington: Illinois Agricultural Association, 1965), p. 181; "Earl Smith quits after 20 years service to IAA," *Prairie Farmer*, 8 December 1945, p. 8; "He's new IAA president," *Prairie Farmer*, 8 December 1945, p. 8.

7. Thus, during the 1930s, cotton and wheat farmers routinely approved marketing quotas by lopsided margins, while corn farmers just as routinely turned them down. The differences made economic and political sense. Gardner found a negative relationship between the demand elasticities of farm commodities and the level of government support for

bad bargain, and their Farm Bureau leaders worked desperately to head off Kline's election. They tried to coax Ed O'Neal and Earl Smith out of retirement and into the presidential race. Both declined. They tried to cut a deal with presidential hopeful Hassil E. Schenck, the president of the Indiana Farm Bureau. The agreement fell through. They tried to elect a sympathetic vice president, Georgia tomato farmer H. L. Wingate. Instead, the convention chose an opponent, Arkansas rice grower Romeo E. Short. Flexible price supports won the day in the Farm Bureau, but the issue divided it deeply.[8]

The Farm Bureau's skirmish over flexibles foreshadowed the proposal's reception in Congress. The Senate Agriculture Committee, led de facto by Vermont Republican George D. Aiken, approved the administration's bill, and the Senate easily passed it. The House Agriculture Committee, on the other hand, snubbed the Truman proposal and submitted its own alternative, written by its chairman, Kansas Republican Clifford R. Hope: a two-year extension of price supports at 90 percent of parity for the basic commodities and milk. The House routinely endorsed it.[9]

In the conference committee, convened late in the spring of 1948, Hope and Aiken wired the two bills together, extending fixed supports until 1949 and implementing flexibles thereafter. This obvious compromise, however, quickly ran aground. Four House conferees, Wisconsin Republican Reid F. Murray and three southern Democrats, all

---

them. See Bruce L. Gardner, "Causes of U.S. farm commodity programs," *Journal of Political Economy,* 95 (April 1987), pp. 302–9; and Bruce L. Gardner, "Efficient redistribution through commodity markets," *American Journal of Agricultural Economics,* 65 (May 1983), pp. 229–30.

8. "AFBF chooses Kline," *WF,* 3 January 1948, p. 10; Eugene Butler, "What's new in agriculture," *Progressive Farmer* (hereafter *PF*), February 1948, p. 8; Eugene Butler, "What's new in agriculture," *PF,* November 1947, p. 8; *WDWF* No. 218, 15 November 1947; *WDWF* No. 224, 27 December 1947; *WDWF* No. 229, 31 January 1948; *KAL* No. 497, 13 December 1947; "H. L. Wingate, revolutionary," *Fortune,* October 1941, pp. 72–77; Interview with Roger Fleming, December 1986; Allen J. Matusow, *Farm policies and politics in the Truman years* (Cambridge: Harvard University Press, 1967), pp. 135–38. Short shared one intriguing trait with his midwestern allies: their crops, rice and hogs, were the only two commodities whose original AAA processing tax was shifted substantially back onto producers. See *An analysis of the effects of the processing taxes levied under the Agricultural Adjustment Act,* Bureau of Agricultural Economics, U. S. Department of Agriculture, 1937, pp. 6–7, 18–19, 59.

9. *KAL* No. 502, 21 February 1948; *WDWF* No. 240, 17 April 1948; Eugene Butler, "What's new in agriculture," *PF,* November 1947; *Hearings before the House Committee on Agriculture,* "Long-range agricultural policy," 80th Congress, 1st session, 1947, Parts 5 to 13; Theodore Saloutos, "Agricultural organizations and farm policy in the South after World War II," *Agricultural History,* 53 (January 1979), p. 389.

supporters of high and rigid price supports, refused to sign the conference report, and as adjournment neared, the committee deadlocked. Finally, GOP leaders persuaded Murray to resign from the conference. His replacement, Indiana Republican George W. Gillie, approved the compromise, and the conference issued its report (still without the signatures of the three House Democrats) just hours before adjournment. In a matter of minutes, the two chambers approved the Hope-Aiken Act and thereupon closed shop.[10]

Come November, though, farm voters delivered a surprising verdict. Against all expectations, Democratic president Harry S Truman defeated GOP governor Thomas E. Dewey, and the Democrats reclaimed control in both houses of Congress.

As pundits searched for reasons, suspicions turned to the farm vote. In the presidential contest, commentators noted, the Democratic ticket trailed its 1944 totals in industrial regions but led them in the midwestern farm belt. Despite the mobilization of organized labor around the issue of the Taft-Hartley Act, the president lost the northeastern industrial states, where Franklin D. Roosevelt had beaten Dewey four years before. On the other hand, they continued, Truman won in three agricultural states, Ohio, Wisconsin and Iowa, where Roosevelt had earlier lost to Dewey. Truman's victory, they reasoned, came on the strength of the farm vote.[11]

In congressional contests, moreover, the Democrats scored their most impressive gains in the agricultural states. In the Senate, they claimed GOP seats in Minnesota, Illinois, Iowa, Kentucky, Oklahoma,

10. *Congressional Record,* 80th Congress, 2d session, Part 7, pp. 9338–9347; Interview with Hyde Murray (Reid Murray's son), December 1986; *KAL* No. 511, 26 June 1948; Richard Wilson, "The farmer's Washington," *Successful Farming* (hereafter *SF*), August 1948, p. 12; Richard Wilson, "The farmer's Washington, *SF,* October 1948, p. 16; *WDWF* No. 249, 20 June 1948; Matusow, *Farm policies,* pp. 134–44; Tom G. Hall, "The Aiken bill, price supports, and the wheat farmer in 1948," *North Dakota History,* 39 (Winter 1972), pp. 13–22, 47. The 1948 act also redefined parity. It based the index on a ten-year moving average of farm and nonfarm prices rather than on the original 1909–1914 average.

11. Mark Sullivan, "The farmers' defection," *Washington Post,* 8 November 1948, p. 8; "What does the election mean to farmers?" *WF,* 20 November 1948, pp. 18–19; Wesley McCune, "Farmers in politics," pp. 41–51 in Donald C. Blaisdell, ed., "Unofficial government: Pressure groups and lobbies," *Annals of the American Academy of Political and Social Science,* 319 (September 1958), p. 45; *WDWF* No. 272, 27 November 1948; *KAL* No. 522, 13 November 1948; "Hog raisers may get direct payments," *WF,* 21 May 1949, p. 20; "Was the '48 election rigged?" *U.S. News and World Report,* 6 June 1952, p. 20; Irwin Ross, *The loneliest campaign: The Truman victory of 1948* (New York: New American Library, 1968), pp. 256–60; Lauren Soth, *Farm trouble* (Princeton: Princeton University Press, 1957), pp. 12–13.

Idaho and Wyoming, plus Delaware and West Virginia. In the House, they picked up eight seats in Ohio, three in Minnesota, five in Indiana, eight in Missouri—all told, over thirty seats in the rural Middle West. In both the presidential election and in congressional elections, the *New York Times* concluded, "the farm vote bitterly disappointed the Republicans. Where it did not turn on them outright, the Democrats made sharp inroads in the grain belt."[12]

Since 1948, more disinterested observers have questioned the importance of the farm vote to Truman's "miracle of electioneering." Even if they are correct, however, their "conclusion [is] the opposite of what was believed by Congressmen in 1948–49." In the fall campaign, rural lawmakers averred, Truman had planted doubts about the GOP's commitment to the farm program, and farmers' worries had derailed Dewey's drive for the White House. The "do-nothing" Republican Congress, Truman told farm audiences, had "stuck a pitchfork in the farmer's back." By limiting the government's power to build grain storage, Democratic campaigners charged, Republicans had threatened farmers with default on government price support obligations, taking the first step in a plan to abolish the program entirely. The president's fear campaign in the farm belt, the press agreed, registered with farmers. "Riding the crest of the greatest farm prosperity in history," the *Times* concluded, "they wanted to keep the high level, and their anxiety over the future was best answered by Mr. Truman."[13]

12. William S. White, "Truman wins with 304 electoral votes: Sweep in Congress," *New York Times,* 4 November 1948, p. 1; *WDWF* No. 269, 6 November 1948; "Gillette gains in Senate race," *WF,* 16 October 1948, pp. 26–27; "Farm, labor vote carries Missouri," *New York Times,* 4 November 1948, p. 10; William M. Blair, "Farm revolt laid to anxiety on aid," *New York Times,* 4 November 1948, p. 15; "Truman sweep," *New York Times,* 7 November 1948, p. H 1; John W. Ball, "Sweeping Truman victory goes down to grass roots," *Washington Post,* 4 November 1948, p. 3; Murray interview; John Earl Haynes, "Farm coops and the election of Hubert Humphrey to the Senate," *Agricultural History,* 57 (April 1983), pp. 201–11; Paul H. Douglas, *In the fullness of time* (New York: Harcourt Brace Jovanovich, 1971), chap. 13; Edward L. Schapsmeier and Frederick H. Schapsmeier, "Paul H. Douglas: From pacifist to soldier-statesman," *Journal of the Illinois State Historical Society,* 67 (June 1974), p. 307.

13. Arthur Krock, "Truman wins with 304 electoral votes: Ohio poll decides," *New York Times,* 4 November 1948, p. 1; Congressional Quarterly Service, *U.S. agricultural policy in the postwar years, 1945–1963* (Washington: Congressional Quarterly Press, 1963), p. 25; "Address at Dexter, Iowa, on the occasion of the National Plowing Match, September 18, 1948," *Public papers of the Presidents of the United States: Harry S Truman, 1948* (Washington: Government Printing Office, 1964), p. 506; Blair, "Farm revolt," p. 15; "Let CCC build more bins," *WF,* 16 October 1948, pp. 32–33; *WDWF* No. 270, 13 November 1948; Matusow, *Farm policies,* pp. 174–91; Charles M. Hardin, "Farm price policy and the farm vote," *Journal of Farm Economics,* 37 (November 1955), pp.

For many congressional agrarians, however, the lessons of Dewey's defeat went even further, casting doubt upon the political wisdom of flexible price supports. The Hope-Aiken Act was not an issue in Truman's campaign—it was his program, after all—but the conclusion that farmers opposed it was easy to draw, especially if one was already inclined to it. In accepting the need for more moderate price supports, a Washington wit observed, the 1948 Agriculture Act promised "more Aiken than Hope for farmers," and Democratic congressional candidates made the most of its GOP paternity. In the fall of 1948, close watchers of farm politics detected "strong opposition to less than 90 percent of parity supports," and Republican candidates watched the votes slip away. "Farmers didn't understand the Aiken bill," Clifford Hope wrote in postmortem, "and it simply gave the Democrats a chance to say that Republicans had passed a price support bill with supports at 60% of parity."[14]

When the House Agriculture Committee convened in January 1949, six of its sixteen Republicans were no longer present; one had retired, five more had lost. Indiana's George W. Gillie, who had replaced Reid Murray on the conference committee and who had provided the decisive vote for flexibles, was one of the casualties. Murray was back for another term.[15]

At the opening of the Eighty-first Congress, therefore, GOP agrarians rushed to renounce the Hope-Aiken Act. "I think what the record should show is that the House conferees and members of the House, in accepting the conferees' report, did not express any approval or disapproval of the Aiken bill in doing so," Clifford Hope stressed. "The Aiken bill was accepted with the understanding that it would be studied fur-

---

601–24; Thomas G. Ryan, "Farm prices and the farm vote in 1948," *Agricultural History*, 54 (July 1980), pp. 387–401; Ross, *Loneliest campaign*, pp. 182–86, 256–60; Roger Fleming, "Political history of the farm price support issue," pamphlet, American Farm Bureau Federation, 1955, p. 10.

14. *WDWF* No. 268, 30 October 1948; James L. Forsythe, "Postmortem on the election of 1948: An evaluation of Congressman Clifford R. Hope's views," *Kansas Historical Quarterly*, 38 (Autumn 1972), p. 341 and pp. 338–59; Edward L. Schapsmeier and Frederick H. Schapsmeier, *Ezra Taft Benson and the politics of agriculture: The Eisenhower years, 1953–1961* (Danville, Ill.: Interstate Printers and Publishers, 1975), p. 278n; *WDWF* No. 270, 13 November 1948; Murray interview.

15. The contribution of the Hope-Aiken controversy to Gillie's loss is not clear from any of my sources. His district, the Indiana Fourth, was normally safe Republican territory, but in 1948 Gillie dropped ten points below his usual totals and lost to Democrat Edward H. Kruse. In Allen County, he fell nearly fourteen points below his normal tally, suggesting retaliation against his vote for Taft-Hartley by the unions in Fort Wayne. Had he run as well in the seven surrounding rural counties as he commonly did, however, he would still have slipped by.

ther in this session of Congress. I think it is only fair to say that none of us knew exactly what the full implications of the bill were at that time." With the benefit of hindsight, however, the implications *were* clear. "The farmers of America are against this sliding scale support business," Iowa Republican Ben Jensen concluded. "It's not just Southern farmers who are putting up the fight—it's farmers all over the country."[16]

For farm state politicians, then, the 1948 election underscored farmers' sensitivity to threats to farm price supports. By rejecting GOP candidates, it seemed, farmers rejected lower prices. By rejecting lower prices, they rejected flexible farm supports. And by rejecting flexible farm supports, they rejected the position of the American Farm Bureau Federation.

For party politicians, accordingly, the 1948 election gave a first glimpse of the Farm Bureau's vincibility. It suggested the Federation did not, in fact, speak for farmers. It suggested dissipation of competitive advantage.

Partisan Challenge: The Brannan Plan

Down on Independence Avenue, in the gargantuan complex of the Department of Agriculture, the results of the 1948 election set political minds in motion. Within months, they had arrived at a proposal.

On 7 April 1949, Agriculture Secretary Charles F. Brannan appeared before a joint session of the House and Senate Agriculture Committees to submit his ideas for a radically different long-range farm program. In its barest essentials, the "Brannan Plan" proposed to maintain farm incomes at generous levels without raising consumer prices. It created a list of ten new "basic" commodities entitled to mandatory government price supports: corn, cotton, tobacco, wheat, milk, eggs, chickens, hogs, cattle and lambs. For the "storables" (cotton, tobacco and grains), the program shored up farm prices with conventional loan and storage instruments. For the "perishables" (all others), however, the program al-

16. *Hearings before the Special Subcommittee of the House Agriculture Committee,* "Agricultural Act of 1948 (Aiken bill)," 81st Congress, 1st session, Serial D, 1949, pp. 15–16; Eugene Butler, "What's new in agriculture," *PF,* February 1949, p. 10; *WDWF* No. 270, 13 November 1948; *WDWF* No. 272, 27 November 1948; *WDWF* No. 275, 18 December 1948; "ERP backed in new Congress," *Washington Post,* 7 November 1948, p. 2; *WDWF* No. 249, 20 June 1948; *KAL* No. 511, 26 June 1948. Flexible price supports were well suited to insinuating language. Opponents called them the "sliding scale" to make the point, as Clifford Hope phrased it, that "things don't slide *up.*" The Farm Bureau, on the other hand, preferred the term "variable supports." See Duncan Norton-Taylor, "Mr. Benson's flexible flyer," *Fortune,* March 1954, p. 89; and Fleming, "Political history of the farm price support issue," p. 15.

lowed prices to drop to free market levels and made up the price difference with direct payments to producers. By means of direct payments, the Brannan Plan promised parity income for farmers and market prices for consumers.[17]

The idea of using direct payments to maintain farm income was not new to Charles Brannan; variants had floated around the Department of Agriculture for almost a decade. Original to the secretary, however, was a conception of how the idea might be used politically. First, just by the fact of its offering, it distanced the Truman administration from flexible price supports, a policy that appeared to be heading nowhere quickly. Second, and more important, with its dual promise of lower food prices and higher farm income, it positioned Brannan as the champion of the two constituencies that had kept Harry Truman in the White House: labor and farmers. "If Brannan is right," the *New Republic* observed, "the political miracle of 1948 will become a habit as farmers, labor and consumers find common political goals."[18]

In the insular world of agricultural politics, though, the Brannan Plan was additionally a daring partisan challenge to the policy leadership of the farm lobby. In deliberate departure from past Department practice, Brannan had developed the proposal in secret, without the consultation of any of the farm groups. Even so, the National Farmers Union, led by Brannan's friend and ally James G. Patton, enthusiastically endorsed it.[19]

17. *Hearings before the Special Subcommittee of the House Agriculture Committee,* "General farm program," 81st Congress, 1st session, Serial P, 1949 (hereafter *Hearings,* "Brannan Plan," 1949), passim; Reo M. Christenson, *The Brannan Plan: Farm politics and policy* (Ann Arbor: University of Michigan Press, 1959); Matusow, *Farm policies,* pp. 196–99.

18. Angus McDonald, "The Fair Deal's farm program," *New Republic,* 2 May 1949, p. 13; "Hog raisers may get direct payments," *WF,* 21 May 1949, p. 20; *KAL* No. 533, 16 April 1949; *KAL* No. 543, 3 September 1949; Eugene Butler, "What's new in agriculture," *PF,* May 1949, p. 10; " 'I'm waiting to see,' say farmers," *WF,* 2 July 1949, p. 14; "The Brannan farm plan," *Consumer Reports,* June 1949, pp. 278–80.

19. *KAL* No. 534, 30 April 1949; Eugene Butler, "What's new in agriculture," *PF,* June 1949, p. 10; Matusow, *Farm policies,* pp. 194–95. The Farmers Union repudiated its initial hostility for the New Deal in 1937, when a faction of moderates (including Patton) captured the organization. During the late 1930s and early 1940s, alone among the farm groups, it supported the Farm Security Administration, the incorporation of the Farm Credit Administration into the USDA, and the wartime system of price controls, all initiatives dear to the hearts of Democratic liberals. Under Patton's leadership, the NFU styled itself into the "progressive" farm organization, and supported the whole array of Fair Deal legislation. Patton's friendship with Brannan dated to their days together in Colorado, where Patton headed the Farmers Union and Brannan directed the regional office of the Farm Security Administration. See John A. Crampton, *The National Farmers Union: Ide-*

The Farm Bureau, on the other hand, bitterly opposed the Brannan proposal, for reasons both practical and political. On a policy level, the Farm Bureau argued, direct subsidies were a surefire way to make farmers dependent on the whims of taxpayers, and the Federation fought them now as it had throughout the war. Now, though, the dispute ran much deeper, and Farm Bureau leaders rose to it. "I wonder what the C.I.O. reaction would be," a Federation spokesman asked, "if Secretary of Labor Tobin took into Congress some legislative program labor had never even heard of?" In the eyes of the Farm Bureau—and in the eyes of the secretary as well—Brannan had set out to show who really spoke for farmers.[20]

Brannan's idea of a partisan program for farmers was not automatically attractive to politicians on Capitol Hill, even in the aftermath of the 1948 election. In one of its particulars, the secretary had judged the situation correctly: rural lawmakers were exasperated with the Farm Bureau leadership and its stubborn attachment to flexible price supports.[21]

In two other particulars, however, Brannan clearly misjudged. First, given its internal divisions, the Farm Bureau was in no position to hold

ology of a pressure group (Lincoln: University of Nebraska Press, 1965); *KAL* No. 205, 28 November 1936; *KAL* No. 288, 23 December 1939; *KAL* No. 294, 16 March 1940; *KAL* No. 313, 7 December 1940; *KAL* No. 361, 26 September 1942; Richard Wilson, "It's Reno for the Bureau," *SF*, September 1942, p. 16; *KAL* No. 372, 27 February 1943; "Patton is willing," *Time*, 14 September 1942, p. 22; Oren Stephens, "FSA fights for its life," *Harper's*, April 1943, pp. 478–87; James G. Patton and James Loeb, Jr., "The challenge to progressives," *New Republic*, 5 February 1945, pp. 187–206; A. G. Mezerik, "The Brannan Plan," *New Republic*, 28 November 1949, p. 12; Benton J. Stong, "Rock-ribbed farmers," *New Republic*, 28 February 1949, pp. 16–18; James G. Patton, *The case for farmers* (Washington: Public Affairs Press, 1959); William C. Pratt, "Glenn J. Talbott, the Farmers Union, and American liberalism after World War II," *North Dakota History*, 55 (Winter 1988), pp. 3–13.

20. Richard Wilson, "The farmer's Washington," *SF*, June 1949, p. 16; Allan B. Kline, "Government . . . and the farm minority," *Nation's Agriculture*, March 1949, p. 7; "Crop controls or bankruptcy," *WF*, 17 December 1949, p. 8; Roger Fleming, "Price—and more too," *Nation's Agriculture*, November 1949, p. 20; Richard Wilson, "The farmer's Washington," *SF*, September 1949, p. 18; *WDWF* No. 327, 17 December 1949; "Fight on production payments," *WF*, 7 May 1949, p. 33; "The farm plan won't die," *New Republic*, 26 December 1949, p. 7; Matusow, *Farm policies*, pp. 204–5; Grant McConnell, *The decline of agrarian democracy* (Berkeley and Los Angeles: University of California Press, 1953), chap. 12.

21. See *Hearings before the Special Subcommittee of the House Agriculture Committee*, "General farm program," 81st Congress, 1st session, Serial R, 1949 (hereafter *Hearings*, 1949), pp. 448, 443–50; Eugene Butler, "What's new in agriculture," *PF*, February 1949, p. 10; "Won't limit corn acres this year," *WF*, 5 February 1949, p. 27.

lawmakers to anything. As Kline candidly admitted, the Farm Bureau itself could hardly agree on farm policy:

W. R. (BOB) POAGE (D., Tex.): Was there just a groundswell of voice from the cotton-producing areas that came up here and urged you overwhelmingly, saying, "This is what the cotton people want to be allowed to do"? . . .

KLINE: There certainly was and as a result we have the compromise which we have.

POAGE: I am not trying to put you on the spot with any of your officers, . . . but do you remember any of the people from my section of the country who urged such a procedure [flexible supports] in your convention?

KLINE: No, I don't remember any.

On the price support issue, the Farm Bureau was dealing from weakness, and its leaders and its congressional allies very well knew it. In reality, therefore, Congress's choices were not the Farm Bureau plan or the Brannan plan. Rather, its leading options were a high and rigid farm support program or a lower but more flexible farm support program, each of which had its champions in the American Farm Bureau.[22]

Second, the secretary overestimated the damage the 1948 election had inflicted on the Farm Bureau's standing in Congress. In 1949, despite their disagreements and despite their doubts, lawmakers from both parties went out of their way to solicit the Farm Bureau, as indeed they consistently had. "We will probably ask Mr. Kline to meet with us in a night session," Georgia Democrat Stephen Pace decided, when it became clear after a day of testimony that the Committee was still eager to hear from him.

PACE: I think the importance of the views of your organization and the membership of your organization is such that you should be heard throughout at the earliest possible moment.

22. *Hearings*, 1949, pp. 488, 446; "Controls look good to farmers," *U.S. News and World Report*, 22 April 1949, p. 17; Eugene Butler, "What's new in agriculture," *PF*, July 1949, p. 15; *WDWF* No. 295, 7 May 1949. Despite Kline's candor, Farm Bureau dissidents took no chances, and they appeared immediately after him to contradict him directly. See *Hearings*, 1949, pp. 507–18; and *Hearings before the House Agriculture Committee*, "Farm program of the American Farm Bureau Federation," 80th Congress, 2d session, 1948, p. 47. On the Farm Bureau disputes over policy in 1948, see Eugene Butler, "What's new in agriculture," *PF*, January 1949, p. 8; *WDWF* No. 275, 18 December 1948; *WDWF* No. 284, 19 February 1949; *KAL* No. 524, 11 December 1948; *KAL* No. 525, 24 December 1948; "Won't limit corn acres this year," *WF*, 5 February 1949, p. 27; Fred Bailey, "Washington roundup," *Country Gentleman*, March 1949, p. 12; "Compromise on supports," *WF*, 1 January 1949, p. 23; Eugene Butler, "What's new in Washington," *PF*, March 1949, p. 10; Matusow, *Farm policies*, pp. 192–94; William Bruce Storm, "An analysis of the Illinois Agricultural Association as a pressure group for farmers," Ph.D. dissertation, University of Chicago, 1950, pp. 313, 318, 491.

CLIFFORD R. HOPE (R., Kan.): Mr. Chairman, you are not going to get very many members here at night. Certainly this great organization is entitled to come here during the daytime. We do not have to have a night session, surely, for the American Farm Bureau Federation.

The Farm Bureau's access to the House Agriculture Committee survived the 1948 election. Without an unambiguous indication that the Farm Bureau no longer spoke for farmers, lawmakers clung to the Farm Bureau's counsel.[23]

Capitol Hill, accordingly, handled the Brannan Plan cautiously. Midwestern Republicans and southern Democrats decried its cost, its "regimentation" of farmers, its explicitly partisan intent. "It is not the job of government agency personnel to formulate agricultural policy," fumed New Mexico senator Clinton P. Anderson, Brannan's predecessor. "I want to see farm legislation developed by farmers through their own farm organizations in co-operation with members of Congress."[24]

Faced with widespread congressional resistance to his ideas, Brannan heaved his proposal onto the high support bandwagon. He endorsed a measure that combined elements of the old Hope bill and the new Brannan Plan, authored by Georgia Democrat Stephen Pace. Like the Brannan proposal, the Pace bill applied direct subsidies to three perishable commodities of the secretary's choosing. Like the Hope Act, it provided high and rigid price supports for ten other commodities, including corn, cotton, tobacco, wheat, hogs and milk. The House Agriculture Committee approved it on a party-line vote.[25]

Congressional opponents of the Brannan Plan, rallied by the Farm Bureau, countered the Pace bill with tempting alternatives. In the Senate, Clinton P. Anderson offered a compromise to lift the lower limit of the flexible price support scale from 60 percent of parity to 75. In the House, Tennessee Democrat Albert Gore proposed a substitute to extend price supports at 90 percent of parity for still another year. Lawmakers stampeded, senators to the Anderson bill, representatives to the Gore amendment. The conference committee combined the two bills into the Agricultural Act of 1949.[26]

23. See *Hearings*, 1949, pp. 451–52, 460–63, 517.

24. Christenson, *Brannan Plan*, p. 57; *Hearings*, 1949, pp. 160–63, 511–12; *Hearings*, "Brannan Plan," 1949, passim; Eugene Butler, "What's new in agriculture," *PF*, July 1949, p. 15; *WDWF* No. 291, 9 April 1949; Clifford R. Hope, "Something for everybody," *Nation's Agriculture*, June 1950, pp. 9–10.

25. Interview with Wesley McCune (an aide to Brannan), November 1986; Eugene Butler, "What's new in agriculture," *PF*, August 1949, p. 16; "Plan to reseal 1948 corn," *WF*, 4 June 1949, p. 16; Matusow, *Farm policies*, pp. 208–9.

26. "Why the farm plan lost," *New Republic*, 1 August 1949, p. 7; Matusow, *Farm policies*, pp. 209–18; *KAL* No. 540, 23 July 1949; Eugene Butler, "What's new in agricul-

The Farm Bureau gave a cheer. "Once again," a Farm Bureau commentator wrote, "American agriculture has rebuffed those who would place the national farm program on a partisan political basis."[27]

The price for the Farm Bureau's victory over the Brannan Plan, however, was a retreat from flexible price supports. In the shadow of the 1948 election, the secretary had almost carried the day, simply by promising more for the farmer than the Farm Bureau did. As Wayne Darrow put it, the "Brannan Plan has congressmen of both parties scared. Many are afraid to vote for it in the face of almost solid farm organization opposition, and possible high costs. Many are afraid to vote against it lest it prove popular with voters in 1950."[28]

Thus, for rural lawmakers—and doubly for the Farm Bureau and Charles Brannan—the 1950 midterm elections were a crucial showdown, an important sounding of the Farm Bureau's competitive advantage. The "Democrats fully expect to gain congressional strength in the Midwest in the elections this year," a midwestern farm journal observed, "because of the *opposition* of the American Farm Bureau Federation to the Brannan Plan. Democratic politicos remember that the Farm Bureau was not strong for Truman in the last election. They think that the rank and file of the Farm Bureau did not follow its leadership. Therefore, they reason, it makes political sense for Brannan to continue to fight Allan Kline."[29]

To carry the Democratic standard into battle, the secretary recruited a proxy on Allan Kline's home turf. Brannan's under secretary, Albert J. Loveland, the Iowa Triple A's longtime chairman, joined the race against Republican senator Bourke B. Hickenlooper, the Iowa Farm Bureau's longtime champion. As Brannan intended, Loveland's entry turned the contest in Iowa into a referendum on the Brannan Plan. "If Loveland wins," a Des Moines journal observed, "Washington political observers believe the effect will be very strong. . . .On the other hand, if Loveland is beaten, the Brannan Plan will be sunk."[30]

From Brannan's perspective, however, the campaign was a nation-

ture," *PF*, September 1949, p. 10; *WDWF* No. 306, 23 July 1949; *WDWF* No. 317, 8 October 1949.

27. Gordon H. Allen, "Washington from the inside," *Nation's Agriculture*, September 1949, p. 6; J. Roland Pennock, "Party and constituency in postwar agricultural price-support legislation," *Journal of Politics*, 18 (May 1956), pp. 171–81.

28. *WDWF* No. 302, 23 June 1949.

29. Richard Wilson, "The farmer's Washington," *SF*, February 1950, p. 8.

30. Richard Wilson, "The farmer's Washington," *SF*, May 1950, p. 8; Fred Bailey, "Washington roundup," *Country Gentleman*, August 1949, p. 12; Murray D. Lincoln, *Vice president in charge of revolution* (New York: McGraw Hill Book Co., 1960), pp. 232–33; *KAL* No. 557, 18 March 1950; *KAL* No. 563, 10 June 1950; *WDWF* No. 372,

wide disaster. In an orgy of red-baiting, Republican and Democratic opportunists equated the Fair Deal with socialism and cited the Brannan Plan as a foremost example. Democratic incumbents rapidly renounced it, but they could not escape. In an Oklahoma primary, Democratic representative A. S. (Mike) Monroney knocked off Senator Elmer Thomas, the chairman of the Senate Agriculture Committee and Brannan's most prominent Senate ally. In Illinois, former GOP congressman Everett M. Dirksen dispatched Senator Scott W. Lucas, the majority leader of the United States Senate. Finally, in Iowa, Republican senator Bourke B. Hickenlooper defeated Brannan's handpicked candidate, Albert J. Loveland, by almost ninety thousand votes.[31]

The 1950 elections, therefore, were an insurmountable setback for Charles Brannan. For farmers, like other voters, the war in Korea and the alleged communists in the State Department evidently overshadowed domestic worries. But "the commonly accepted interpretation that farmers voted against Brannan and his plan," Darrow observed, "gives Farm Bureau president Kline and his followers at least a temporary advantage on the Hill." By this time preoccupied with the Korean conflict, the USDA quietly dropped the Brannan Plan, and Congress extended high and rigid price supports through two years after the end of the war.[32]

28 October 1950; " 'Support stock,' says Brannan," *WF*, 3 June 1950, p. 26; "What does new law do for corn?" *WF*, 17 July 1948, p. 778. In many respects, Loveland was a poor candidate for a showdown. He had never held elected office, and he had to maneuver through a crowded Democratic primary even to get to Hickenlooper. Moreover, early *Wallaces' Farmer* polls showed him trailing the incumbent by more than ten percentage points. Richard Wilson, "The farmer's Washington," *SF*, February 1950, p. 8; "How farmers may vote," *WF*, 18 February 1950, p. 6; " 'Scandal in butter is on the way,' " *WF*, 18 March 1950, p. 21.

31. "Charlie Brannan's plan," *WF*, 17 June 1950, p. 8; *WDWF* No. 374, 11 November 1950; "Nationwide roundup," *Country Gentleman*, December 1950, p. 4; *KAL* No. 574, 11 November 1950; Richard Wilson, "The farmer's Washington," *SF*, June 1950, p. 18; "They'll watch Loveland," *WF*, 17 June 1950, p. 28; "How farmers may vote," *WF*, 2 September 1950, p. 10; "How farmers say they'll vote," *WF*, 7 October 1950, p. 20; "More corn, more beans in '51," *WF*, 21 October 1950, p. 24; "Mr. Brannan and the Farm Bureau," *PF*, August 1950, p. 75; "One will head Senate Agricultural Committee," *Nation's Agriculture*, September 1950, p. 8; "Illinois shuns bossism," *New Republic*, 20 November 1950, pp. 8–9; "Democratic gains," *New Republic*, 20 November 1950, pp. 9–10; Eric Manheimer, "The public career of Elmer Thomas," Ph.D. dissertation, University of Oklahoma, 1952, pp. 210–17; Edward L. Schapsmeier and Frederick H. Schapsmeier, "Scott W. Lucas of Havana: His rise and fall as Majority Leader in the United States Senate," *Journal of the Illinois State Historical Society*, 70 (November 1977), pp. 310–18; Edward L. Schapsmeier and Frederick H. Schapsmeier, *Dirksen of Illinois: Senatorial statesman* (Urbana: University of Illinois Press, 1985), chap. 3.

32. *WDWF* No. 374, 11 November 1950; "Election year package for the farm states," *Business Week*, 29 September 1951, p. 26; *KAL* No. 619, 2 August 1952; Don

In the late 1940s, in short, Brannan's challenge to the policy leadership of the farm lobby died aborning. In the 1948 elections, in farmers' rejection of lower prices, Brannan had seen an hopeful indication of a new Farm Bureau weakness, and with the Brannan Plan he had attempted to exploit it.

But Brannan's hopes were premature. Despite the outcome of the 1948 elections, and despite congressional displeasure with the Farm Bureau program, rural lawmakers were as yet unwilling to make the break. Lacking a firm indication that the Federation no longer spoke for farmers, lawmakers maintained their old alliance with the American Farm Bureau, and the 1950 elections only confirmed them in their habits.

Even so, the 1949 Agriculture Act and the stopgap policies of the Korean War simply delayed the day of reckoning. The bitter conflict over long-range farm policy carried over to the 1950s. It engulfed the House Agriculture Committee in the most heated partisanship it had ever known. It bequeathed the Farm Bureau a diminution of its access.

Forcing the Issue: Republican Policy and Farm Bureau Access

In 1953, as Dwight D. Eisenhower took office, any competent observer of farm politics could detect substantial grass-roots opposition to flexible price supports, the long-range policy of the American Farm Bureau.

The Korean War halted, a precipitous drop in commodity prices had rekindled agrarian demands for high and rigid farm supports. That summer, in the first referendum on production quotas since 1942, wheat farmers approved stricter acreage limits and higher loan rates by a vote of five to one. That winter, cotton and peanut producers endorsed their own marketing quotas by margins of nine to one.[33]

Within the farm organizations, moreover, the commitment to flexibles appeared to be weakening. Within the Farm Bureau and the Grange, the two farm organizations that remained friendly to the Aiken Act, radicals pressed their leaders to disown their prior endorsements.

Lerch and Eugene Butler, "What's new in agriculture," *PF,* February 1952, p. 12; Don Lerch and Eugene Butler, "What's new in agriculture," *PF,* April 1952, p. 192; "Price supports at 90 percent," *WF,* 19 July 1952, p. 39; Fred Bailey, "Washington roundup," *Country Gentleman,* August 1952, p. 10; "Mr. Brannan and the Farm Bureau," *PF,* August 1950, p. 75.

33. *WDWF* No. 519, 22 August 1953; *WDWF* No. 521, 12 September 1953; Eugene Butler and Jay Richter, "What's new in agriculture," *PF,* January 1954, p. 8; *KAL,* 19 December 1953; " 'Regimentation' wins," *New Republic,* 24 August 1953, pp. 3–4; Ezra Taft Benson, *Cross fire: The eight years with Eisenhower* (Garden City, N.Y.: Doubleday and Co., 1962), pp. 144–49.

In both, they succeeded, but only partially. At the annual meeting of the National Grange, master Herschel Newsom called for a one-year delay in implementing the flexibility provisions of the 1949 Agriculture Act. At the annual convention of the American Farm Bureau, on the other hand, delegates reaffirmed their endorsement of variable price supports. Bowing to the wishes of the southern federations, however, they also approved 90 percent price guarantees in the first year of marketing quotas, and they also named a new vice president, Alabamian Walter Randolph, an advocate of high and rigid farm policy. Under pressure from the rank and file, the farm lobby leadership relented.[34]

Finally, the congressional agriculture committees, each on a cross-country tour, found that "more farmers than ever before want price supports at 90 percent of parity or higher." The panels heard from farmers and merchants and county farm bureaus, and many of the witnesses opposed the flexible price support plan of the American Farm Bureau. "It is becoming more and more apparent," North Dakota senator Milton Young concluded, "that the great majority of farmers want 90 percent of parity supports—regardless of what some farm organizations say."[35]

Also in 1953, however, also as Eisenhower took office, informed observers of farm politics could see a growing impatience for a policy confrontation.

Despite his artful pledge to "stand behind . . . the price supports now on the books," the general chose an enemy of the New Deal farm program to lead the Department of Agriculture. Ezra Taft Benson, the secretary-designate, was a deeply religious Mormon who had directed the lobbying efforts of the National Council of Farmer Cooperatives from 1939 until 1943. A zealous economic libertarian, Benson clearly bore the imprint of the Co-op Council, which represented producers of perishable commodities who did not much benefit from the price support and adjustment programs. Accordingly, he had long been cool toward federal farm policy, and he made no attempt now to indicate a

34. Glenn Martz, "Washington from the inside," *Nation's Agriculture,* February 1954, p. 14; "Farm troubles in Washington," *WF,* 21 November 1953, pp. 22–23; "Bureau still wants flexible supports," *WF,* 2 January 1954, p. 20; *WDWF* No. 536, 19 December 1953; *WDWF* No. 538, 2 January 1954; *KAL,* 21 November 1953; *KAL,* 19 December 1953; "Prairie fires: Ablaze and spreading," *New Republic,* 26 October 1953, p. 3.

35. "What farmers reported," *WF,* 7 November 1953, p. 44; Wayne E. Swegle and J. S. Russell, "What's ahead in price supports?" *SF,* November 1953, p. 68; Kenneth S. Davis, "Eisenhower and the forty farmers," *New Republic,* 9 November 1953, pp. 11–12; "Lonesome Benson," *New Republic,* 28 December 1953, p. 3; *Hearings before the House Agriculture Committee,* "Long range farm program," 83d Congress, 1st session, Serial R, 1953, parts 1–17.

significant change of heart. At his confirmation hearings, Republican senators tried to coax Benson into an endorsement of price supports at 90 percent of parity, but he would have nothing of it. "There's growing suspicion [on Capitol Hill]," Wayne Darrow quipped, "that a Pharaoh is in power who knows not Joseph."[36]

Benson and his advisers, most of them likewise drawn from the cooperatives and from agribusiness, regarded proponents of high and rigid price supports as apostates who would gladly sell themselves into political bondage for a paltry few dollars. The issue, as they saw it, was "freedom to farm." Knowing that they lacked the political wherewithal to scrap the farm program outright, the Republican leadership of the USDA instead committed itself to flexible price supports. Ezra Taft Benson, that is, pledged the Republican Party to the price support policy of the American Farm Bureau.[37]

Benson's appointment breathed life into old, internecine conflicts and split the House Agriculture Committee. On the one side were representatives of milk, meat, fruit and vegetable producers, the emissaries of farmers who used "basic" commodities as inputs or whose crops were not supported. "I do say," Pennsylvania Republican Paul B. Dague told Benson, "that your bill will have no trouble with me, nor will your philosophy have any serious trouble in my congressional district. The majority of my constituents are, I think, wholeheartedly in support of you and your program and they have so told me." On the other side, how-

36. Matusow, Farm policies, p. 246; WDWF No. 486, 3 January 1953; Wesley McCune, Ezra Taft Benson: Man with a mission (Washington: Public Affairs Press, 1958), pp. 5–11; Schapsmeier and Schapsmeier, Benson, pp. 36, 284n; Benson, Cross fire, pp. 30–39; "Benson will take Brannan's job," WF, 6 December 1952, p. 32; "Don't expect help on perishables," WF, 17 January 1953, p. 24; KAL No. 628, 6 December 1952; KAL No. 630, 3 January 1953; KAL No. 632, 31 January 1953; KAL No. 633, 14 February 1953; James L. Guth, "The National Cooperative Council and farm relief, 1929–1942," Agricultural History, 51 (April 1977), pp. 441–58; Charles M. Hardin, "The Republican Department of Agriculture—A political interpretation," Journal of Farm Economics, 36 (May 1954), pp. 210–27.

37. Ezra Taft Benson, Freedom to farm (Garden City, N.Y.: Doubleday and Co., 1960); "Facing up to farm forces," Business Week, 14 February 1953, p. 30; Wesley McCune, Who's behind our farm policy? (New York: Frederick A. Praeger, 1956); KAL No. 630, 3 January 1953; WDWF No. 486, 3 January 1956; Jean Begeman, "Businessmen at the plow," New Republic, 16 February 1953, pp. 14–15. Among the more extreme of Benson's advisers was James McConnell, the administrator of the Commodity Stabilization Service and later the assistant secretary. McConnell was formerly an official of a giant, ultraconservative New York cooperative, the GLF Exchange. The supporters of 90 percent, he commented, "are largely innocent dupes being manipulated by very clever professional socialists." "Benson 'cleans house,'" WF, 6 March 1954, p. 6; "Views of new CSS head," WF, 17 April 1954, p. 63.

ever, were representatives of corn, cotton, wheat, tobacco and dairy producers, the emissaries of farmers who produced "basics" as cash crops and whose crops were supported. "Contrary to my friend, Mr. Dague, I would be in a lot of trouble in my district if I accepted the principles of the bill under consideration," Oklahoma Democrat Carl Albert responded.[38]

The Committee's division, however, did not immediately foreclose Farm Bureau access. In 1954, its relationship with the American Farm Bureau Federation remained cordial and respectful. Almost without exception, its members shied from confrontation and fumbled toward accommodation, even though a solid majority opposed the administration's flexible farm plan.

First, in 1954, opponents of the Farm Bureau plan were careful to justify their disagreement. "If you and your organization can convince me that by the adoption of the program you propose I can still keep for my farmers this magic symbol which has come to represent agricultural prosperity, that is, 90 percent of parity, . . . if that can be done I accept your proposal," Georgia Democrat W. M. (Don) Wheeler promised Allan B. Kline. "I don't know whether I can sell it to my people or not."[39]

Second, opponents of the Farm Bureau plan were careful to downplay the significance of the conflict. "With all your predecessors this committee has worked as harmoniously as any committee in Congress, and with the help of the Farm Bureau and the Grange and the other big organizations we have built a program that has operated and is operating . . . well," North Carolina Democrat Harold D. Cooley continued. "Why cannot we compose our differences? It seems to me that we have composed a lot of them right here this morning."[40]

Finally, opponents of the Farm Bureau plan were careful to underscore their readiness to cooperate. "Mr. Kline," Carl Albert concluded, "I want to join my colleagues in saying that I think you have . . . shown yourself to be one of the great authorities on American agriculture. That does not mean that we cannot in a friendly manner all of us—sometimes

---

38. *Hearings before the House Agriculture Committee*, "Long range farm program," 83d Congress, 2d session, Serial R, 1954 (hereafter *Hearings, 1954*), pp. 2293–94, 2635–37, 3093–3102, 3490–91, 3598. See also Carl Albert (with Danney Goble), *Little giant: The life and times of Speaker Carl Albert* (Norman: University of Oklahoma Press, 1990), pp. 173–83, 210–11. For a good summary of internal political conflicts in agriculture, see John Heinz, "The political impasse in farm support legislation," *Yale Law Journal*, 71 (1962), pp. 955–61.

39. *Hearings, 1954*, pp. 2866–67, 2587–89, 2582–84, 2822, 2832-33, 2871, 3639.

40. *Hearings, 1954*, p. 2765.

perhaps we are not too friendly—try to resolve some of these differences and see what we can best do for American agriculture and for our country as a whole."[41]

In 1954, in sum, the Farm Bureau maintained its access to the House Agriculture Committee; the panel's eagerness to paper over their differences was the very measure of its solicitude. "I do not want it to appear that I am feuding with the Farm Bureau, Mr. Kline, or anyone else," Mississippi Democrat Thomas G. Abernethy stressed. "I violently differ with Mr. Kline and his views. However, I respect his right to express his views and trust that he respects mine." In 1954, despite GOP leadership, the Committee reported a measure to extend 90 percent price supports for two more years. It opposed the policy of the American Farm Bureau, but it was distinctly apologetic in doing so.[42]

It is no great mystery why. Despite the disagreements of seven years, the popularity of the flexible price support program of the American Farm Bureau had never been put directly to a test. Lawmakers found indications that farmers opposed it in the votes of 1948, in the proofs of referenda, in the witness of dissenters, but the breadth, intensity and durability of the agrarian unrest were three great unknowns. As of 1954, that is, the competitive advantage of the American Farm Bureau was perturbed but intact. The degree to which the Federation still spoke for farmers had not yet been wholly discerned.

In the late 1950s, however, two distinct but related incidents conspired to upset the congressional tradition of bipartisan deference to the farm lobby. First, Ezra Taft Benson and the American Farm Bureau allied on a particularistic farm policy, a program designed above all to benefit Republican farmers in the Corn Belt. Second, and roughly simultaneously, Democrats in the Middle West racked up victory after victory in campaigns against that same policy. As the Democrats implicated the Farm Bureau in Republican farm policy, they drew the farm lobby into a partisan controversy. Moreover, as the Democrats tested the organization's competitive advantage and found it wanting, they restricted the

41. *Hearings,* 1954, pp. 2855, 2845–51, 2762, 2770, 2807–19, 2821.

42. *Hearings,* 1954, p. 3656; "We'll try to write the bill farmers want," *SF,* March 1954, p. 50; *WDWF* No. 544, 13 February 1954; "Vote against flexibles," *WF,* 19 June 1954, p. 24. The Committee vote was reported as twenty-one to eight. The opposition to the committee bill probably comprised seven Republicans and one Democrat. It was concentrated regionally, in the Northeast, California and Florida, in states whose products did not benefit from the price support program. In all likelihood, only two midwestern representatives voted against the committee bill. One was certainly Nebraska Republican Robert D. Harrison. The other could have been Colorado Republican William S. Hill, Indiana Republican Ralph Harvey or Oklahoma Republican Page Belcher. I consider Harvey (from the Corn Belt) the most likely.

access of the American Farm Bureau. In the late 1950s, in sum, Democrats turned toward partisanship and turned from the Farm Bureau. The first step in the process was the Farm Bureau's convergence with Ezra Taft Benson. In 1954, impatient with the delays in implementing flexible price supports, the Federation took the lead in advancing the administration's farm program. Having lost its case in the House Agriculture Committee, as it expected, it mobilized against high and rigid price supports on the House floor. At its behest, Nebraska Republican Robert D. Harrison offered an ingenious amendment to his own committee's bill. For one year, it raised the lower bound of flexible price supports to 82.5 percent, halfway between the 90 percent of the Committee bill and the 75 percent of the 1949 Agriculture Act. The result "was a clear-cut Benson–Farm Bureau victory. . . . The Benson–Farm Bureau campaign for flexibles—combined with superb GOP discipline on the House floor—swung some 15 to 20 Farm Bloc votes to flexible supports." Added to a large urban vote for Benson, the Farm Bureau substitute carried.[43] Seven years after it began its campaign for lower farm price supports, the American Farm Bureau at last had succeeded in winning them.[44]

The Federation celebrated its victory by hardening its commitment to the particular interests of the Corn Belt. Allan B. Kline delayed his retire-

43. *WDWF* No. 565, 10 July 1954; Albjerg, "Kline," p. 366; *WDWF* No. 559, 29 May 1954; *WDWF* No. 564, 3 July 1954; *KAL*, 5 June 1954; *KAL*, 3 July 1954; "House vote on variable price supports," *Nation's Agriculture*, October 1954, pp. 14–15; "Senate vote for and against Farm Bureau position on variable price supports," *Nation's Agriculture*, October 1954, p. 16; Glenn Martz, "Washington from the inside," *Nation's Agriculture*, February 1954, p. 14; "Vote against flexibles," *WF*, 19 June 1954, p. 24; "Corn loan to drop next year," *WF*, 17 July 1954; Benson, *Cross fire*, pp. 183–210; David Miller Tiffany, "Agricultural policy-making in the Eisenhower Administration," Ph.D. dissertation, State University of New York at Binghamton, 1974, pp. 157–59. Pennock and Mayhew found that representatives on this vote, the most important of the decade, hewed fairly closely to district interests. Representatives of districts with cross-pressures (farm belt Republicans with mixed constituencies and urban Democrats) divided fairly evenly. See Pennock, "Party and constituency," pp. 184–97; and David R. Mayhew, *Party loyalty among congressmen: The difference between Democrats and Republicans, 1947–1962* (Cambridge: Harvard University Press, 1966), pp. 30, 49.

44. In the 84th Congress (1955–56), the Democrats, back in control, managed barely to restore 90 percent supports in the House, lost them in the Senate, then regained them in the Senate, then lost them to Eisenhower's veto. The House Agriculture Committee, in a macabre protest, bought a child's coffin and gave high and rigid price supports a "funeral." Murray interview; *KAL*, 26 February 1955; *KAL*, 12 March 1955; *KAL*, 7 May 1955; Eugene Butler and Jay Richter, "What's new in agriculture," *PF*, June 1955, p. 10; *WDWF* No. 652, 10 March 1956; *WDWF* No. 654, 24 March 1956; *KAL*, 24 March 1956; *KAL*, 21 April 1956; *KAL*, 5 May 1956; *KAL*, 19 May 1956; *WDWF* No. 663, 26 May 1956.

ment right up to the 1954 convention, specifically to avert the promotion of vice president Walter Randolph, a high-support Alabamian. Convention delegates then passed Randolph over and selected Charles B. Shuman, the leader of the Illinois Agricultural Association and Kline's protégé, as the Federation's next president. Although nominally a Democrat, Shuman reckoned himself the most conservative member of the Federation's board; once, when he spoke in favor of a *larger* government appropriation, his colleagues on the board erupted with applause and laughter. With the Farm Bureau's leadership secure in conservative hands, the delegates again overruled southern objections and resolved in praise of the 1954 Agriculture Act. The organization's true moniker, its critics now joked, was not "the American Farm Bureau Federation" but "the American Corn Bureau Federation."[45]

Finally, just over a year later, the Eisenhower administration followed the Farm Bureau's lead. In 1956, the Department of Agriculture proposed to create a subsidized land retirement program, or "soil bank," to conserve natural resources and to maintain farm income. The Soil Bank idea was a longtime favorite of the midwestern Farm Bureaus, and the American Farm Bureau had endorsed it, by name, in 1955. Under its provisions, the federal government paid farmers to cut production of wheat, cotton, tobacco, peanuts and rice below established *allotments*. It paid midwestern farmers, however, to cut production of corn below established *bases*. Allotments were a fraction of bases; therefore Benson proposed that corn farmers, relative to other farmers, receive equal benefits but make smaller sacrifices. "The new farm program," Darrow observed, "crowns corn king of crops."[46] Intent on consolidating its own farm policy gains, the Eisenhower administration reproduced the commodity particularism of the American Farm Bureau Federation.

45. "The farmer's four voices," *Time,* 7 May 1956, p. 31; "Shuman is new AFBF head," *WF,* 1 January 1955, p. 22; Eugene Butler and Jay Richter, "What's new in Washington," *PF,* November 1955, p. 10; "Will Congress help prices?" *WF,* 19 March 1955, p. 9; John Strohm, "Farm Bureau's new president," *Better Farming,* March 1955, p. 27; Storm, "Illinois Agricultural Association," pp. 301–2. In addition, the Farm Bureau called upon the USDA to reinstate cross-compliance requirements, the practical effect of which was to prevent farmers from expanding feed grain production on acres diverted from cotton and wheat on penalty of loss of all program benefits. Cross-compliance had long been a sore point between midwestern Farm Bureaus, which favored it, and southern Farm Bureaus, which opposed it.

46. *WDWF* No. 664, 1 June 1956; Eugene Butler and Jay Richter, "What's new in Washington," *PF,* January 1956, p. 8; Art Thompson, "Ike's men push farm bill," *WF,* 17 March 1956, pp. 102–3; "Land rental plan gains favor," *WF,* 1 October 1955, p. 56; "Big snowball for lawmakers," *WF* 19 November 1955, p. 6; "Hill calls for crop control," *WF,*

The attention that the administration and the Farm Bureau lavished onto the Corn Belt had significant partisan implications. On the one hand, it stiffed the diehard Democrats who grew cotton in the South and the steadfast Republicans who raised wheat on the Plains. On the other hand, it gave freely to corn farmers, whose propensity to abandon the GOP, 1948 had shown, was directly related to the condition of finances. "Stripped of its high-sounding platitudes," a Corn Belt journal noted, "the new plan is a bold bid for the farm vote in the 1956 presidential-congressional races."[47]

To the House Agriculture Committee, the political motives behind the Soil Bank bill were transparent. Benson's proposal met the jeers of southern representatives of cotton, all Democrats, and western representatives of wheat, mostly Republicans. "You are so obsessed with the idea that a certain group of farmers should receive a treatment that is not accorded to the general masses of farmers," Texas Democrat W. R. (Bob) Poage complained. "I am just going on the principle that we ought to treat farmers, whether they are Republican or Democratic farmers, whether they are farmers in Texas or farmers in Iowa, that we ought to treat them alike."[48]

Accordingly, the Soil Bank precipitated the destruction of the bipartisan farm bloc. On the House Agriculture Committee, the Democrats returned Benson's partisanship in kind. In a particularly stormy session, punctuated by cheers and applause, the likes of which had not been seen

---

19 November 1955, p. 28; *KAL,* 10 September 1955; *KAL,* 17 December 1955; Tiffany, "Agricultural policy-making," pp. 170–73. The actual distribution of Soil Bank payments, released in 1957 at Carl Albert's request, confirmed the bias. Sixty-nine percent of the money went to Corn Belt farmers; only 17 percent went to wheat growers and only 11 percent went to cotton growers. See *Hearings before the House Agriculture Committee,* "Soil bank program," 85th Congress, 1st session, Serial A, 1957, p. 61; Eugene Butler and Jay Richter, "What's new in Washington," *PF,* February 1957, pp. 8, 10.

47. "The farmer's Washington," *SF,* March 1956, p. 16; *WDWF* No. 644, 14 January 1956; "The farmer's Washington," *SF,* June 1956, p. 14; "How farm belt sees prices and politics," *Business Week,* 26 May 1956, pp. 28–30; "Why the farm vote worries the Republicans," *U.S. News and World Report,* 11 November 1955, pp. 28–29. For the 1956–57 crop year, moreover, the Eisenhower administration announced a federal loan of $1.25 on corn for farmers who had not complied with acreage restrictions, compared to a $1.50 corn loan for farmers who had complied. In effect, corn producers could raise as much as they liked and still qualify for government price support. The noncompliers loan, which lasted for the duration of Eisenhower's second term, applied only to corn, nothing else. *WDWF* No. 692, 15 December 1956.

48. *Hearings before the House Agriculture Committee,* "General farm legislation," 84th Congress, 2d session, Serial MM, 1956 (hereafter *Hearings,* 1956), p. 66 and pp. 48–50, 61–86.

in thirty years, Bob Poage, a Unitarian, parried sacred and profane with the Mormon apostle:

POAGE: I am glad to find that this program, whatever it is, goes back to the days of Joseph, and that we have a good nonpartisan foundation for it. . . . I believe you will agree with me that it ought not to be presented here as a political issue.

BENSON: I agree with you wholeheartedly.

POAGE: I wonder if you would agree with the philosophy of this advertisement? . . . It says, "Help Eisenhower pass the new farm program." . . . And it says that it was sponsored and paid for by the National Republican Senatorial and Congressional Committees, Washington, D.C. . . . Do you think the way to create nonpartisan support for a program is to put out this kind of advertising? (Applause.)

BENSON: Well, that is a matter of opinion. . . . I would like both parties to support this program in the same fashion.

POAGE: And claim that it is a partisan proposition? . . . Did I not understand a minute ago that you said this program started with Joseph and not with President Eisenhower? . . .

BENSON: He probably was a Republican, but I am not sure.

POAGE: Because of his taking of the golden vessels that belonged to his brethren when they came down and bought corn—it is reported that he did that. (Applause.)

BENSON: He was also their benefactor, wasn't he. Don't you get too deep in the scriptures now. . . . I will take this [advertisement] home and read it and then I will give you my opinion.

POAGE: All right. Frankly, I can give you mine right now. If we are going to have a bipartisan farm program . . . that is not the way to get it; the way to get it is to sit here and try to work something out that will benefit the farmers. . . . I do not think the majority of the American people want simply a Democratic program. I know they don't want simply a Republican program. I think they want a farm program.

BENSON: I am sure that is right. (Applause.)[49]

Once loosed, the epidemic of partisanship was not easily controlled. Ultimately embarrassed by Eisenhower's veto of an alternative, Christmas-tree bill, the Democrats concentrated on settling the score. In 1957, on the House floor, they combined to kill a bill to raise the price support for corn. From there, the fight moved to the Senate, where midwestern senators told Agriculture Committee chairman Allen Ellender (D., La.) "to abandon his mulishness about getting up a corn bill. Otherwise, so they are reported to have said, no cotton or tobacco proposal would ever get out of committee, either." Ellender reported the corn bill,

49. *Hearings*, 1956, pp. 55–57.

but the Senate Democrats defeated it. "The gingham dog and the calico cat are eating each other up," the *Washington Farmletter* reported. "The Democrats beat the Andresen bill. Republicans with a little assist from Democrats will beat the Cooley bill. Compromises such as the Harrison bill will be beaten by the Democrats with some GOP help. . . .The Farm Bloc is now split along party lines as well as commodity lines."[50]

In the midfifties, then, the farm program of the Farm Bureau and the Eisenhower administration, with its exclusive affinity for corn producers, split the farm bloc along party lines for the first time in anyone's memory. "During my time on this committee, since the days of the old McNary-Haugen bill, I and other members of this committee have religiously tried to keep politics away from farm legislation," Minnesota Republican August H. Andresen told Benson. "I believe that is the way it should be."[51]

The farm program of the Eisenhower administration, however, was not only the responsibility of Ezra Taft Benson. The Farm Bureau's complicity in the Corn Belt conspiracy drew partisan fire from the House Agriculture Committee. "I do not see why we are so disturbed about corn," Committee chairman Harold D. Cooley objected to Charles Shuman. "What I do on this committee is try to follow the advice of the men who are from the real corn-growing areas when they talk about the corn program, and the same way when we talk about a wheat area program, I like to listen to Mr. Hope [R., Kan.], who is from the wheat-growing area." For the House Committee's Democrats, by the

50. "Final try on corn bill," *WF*, 6 April 1957, p. 18; *WDWF* No. 704, 9 March 1957; *KAL*, 25 February 1956; *KAL*, 24 March 1956; *KAL*, 21 April 1956; *KAL*, 5 May 1956; *KAL*, 19 May 1956; *WDWF* No. 652, 10 March 1956; *WDWF* No. 663, 26 May 1956; *KAL*, 9 March 1957; *KAL*, 1 June 1957; Eugene Butler and Jay Richter, "What's new in Washington," *PF*, May 1957, p. 8; Art Thompson, "Farm bloc splits on corn bill," *WF*, 16 March 1957, p. 13; "No new corn bill for 1957," *WF*, 20 April 1957, p. 20; John Harms, "End of an era in farm programs," *SF*, August 1957, p. 37; Roy F. Hendrickson, "7 reasons why we may lose our farm programs," *SF*, September 1957, p. 55; *WDWF* No. 695, 5 January 1957; *WDWF* No. 702, 23 February 1957; *WDWF* No. 703, 2 March 1957; *WDWF* No. 704, 9 March 1957; *WDWF* No. 709, 13 April 1957; Carroll Kilpatrick, "What happened to the farm bloc?" *Harper's*, November 1957, p. 58; John Osborne, "Crafty Ezra Benson," *Fortune*, April 1958, p. 194; Murray interview. Pennock, Mayhew and Wilson noted the increasingly partisan divisions on floor votes in this period. See Pennock, "Party and constituency," pp. 184–209; Mayhew, *Party loyalty*, chap. 2; and Graham K. Wilson, *Special interests and policymaking: Agricultural policies and politics in Britain and the United States of America, 1956–1970* (London: John Wiley and Sons, 1977).

51. *Hearings*, 1956, pp. 86, 22. For recriminations against the Farm Bureau because of its narrow preoccupation with Corn Belt farmers, see pp. 66, 425, 436.

mid-1950s, the American Farm Bureau Federation had come to be little more than an emissary of the Corn Belt, an adjunct of the GOP.[52]

In the mid-fifties, therefore, the American Farm Bureau moved into alliance with the Eisenhower administration. Each for its own reasons, the Farm Bureau and the administration adopted the parochial interests of the Corn Belt as their own. Directly, their refusal to accommodate the needs of other sections undermined the farm bloc's traditional bipartisanship. Indirectly, but more importantly, their alliance eroded the Farm Bureau's congressional access.

The alliance between the Farm Bureau and the Eisenhower administration staked the Farm Bureau's reputation to the GOP's performance. The farm program of the American Farm Bureau was the same as the farm program of the Republican Party, upon which farm voters could pass judgment. The electorate's verdict, moreover, fast became clear. From election to election, the evidence mounted against the administration; for the duration of the Eisenhower presidency, the farm vote was a torment for the Republicans and a windfall for the Democrats. In large parts of the farm belt, that is, elections discountenanced the policy of the American Farm Bureau. Elections revealed the depletion of its competitive advantage.

The reaction against Eisenhower's farm policy surfaced quickly. In October 1953, Democrat Lester R. Johnson scored a surprise victory in Wisconsin's Ninth District (Eau Claire), a seat that Republicans had held for more than half a century. Setting the pattern for Democratic campaigns to come, Johnson railed against low milk prices and Ezra Taft Benson's express desire to drop them still further.[53]

As the 1954 midterms approached, midwestern Democrats picked up Johnson's call. "Ezra Taft Benson," one reporter observed, "has become the [Democrats'] fall guy, replacing the tired image of Herbert Hoover." "I think we have a real problem on our hands," Nebraska sen-

---

52. *Hearings,* 1956, pp. 425, 436. Cooley to Shuman in 1959: "I understand you are supporting the Secretary and he is supporting you." *Hearings,* 1959, p. 146. Asked if he thought Eisenhower would veto a farm bill if Congress managed to pass one, Bob Poage replied, "He won't, if the corn-hog people are hurting badly enough." "Which way farm legislation," *PF,* June 1959, p. 36.

53. E. B. Richards, "Bitter harvest in Wisconsin," *New Republic,* 26 October 1953, p. 13; "The winner explains," *New Republic,* 26 October 1953, p. 5; *WDWF* No. 521, 5 September 1953; *WDWF* No. 527, 17 October 1953; *WDWF* No. 528, 24 October 1953. The parties were sensitive to the significance of Johnson's campaign. The Democrats sent Charles Brannan to speak for Johnson; the Republicans sent Benson to speak in his own defense. Tiffany, "Agricultural policy-making," p. 90.

ator Carl T. Curtis, a Republican, wrote to Benson. "Some careful observers liken it to 1948."[54]

The 1954 elections, however, lacked 1948's dramatic surprises. On the one hand, the Democrats regained control of the House and the Senate, partly on the strength of their showing in the farm belt. In Minnesota and Illinois, Hubert H. Humphrey and Paul H. Douglas retained hotly contested Senate seats with well-timed jabs at flexible price supports. In Missouri, the Democrats carried two House districts where Benson had campaigned; altogether eighteen of the twenty-two Democratic pickups in the House had belonged to his GOP supporters. On the other hand, the Republicans successfully defended doubtful Senate seats in Kansas, Nebraska and South Dakota, and they upset Senator Guy M. Gillette in Iowa. "The Democrats are privately disappointed that farmers did not rise against the Eisenhower policy of flexible price supports," *Business Week* reported. "As they read the election results— particularly the defeat of Democratic Senator Guy Gillette of Iowa— Eisenhower got at least a draw on this issue. But they don't accept this as a sign that their own policy of rigid price supports has lost its old glamor—instead, they believe that their case was not presented powerfully enough."[55]

In 1955, as if in confirmation, reports of deepening farmer displeasure dejected farm state Republicans and cheered farm state Demo-

---

54. Robert Engler, "What remedies will Congress choose?" *New Republic*, 25 January 1954, p. 12; Schapsmeier and Schapsmeier, *Benson*, p. 93; Richards, "Bitter harvest in Wisconsin," p. 13; "Congress sizes up '54 issues," *U.S. News and World Report*, 18 December 1953, pp. 30–31; *WDWF* No. 539, 9 January 1954; *WDWF* No. 545, 20 February 1954; *KAL*, 3 December 1953; *KAL*, 16 January 1954; *KAL*, 27 February 1954; "Why were dairy supports cut?" *WF*, 6 March 1954, pp. 92–93; Robert G. Lewis, "Midwest report: The prairie farmer revolts," *Nation*, 25 September 1954, pp. 251–53.

55. "Changing the guard in Congress," *Business Week*, 13 November 1954, p. 28; "The farm vote," *New Republic*, 15 November 1954, p. 3; "People of the week," *U.S. News and World Report*, 12 November 1954, p. 14; "What's ahead now—Leaders appraise the election," *U.S. News and World Report*, 12 November 1954, p. 74; V. O. Key, Jr., "The 'moral victory' of the Republicans," *New Republic*, 6 December 1954, pp. 9–11; "Kansas City: The issue is farm policy," *Business Week*, 9 October 1954, pp. 54–60; "Here's what voters did," *U.S. News and World Report*, 12 November 1954, p. 29; "How farmers really voted in '54," *U.S. News and World Report*, 7 January 1955, pp. 37–39; *KAL*, 6 November 1954; *WDWF* No. 582, 6 November 1954; "Iowa's farm vote," *WF*, 15 January 1955, p. 9; "Did farmers vote approval of Benson?" *WF*, 19 May 1955, p. 41; Democratic political advertisement, *WF*, 16 October 1954, p. 27; "Will farm law be changed," *WF*, 20 November 1954, p. 20; Tiffany, "Agricultural policy-making," pp. 109–11; Carl Solberg, *Hubert Humphrey: A biography* (New York: W. W. Norton and Co., 1984), pp. 167–68.

crats. In North Dakota, the Nonpartisan League (NPL) announced that it would leave the Republicans for the Democrats starting in the 1956 elections, after fifty stormy years of union. In Missouri and Iowa, skidding hog prices touched off protests; they soon coalesced into the militant National Farmers Organization (NFO) and spread into Nebraska and Kansas. Throughout the Corn Belt, finally, agrarian antipathy toward Ezra Taft Benson intensified; of Iowa farmers, 48 percent rated his job performance "poor," only 7 percent rated it "good."[56]

Farm belt Republicans braced for a difficult 1956 campaign. "On the Republican farm front," Kiplinger noted, "some members freely predict that unless drastic action is taken soon they won't be back for the next Congress." They appealed to the president to sweeten the deal for farmers, and the White House forced Benson to offer up the Soil Bank bill. Even in the heart of the Corn Belt, however, the Soil Bank did not overcome the Republicans' biggest campaign liability, and GOP office seekers ran for cover. "In 1956, when Benson came to Iowa," a farm editor remembered, "the Republican candidates scattered like chickens under the shadow of a hawk."[57]

Meanwhile, persistent agrarian unrest whetted Democratic appetites for victories in a region traditionally short on them.[58] In 1955 and 1956, Democratic party strategists maneuvered to sharpen the partisan differences. First, the Democratic House passed a measure to restore price supports at 90 percent of parity, the Democratic Senate passed a

56. " 'Hold on to your hat, Mr. Benson,' " WF, 21 January 1956, p. 14; "How farm belt sees prices and politics," Business Week, 26 May 1956, pp. 28–30; Haldore Hanson, "Will the farmers beat Eisenhower?" New Republic, 16 April 1956, pp. 8–10; Dale Kramer, "An agrarian tide—standing still," New Republic, 16 April 1956, pp. 11–12; Charles F. Ransom, "Farmers defy G.O.P.," Nation, 26 November 1955, pp. 455–56; "Why the farm vote worries the Republicans," U.S. News and World Report, 11 November 1955, pp. 28–29; "How the polls are running in the farm belt," U.S. News and World Report, 16 December 1955, pp. 32–36; KAL, 10 September 1955; KAL, 5 November 1955; Art Thompson, "Ask Secy. Benson to quit," WF, 1 October 1955, pp. 26–27; KAL, 7 April 1956; "Refuse quick aid to farmers," WF, 4 February 1956, p. 32; "See no let-up in farm squeeze," WF, 17 December 1956, p. 31; Schapsmeier and Schapsmeier, Benson, pp. 146–48; Ross B. Talbot, "The North Dakota Farmers Union and North Dakota politics," Western Political Quarterly, 10 (December 1957), pp. 875–901.

57. KAL, 28 January 1956; Donald R. Murphy, "How will Corn Belt farmers vote?" New Republic, 6 October 1958, p. 7; KAL, 10 September 1955; "Get queries on hog prices," WF, 17 September 1955, p. 6; "The farmer's Washington," SF, March 1956, p. 16; "The farmer's Washington," SF, June 1956, p. 14; WDWF No. 644, 14 January 1956; Schapsmeier and Schapsmeier, Benson, pp. 126–40, 153–56.

58. In 1956, Democrats held only 44 of the 129 House seats in the twelve midwestern states, and only 14 of those seats were rural (6 of which were in Missouri alone). In states without major cities—Kansas, Nebraska, Iowa and the Dakotas—Democrats had no representatives at all.

variant, and the president vetoed it. Second, Senate leaders persuaded New Mexico Democrat Clinton P. Anderson, whose sympathy for flexible price supports was now something of an embarrassment to the party, to resign from the Senate Agriculture Committee. They replaced him with Missouri Democrat Stuart Symington, a supporter of 90 percent.[59]

Finally, the Democrats' 1956 Convention gave the vice-presidential nomination to Tennessee senator Estes Kefauver, whose victory in the Minnesota primary had surprised Adlai Stevenson and alarmed the White House. Armed with a platform commitment to price supports at 90 percent of parity, the Stevenson-Kefauver ticket hammered away at GOP farm policy. "The only way to break up the New York Yankees," they told their audiences, "is to get Ezra Taft Benson to manage their farm system."[60]

In the 1956 elections, the midwestern farm vote tilted decisively back toward the Democrats—not enough to tip the presidential election to Adlai Stevenson, to be sure, but sufficient to offset Republican coattails in the rest of the country.

In Senate races, observers noted, agrarian discontent contributed to Democratic victories in Colorado, Idaho, Washington and Oregon. Renegade Senator Wayne Morse, once a Republican but now a Democrat, turned back Interior Secretary Douglas McKay in Oregon, and poultry farmer Frank F. Church turned out Senator Herman Welker in Idaho. In South Dakota, farmer unrest threw a scare into Senator Fran-

59. *KAL,* 26 February 1955; *KAL,* 7 May 1955; *KAL,* 25 February 1956; *KAL,* 24 March 1956; *KAL,* 21 April 1956; *KAL,* 5 May 1956; *KAL,* 19 May 1956; Art Thompson, "Ike's men push farm bill," *WF,* 17 March 1956, pp. 102–3; "What farm bill means to you," *WF,* 21 April 1956, p. 14; *WDWF* No. 647, 4 February 1956; *WDWF* No. 652, 10 March 1956; *WDWF* No. 654, 24 March 1956; *WDWF* No. 663, 26 May 1956; Duncan Norton-Taylor, "Mr. Benson's flexible flyer," *Fortune,* March 1954, p. 88; Benson, *Cross fire,* p. 315; *WDWF* No. 654, 24 March 1956; *WDWF* No. 656, 7 April 1956.

60. Benson, *Cross fire,* p. 331; *KAL,* 24 March 1956; *KAL,* 7 April 1956; *WDWF* No. 654, 24 March 1956; Dale Kramer, "Pigs and pocketbooks," *Reporter,* 18 October 1956, pp. 25–27; Hanson, "Will the farmers beat Eisenhower?" p. 9; "Why some farmers are deserting Ike," *U.S. News and World Report,* 19 October 1956, pp. 44–45; "Midwest sticking with Ike and he's almost over the top," *U.S. News and World Report,* 19 October 1956, pp. 41–50; "Stevenson-Kefauver *leading* Ike-Nixon," *WF,* 6 October 1956, p. 18. Another indication of Democratic optimism about the farm issue was the number of prominent challengers they brought out of storage. Former Agriculture Secretary Claude R. Wickard penciled himself in against Senator Homer E. Capehart in Indiana. Former Agriculture Secretary Charles F. Brannan entered (but lost) the Democratic primary for the Senate in Colorado. Finally, former Agricultural Adjustment administrator Rudolph M. (Spike) Evans contested Senator Bourke B. Hickenlooper in Iowa. "The next Senate," *New Republic,* 19 December 1955, p. 4; Richard Austin Smith, "Five hot Senate races," *Fortune,* October 1956, p. 168ff.; *KAL,* 7 April 1956; *WDWF* No. 681, 29 September 1956.

cis H. Case. He narrowly defeated Kenneth Holum, whom senior senator Karl E. Mundt had shellacked two years earlier. "The price situation and the continued agitation that 'prices are made in Washington' made Republican farm policies a dominant issue," Case explained. "My Democratic opponent . . . campaigned on the argument that he would be the only dirt farmer sent to Congress from South Dakota." Thanks to its gains in the West, the Democratic Party netted one seat in the Senate.[61]

In midwestern House races, moreover, the 1956 elections were milestones for the party of Jackson. First, in South Dakota, history professor George S. McGovern ousted Representative Harold O. Lovre. McGovern was the first Democrat to win national office from South Dakota since 1936. Second, in Kansas, stockman J. Floyd Breeding won the seat vacated by Clifford R. Hope, a thirty-year veteran. Breeding was the first Democrat to claim the district since 1916. Third, in Missouri, hillbilly band promoter Charles H. Brown upset Congressman Dewey Short, the only Missouri Republican to weather Truman's sweep. Brown was the first Democrat to win in the Ozarks since 1916. Finally, in Iowa, the Reverend Merwin Coad defeated Representative James I. Dolliver, the nephew of former Iowa senator Jonathan P. Dolliver. Coad was the first Democrat to capture the district since 1852. Altogether, the Democrats picked up a half dozen House seats in the rural Middle West, enough to net two in the lower chamber.[62]

61. "What happened in the election," *U.S. News and World Report,* 16 November 1956, p. 47; "Ike vs. Democratic Congress—who will hold the real power," *U.S. News and World Report,* 16 November 1956, pp. 43–44; *KAL,* 17 November 1956; "Close race for U.S. Senator," *WF,* 3 November 1956, p. 20; *WDWF* No. 687, 10 November 1956. The special economic volatility of farm voters in the 1950s caught the attention of the authors of *The American voter.* "In national elections since 1948," they wrote, "the two-party vote division among farmers outside the South has fluctuated more sharply than it has within any of the other major occupational groupings." Angus Campbell, Philip E. Converse, Warren E. Miller and Donald E. Stokes, *The American voter* (New York: John Wiley and Sons, 1960), p. 402, and more generally chap. 15.

62. "16 of 46 freshmen representatives are from Midwest," *Congressional Quarterly Weekly Report,* 21 December 1956, p. 1464; "'Why I won'—'why I lost,'" *U.S. News and World Report,* 16 November 1956, p. 140; "Hard facts of the farm vote," *U.S. News and World Report,* 23 November 1956, pp. 49–52; *KAL,* 17 November 1956; *WDWF* No. 687, 10 November 1956; Eugene Butler and Jay Richter, "What's new in Washington," *PF,* January 1957, p. 10; "What hit the Republicans in the Midwest—here's the way they see it," *U.S. News and World Report,* 1 February 1957, pp. 59–62; Tiffany, "Agricultural policy-making," p. 213; George S. McGovern, *Grassroots: The autobiography of George McGovern* (New York: Random House, 1977), pp. 65–71; Robert Sam Anson, *McGovern: A biography* (New York: Holt, Rinehart and Winston, 1972), pp. 75–85. To the Republican faithful, a Democratic representative from Iowa, especially a Democratic minister, signified the millennium. "Iowa will go Democratic," Jonathan Dolliver had

Unsurprisingly, representatives from both parties took the 1956 soundings as a censure of Republican farm policy. "Return to 90% supports is sure to be pushed once more this year by [the] Democrats," Kiplinger wrote in postmortem. "It was one of their strongest campaign issues in the farm belt and many Democrats will feel obligated to try . . . just for the record. They will get some help from Midwestern Republicans, probably more than they got this year. Elections scared some of them."[63]

In fact, though, the GOP's terror in the farm states had only begun. In a 1957 special election to fill the seat of the late Senator Joseph McCarthy, Wisconsin Democrat William Proxmire soundly defeated former GOP governor Walter J. Kohler, Jr. A three-time loser in bids for the statehouse (twice to Kohler), Proxmire staked his campaign on opposition to the agriculture secretary, and upon his election he wired Eisenhower, "Respectfully but with great urgency I appeal to you to take immediate action to replace Ezra Taft Benson."[64]

Five months later, in February 1958, another bombshell hit, when voters in Minnesota's First District (Rochester) went to the polls to elect a successor to August H. Andresen, the House Agriculture Committee's ranking Republican. "For years before his death," a reporter noted, "Mr. Andresen used to carry his district by lopsided majorities. It was a rock-strong Republican district. In this week's election Republicans apparently won again, but [the] victory of Albert Quie was by less than one-half of one percent." The First District had not elected a Democrat to Congress in sixty-six years, but Democrat Eugene Foley pitched into Ezra Taft Benson, drew 54 percent of the farm vote, and lost by only six hundred votes of eighty-eight thousand cast. Had he been a Scandinavian and a Lutheran, like Andresen and Quie, he might well have won.[65]

The uprising in America's dairyland sent GOP lawmakers scurrying again for cover. A. L. Miller of Nebraska and Walter H. Judd of Minnesota petitioned Ezra Taft Benson to resign for the good of the party.

---

prophesied, "when Hell goes Methodist." Presumably, Hell had gone dry. James C. Larew, *A party reborn: The Democrats of Iowa, 1950–1974* (Iowa City: Iowa State Historical Department, 1980), p. iii.

63. *KAL*, 17 November 1956; Interview with George S. McGovern, November 1986.

64. Schapsmeier and Schapsmeier, *Benson*, p. 193; *KAL*, 21 September 1957; Eugene Butler and Jay Richter, "What's new in Washington," *PF*, October 1957, p. 12; "Benson outlines 1958 program," *WF*, 19 October 1957, p. 6; *WDWF* No. 729, 31 August 1957; *WDWF* No. 749, 18 January 1958.

65. *KAL*, 22 February 1958; *WDWF* No. 754, 22 February 1958; "Why Republicans worry about the farm states," *U.S. News and World Report*, 28 February 1958, pp. 56–57; "At the grass roots: Good news for the Democrats," *U.S. News and World Report*, 14 March 1958, pp. 66–67.

Charles Hoeven of Iowa carefully distanced himself from his party's farm policies. Hal Holmes of Washington retired rather than face the ordeal again.[66] The Democrats pushed even harder. Angling for a timely veto, the Senate Agriculture Committee proposed to freeze farm price supports permanently at current levels, to prevent Secretary Benson from lowering them any further. In the Senate and the House, helpless farm state Republicans joined them to pass it. Obligingly, the president killed it.[67]

In November 1958, the stream of Democratic victories in the Middle West became a torrent. Across the nation, but nowhere more so than in the farm belt, the Democrats routed the Republicans.

In the Senate, five out of the fourteen Democratic pickups came in the agricultural states of the Midwest. Democrats defeated GOP incumbents in Ohio, Michigan, Indiana, Minnesota and Wyoming, and in many of the races, Ezra Taft Benson was *the* issue of the campaign. "I didn't win because of McGee, really," Wyoming senator Gale W. McGee recalled. "I won because of the anti wave in the West . . . against Ezra Taft Benson." In four years, the Democrats had doubled their holdings of midwestern Senate seats.[68]

In the House, likewise, the Democrats picked up six GOP seats in Indiana, three in Illinois, three in Iowa, two in Ohio, two in Wisconsin, two in Nebraska, and two in Kansas. They cut a wide swath through the GOP side of the House Agriculture Committee. In Colorado, they captured the district of William S. Hill, departing as its ranking Republican.

66. Schapsmeier and Schapsmeier, *Benson*, p. 198; "What farmers are saying in an election year," *U.S. News and World Report*, 25 April 1958, p. 52; Donald R. Murphy, "How will the Corn Belt farmers vote?" *New Republic*, 6 October 1958, pp. 6–7; Dale Kramer, "Hog-tied farmers in the Corn Belt," *Reporter*, 29 May 1958, pp. 21–24; *KAL*, 8 March 1958; *KAL*, 1 November 1958; Oral History Interview with Catherine May Bedell, Association of Former Members of Congress Oral History Project, Library of Congress, 1979, p. 25.

67. "Report asks for bi-partisan board," *WF*, 1 March 1958, p. 8; "Veto expected on price support freeze," *WF*, 5 April 1958, p. 8; *WDWF* No. 756, 8 March 1958; *WDWF* No. 757, 15 March 1958; *WDWF* No. 758, 22 March 1958; *WDWF* No. 760, 5 April 1958; Tiffany, "Agricultural policy-making," p. 259.

68. Oral History Interview with Gale W. McGee, Association of Former Members of Congress Oral History Project, Library of Congress, 1979, p. 7; Interview with Edward J. Thye, Minnesota Historical Association, 1963, p. 34; "Some winners and why they won," *New Republic*, 17 November 1958, pp. 5–6; *KAL*, 15 November 1958; Eugene Butler and Jay Richter, "What's new," *PF*, December 1958, p. 8; *WDWF* No. 790, 8 November 1958; "Late news of the nation," *Nation's Agriculture*, December 1958, p. 9. McGee's son recalled the election differently, seeing it as a national Democratic swing that overcame opposition in rural areas: David McGee, "A family affair," *Reporter*, 9 March 1967, pp. 43–48.

In Indiana and Nebraska, they ousted Ralph Harvey and Robert Harrison, two Republican stalwarts. In Wisconsin, they defeated Donald E. Tewes, its only GOP freshman. In Iowa, they came within 5,100 votes of Charles B. Hoeven; in Oklahoma, within 3,700 of Page Belcher; in Kansas, within 240 of Wint Smith. In 1958, the Democrats won a majority of the seats in the twelve midwestern states for the first time since 1936, for only the sixth time in history.[69]

In the late 1950s, in sum, the Republicans took a severe beating in the farm belt. In regular elections and in special elections, in dairy states and in wheat states and in corn states, Democratic attacks on Ezra Taft Benson and the deplorable condition of farm finances swayed rural voters.[70] Between 1953 and 1959, the number of Democrats in midwestern congressional contingents doubled. The count in rural constituencies more than tripled.[71]

In the late 1950s, likewise, the Farm Bureau took a severe beating in Congress. By its words and by its actions, it had cast its lot with Ezra Taft Benson. Its competitive advantage buckled under the weight of GOP losses.

By the end of the decade, accordingly, the American Farm Bureau Federation found its access to the House Agriculture Committee much reduced, particularly—but not exclusively—on the Democratic side. In 1958, for instance, Wayne Darrow interviewed eight members of the House Agriculture Committee. "All said F.B. influence is much less than a few years ago," he reported, "old timers said 10 years. . . . [Six] said

69. WDWF No. 790, 8 November 1958; "The farmer's Washington," SF, January 1959, p. 28; "What we want from Congress this year," SF, March 1959, pp. 62–63; "How many farm Democrats?" WF, 17 January 1959, p. 27; "Who won, who lost—and the nation," U.S. News and World Report, 14 November 1958, pp. 38–41; "How they voted—farmers, workers, Negroes," U.S. News and World Report, 14 November 1958, pp. 51–52; Ralph Harvey, Autobiography of a Hoosier congressman (Greenfield, Ind.: Mitchell-Fleming Printing, 1975), p. 62; Anson, McGovern, pp. 87–90. The Democrats reached an additional milestone in 1958. North Dakota elected the first Democratic representative in its history, Quentin N. Burdick, in the place of his father, Usher L. Burdick, an NPL-Republican. (Usher Burdick's son-in-law, Robert W. Levering, also won election to the House, as a Democrat from Ohio.)

70. The efficacy of campaigns against Ezra Taft Benson persisted right up to the end of Eisenhower's term. In August 1960, Democratic representative Quentin N. Burdick won a North Dakota Senate seat by defeating Republican governor John E. Davis. His campaign slogan: "Beat Benson with Burdick." Schapsmeier and Schapsmeier, Benson, p. 241.

71. In recognition of their campaign debts to farmers, more than sixty members of the House requested one of the nine vacant seats on the House Agriculture Committee after the 1958 election. WDWF No. 799, 10 January 1959; Don F. Hadwiger and Ross B. Talbot, Pressures and protests: The Kennedy farm program and the wheat referendum of 1963 (San Francisco: Chandler Publishing Co., 1965), p. 51.

Farm Bureau influence is negative—it can defeat bills but it can't pass them."[72]

In the House Agriculture Committee, the extent of the Farm Bureau's losses varied by party and by region. On the GOP side, representatives from the East Coast and the West Coast and the heart of the Corn Belt defended the Farm Bureau as readily as ever. Republican representatives from other areas, however, hesitated. When North Carolina Democrat Harold D. Cooley chided the Republicans for their reluctance to introduce the Benson farm program, California Republican Charles M. Teague was the only volunteer. The midwestern Republicans held their tongues.[73]

On the Democratic side, conversely, midwestern Democrats held their distance from the Farm Bureau but they refrained from direct attacks on it. Their southern colleagues had no such compunctions. For the first time in almost thirty years, southern Democrats opposed the Farm Bureau bluntly, casting aspersions on its leadership and authority. In 1959, for instance, Charles B. Shuman proposed a program of "stop-loss" price supports at 90 percent of a three-year average of market prices. In response, Committee Democrats challenged him to name a single state Farm Bureau that had endorsed the idea *before* the organization's national convention. Shuman could not. "In his statement to the committee Mr. Shuman said he would be glad to furnish the information as to the States which did recommend the principle," an anonymous Committee member observed in a peevish footnote to Shuman's testimony. "Subsequently the American Farm Bureau Federation supplied voluminous material relating to the recommendations by the State farm bureaus on price support and adjustment programs. No incident was cited where, prior to approval by the national convention, a State farm bureau had ratified specifically the principle of price supports at 90 percent of the 3-year average market price."[74]

Unlike in the early part of the decade, moreover, the Democrats made no effort to minimize their differences with the Farm Bureau's leadership. "You are speaking for my farmers, but you are not having any influence on me," Committee chairman Harold D. Cooley, a North Carolina Democrat, told Shuman. "I recognize that, Mr. Chairman," the Farm Bureau president conceded.[75] The boldness of the statement,

72. *WDWF* No. 751, 1 February 1958.

73. *Hearings before the House Agriculture Committee,* "General farm legislation," 86th Congress, 1st session, Serial GG, 1959 (hereafter *Hearings, 1959*), pp. 177, 153–56, 181–85.

74. *Hearings, 1959,* p. 144, pp. 141–43, 146–56, 159–71, 178–80, 188–92.

75. *Hearings, 1959,* p. 145.

the resignation of the reply—both were unimaginable just a decade earlier.

By the late 1950s, then, the Farm Bureau had lost a substantial part of its access to the House Agriculture Committee. The Democrats abjured it for a mixture of reasons: for its hand in a partisan program, for its insistence on lower price supports, for its doctrinaire conservatism. Likewise, the Republicans tolerated it for a variety of motives: for its defense of a partisan program, for its loyalty to flexible price supports, for its congenial conservatism.

Taken as a whole, however, the Democratic attacks and the Republican discomfort came back to one thing: the Farm Bureau seemed to have lost its punch in congressional elections. The elections of the 1950s had exposed the shallowness of its competitive advantage.

To be sure, the policy message of the farm belt elections was hardly explicit. The voters did not discriminate carefully between Benson's friends and Benson's foes. "High price supports vs. flexible [price] supports," Kiplinger pondered in 1956. "Nothing clear-cut shows up in the vote on this question. Some high-support Republicans lost out. So did some of their candidates favoring flexible supports. The farm vote seemed to indicate a general irritation among farmers at the farm program rather than dissatisfaction on the specifics."[76]

The political message, however, could not have been clearer. The American Farm Bureau had allied itself with Ezra Taft Benson, and the apparent electoral reaction against his policies undermined confidence in its ability—and willingness—to represent farmers' opinions accurately to lawmakers and to represent legislators' actions accurately to constituents.

The American Farm Bureau, it appeared, did not necessarily speak for farmers, not even for its own members. "This fall and every fall I go around to various counties," Iowa Democrat Merwin Coad announced to Farm Bureau president Charles B. Shuman. "In almost every county a delegation from your organization comes to call on me. I appreciate their coming and I listen to their views. Last fall a delegation in a given

---

76. *KAL*, 17 November 1956; "Analysis of 263 congressional districts," *Congressional Quarterly Weekly Report*, 15 February 1957, pp. 201–3; "Does Benson hurt GOP in Midwest?" *Congressional Quarterly Weekly Report*, 14 March 1958, pp. 310–12; "Benson loses Midwest farm support in House," *Congressional Quarterly Weekly Report*, 21 November 1958, pp. 1475–76; "Late news of the nation," *Nation's Agriculture*, December 1958, p. 9; Interview with George S. McGovern, November 1986; Fleming, "Political history of the farm price support issue," pp. 19–22; Thomas V. Gilpatrick, "Price support policy and the Midwest farm vote," *Midwest Journal of Political Science*, 3 (November 1959), pp. 319–35.

county came to me and for 15 minutes they gave me the policy of the American Farm Bureau Federation, and after that they then said, 'That is the official policy of the Farm Bureau Federation. Now we want to tell you what we think.' Then they told me. Which was I to follow?"[77]

The American Farm Bureau, it also appeared, did not always convey an advantageous picture of congressional performance to its farmer constituents. In 1956, Minnesota senator Edward J. Thye, a Republican who opposed flexible price supports, complained to Shuman:

THYE: As I look at [your] publication I find myself rated .400, and I find a great number who have been elected with overwhelming farm votes listed as .000 in your publication. . . . I am just wondering if it is not well that we give the membership a bird's-eye view here.

SHUMAN: Senator, I might say that I am glad we used this comparison to a baseball team. . . . You will notice that we did not recommend to our members that any of the members of this team be retired. We simply reported on their performance in this game. We hope in the next game they will have a better batting average.

THYE: But I would say, Mr. Shuman, this is October [1956]. Four weeks from today is election day. . . . You represent the American Farm Bureau, one of the great organizations representing agriculture and one with which I have been affiliated ever since I became a recognized producer. . . . I am entirely in sympathy with your organization. . . . But I do wonder whether by this kind of publication in which you are the master in setting up a score by which you are going to judge men's actions . . . whether you are doing injury to somebody who is serving . . . very commendably . . . in this election year when the vote is to be counted 4 weeks from tomorrow. I cannot help but bring that thought out, because we are trying to determine what is right and what is wrong.[78]

For agrarian representatives in Congress, in short, the elections in the Midwest demonstrated a decisive lapse in the Farm Bureau's competitive advantage—the Farm Bureau said one thing, but elections said an-

77. *Hearings*, 1959, p. 159. Many lawmakers believed that the Farm Bureau's growing insurance program allowed the Federation's leadership to ignore members who supported liberal price support policies, raising an interesting point. Losses of access may be an important constraint on group leaders who seek to develop services to maintain membership. Congressional judgments of competitive advantage, that is, may force leaders to trade off political credibility with membership stability. See *Hearings*, 1956, p. 369; John Harms, "End of an era in farm programs," *SF*, August 1957, p. 62; and Mancur Olson, Jr., *The logic of collective action: Public goods and the theory of groups* (Cambridge: Harvard University Press, 1971), chap. 6.

78. *Hearings before the Special Senate Committee to Investigate Political Activities, Lobbying and Campaign Contributions*, "Campaign contributions, political activities and lobbying," 84th Congress, 2d session, 1956, pp. 653–54, and pp. 651–60. The Farm Bureau was not sorry to see Thye lose to Democratic representative Eugene McCarthy in 1958. See "Late news of the nation," *Nation's Agriculture*, December 1958, p. 9.

other. In the late 1950s, midwestern representatives had tested the Farm Bureau's competitive advantage, and they had found it wanting. The Farm Bureau's access to the House Agriculture Committee suffered from the revelation. As one reporter summarized, "many farm leaders in Congress question whether either [the Farm Bureau or the Farmers Union] speaks for its own membership on farm policy matters."[79]

Healing the Breach: Voluntary Farm Programs and the Decline of Partisanship

The conduct of agricultural politics in the Kennedy administration was a striking confirmation of the new politics of agriculture, which was in turn a striking contrast to the old politics of agriculture. For thirty years, congressional orientations toward the farm program had been dependably bipartisan; now they were partisan. For thirty years, congressional relations with the farm lobby had been universally solicitous; now they, too, were partisan.

Seduced by the prospect of electoral gains in the farm belt during the Eisenhower administration, the Democrats had committed themselves to a high-price farm policy, and now that they controlled the White House, they took steps to achieve it. President John F. Kennedy appointed Minnesota governor Orville L. Freeman, a confidant of Senator Hubert H. Humphrey, to the top position in the Agriculture Department, and he adopted a Humphrey initiative, the "supply management" bill, as the basis for his farm plan. The Kennedy administration proposed to achieve high prices by regulating farm output with a set of strict, comprehensive production controls.[80]

79. Harms, "End of an era in farm programs," p. 62. As Truman averred, one factor in the Farm Bureau's loss of access was the loss of its "cohesion"—it could not agree internally on farm price support policy. As this section has shown, however, the loss of cohesion was not in itself decisive. Even in the 1920s and 1930s, major factions within the Federation dissented from the national leadership's position, especially the New York and Ohio federations, but this did not undermine the American Farm Bureau's access. The Farm Bureau's loss of cohesion in the 1950s was consequential only because it caused a discrepancy between the messages that the Farm Bureau conveyed and the lessons that elections taught. See David B. Truman, *The governmental process* (New York: Alfred A. Knopf, 1951), chap. 6; Christiana McFadyen Campbell, *The Farm Bureau and the New Deal* (Urbana: University of Illinois Press, 1962), chap. 5; and Lincoln, *Vice president,* chaps. 4–7, 10.

80. For thorough accounts of Kennedy administration farm policy, see Hadwiger and Talbot, *Pressures and protests;* and Willard W. Cochrane and Mary E. Ryan, *American farm policy, 1948–1973* (Minneapolis: University of Minnesota Press, 1976), pp. 36–50.

The supply management proposals intensified the conflicts the Soil Bank program had opened, and the House Agriculture Committee's deliberations turned more partisan than they had ever been before. It is "the committee that is perhaps the most bitterly divided in a partisan sense," Missouri Democrat Richard Bolling observed in 1965. "At one time, the farm bloc presented a united front on the committee. However, in recent years this has broken into two rival groups. On the one hand, there are the cotton, tobacco, peanut, and rice interests represented by the Southerners; and on the other hand, the wheat and corn interests represented by the Republicans."[81]

Beginning in 1961, Republican ranks closed against the Freeman plan, and congressional Democrats, their unity threatened by wavering southerners, sputtered with helpless fury. "I think it is perfectly evident," Missouri Democrat Paul C. Jones sniped, "that the Republican leadership has said, 'We do not want any bill to pass.' I think that is apparent. . . . I think the normal thing would be . . . [to get] a bill out by compromise." "I do not know on what premise the gentleman says that the Republican leadership is against any bill," ranking Republican Charles B. Hoeven shot back. "The Republican minority has not been taken into the confidence of the majority in an attempt to work out a compromise bill. . . . The minority has been kept completely in the dark. . . . We never have been asked to work out a compromise."[82]

Conforming with their practice of the recent past, the leaders of the farm lobby committed to partisan teams. On the one side, the National Farmers Union and the National Grange allied with the Democrats, leading a coalition of a dozen farm groups in support of the administration. On the other side, the American Farm Bureau, its midwestern and southern factions for once in agreement, allied with the Republicans, leading the opposition in vituperative attacks. "The purpose of this [Freeman] bill," Farm Bureau president Charles B. Shuman charged, "is cheap food produced by docile, licensed, and properly managed farmers."[83]

81. Richard Bolling, *House out of order* (New York: Dutton, 1965), p. 96. See also Heinz, "Political impasse," pp. 952–78.

82. *Hearings before the House Agriculture Committee,* "Agricultural Act of 1961," 87th Congress, 1st session, Serial E, 1961 (hereafter *Hearings,* 1961), pp. 976, 46–133, 946–77.

83. "Farm organizations battle over bill," *WF,* 17 June 1961, p. 6; *WDWF* No. 901, 24 December 1960; *KAL,* 1 April 1961; *KAL,* 27 May 1961; *KAL,* 23 December 1961; "The farmer's Washington," *SF,* July 1961, p. 17; "Big changes made in omnibus bill," *WF,* 1 July 1961, p. 6; Hadwiger and Talbot, *Pressures and protests,* pp. 57–58. The Farm Bureau's unaccustomed unity stemmed from southern fears that the supply management program would arrest the expansion of grain and soybean production in the South. On the

By 1961, with nearly a decade of experience, the members of the House Agriculture Committee regarded the farm organizations' testimony as a simple extension of party warfare. The Democrats defended the Farmers Union and attacked the Farm Bureau. For instance, Texas Democrat Bob Poage assailed Farm Bureau lobbyist Marvin McLain for attempting to tar the supply management bill with the name of its originator, University of Minnesota economist Willard W. Cochrane, whom many lawmakers found nettlesome.

POAGE: I think this is very unfortunate and unseemingly [sic], and for the American Farm Bureau Federation to call this the Cochrane-Freeman bill, when there is a well-established practice in Congress to call a bill by the name of the author. The author of this bill is Harold D. Cooley, the chairman of the Committee on Agriculture of the House of Representatives. And I think it is the Cooley bill.

McLAIN: I saw yesterday a [press] release, and this will amuse you . . . that was put out by the [Agriculture] Department, in which it called the bill the Freeman-Kennedy bill.

POAGE: They can call it whatever they please, but the purpose of calling this something else . . . is to try to use ridicule to try to destroy that which we cannot discredit with logic. Is that not the purpose of that type of name calling?[84]

The Republicans, for their part, defended the Farm Bureau and attacked the Farmers Union. Reuben Johnson, the Union's legislative director, made a tally of a recommittal vote on a farm bill and scolded the Committee's Republicans for their solid lineup against it. The Republicans struck right back. "I voted for the emergency feed grain bill in the form it came out of the conference committee," Minnesota Republican Albert Quie wrote in an angry rebuttal. "This recounting of the facts of this case surely should show just how unfair and politically partisan such a use of the recommittal vote cited by Mr. Johnson is."[85]

The farm lobby fight, in short, was as partisan a fight as the Committee's. It was the "bitterest farm bill brawl in memory," Kiplinger wrote, "and [the] major farm organizations are tearing each other apart to win out."[86]

---

changing cultivation patterns in the South, see Harry D. Fornari, "The big change: Cotton to soybeans," *Agricultural History,* 53 (January 1979), pp. 245–53.

84. *Hearings,* 1961, p. 1008, and pp. 266, 291–92, 564–65, 997-1008; *Washington Farmletter* (hereafter *WFL*) No. 993, 29 September 1962.

85. *Hearings,* 1961, p. 1041, and pp. 267–83, 293, 1011, 1033–44.

86. *KAL,* 27 May 1961. One striking irony is that academics were leveling their most vigorous criticism at the parochial, bipartisan farm bloc precisely at the time it was least like that. See Grant McConnell, *Private power and American democracy* (New York: Alfred A. Knopf, 1966), chap. 7; Theodore J. Lowi, "How the farmers get what they want," *Reporter,* 21 May 1964, pp. 34–37.

For more than two years, partisan skirmishes characterized farm politics both inside the Committee and outside on the floor. The Farm Bureau, anxious that the policy gains of the Eisenhower years not be reversed, urged its Republican allies not to yield a single inch. As one GOP senator put it, "the Farm Bureau is so uncompromising that it won't accept the omnibus bill [even] if everything is knocked out except its number." Faced with a unified opposition party, and worried that southern hesitations might allow the GOP to win, the administration threw entire sections of the Freeman bill overboard even before it left the committee. On the floor, it pressured northern liberals; New York Democrat Otis G. Pike, for one, complained that his arm ached from all the twisting the White House had given it. The strategy ultimately worked. The farm bill staggered through Congress with a few votes to spare.[87]

At first, the Democrats were willing to shoulder such extraordinary political costs for quite meager political payoffs. The Farm Bureau's vitriolic conservatism had gotten their backs up. "From the White House on down," Wayne Darrow reported, in 1962, "the Administration sees this primarily as a fight with the Farm Bureau."[88]

As the Democrats fought one exhausting battle after another, though, and as their casualties began to mount, their enthusiasm for the fight rapidly faded. First, the feuding on Capitol Hill forced them to devote an inordinate sum of resources to the simplest farm legislation. In 1962, for example, the administration's mandatory wheat and feed grains program stalled in the House Agriculture Committee, blocked by a coalition of Republicans and a few southern Democrats. Finally, after many weeks of head counts, promises, threats and delays, the Committee reported Freeman's bill, but by only a single vote. "All this [fighting] is par for the course in the stormy House Agriculture Committee, which has a House-wide reputation for feuding, delay, and disagreement," the *Washington Farmletter* noted. "Hard as it is to get a farm bill through the House, it's still harder to get anything of substance out of the Ag Committee."[89]

87. *WDWF* No. 926, 17 June 1961; Hadwiger and Talbot, *Pressures and protests*, p. 199; Donald T. Donnelly, "Washington from the inside," *Nation's Agriculture*, December 1962, p. 11; Eugene Butler and Jay Richter, "What's new," *PF*, June 1961, p. 6; "Long range farm proposals hit snag," *WF*, 15 April 1961, p. 8; *WDWF* No. 920, 6 May 1961.
88. *WFL* No. 977, 9 June 1962.
89. *WFL* No. 968, 7 April 1962; *WFL* No. 955, 6 January 1962; *WFL* No. 973, 12 May 1962; *WFL* No. 979, 23 June 1962; "What's new in Washington," *SF*, August 1962, p. 15; "Here's new farm plan for 1963," *WF*, 6 October 1962, p. 8; *KAL* "Special letter: What's ahead for agriculture," ca. December 1962; Hadwiger and Talbot, *Pressures and protests*, p. 168; Albert, *Little giant*, pp. 272–73. The administration's efforts to pass a

Second, the administration's insistence on strict, mandatory production controls jeopardized the Democrats' recent gains in the Middle West. The 1962 midterms retired three votes for the Kennedy program, all in districts where incumbent supporters of the administration, because of redistricting, went head-to-head with incumbent opponents. In the GOP primary in the new Nebraska First District, Ralph F. Beermann defeated Phil Weaver, the only Republican to vote in favor of the 1961 farm bill. In the new Kansas First, freshman Republican Bob Dole ousted three-term Democrat J. Floyd Breeding. And in the new Illinois Twentieth, freshman Republican Paul Findley dislodged ten-term Democrat Peter F. Mack, Jr.[90]

Finally, in May 1963, the Democratic farm program met with a stunning, decisive reversal. In a referendum on the 1964 wheat program, farmers spurned the administration's offer of two-dollar wheat and a 10 percent acreage cut. For the first time ever, they disapproved production quotas, and the vote was not even close. Nationally, only 48 percent approved the program, far short of the two-thirds required. Only fifteen states, with just 37 percent of the national wheat allotment, gave it a simple majority, and the largest wheat state, Kansas, mustered only 42 percent in favor. Through skilful exploitation of typically low referendum turnout, the American Farm Bureau Federation had engineered a dramatic setback for the Kennedy administration farm program.[91]

---

feed grains act in 1963 had the same Sisyphean quality. See Hadwiger and Talbot, *Pressures and protests*, pp. 297–98.

90. "USDA plans for new farm legislation," *WF*, 1 December 1962, p. 8; *WFL* No. 999, 10 November 1962; Donald T. Donnelly, "Late news of the nation," *Nation's Agriculture*, September 1962, p. 11; Donald T. Donnelly, "Washington from the inside," *Nation's Agriculture*, November 1962, p. 2; Donald T. Donnelly, "Washington from the inside," *Nation's Agriculture*, December 1962, p. 11; "Whose victory was it?" *New Republic*, 17 November 1962, pp. 5–6; " 'Why I won'—'Why I lost,' " *U.S. News and World Report*, 19 November 1962; pp. 64–72; "Some election results you may have missed," *U.S. News and World Report*, 26 November 1962, p. 56; *WFL* No. 989, 1 September 1962. The context of the elections made Democrats more wary than the results might have indicated. In September 1962, a growers' referendum on the 1963 wheat program had barely recorded the requisite two-thirds in favor, and it fell short of two-thirds in Kansas, Montana, Oklahoma and Washington, four of the top five wheat states. After the 1962 midterm elections, Democratic leaders in Congress began to complain about the difficulty they had in finding lawmakers willing to serve on the agriculture committees. See "Foresee compromise farm program," *WF*, 15 September 1962, p. 8; *WFL* No. 1006, 29 December 1962; *WFL* No. 1009, 19 January 1963.

91. Hadwiger and Talbot, *Pressures and protests*, pp. 244–315; *WFL* No. 1005, 22 December 1962; *WFL* No. 1006, 29 December 1962; Donald T. Donnelly, "Washington from the inside," *Nation's Agriculture*, February 1963, p. 11; Donald T. Donnelly, "Washington from the inside," *Nation's Agriculture*, March 1963, p. 18; Donald T. Donnelly,

The wheat program's failure forced Democratic officials to pause and take stock. Despite extraordinary efforts over the past two years, the administration had barely emerged standing after every confrontation with Congress. It had lost ground in midwestern elections. Finally, to top it off, it had lost its program. "By measure of wooing farmers' votes for the Administration," a midwestern journal observed, "New Frontier farm programs *haven't delivered.* White House advisers who've long argued Washington is spending more for the farm vote than it's getting are now being heard."[92]

Understandably, the first impulse of official Washington was to write off the wheat program. "Farmers have voted themselves out of a program of their own free choice and are now free to plant the face of the earth in wheat," House Agriculture Committee chairman Harold D. Cooley (D., N.C.) huffed. "We don't intend to interfere with that decision."[93]

In time, however, the prospect of a record-breaking wheat crop piled atop a record-breaking surplus caused cooler heads, most of them attached to midwestern Democrats, to reconsider. With 1964 campaigns a year away, a reporter noted, "Congressmen aren't designed to withstand the pressure of $1.25 wheat." Accordingly, farm belt Democrats undertook to invent a new farm program, but in a climate that was more open to innovation than at any time in the past decade, precisely because of the defeat of the wheat referendum. "Some observers see a silver lining. . . . And indeed there may be one," *Wallaces' Farmer* observed. "For the first time within memory, Washington is no longer crusading for this or that farm program. There is a spark of hope that perhaps the resulting void can be filled by some reasoned 'middleground.'"[94]

The Democrats from the farm states located it quickly. In June 1963,

---

"Washington from the inside," *Nation's Agriculture,* April 1963, p. 10; "What's new in Washington," *SF,* March 1963, p. 27; "Wheat vote will leave scars!" *WF,* 20 April 1963, p. 10; "Little interest in wheat referendum," *WF,* 20 April 1963, p. 20; "May 21 wheat referendum," *WF,* 18 May 1963, pp. 14-15; *WFL* No. 1007, 5 January 1963; *WFL* No. 1017, 16 March 1963; *WFL* No. 1021, 13 April 1963; *WFL* No. 1026, 18 May 1963; "Farmers slap down wheat plan," *Business Week,* 25 May 1963, p. 29; "Abundance aborted," *Nation,* 15 June 1963, pp. 497–98; "Farmers say no," *New Republic,* 1 June 1963, p. 6.

92. "What's new in Washington," *SF,* June 1963, p. 13 (emphasis in original).

93. "What's new in Washington," *SF,* July 1963, p. 15; *WFL* No. 1027, 25 May 1963; Hadwiger and Talbot, *Pressures and protests,* pp. 316–17.

94. "Can AFBF get new wheat program?" *WF,* 1 June 1963, p. 16; "New direction for farm programs?" *WF,* 4 May 1963, p. 8; "Wheat vote creates new policy battle!" *WF,* 15 June 1963, p. 6; *WFL* No. 1027, 25 May 1963; *WFL* No. 1028, 1 June 1963; "Smooth sailing for LBJ farm program," *WF,* 5 December 1964, p. 8.

South Dakota senator George S. McGovern offered the idea of a voluntary wheat certificate program. The recently defeated mandatory wheat program, like every other commodity program since 1939, would have required farmers to observe production limits under penalty of prosecution. McGovern's plan, in contrast, provided more generous price supports for farmers who observed their acreage quotas "voluntarily." Congress wedded it to a cotton bill and passed it in April 1964.[95]

From a political standpoint, the genius of voluntarism was twofold. First, for the producers, it removed the most objectionable aspect of the farm programs, the compulsion, while preserving the most appealing, the payments. "Inside-the-White House theory on farm programs," a midwestern journal commented, "boils down to this: what farmers really want from Washington are the benefits of farm programs but without the restrictions usually involved." Indeed, the model for the McGovern wheat plan, a voluntary feed grains program passed as a stopgap in 1961, had already won wide acceptance from corn growers, who were not ordinarily noted for their rapport with the farm program. For almost a year, extending the idea to other crops had been the subject of discussion within the farm policy community.[96]

Second, the voluntary plan invited cooperation from across the aisle, as the Democrats had explicitly calculated. "We've got to give enough," one told a reporter, "to get some Republicans who have a stake in this farm thing to vote with us." The McGovern bill reproduced the main features of a voluntary wheat plan offered earlier by three GOP representatives, Albert Quie of Minnesota, Bob Dole of Kansas and Don Short of North Dakota.[97]

By neutralizing the Republicans' most telling issue—coercion—the

95. "What's new in Washington," *SF*, August 1963, p. 19; *WFL* No. 1031, 22 June 1963; *WFL* No. 1037, 3 August 1963; Hadwiger and Talbot, *Pressures and protests*, chap. 14; *WFL* No. 1055, 6 December 1963; *WFL* No. 1068, 6 March 1964; *WFL* No. 1072, 3 April 1964; *WFL* No. 1073, 10 April 1964; McGovern interview. For the full story of the 1964 wheat-cotton bill, see Varden Fuller, "Wheat, cotton and political arithmetic," *California Monthly*, July/August 1964, p. 12.

96. "What's new in Washington," *SF*, December 1964, p. 7; "Whose victory was it?" *New Republic*, 17 November 1962, p. 6; "Freeman may change program goals!" *WF*, 18 August 1962, p. 6; *WFL* No. 995, 13 October 1962; "What's new in Washington," *SF*, January 1963, p. 15; Jack Heinz, "Those annoying farmers: Impossible but not really serious," *Harper's*, July 1963, p. 64; Heinz, "Political impasse," pp. 974–75. In fact, corn growers had voted down the 1962 feed grains program, but such an occurrence was so common that it received little notice. See *WFL* No. 1027, 25 May 1963.

97. "New worry for politicians: Dollar wheat and the '64 vote," *U.S. News and World Report*, 16 September 1963, p. 88; Hadwiger and Talbot, *Pressures and protests*, pp. 316–17.

voluntary farm programs of the late sixties put agricultural politics back on its traditional bipartisan footing. By 1965, a renewed spirit of cooperation across party lines was already evident. First, Republicans and Democrats once again each borrowed freely from the other's best ideas. Albert Quie proposed a bill to provide direct payments of subsidies to wheat and corn farmers, a notion reminiscent of the earlier, Democratic Brannan Plan. "The amazing spectacle of a Republican urging compensatory payments has most people flabbergasted," a farm reporter noted. Second, Republicans again rushed to take credit for popular Democratic proposals. Bob Dole was so anxious to be identified with a Democratic farm bill that his office called the *Washington Farmletter* to correct the erroneous report that he had voted against it in committee. Finally, Republicans again joined Democrats to pass the farm program. Nineteen Republicans voted for the 1965 Food and Agriculture Act, including all five from Kansas, all four from Minnesota and both from South Dakota. No omnibus, Democratic farm bill had won so many GOP votes since 1954. The voluntary programs had renewed the basis for bipartisan cooperation.[98]

The reconstruction of the farm bloc was no temporary aberration. After 1965, bipartisan cooperation deepened and spread. On the House Agriculture Committee, the partisan atmosphere relaxed considerably. By 1968, for instance, two strong partisans, Kansas Republican Bob Dole and Agriculture Secretary Orville Freeman, could make light of their ideological differences.

DOLE: One of the strong points of the 1965 program, so far as I was concerned, was the fact of taking it out of the political arena until 1969. Do you have any comment on the political arena question?

FREEMAN: I am completely apolitical, as you know. (Laughter.)

DOLE: I understand that—apolitical. I also have the same problem.

By 1973, likewise, two strong party leaders could trust each other completely. At one point in the Agriculture Committee's deliberations, Bob Poage of Texas, the Democratic chairman, turned the hearings over to Charles M. Teague of California, the ranking Republican. As Teague

98. "Smooth sailing for LBJ farm program!" *WF*, 5 December 1964, p. 8; *WFL* No. 1136, 25 June 1965; *WFL* No. 1139, 16 July 1965; *WFL* No. 1140, 23 July 1965; *WFL* No. 1145, 27 August 1965; *WFL* No. 1148, 17 September 1965; "How 'new' is the 'new' farm bill?" *WF*, 6 November 1965, p. 8; "What's new in Washington," *SF*, August 1965, p. 7; Eugene Butler and Jay Richter, "What's new in Washington," *PF*, August 1965, p. 8. Nineteen Republican votes is more impressive when put in perspective—there were many fewer farm belt Republicans in 1965 than there had been in 1954. In 1954, for example, the entire Iowa House delegation was Republican; in 1965, six of the seven were Democrats.

himself noted, he was the first Republican to preside over the Committee—however briefly—in twenty years, since the GOP had last controlled it.[99]

After 1965, moreover, the distinctions between Republican and Democratic farm policy blurred, except among a handful of conservative Republican and liberal Democratic ideologues. In 1973, for example, the Committee was unimpressed by the Nixon administration's plan to phase out the farm programs; neither Republicans nor Democrats took the proposal very seriously.[100] In 1977, likewise, the Committee united in its unhappiness that the Carter administration's farm bill was not more generous to farmers. "Mr. Secretary, what has happened?" Kansas Republican Keith G. Sebelius asked Bob Bergland, his Democratic comrade on the Committee until a few months before. "You suggested that he go down and see Mr. Carter," Nebraska Republican Charles Thone interjected, to the laughter of his colleagues. "I would suggest that is exactly what has happened."[101]

99. *Hearings before the House Agriculture Committee*, "Extend the Food and Agriculture Act of 1965," 90th Congress, 2d session, Serial SS, 1968 (hereafter, *Hearings, 1968*), p. 284; *Hearings before the House Agriculture Committee*, "General farm program," 93d Congress, 1st session, Serial 93-K, 1973 (hereafter *Hearings, 1973*), p. 175.

100. In fact, the rebellion against the Nixon administration's farm policy was led by Republicans on the Senate Agriculture Committee. North Dakota Republican Milton R. Young offered a proposal for compensatory payments to farmers to make up the difference between the market price and the legislated "target price." In its basic orientation, this was the same program that Charles Brannan had proposed in 1949. See Donald T. Donnelly, "Washington: Assignment agriculture," *American Farmer*, October 1973, p. 10; *KAL*, 11 May 1973; "Washington report," *SF*, August 1973, p. 7; *WFL* No. 1528, 19 January 1973; *WFL* No. 1529, 26 January 1973; *WFL* No. 1544, 11 May 1973; *WFL* No. 1546, 25 May 1973; "Back to Brannan," *New Republic*, 23 June 1973, p. 7.

101. *Hearings before the House Agriculture Committee*, "General farm bill," 95th Congress, 1st session, Serial 95-H, 1977 (hereafter *Hearings, 1977*), p. 166 and pp. 155–219; *Hearings, 1973*, pp. 1–58; "New farm bill faces hard fight," *Farm Journal*, April 1973, p. 32; *KAL*, 16 March 1973; "What's new from Washington," *PF*, May 1973, p. 12; *WFL* No. 1535, 9 March 1973; *WFL* No. 1540, 13 April 1973; *WFL* No. 1546, 25 May 1973; *WFL* No. 1552, 6 July 1973; Ralph D. Wennblom, "New farm bill ties targets to cost of production," *Farm Journal*, February 1977, p. 9; Ralph Wennblom, "What's in the administration's new farm bill?" *Farm Journal*, May 1977, p. 15; *KAL*, 25 March 1977; *KAL*, 8 April 1977; Michael S. Lyons and Marcia Whicker Taylor, "Farm politics in transition: The House Agriculture Committee," *Agricultural History*, 55 (April 1981), p. 136; Robert P. Weber, "Home style and committee behavior: The case of Richard Nolan," pp. 71–94 in Morris P. Fiorina and David W. Rohde, eds., *Home style and Washington work* (Ann Arbor: University of Michigan Press, 1989). See also *Hearings before the House Agriculture Committee*, "General farm program and food stamp program," 91st Congress, 1st session, Serial Q, 1969 (hereafter *Hearings, 1969*), pp. 1–46; and *Hearings before the House Agriculture Committee*, "General farm bill of 1981," 97th Congress, 1st session, Serial 97-G, 1981 (hereafter *Hearings, 1981*), pp. 431–507.

After 1965, in short, the strident partisanship of the Eisenhower and Kennedy years faded rapidly from memory. In 1970, one reporter noted, "party lines, as is usual in farm bill battles, are fuzzy." In 1972, another observed, "rarely are farm bills passed or defeated on a party-line basis." An exhaustive study of the politics of the Reagan administration's 1985 farm bill made no mention of partisan politics. The architect of the voluntary farm programs remembered the reasons for the rapprochement in a 1986 interview. "The [Democrats'] search for the 'middle ground,'" former USDA economist John A. Schnittker confirmed, "was the basis for the decline in partisanship."[102]

The Aftermath: Farm Bureau Access in an Era of Good Feeling

With some justification, the leaders of the American Farm Bureau Federation considered the 1963 wheat referendum an opportunity to restore the Federation's flagging position as the nation's hegemonic farm organization. "To understand the meaning of the referendum," a Washington correspondent commented, "you need to understand what it is being *made* to mean. It is a battleground, the site chosen for a showdown between the American Farm Bureau Federation and Secretary of Agriculture Orville L. Freeman. More than wheat is at stake in the vote. *Here's why:* The real prize will be political prestige and influence. It is less a question of *what* than of *who*. Farm Bureau says that it speaks for its farmer members. Freeman tells Congress this is not true—and he would like to have this honor. Congress, confused now, will side with the winner."[103]

102. *WFL* No. 1406, 4 September 1970; Fred Bailey, Jr., "What the election means to farmers," *SF*, October 1972, p. 7; Interview with John A. Schnittker, November 1986; William P. Browne, *Private interests, public policy, and American agriculture* (Lawrence: University Press of Kansas, 1988); *KAL*, 6 August 1971; "Credit Page Belcher with a bipartisan farm bill," *PF*, September 1971, p. 56; Alan Ehrenhalt, "House Agriculture: New faces, new issues," *Congressional Quarterly Weekly Report*, 22 February 1975, pp. 381–84; Arthur Maass, *Congress and the common good* (New York: Basic Books, 1983), pp. 38–39. The chronology of partisanship on the House Agriculture Committee is supported by the recollections of a member who served immediately before the farm bloc split on party lines and immediately after it reconciled. William C. Wampler, a Republican from Virginia, served on the Committee in 1953 and 1954, but he lost a reelection bid in 1954. In 1967, he returned to Congress and to Agriculture. He recalled that partisan objections were seldom voiced in 1954; he noticed no appreciable difference in 1967. Interview with William C. Wampler, December 1986.

103. "What's new in Washington," *SF*, March 1963, p. 27 (emphasis in the original); *WFL* No. 1005, 22 December 1962; *WFL* No. 1006, 29 December 1962; Eugene Butler and Jay Richter, "What's new," *PF*, January 1963, p. 8.

The political fallout from the referendum, however, disappointed the Farm Bureau's hopes. Its victory failed to recoup the congressional access it had already lost. In fact, in inspiring the search for a bipartisan farm policy, the referendum further subverted its access.

The voluntary farm programs damaged the Farm Bureau twice over. First, their popular success undermined the credibility of the Bureau's claim that producers would rather do without them. In 1961, for instance, Virginia Democrat Pat Jennings quizzed two Federation lobbyists about the puzzling discrepancy between the Farm Bureau's position on the feed grains program and farmers' participation in it.

JENNINGS: You said the majority of your members felt [the Farm Bureau proposal] was best. On the emergency feed grain program for 1961, I believe you were opposed to that, were you not? . . .

JOHN LYNN: Yes.

JENNINGS: How do you account for the fact that so many farmers have signed up for this program?

LYNN: Mr. Jennings, I started out working with these programs in 1933 and this is the most lush program that has ever been presented to farmers.

JENNINGS: Did Farm Bureau members sign up?

LYNN: Everyone that wanted to. We certainly did not do anything to stop them. We said to Farm Bureau members: "Look at the facts; . . . what will mean the most money to you in 1961?" And that is exactly what they have done. We have officials in the Farm Bureau that are participating in this program. We have no criticisms to offer it, either. . . .

JENNINGS: Why are you opposed to it?

LYNN: We do not think it will solve the feed grain problem.

MARVIN MCLAIN: Or solve any other problem.

The popularity of the voluntary program, in short, flew in the face of the Farm Bureau's counsel. "Even though Charlie Shuman would rant and rave about it," former USDA official Edwin A. Jaenke recalled, "he really didn't have any support in the country, and the politicians saw that."[104]

Second, by robbing the Republicans of their most effective campaign issue in the farm belt, coercion, the voluntary programs cheated the Farm Bureau out of its last remaining point of compatibility with farm state Republicans. As a *Wallaces' Farmer* correspondent shrewdly noted, "some GOP lawmakers who beat the drums for Farm Bureau in advance of the referendum did so, it now appears, to get off the hook on farm legislation." By the offer of the voluntary program in 1964, the

104. *Hearings,* 1961, p. 997; Interview with Edwin A. Jaenke, December 1986; "AFBF attacks feed grain program," *WF,* 16 March 1963, p. 9; "Record signup in feed grain program," *WF,* 18 April 1964, p. 8.

Democrats forced the Farm Bureau and the Republicans onto the record against a generous farm bill.[105]

For farm belt Republicans, the consequences were disturbing. Already burdened by Barry Goldwater and his denunciations of the farm program, the opponents of the voluntary wheat and feed grains programs fared poorly. In Iowa, four of six GOP members who had voted against the feed grains bill lost; a fifth retired. In Nebraska and North Dakota, Ralph Beermann and Don Short opposed the plans and lost their seats. In Kansas, Bob Dole voted against the wheat bill and eked out a five-thousand-vote victory, the closest election of his career. "It turned out that the farm . . . vote made a difference in the election after all," Darrow noted. "It defeated a score or more Republicans running for Congress and accounted for more than half of the increased Democratic majority in the next House." In the late 1950s, the Farm Bureau program had been a GOP liability. In the early 1960s, it had been a harmless extension of partisan warfare. In the late 1960s, it had become a liability once more.[106]

In the midsixties, then, the voluntary farm programs undermined whatever tenuous claim the Farm Bureau had to the loyalties of farm belt Republicans, and the Farm Bureau's access to the House Agriculture Committee suffered still more. Except for a few conservative ideologues, the Committee's GOP members lost interest in defending it. Except for a few liberal ideologues, conversely, the Committee's Democratic members gradually lost interest in attacking it, precisely because that was no longer necessary. By the late 1960s, the Farm Bureau's inability or unwillingness to represent farmers was the stuff of Committee lore. "I am perplexed . . . by the presentation of the Farm Bureau Federation," Washington Democrat Thomas S. Foley announced in 1969. "I do not know how we are to evaluate presentations that come before us from the Farm Bureau when members have so many constituents who do not agree with those presentations. But we are not going to resolve that today."[107]

Starting in the late 1960s, the House Agriculture Committee de-

105. "Wheat vote creates new policy battle!" *WF*, 15 June 1963, p. 6; "Can AFBF get new wheat program?" *WF*, 1 June 1963, p. 16; *WFL* No. 1027, 25 May 1963; *WFL* No. 1071, 27 March 1964; *WFL* No. 1073, 10 April 1964; Hadwiger and Talbot, *Pressures and protests*, pp. 311–15.

106. *WFL* No. 1103, 6 November 1964; *KAL*, 6 November 1964; Eugene Butler, "Johnson vs. Goldwater," *PF*, October 1964, p. 112; "Smooth sailing for LBJ farm program!" *WF*, 5 December 1964, p. 8; "Congress: Running hard to stand still," *Business Week*, 10 October 1964, p. 58; "Normally Republican Midwest shows Democratic trend," *Congressional Quarterly Weekly Report*, 23 October 1964, p. 2494.

107. *Hearings*, 1969, pp. 1121, 172, 242–44, 1155.

clared its independence from the Farm Bureau and proclaimed its independence a virtue. In 1969, for example, Washington Republican Catherine May assisted USDA Secretary Clifford M. Hardin's denial of Farm Bureau involvement in the Nixon administration's farm policy.

MAY: There have been from time to time reports in the press, and perhaps rumors that you and your Department are already committed to one specific farm program proposed by either an individual or a group of individuals or a farm organization. Would you comment on that report?

HARDIN: I would be very happy to, Mrs. May. No; we are not committed to any program proposed by any organization . . . nor are we committed individually or collectively to any one set of proposals or techniques for modifying the program.

In 1985, similarly, "the Farm Bureau proposal that was eventually drafted encountered difficulty in finding a sponsor willing to be politically positioned with the AFBF, and, when the proposal was sponsored, it was lost in an extensive array of bills introduced in Congress by members who wanted some share of the credit for attending to the farm crisis." The Farm Bureau program was a liability that nobody on the Committee quite wanted to assume.[108]

Congressional wariness toward the Farm Bureau had much to do with the organization's diehard conservatism, of course, but its ideological extremity was not the whole problem. In fact, starting in 1970, with the retirement of Charles B. Shuman, the Farm Bureau steadily moderated its policy positions. Under the direction of Shuman's handpicked successor, William Kuhfuss of Illinois, the AFBF softened its ideological edge even while it maintained its oppositional outlook on national farm policy.[109]

108. *Hearings, 1969,* p. 21; Browne, *Private interests,* p. 224. The Farm Bureau expected Nixon's victory in 1968 to give it the political wherewithal to phase the farm programs out. It therefore regarded Hardin's cooperation with congressional Democrats as sheer treachery. *KAL,* 21 March 1969; *KAL,* 30 May 1969; *KAL,* 11 July 1969; Eugene Butler and Jay Richter, "What's new in Washington," *PF,* July 1969, p. 6; "New farm program proposed by Farm Bureau," *WF,* 12 April 1969, p. 20; Donald T. Donnelly, "Washington: Assignment agriculture," *Nation's Agriculture,* September 1970, p. 11; "Washington report," *SF,* November 1970, p. 7; *WFL* No. 1440, 30 April 1971.

109. *WFL* No. 1420, 11 December 1970; *KAL,* 11 December 1970; "Kuhfuss heads AFBF, replaces Shuman," *WF,* 23 January 1971, p. 101. The Farm Bureau's flirtation with the extreme right dated back at least to World War II, especially on labor issues, but its involvement in reactionary politics seems to have increased after the war. For allegations of of the Farm Bureau's ties with the radical right, see Wesley McCune, *Who's behind our farm policy?* (New York: Frederick A. Praeger, 1956); and Samuel R. Berger, *Dollar harvest: The story of the Farm Bureau* (Lexington, Mass.: Heath Lexington Books, 1971). Both writers were longtime critics of the Farm Bureau. McCune had ties to Charles Bran-

Within the organization, though, support for the basic outlines of the federal farm program continued to grow. From 1953 to 1968, Farm Bureau membership in the Midwest hovered around 775,000, but Farm Bureau membership in the South spurted from 550,000 to 825,000. As southern membership eclipsed midwestern membership, discontent with the laissez-faire policies of the Federation's Corn Belt leadership mounted and finally came to a head. In 1976, the first Farm Bureau uprising in half a century cashiered Kuhfuss for a westerner, Allan Grant of California. Southern delegates supported the coup on the understanding that one of their own, Robert Delano of Virginia, elected vice president, would succeed Grant. Buoyed by their success, Farm Bureau moderates cleaned house, expanding the representation of the South in the Federation's hierarchy and forcing executive secretary Roger Fleming, a hard-line Corn Belt conservative, out of the Farm Bureau's Washington office. The new leadership was much more to their liking. Under the direction of Grant and Delano, the Federation tilted away from its doctrinaire conservatism and accepted most elements of the national farm program, even though it often wished to see them less lavishly funded.[110]

The make-over of the Farm Bureau's leadership, however, did not reverse its losses. The elections of the fifties and sixties had already demonstrated the lapse of its competitive advantage beyond any reasonable doubt.

Lawmakers had come to regard the views of the Farm Bureau—whatever their content—as nothing special, and the Agriculture Committee treated the Farm Bureau's leaders in a manner that would have been unimaginable in the days of Ed O'Neal and Allan Kline. In 1973, for instance, its chairman, Bob Poage, introduced the Farm Bureau as "one of the farm organizations," and he fretted that the Committee was

---

nan and the Farmers Union. Berger was an aide to Representative Joseph Resnick (D., N.Y.), a member of the Agriculture Committee (1965–68) and a dedicated Farm Bureau antagonist.

110. "Membership paid to the American Farm Bureau Federation," mimeo, American Farm Bureau Federation, 1982; "The story behind the Farm Bureau shake-up," *Farm Journal*, February 1976, p. 10; *KAL*, 16 January 1976; "What's new from Washington," *PF*, February 1976, p. 13; E. D. Wilborn, "What the South gained in Farm Bureau struggle," *PF*, March 1976, p. 32; "Washington report," *SF*, February 1976, p. 4; "Changes in national Farm Bureau leadership," *WF*, 14 February 1976, p. 98; F. R. Jimson, "Farm politics," *WF*, 28 February 1976, p. 14; "Washington," *Farm Journal*, January 1977, p. 8; F. R. Jimson, "Farm politics," *WF*, 12 February 1977, p. 14; "Oppose government farm payments, grain reserve," *WF*, 12 February 1977, p. 95; "Farm Bureau wants five year extension of farm bill," *WF*, 12 March 1977, p. 41; F. R. Jimson, "Farm politics," *WF*, 25 June 1977, p. 10; *Hearings*, 1977, pp. 70–138; *Hearings*, 1981, pp. 235–51.

devoting too much time to its president, William Kuhfuss. In 1977, the Committee's chairman, Tom Foley, put a new Farm Bureau president, Allan Grant, onto a "roundtable" of a half dozen farm group leaders. And in 1981, finally, its chairman, "Kika" de la Garza, sandwiched the latest Farm Bureau leader, Robert Delano, with seven other witnesses. On opening the floor for discussion, forty-five minutes elapsed before North Carolina Democrat Charles Whitley asked Delano, a Virginian, about the tobacco program. Whitley's was the first question directed to Delano that morning. In fact, it was the *only* question directed to Delano—the leader of the nation's largest farm organization—all morning.[111]

To be sure, the Farm Bureau retained some of its influence on farm price support policy. In 1979, it was the leading vote getter in a *Successful Farming* poll; 80 percent of the Capitol Hill staffers the magazine surveyed judged it a group with a "big impact on agricultural policy" (including price supports). In the heart of the Corn Belt and in the West, its conservative program continued to meet with considerable sympathy. Nevertheless, the Farm Bureau's claim on the attention of farm state lawmakers was clearly not what it once had been. "I think we understand each other well enough to know that we can differ on many views and still appreciate the other fellow's viewpoint," Bob Poage told Farm Bureau lobbyist John Lynn in 1965. "I disagree with some of yours as you do with some of mine." For most of the members on the House Agriculture Committee, the Farm Bureau's counsel had lost its gravity, its urgency. The American Farm Bureau had sacrificed its competitive advantage; it had forfeited its access to congressional deliberations.[112]

Conclusion

In the thirties and forties, the American Farm Bureau Federation monopolized access to the House Agriculture Committee. In the South, in the Midwest and in the West, Democrats and Republicans alike solicited the favor of its leaders. In the Corn Belt, in the Cotton Belt and in the Wheat Belt, representatives weighed its views with care.

111. *Hearings*, 1973, pp. 29, 48; *Hearings*, 1977, pp. 47–138; *Hearings*, 1981, pp. 143–72, Whitley's question at pp. 157–59. In contrast, the 1981 hearings opened with effusive accolades for the leaders of the American Agriculture Movement and the National Farmers Organization, two protest-oriented organizations on the radical end of the spectrum. See pp. 87–116.

112. Marcia Zarley, "Washington report," *SF*, October 1979, p. 4; *Hearings before the House Agriculture Committee, Subcommittee on Livestock and Feed Grains and Subcommittee on Wheat,* "Wheat and feed grains," 89th Congress, 1st session, Serial J, 1965, p. 216. See also Browne, *Private interests*, pp. 105–6.

Gradually, however, the Farm Bureau's access eroded. By the late fifties, the Democrats had renounced it; by the late sixties, the Republicans had forsaken it. By the seventies, the House Agriculture Committee reacted to the Farm Bureau's counsel in ways that would hardly have been conceivable a generation before. In 1937, Marvin Jones asked Ed O'Neal to run the hearings; in 1977, Tom Foley put Allan Grant on a roundtable. In 1947, the Agriculture Committee devoted a special session to the Farm Bureau's testimony; in 1981, it scarcely asked it a question. In the thirties and forties, in short, the House Agriculture Committee put Farm Bureau leaders at center stage; in the sixties and seventies, it put them in the cast. By the early eighties, the Farm Bureau's voice was an important voice, but it was no more noteworthy than many others.

Next to its improbability, the most striking aspect of the break was its timing. The Farm Bureau's access to the House Agriculture Committee diminished in the late 1950s and the early 1960s. The timing, as before, is significant.

First, it suggests that the erosion of Farm Bureau access did not follow directly from policy disagreements. In the late thirties, after all, the farm lobby and Congress had divided sharply over mandatory programs, but their relationship had survived it. In the late forties, likewise, the farm lobby and Congress had divided sharply over flexibles, but their relationship had outlasted it. To be sure, the fight over flexibles laid the groundwork for the erosion of Farm Bureau access, but it did not in itself cause it. The conditions were not right until later.

Second, it suggests that the erosion of Farm Bureau access did not follow directly from the construction of farm policy as a partisan issue. In the late 1940s, after all, Charles Brannan had offered a partisan program, but the farm bloc had endured it. In the early 1950s, Ezra Taft Benson had designed a sectarian policy, but the farm bloc had lingered despite it for another several years. To be sure, Benson's adoption of the Farm Bureau program set the stage for the erosion of its access, but it did not in itself cause it. The conditions were not right until later.

Rather, the policy divisions of the postwar period and Ezra Taft Benson's exploitation of them each contributed to the fulfillment of the conditions for the Farm Bureau's loss of access. The Farm Bureau's contention that farmers would accept lower prices was testable, but as long as candidates disbelieved it, it would not in fact be examined—nobody would run on it. The Republican Party's adoption of the argument, however, insured that the contention would receive its due. It did, and the answers were revealing. Starting in 1953 and peaking in 1958, the elections of the fifties repeatedly repudiated the farm program of the

American Farm Bureau. The elections of the late 1950s, that is, signaled the lapse of the Farm Bureau's competitive advantage; they destroyed lawmakers' confidence in the value of its counsel. Thereafter, legislators limited their dependence on the American Farm Bureau.

In fact, the progress of agricultural politics in the postwar years highlighted important constraints on both pressure politics and party politics. As the fifties and sixties demonstrated, the ability of interest groups to direct policy discussion was severely and properly limited. The Farm Bureau asserted that farmers preferred freedom to security, but elections exposed the shallowness of its grassroots support. Interest groups could not make arbitrary claims, because lawmakers had a means by which to check them. As one lobbyist put it, "The worst thing you can do . . . is to claim widespread member support when there is none. There are too many clues available elsewhere."[113]

As the fifties and sixties also attest, however, the capability of political parties to order policy discussion was also severely constrained. Charles Brannan was unable to make farm policy a partisan issue merely by identifying it as such, and Orville Freeman was unable to maintain farm policy as a partisan issue merely by desiring that it would be. Brannan had no way to require Democrats to adopt it; Freeman had no way to forbid Republicans to embrace it. Ezra Taft Benson's successful construction of farm policy as a partisan issue required an unflinching commitment to it, a willingness to abide by it despite frightful electoral consequences. For agricultural policy to turn toward partisanship, therefore, the party program had not only to appeal to advocates, but its contrary had also to appeal to the opposition. Ezra Taft Benson was willing to accept the consequent risk of rejection, but more often, party politicians are not. Wise politicians choose their arenas carefully. More often, they have bigger games to play.

113. Quoted in William P. Browne and Charles W. Wiggins, "Interest group strength and organizational characteristics: The general farm organizations and the 1977 farm bill," pp. 109–21 in Don F. Hadwiger and William P. Browne, eds., *The new politics of food* (Lexington, Mass.: Lexington Books, 1978), p. 117.

6   Constraints, Alternatives
and Access in
Agriculture, 1949–1981

> We are playing to the cheers of an ever-decreasing
> grandstand.
>
>   USDA official Don Paarlberg[1]

At the time World War II ended, the federal government provided price
supports for 166 agricultural commodities ranging from cotton and
wheat to eggs and tung nuts. For twenty commodities—six "basic commodities" and fourteen "Steagall commodities"—the Steagall Amendment of 1941 (as amended) obligated the government to maintain prices
at 90 percent of parity for two years beyond the cessation of hostilities.[2]
    The results were predictable. Farmers responded to the Steagall guar-
antees with mountainous surpluses of potatoes (among other things).
The Commodity Credit Corporation (CCC) purchased nearly a quarter
of the potato crop in 1946, 1947 and 1948 and turned the bulk of the
surplus into alcohol, starch and livestock feed. Much of the rest went to
waste. In one well-publicized incident, local agents of the United States
Department of Agriculture (USDA), unable to figure out what to do with
thirty thousand bushels, piled the tubers in an Alabama field, doused
them with kerosene, and set them on fire. The "political conflagration,"
Matusow wrote, "lit up the Washington skies." Government-financed
destruction of food, juxtaposed against famine in Europe and inflation
at home, deeply offended public sensibilities. Editorial writers raged in
protest, and Congress launched an investigation (which concluded that
potatoes should not be burned). The potato fiasco provoked the greatest
public outcry against the farm program since 1933, when the Agri-

---

1. Quoted by Hyde Murray in author's interview, December 1986. Paarlberg was As-
sistant Secretary for Marketing and Foreign Agriculture under President Eisenhower and
Director of the Office of Agricultural Economics under Presidents Nixon and Ford.
    2. Murray R. Benedict, *Farm policies of the United States, 1790–1950* (New York:
Twentieth Century Fund, 1953), pp. 415–16; Walter W. Wilcox, *The farmer in the Second
World War* (Ames: Iowa State College Press, 1947), pp. 243–46.

cultural Adjustment Administration (AAA) marched six million little pigs off to slaughter.[3]

The House Agriculture Committee, nevertheless, greeted the uproar with exceptional calm. It warned potato growers that they had one more chance to get their house in order before Congress abandoned them, but it assured them that whatever kind of program they wanted, the Committee would get it for them. "The position of the potato growers would have great influence on the committee on the fundamental questions facing the potato growers of the country," said Stephen Pace, a Georgia Democrat who was the chairman of the special subcommittee appointed to reexamine the farm program. "Now the question is do they want to tell us the amount of the support, and how it will be handled, and what they will have to do or not to do, or do they want it determined entirely by the Secretary of Agriculture, or do they want to consult with the committee and they themselves, with our assistance, write their own ticket. . . . I think that is the only issue as I understand it." The public backlash against the potato program—the greatest threat to the price support system since it was created—was nothing to worry about. The Agriculture Committee had the votes.[4]

The potato episode was typical of the way the Agriculture Committee and its allies, the farm producer groups, regarded the limits set by an urban, industrial society. From time to time, they knew, the expense of the commodity subsidy programs became a political problem. The AAA's appropriation for 1940, for instance, was saved from the "economy bloc" only by the intervention of New York mayor Fiorello La Guardia, who lined up the support of the city's delegation in exchange for the farm bloc's support for a relief appropriation.[5]

3. Allen J. Matusow, *Farm policies and politics in the Truman years* (Cambridge: Harvard University Press, 1967), p. 128 and pp. 124–30; *Hearings before the Subcommittee on Food Shortages of the House Agriculture Committee,* "Potato surpluses and the prevention of wastage," 80th Congress, 1st session, 1947; George T. Blakey, "Ham that never was: The 1933 emergency hog slaughter," *Historian,* 30 (November 1967), pp. 41–57.

4. *Hearings before the Special Subcommittee of the House Agriculture Committee,* "General farm program," 81st Congress, 1st session, 1949, Serial U, p. 959; "New Congress may kill supports," *Wallaces' Farmer* (hereafter *WF*), 21 August 1948, p. 16; *Wayne Darrow's Washington Farmletter* (hereafter *WDWF*) No. 227, 17 January 1948. The potato industry failed to work out a compromise acceptable to all of its growers, despite the Committee's invitation to caucus in the committee room while members went to the floor to vote. Congress finally terminated the program in 1950. See *Hearings,* 1949, pp. 934–80; "1950s never-normal granary," *Business Week,* 4 March 1950, pp. 31–32.

5. Orville M. Kile, *The Farm Bureau through three decades* (Baltimore: Waverly Press, 1948), pp. 274–76.

In 1948, likewise, the high and rigid price guarantees of the wartime program threatened to drain the Treasury, and the Truman administration joined with the Republican Senate in support of a more flexible price support system. "If we continue the high level of 90 percent support," Vermont senator George D. Aiken warned the "90 percenters" in the House, "the time will not be far distant when the American people will rise up and say they will no longer have any price-support program." Rapid wartime migration had profoundly altered political realities, the advocates of flexibility argued, and it was time for the farm bloc to get used to it. "I think you are going to have to tell your constituents that perhaps the people who have something to say about how much money from the American Treasury will go to maintain their price supports will have to be convinced that they are getting either a direct or a collateral benefit out of that expenditure," Agriculture Secretary Charles F. Brannan told the House Committee. "We do it by making the programs . . . in the national interest, and not specific class legislation."[6]

To members of the congressional farm bloc, however, the future was still a long way off. In the meantime, they had more pressing matters to contemplate. "Mr. Secretary, I recognize that on the one side we have the taxpayer and the consumer to consider," Oklahoma Democrat Carl Albert told Brannan. "But on the other side we have another practical situation, and that is how far . . . the farm population of this country will go." The farmers, he believed, were not yet ready to budge.[7]

In the late 1940s, Albert's farm bloc sentiments were widely shared. For one thing, belief in the potency of the farm vote was at an all-time high, reinforced by the circumstances of Truman's miraculous victory in 1948. "Maybe labor carried the Congress for Harry," the agrarians boasted, "but we put him in the White House." For another thing—far more important—the Committee was still fairly representative of Congress as a whole, and it had all the votes it needed on the floor. In the late 1940s, the United States Congress was still an overwhelmingly rural institution (see table 1). Representatives of farm districts constituted a numerical majority in the House of Representatives right up to the eve of World War II, and they maintained their hegemony after it. In the late

6. Congressional Quarterly Service, *U.S. agricultural policy in the postwar years, 1945–1963* (Washington: Congressional Quarterly Press, 1963), p. 24; *Hearings before the Special Subcommittee of the House Agriculture Committee*, "General farm program," 81st Congress, 1st session, Serial O, 1949 (hereafter, *Hearings*, 1949), p. 77.

7. *Hearings*, 1949, p. 78. See also Carl Albert (with Danney Goble), *Little giant: The life and times of Speaker Carl Albert* (Norman: University of Oklahoma Press, 1990), pp. 147–49.

Table 1.   Farm representation in Congress, 1930–1980

Reapportionment/ census year	Farm population (%)	Representation in Senate[a] (%)	Representation in House[b] (%)
1930	24.9	88	55
1940	23.2	88	51
1950	15.3	75	37
1960	8.7	48	12
(1965)	(6.4)		(11)
1970	4.8	30	3
1980	3.3	8	≪1

Sources. Farm population: U.S. Bureau of the Census, Historical statistics of the United States, Series K-2, K-17 to K-81; U.S. Bureau of the Census, Statistical abstract of the United States. Congressional districts, 1930–1950: Wayne Darrow's Washington Farm-letter No. 776, 2 August 1958; 1950: U.S. Bureau of the Census, 1956 county and city data book; 1960–1970: U.S. Bureau of the Census, Congressional district data book, 88th Congress, 89th Congress, 90th Congress and 93d Congress; 1980: Thomas E. Cavanaugh, ed., The JCPS congressional district fact book (Washington: Joint Center for Political Studies, 1984), p. 32.
[a]Percentage of Senate membership representing states with over 10 percent of the population on farms.
[b]Percentage of House membership representing districts with over 20 percent of the population on farms.

1940s, the House Agriculture Committee was still one of the most representative committees in Congress, and it realized full well that it could get pretty much what it wanted on the floor.[8]

The political importance of farmers, however, was fast on the wane. During the 1940s, 10.6 million Americans—roughly one in every twelve—either left their farms or saw their farms incorporated into metropolitan areas. Another 10.5 million joined the exodus in the 1950s before the migration slowed to 7.4 million in the 1960s.

The implications for congressional representation were epoch making. In 1950, representatives of farm districts held 38 percent of the seats in the House of Representatives. By 1960, they held only 12 percent; by 1970, 3 percent. In 1930, 240 or so House members represented sizable numbers of farmers. A half century later, only one did.[9]

8. Richard Wilson, "The farmer's Washington," Successful Farming (hereafter SF), February 1949, p. 14; " 'Fair Deal' hurdle: Rural votes," U.S. News and World Report, 15 April 1949, p. 17; Lauren Soth, Farm trouble (Princeton: Princeton University Press, 1957), pp. 12–13. Table 1 probably underestimates the size of the agricultural bloc because it excludes the numbers of people who lived in rural areas but not on farms. In 1949, by one count, 276 House districts—63 percent—were rural.
9. Republican Vin Weber, from the Second District of Minnesota (Marshall).

In the fifties and sixties, the constraints of an increasingly urban Congress converged steadily on an increasingly unrepresentative Agriculture Committee. In 1953, when rural lawmakers again refused to support legislation designed for urban areas, Manhattan Republican Jacob Javits threatened closer scrutiny for the agricultural price support system. "As a representative of a city district," his West Side colleague, Franklin D. Roosevelt, Jr., added, "I have continually preached to my people that we must help support the farm and rural areas of this country, because we can be prosperous only if the whole country is prosperous; but the day is coming . . . when my people will not listen to that any more and they will misunderstand if I continue to support farm programs."[10]

In 1954 and after, Ezra Taft Benson's proposals gave many city lawmakers their first opportunity—or their first need—to put their words into action. By calculation or by coincidence, Benson's flexible farm supports held great appeal in city constituencies. "There are some Republican leaders who believe that Benson is more of an asset than a liability to the party," *Wallaces' Farmer* reported in 1957. "They contend . . . that Benson has considerable popularity in urban areas. . . . These are rather frightening ideas [for farmers]—a secretary of agriculture who appeals to city people more than [to] farmers." In the past, urban representatives had tended to favor farm supports out of a sense of party loyalty—most of them were Democrats. With Republicans scouting price support votes for an issue, however, many were no longer so willing to collaborate. Three-quarters of the legislators from urban areas, including two-thirds of the Democrats, voted to implement flexible price supports in 1954. "The Secretary's crusade against high supports," Darrow judged, "registered in the city vote—swung at least 20 city Democrats to flexibles."[11]

On the whole, however, urban Democrats continued to give the farm programs forbearance. On the one hand, the small, hidden impact of agricultural subsidies on consumer prices—and the relative safety of

10. Robert Engler, "The farm bloc and your food dollar," *Nation,* 19 September 1953, p. 232.
11. "Big question: Is Benson in or out?" *WF,* 16 November 1957, p. 6; *WDWF* No. 565, 10 July 1954; Eugene Butler and Jay Richter, "What's new in Washington," *PF,* January 1957, p. 8; "How Ike would give the farmers more money," *U.S. News and World Report,* 27 April 1956, p. 29; Wesley McCune, "Farmers in politics," pp. 41–51 in Donald C. Blaisdell, ed., "Unofficial government: Pressure groups and lobbies," *Annals of the American Academy of Political and Social Science,* 319 (September 1958), p. 51. For the consumerist view of flexible price supports, see Council on Consumer Information, *Consumers look at farm price policies* (Oxford, Ohio: Council on Consumer Information, 1954), pp. 28-33.

their seats—had always given them a fair amount of leeway on farm policy votes. On the other hand, the odium of Ezra Taft Benson's name had turned the normally Republican Middle West into a Democratic happy hunting ground, tipping scores of rural House seats Democratic in 1954, 1956 and 1958. City Democrats, consequently, again pulled their punches in the name of broader partisan objectives.[12]

By the late 1950s, however, as the urban population continued to grow and the rural population continued to shrink, urban representatives found it harder and harder to resist encroachments onto Agriculture's turf. First, the Eisenhower administration's agitation against the farm program debased the symbolism of farm policy votes. In 1958, for instance, Agriculture proposed legislation to raise dairy and wheat supports, the latter through the levy of a processing tax on millers. Its opponents vilified the "bread tax," and the House voted it down. The decision "came a cropper on the wheat and dairy programs, . . . interpreted by city congressmen as being anti-consumer proposals. These ideas have never been sold to the city man and it was inevitable that this reaction would occur."[13] For urban representatives, votes to raise the prices of such staples as bread and milk were difficult votes to explain.

Second, the commodity programs were the preserve of conservative southern Democrats who had long opposed every item dear to the urban liberal's heart. Under the pressure of the civil rights movement, southern congressmen had increasingly hardened into sullen intransigence, precisely at the moment that northern liberals had reinstated social reform on the congressional agenda. In 1958, urban Democrats in the House killed an omnibus farm support bill by voting down its rule, retaliating against the unfavorable votes of top Agriculture Committee Democrats. In 1959, similarly, city Democrats targeted the cotton, tobacco and peanut programs for a strike in reprisal for the southern votes that passed the antilabor Landrum-Griffin Act. "This city Democrat resentment toward Southern leaders isn't new," Darrow observed. "But it's come into the open now, and is much more intense and bitter." The hostility of rural representatives to the liberals' social agenda increased the hostility of urban representatives to the agrarians' economic agenda.[14]

By the late 1950s, finally, the farm program loomed large as a target

12. David R. Mayhew, *Party loyalty among congressmen: The difference between Democrats and Republicans, 1947–1962* (Cambridge: Harvard University Press, 1966), chap. 2.

13. *Kiplinger Agricultural Letter* (hereafter *KAL*), 28 June 1958.

14. *WDWF* No. 831, 22 August 1959; *WDWF* No. 771, 28 June 1958.

for pruning. Farmers armed with nitrogen fertilizer and plant hybrids had made a mockery of production control, and the major price supported crops—especially wheat and feed grains—were in desperate oversupply. As surpluses mounted, program costs increased. In 1959, farm subsidies cost the Treasury $4.6 billion, about 5 percent of federal spending and the nation's third largest expense, after defense and debt service. (The government ran up bills of a million and a half dollars a day for storage alone.) As costs increased, further, the public's tolerance for even more expensive production control programs wore thin. In 1959 urban lawmakers introduced legislation to abolish the farm price support system altogether. The bills would certainly not go far, *Successful Farming* predicted, accurately, but they were significant straws in the wind. In Washington, it reminded readers, "potato memories linger."[15]

The presidential election campaign in 1960 underscored the increasing political marginality of farmers. Neither John F. Kennedy nor Richard M. Nixon made much of farm policy in the campaign. For one thing, both had supported Ezra Taft Benson, Kennedy as a senator from Massachusetts, Nixon as the vice president.[16] For another, however, farmers were of vastly smaller relevance to presidential ambitions than they had ever been before. They accounted for only 9 percent of the electorate, and they resided in lightly populated states with few electoral votes. Neither Kennedy nor Nixon, consequently, assigned a great deal of importance to farmers as a voting group. Stigmatized in rural areas by his Catholicism, Kennedy's appeals to farmers fell flat. In fact, he grumbled privately, his calls for higher agricultural prices had probably cost

15. "The farmer's Washington," *SF,* July 1959, p. 28; T.R.B., "The third largest expense," *New Republic,* 8 June 1959, p. 2; Helen Hill Miller, "Who are those farmers?" *New Republic,* 28 December 1959, pp. 8–9; Joseph A. Loftus, "Budget plan hits farm policy snag," *New York Times,* 2 October 1961, p. 25. One joke of the period cited the Iowa farmer who was making so much money not growing corn that he decided to diversify and not grow wheat. For another version, see Ezra Taft Benson, *Cross fire: The eight years with Eisenhower* (Garden City, N.Y.: Doubleday and Co., 1962), p. 499.

16. *WDWF* No. 893, 29 October 1960; *WDWF* No. 894, 5 November 1960; "Benson: GOP asset or liability?" *WF,* 1 October 1960, p. 6; Edward L. Schapsmeier and Frederick H. Schapsmeier, *Ezra Taft Benson and the politics of agriculture: The Eisenhower years, 1953–1961* (Danville, Ill.: The Interstate Printers and Publishers, 1975), pp. 257–58; Don F. Hadwiger and Ross B. Talbot, *Pressures and protests: The Kennedy farm program and the wheat referendum of 1963* (San Francisco: Chandler Publishing Co., 1965), p. 14; Interview with Roger Fleming, December 1986. Both candidates, however, attempted to minimize their identification with Secretary Benson. In 1956, when Kennedy detected the coolness of midwesterners to his presidential aspirations, he thereafter took his farm policy cues from Minnesota senator Hubert H. Humphrey. Nixon was unable so easily to change his stripes, but he did prevail upon Eisenhower to send the secretary abroad for the duration of the campaign.

him votes in cities. At long last, the 1960 election exorcised the ghost of Tom Dewey.[17] The inauguration of the Kennedy administration, therefore, only intensified metropolitan pressures on the House Agriculture Committee. The White House discerned little political payoff from programs that extorted consumers twice, once at the supermarket and once again at tax time. Agriculture Secretary Orville Freeman bluntly told the farm bloc that the price of higher farm supports was tougher production control, and he pressed his exacting "supply management" program against the scattered resistance of southern Democrats and the unanimous opposition of Republicans. Farm leaders who met with USDA officials "noted that official attitudes toward farmers seem to be growing harder, showing less fear of the farmers' political strength. To these leaders, it was significant that Secretary Freeman's talks to farmers emphasized the need for production controls rather than promises of benefits." Freeman's farm bills passed by only handfuls of votes.[18]

In 1964, finally, the harsh new political reality intruded dramatically onto the farm bloc's demesne, when the Agriculture Committee brought forth legislation to sweeten the cotton and wheat programs. The cotton provisions of the Committee's bill implemented subsidy payments to domestic textile mills that used American cotton, then ailing from the competition of foreign textiles and synthetic fibers. The wheat provi-

17. *KAL*, 29 October 1960; *KAL*, 12 November 1960; *WDWF* No. 893, 29 October 1960; *WDWF* No. 901, 24 December 1960; "How will vote affect farm policy?" *WF*, 3 December 1960, p. 6; "To win farmer or housewife: That's the problem," *Business Week*, 1 October 1960, pp. 32–33. Kennedy, accordingly, regarded the farm program as nothing but a headache. "John F. Kennedy is reported to have remarked that he didn't want to hear about agriculture from anyone except John Kenneth Galbraith, and he didn't want to hear about it from him either." John A. Schnittker, "The farmer in the till," *Atlantic*, August 1969, p. 43.

18. "A hard choice for farmers," *U.S. News and World Report*, 12 February 1962, p. 52; "Big push to cut USDA budget," *WF*, 3 March 1962, p. 6; "Take-it-or-leave-it farm bill offers tighter controls," *Business Week*, 25 March 1961, pp. 28–29; "Kennedy's pitch for the city vote," *Business Week*, 10 February 1962, p. 32; *WDWF* No. 947, 11 November 1961; *WDWF* No. 950, 2 December 1961; *WFL* No. 955, 6 January 1962; "What's new in Washington," *SF*, May 1962, p. 15; "Kennedy's new farm program," *WF*, 17 February 1962, p. 8; "What's new in Washington," *SF*, June 1963, p. 13; Eugene Butler and Jay Richter, "What's new," *Progressive Farmer* (hereafter *PF*), April 1961, p. 8; "What's new in Washington," *SF*, October 1963, p. 19; "How to save money with new tax bill," *WF*, 7 September 1963, p. 8. For all the agrarians, moreover, Billie Sol Estes's fraudulent manipulation of Texas cotton allotments hardly helped matters. Julius Duscha, *Taxpayer's hayride: The farm problem from the New Deal to the Billie Sol Estes case* (Boston: Little, Brown and Co., 1964); "Will Estes affair kill Freeman bill?" *WF*, 2 June 1962, p. 6; Julius Duscha, "How Billie Sol used the farm programs," *Reporter*, 21 June 1962, pp. 32–35; "Billie Sol's friends," *New Republic*, 16 July 1962, pp. 5–6.

sions, moreover, rescued growers from the consequences of their adverse vote in the 1963 wheat referendum. In the South and on the Plains, the legislation was a matter of great urgency, especially for Democrats. Up until then, however, the farm bloc had continued to ignore warnings that the fate of its program was linked inextricably to the fate of liberal programs, more or less daring city lawmakers to call its bluff. The liberals finally did. Under President Lyndon B. Johnson's not-so-gentle prodding, House Agriculture Committee chairman Harold D. Cooley pried an authorization for a permanent food stamp program out of his committee, which had long been inhospitable to any welfare programs that did not benefit farmers. On the floor, the urban liberals insisted that the food stamp vote precede the farm bill vote, lest unrepentent conservatives defect. The script went as planned. "Prior passage of [the] food stamp bill paved the way for Democratic unity seldom seen on farm bills," the *Washington Farmletter* observed.[19]

Accordingly, when the House Agriculture Committee met in 1965 to draft a new, comprehensive farm program, it also mourned the passing of an era. "With all the activities going on, such as in Alabama [i.e., the civil rights marchers in Selma], . . . everybody realizes, as usual, agriculture cannot make the most impressive case to get the proper consideration," Texas Democrat W. R. (Bob) Poage told his audience. "And, frankly, it is going to get less and less consideration as we see the results of the Supreme Court [legislative districting] decisions as we have. I do not think we are getting enough consideration now, and I think we are getting more now than we will next year, and more than we will get three years hence. It is inevitable." The farm bloc carried the 1965 farm bill in the same manner as before, with a logroll, this time trading its support for a repeal (ultimately unsuccessful) of Section 14(b), the "right-to-work" provision, of the Taft-Hartley Act. "Their city brethren demanded this in exchange for farm bill votes."[20]

19. *Washington Farmletter* (hereafter *WFL*) No. 1073, 10 April 1964; *WFL* No. 1068, 6 March 1964; C. P. Trussell, "House rules unit clears food bill," *New York Times* (hereafter *NYT*), 20 March 1964, p. 13; C. P. Trussell, "Food plan scored in House as ruse," *NYT*, 8 April 1964, p. 25; "2 Johnson bills passed by House," *NYT*, 9 April 1964, p. 1; "Johnson phone effort credited with House victory on farm bill," *NYT*, 10 April 1964, p. 15; William M. Blair, "New farm law puts emphasis on consumers," *NYT*, 31 May 1964, p. III 1; Randall B. Ripley, "Legislative bargaining and the Food Stamp Act, 1964," pp. 279–310 in Frederic N. Cleaveland, ed., *Congress and urban problems* (Washington: Brookings Institution, 1969), pp. 291–306; "Paying the farmers," *New Republic*, 18 May 1963, p. 7; Paul R. Wieck, "Taking care of farmers, whoever they are," *New Republic*, 28 March 1964, pp. 9-10.

20. *Hearings before the House Committee on Agriculture, Subcommittee on Livestock and Feed Grains,* "Wheat and feed grains," 89th Congress, 1st session, Serial J,

Just sixteen years before, in 1949, the House Agriculture Committee had had all the votes it needed. Now, in 1965, it had the votes no longer, even in an overwhelmingly Democratic Congress. "The collective views of the House of Representatives and its Committee on Agriculture are fundamentally incompatible," former USDA official John A. Schnittker observed in 1970. "Any farm bill representing the *real* views of the agrarian Southern and Midwestern members can pass only when most urban members are absent."[21]

Living with Less: Farm Lobby Access in Lean Times

In the first two decades after the Second World War, rapid migration from the country to the city permanently altered the relationship between the House Agriculture Committee and its parent body. Year by year, the number of votes held by metropolitan representatives increased. Year by year, the probability of passing a farm bill declined.

By the midfifties, the agricultural policy community knew all too well that its time was running out. "We have only a few years left to write a farm policy to suit ourselves," a veteran farm lobbyist told a reporter in 1955. "After that, the rest of the people will be writing one for us."[22]

In the time it had left, however, the farm bloc had enough of a problem suiting itself. The decade-long, bitter, internecine battle over flexible

---

1965, p. 2; WFL No. 1141, 30 July 1965; WFL No. 1140, 23 July 1965; Oral memoirs of William Robert "Bob" Poage, Baylor University Institute for Oral History, 1985, pp. 1289ff. Poage's reference to the Supreme Court, of course, concerned its reapportionment decisions, especially *Baker v. Carr* (1962) and *Wesberry v. Sanders* (1964). The decisions seem to have had a devastating psychological effect on farm leaders, despite having mostly ratified what had already been accomplished through population movements. In 1965, the American Farm Bureau Federation made a constitutional amendment to overturn the decisions its highest legislative priority. See John C. Datt, "Who will govern *your* state?" *Nation's Agriculture*, February 1965, pp. 10–13; and Donald T. Donnelly, "Washington: Assignment agriculture," *Nation's Agriculture*, June 1966, p. 22. For an examination of the effect of the reapportionments on policy priorities in Congress, see Mathew D. McCubbins and Thomas Schwartz, "Congress, the courts, and public policy: Consequences of the one man, one vote rule," *American Journal of Political Science*, 32 (May 1988), pp. 388–415.

21. John A. Schnittker, "Farm payments," *New Republic*, 27 June 1970, p. 11.

22. "What's behind the new farm crisis," *Business Week*, 10 December 1955, p. 112. In 1958, after Benson beat the farm bloc a third time, many farm bloc partisans concluded that its time was out. "The once-powerful farm bloc is powerful no more," Iowa Republican Charles B. Hoeven reckoned. "A farm bill now must meet the approval of consumers as well as farmers." "Benson wins low price props," *Business Week*, 23 August 1958, p. 21; Carroll Kilpatrick, "What happened to the farm bloc?" *Harper's*, November 1957, p. 59; WDWF No. 806, 28 February 1959; WDWF No. 776, 2 August 1958.

price supports left it vulnerable to urban pressures even while it could still muster the votes. "We hear it freely said in Washington that the power of the '*farm bloc*' is broken," Agriculture chairman Harold D. Cooley (D., N.C.) wrote in 1955, after the farm bloc had failed to extend 90 percent supports. "When people say now that the power of the farm bloc is broken, they apparently mean there are fewer men in Congress who can be depended upon—without a lot of persuasion—to support good farm bills. *This is a perilous situation for agriculture.* But the greater danger lies in the fact that the house of agriculture is divided against itself." The titanic struggles between the Congress and the administration, between the Cotton Belt and the Corn Belt, between the Farmers Union and the Farm Bureau, between the Democrats and the Republicans fettered the farm bloc's defense of what it already had.[23]

In the late 1950s, however, the "agricultural anarchy" brought new leadership to the forefront of the farm lobby. In May 1957, E. M. Norton of the National Milk Producers Federation proposed an alliance of sixteen separate commodity organizations, ranging from the United Fresh Fruit and Vegetable Association to the National Association of Wheat Growers. The National Conference of Commodity Organizations (NCCO) debuted a few months later, promoting a hodgepodge program of several recent ideas: direct payments for cotton, a two-price plan for wheat, a self-help plan for milk and a land retirement program for corn. "The move," Darrow reported, "is an effort to break the farm organization stalemate. Norton and [the] other commodity organization leaders feel they're caught between two fires: Farmers Union at one extreme, Farm Bureau at the other. They figure that many of their commodity programs are handicapped and circumscribed by the mighty battles of the big general organizations."[24]

23. Harold D. Cooley, "The real peril to the farm program," *SF,* July 1955, p. 33 (italics in original); "The farmer's Washington," *SF,* July 1957, p. 24; *WDWF* No. 565, 10 July 1954; *Hearings before the House Agriculture Committee,* "General farm legislation," 86th Congress, 1st session, Serial GG, 1959 (hereafter *Hearings,* 1959), pp. 82–83, 90, 178.

24. *KAL,* 1 June 1957; *WDWF* No. 715, 25 May 1957. The original conference participants included the National Milk Producers Federation, the National Soybean Association, the U.S. Poultry and Egg Association, the National Turkey Federation, the American Rice Growers Cooperative Association, the United Fresh Fruit and Vegetable Association, the Vegetable Growers Association of America, the Potato Growers Council, the National Swine Growers Council, the National Federation of Grain Cooperatives, and the National Association of Wheat Growers. A cotton group joined later. What appeared to distinguish them from other commodity groups was an office in or near Washington. *KAL,* 1 June 1957; *KAL,* 10 August 1957; *KAL,* 5 October 1957; "Lower prices won't solve farm problem," *WF,* 7 September 1957, p. 10; *WDWF* No. 716, 1 June 1957; *WDWF* No. 720, 29 June 1957; *WDWF* No. 726, 10 August 1957; *WDWF* No. 733, 28

The NCCO flourished briefly in the late 1950s, then disbanded, its constituent commodity groups maintaining a mostly supportive stance toward Kennedy administration farm policy. The pattern of tighter and looser commodity lobby alliances persisted, though, through the next twenty years. On the one hand, when faced with Democratic presidents, whom they took as friendly, the commodity groups worked haphazardly together in support of the administration. On the other hand, when faced with Republican presidents, whom they took as hostile, the commodity groups coalesced in opposition. In 1969, for instance, the National Grange and the Midcontinent Farmers Association (MFA) together organized the National Farm Coalition (NFC), composed primarily of about twenty different commodity groups dedicated to preserving the farm programs against the expected onslaught of Richard Nixon and the Farm Bureau. In 1973, they did the same.[25]

Short-lived as they were, however, the creation of alliances of commodity groups marked their political coming of age. From the late 1930s until the late 1950s, representatives of each of the major price-supported crops, many of them federations of local groups of longer standing, organized and established in Washington, where they joined a handful of veteran commodity lobbies. In the twenty-five years following the advent of the farm support and adjustment programs, the

---

September 1957; *WDWF* No. 744, 14 December 1957; *WDWF* No. 748, 11 January 1958; *WDWF* No. 749, 18 January 1958; Eugene Butler and Jay Richter, "What's new in Washington," *PF*, November 1957, p. 8.

25. "Nibbled to bits," *New Republic*, 10 July 1961, pp. 3–4; *KAL* "Special letter: What's ahead for agriculture," ca. December 1962; *KAL*, 3 October 1969; Eugene Butler and Jay Richter, "What's new in Washington," *PF*, August 1969, p. 8; Butler and Richter, "What's new in Washington," *PF*, September 1969, p. 8; "Groups oppose long range land retirement program," *WF*, 26 July 1969, p. 14; *WFL* No. 1496, 9 June 1972; "New farm bill faces hard fight," *Farm Journal*, April 1973, p. 32; *KAL*, 5 January 1973; F. R. Jimson, "Farm politics," *WF*, 24 March 1973, p. 13; Jimson, "Farm politics," *WF*, 14 April 1973, p. 11; Jimson, "Farm politics," *WF*, 28 April 1973, p. 7; Hadwiger and Talbot, *Pressures and protests*, pp. 56–59, 87–90, 96–97, 121–23, 228–29, 273–77; William P. Browne, "Farm organizations and agribusiness," pp. 198–211 in Don F. Hadwiger and Ross B. Talbot, eds., *Food policy and farm programs* (New York: Academy of Political Science, 1982), pp. 207–9. NFC members in 1969 included the Grange, the MFA, the Farmers Union, the National Farmers Organization, the National Rural Electric Cooperative Association, the National Association of Farmer-Elected Committeemen, the Grain Sorghum Producers Association, the Soybean Growers of America, the National Association of Wheat Growers, the National Milk Producers Federation, the Pure Milk Products Cooperative, the Pure Milk Association, the Peanut Growers Cooperative Marketing Association, the North Carolina Peanut Growers Association, the Virginia Peanut Growers Association, the Western Cotton Growers Association, the National Corn Growers Association and the National Potato Council.

Table 2.   Founding of leading commodity groups

Organization	Date	Membership
National Wool Growers Association	1865	Growers
American National Cattlemen's Association	1898	Rangeland producers
National Milk Producers Federation	1916	Dairy cooperatives
Burley Tobacco Growers Association	1922	Growers
Eastern Dark-Fired Tobacco Growers Association	1932	Growers
United Fresh Fruit and Vegetable Association	1937	Growers and industry
National Cotton Council	1938	Grower, industry organizations
National Peanut Council	1941	Growers and industry
National Livestock Feeders Association[a]	1943	Cattle feeders
National Potato Council	1948	Growers
National Association of Wheat Growers	1950	Growers
Burley Stabilization Corporation	1953	Growers
National Pork Producers Council	1954	Hog producers
Grain Sorghum Producers Association	1955	Growers
Plains Cotton Growers	1956	Growers and industry
Rice Council of America	1956	Growers and industry
National Corn Growers Association	1957	Growers
U.S. Feed Grains Council	1960	Grower, industry organizations

[a]In 1977, the National Livestock Feeders Association merged with the American National Cattlemen's Association to become the National Cattlemen's Association.

organization of the industry by commodity became nearly complete (see table 2).

As the intramural battles over price support policy dragged on into the sixties, the commodity lobbies collectively gained advantage, relative to the general farm organizations, and particularly relative to the Farm Bureau.

Their competitive advantage lay in part in specialization. "When an issue comes up about milk, for example, I want to know . . . what the members of the National Milk Producers think," Senator Bob Dole (R., Kan.) commented. "That's because I know the Milk Producers Federation represents dairy farmers. I may not always agree with them but I know what dairy farmers think by talking to them. This holds for most any livestock or commodity group." Historically, production of the various price supported commodities was concentrated in particular parts of the country, corn in the upper Mississippi Valley, cotton in the South and Southwest, wheat in the Plains and Northwest, and dairy in the Great Lakes and Middle Atlantic. After the war, moreover, new production technologies concentrated production still further. The commodity lobbies' conduits to their more differentiated constituencies, therefore, were major assets. As a former Wisconsin representative put it, "Congressmen tend to want to look at specifics on a commodity."[26] As the commodity organizations entrenched themselves in Washington, they offered much the same advantage over the general farm organizations as the latter had over the parties four decades before.[27]

In the early sixties, moreover, two circumstances conspired to assure their superiority.

First, the commodity organizations supported existing farm programs, and the Farm Bureau did not. In the late fifties and through the sixties, as farmers rejected the agricultural policies of the Farm Bureau and the GOP's conservative wing, they also confirmed the counsel of the commodity organizations. Collectively, the commodity groups represented the same people the Farm Bureau did. They, however, got the constituency story more nearly right.

Second, the commodity organizations pursued a "moderate" farm policy, rejecting both the extreme laissez-faire of the Farm Bureau and the extreme interventionism of the Farmers Union. Their freedom from ideological commitments soothed representatives from both parties after a decade of partisan backbiting. Moreover, their satisfaction with half a loaf in preference to none relieved beleaguered lawmakers after a

26. Gale Johnson, "Telling your story in Washington," *SF*, May 1978, p. 14; Interview with Lynn E. Stalbaum, December 1986; Interview with William C. Wampler, December 1986; Oral History Interview with Catherine May Bedell, Oral History Project of the Association of Former Members of Congress, Library of Congress, 1979, pp. 25, 62, 72–76; John Heinz, "The political impasse in farm support legislation," *Yale Law Journal*, 71 (1962), pp. 968–69; James T. Bonnen, "Observations on the nature of national agricultural policy decision processes, 1946–76," pp. 309–27 in Trudy Huskamp Peterson, ed., *Farmers, bureaucrats, and middlemen* (Washington: Howard University Press, 1980). As many scholars have noted, the narrowness of the new lobbies also meshed with the increasing fragmentation of congressional committees. Agriculture conformed to the pattern. In 1955, it reorganized its subcommittees. It replaced its few generic subcommittees—named Number 1, Number 2 and Number 3—with sixteen jurisdictional subcommittees, nine of which handled particular commodities. See David R. Mayhew, *Congress: The electoral connection* (New Haven: Yale University Press, 1974), pp. 94–97; Roger H. Davidson, "Subcommittee government: New channels for policy making," pp. 99–133 in Thomas E. Mann and Norman J. Ornstein, eds., *The new Congress* (Washington: American Enterprise Institute, 1981); Browne, "Farm organizations and agribusiness," pp. 200–201.

27. McConnell attributed the preference for more specialized interest groups to a "deep-seated [ideological] faith in the virtue of small units of social and political organization." This analysis suggests, however, that lawmakers' preferences for specialized informants stem instead from the more practical problem of getting reelected. Whether as a result of an ideological orthodoxy or not, decentralization was built into the institutional structure of American government, and specialized informants help lawmakers to cope with it. See Grant McConnell, *Private power and American democracy* (New York: Alfred A. Knopf, 1966), p. 5 and pp. 241–43; more generally, part 1 and chap. 10.

decade under siege. In the phrase of a Texas congressman, the commodity groups were "reasonable," unlike the Farmers Union and Farm Bureau.[28]

Over the course of the sixties, consequently, the commodity organizations won wider and wider access to the deliberations of the House Agriculture Committee. "The commodity groups combined," a senior House aide told a reporter in 1979, "are what the Farm Bureau was in the 1940s, '50s and '60s."[29]

The terms of farm lobby access, however, had since changed radically. Farm lawmakers paid much less heed to what the farm organizations wanted and much greater heed to what they could get the farm organizations to accept.

In 1969, for instance, farm state representatives flatly informed the farm groups that the Committee was perfectly willing to write the program itself, with or without their blessing, if that was what it took to pass one. "Whatever the farmers of the country might agree on, whatever the agriculture committees of the House and Senate might agree on, unless the program costs less, unless it shows real promise in creating

28. Interview with Graham B. Purcell, December 1986; Browne, "Farm organizations and agribusiness," p. 203; Harold D. Guither, The food lobbyists (Lexington, Mass.: Lexington Books, 1980), p. 163; William P. Browne and Charles W. Wiggins, "Interest group strength and organizational characteristics: The general farm organizations and the 1977 farm bill," pp. 109–21 in Don F. Hadwiger and William P. Browne, eds., The new politics of food (Lexington, Mass.: Lexington Books, 1978), p. 110. Throughout the sixties and seventies, the Farm Bureau refused steadfastly to cooperate in the commodity groups' "political logrolling." The Farmers Union dropped in and out of the coalitions, depending upon what was at stake. Interview with Roger Fleming, December 1986; Interview with Reuben L. Johnson, July 1990; Eugene Butler and Jay Richter, "What's new in Washington," PF, November 1957, p. 8; Donald T. Donnelly, "Washington from the inside," Nation's Agriculture, December 1970, p. 5.

29. Marcia Zarley, "Washington report," SF, November 1979, p. 14; Johnson interview; Bonnen, "Observations on the nature of national agricultural policy decision processes"; Michael S. Lyons and Marcia Whicker Taylor, "Farm politics in transition: The House Agriculture Committee," Agricultural History, 55 (April 1981), pp. 128–46; William P. Browne, "Policy and interests: Instability and change in a classic issue subsystem," pp. 182–201 in Allan J. Cigler and Burdett A. Loomis, eds., Interest group politics, 2d ed. (Washington: Congressional Quarterly Press, 1986); Guither, Food lobbyists; Weldon V. Barton, "Coalition-building in the United States House of Representatives: Agricultural legislation in 1973," pp. 141–61 in James E. Anderson, ed., Cases in public policy-making (New York: Praeger, 1976); John G. Peters, "The 1981 farm bill," pp. 157– 73 in Don F. Hadwiger and Ross B. Talbot, eds., Food policy and farm programs (New York: Academy of Political Science, 1982); William P. Browne, Private interests, public policy, and American agriculture (Lawrence: University Press of Kansas, 1988). The farm bill hearings, followed over time, also indicate greater prominence for the commodity lobbies. Starting in the sixties, Agriculture's members recognized them as the equals of the general farm groups. They allotted them more time, granted them earlier appearances and questioned them more expansively (especially when they appeared in coalition).

programs that will give the farmer better income for his labor and capital, we are just spinning our wheels in trying to get support from Congress," Washington Republican Catherine May told Fred Heinkel, the representative of the National Farm Coalition. "I don't know whether you agree with my evaluation, but I think we all have to face the harsh reality of the situation."[30]

When negotiations with the farm groups did not avail, the Agriculture Committee went its own way. The chairman, Bob Poage (D., Tex.), and the senior Republican, Page Belcher (R., Okla.), led it in closed-door bargaining sessions with Agriculture Secretary Clifford Hardin, and by the time the 1970 Agriculture Act came to the floor, none of the major farm organizations supported it. The farm lobby fretted and fumed, but the House passed the farm bill without a single change. "The legislation was put together by Secretary of Agriculture Hardin and members of the Agriculture Committees of the Congress," a farm reporter noted. "The non-government groups which are supposed to represent farmers had little to do with the whole process."[31] A decade earlier, lawmakers would have considered such actions daring, even foolhardy. The politics of the 1970 farm bill showed how much legislators' relationships with the farm lobby had changed.[32]

To be sure, the instance was an extreme one—the Committee preferred not to impose a program on the farm lobby—but it was not atypical. On the one hand, rural legislators were eager to assure the farm organizations that they were on their side. "Is there anyone here who believes we have a cheap food policy in this country?" Missouri Democrat Harold L. Volkmer asked a farm organization panel in 1981. "Yes or no?"

---

30. *Hearings before the House Agriculture Committee*, "General farm program and food stamp program," 91st Congress, 1st session, Serial Q, 1969 (hereafter *Hearings, 1969*), p. 100, pp. 92, 125, 158–60, 499–500, 963, 990, 1010–11.

31. Wayne E. Swegle, "Do farmers care about farm programs?" *SF*, January 1971, p. 20; *KAL*, 12 December 1969; *KAL*, 1 May 1970; *KAL*, 29 May 1970; *KAL*, 9 July 1970; *WFL* No. 1400, 24 July 1970; *WFL* No. 1402, 7 August 1970; *WFL* No. 1411, 9 October 1970; *WFL* No. 1412, 16 October 1970; Donald T. Donnelly, "Washington: Assignment agriculture," *Nation's Agriculture*, September 1970, p. 11; "Credit Page Belcher with a bipartisan farm bill," *PF*, September 1971, p. 56; Poage memoirs, pp. 1300–1301; Clarence D. Palmby, *Made in Washington: Food policy and the political expedient* (Danville, Ill.: The Interstate Printers and Publishers, 1985), pp. 46–50. "Clifford Hardin now has the distinction of being the first Secretary of Agriculture in modern times to be opposed by every major national farm organization," *Successful Farming* noted. "Washington report," *SF*, November 1970, p. 7.

32. Compare 1959, when Agriculture Committee members found it difficult to imagine that they might have to act without the benediction of the farm groups. See *Hearings, 1959*, p. 82–83, 90, 178.

HILTON BRACEY (Midcontinent Farmers Association): I think we would all have to agree with that. . . .
VOLKMER: Does anybody disagree that we should work toward raising grain prices? Does anyone disagree with that?
REAGAN V. BROWN (Texas Agriculture Commissioner): Congressman, does anyone on this panel or anyone in this country have to apologize to the American consumer who is buying food with about 14 percent of his disposable income? . . . In no place else in the world can this be done. . . .
VOLKMER: I believe there probably is no one on the panel who does not agree that production costs to the farmer are going to increase again. Everyone agrees with that—right?
BROWN: Right.
VOLKMER: Thank you very much.[33]

In fact, Committee members sometimes undertook to demonstrate that they were willing to push harder than the farm groups were. "Even though I consider all of you my friends and we have mutual interests toward the same goal, I do not believe we can obtain the best farm program this session if we sit here and agree with each other," South Dakota Democrat Frank Denholm told the representatives of the National Farm Coalition in 1973.

I will therefore disagree with you and seek your response. I am disturbed about leadership of farm organizations today. If you are not interested in writing a farm program when the farmers are in a relatively favorable market position then what do you expect to obtain when they are not? You are not asking for much and I am sure that you are not going to get much. You are being sold out again. The farmers are being neglected in this country and you are being subjected to markets of the world this time instead of just the domestic markets. I suspect that by fall you will have a different view but it may be too late then. . . . You are taken in one at a time. You are taken in by one commodity at a time and nobody has the crust to stand up for the people at home and on the farms of America. If you fellows who lead the farm organizations do not do it, who is going to do it? Do you think a consumer-dominated Congress is going to do it for you?[34]

33. *Hearings before the House Agriculture Committee,* "General farm bill of 1981," 97th Congress, 1st session, Serial 97-G, 1981 (hereafter *Hearings,* 1981), pp. 146–48, 159–61, Part 3, pp. 26-27, 198–99, 217–18, Part 5, pp. 28, 55, Part 7, p. 149; *Hearings,* 1969, pp. 95, 97, 102, 277, 538, 959; *Hearings before the House Agriculture Committee,* "General farm program," 93d Congress, 1st session, Serial 93-K, 1973 (hereafter *Hearings,* 1973), pp. 27, 31–32, 204, 207, 414–16; *Hearings before the House Agriculture Committee,* "General farm bill," 95th Congress, 1st session, Serial 95-H, 1977 (hereafter *Hearings,* 1977), pp. 123, 148, 195, 234, 289, Part 4, pp. 165–67, 175–76.
34. *Hearings,* 1973, pp. 136–37, 133, 168, 262–63, 493–96; *Hearings,* 1969, pp. 547, 1151; *Hearings,* 1977, p. 291; *Hearings,* 1981, p. 29.

On the other hand, farm state lawmakers took pains that the farm lobby appreciate the difficulties under which they labored. The farm groups could rest assured that the Committee was on their side, they stressed, but the Committee could only do so much. "I think the payment limitations are not fundamentally sound," Bob Poage told cotton growers who came in 1973 to complain about them. "And yet I believe that the majority of the Congress wants to do it. I think you gentlemen must recognize that while this committee will not do it to you, the majority of this Congress probably will. You have to get to work on these people who are living in these areas where they are not interested in cotton."[35]

Moreover, they emphasized, as much as the Committee sympathized with the farm organizations, it simply could not accommodate their demands beyond a certain point. "My general impression is that [price support] rates should go up," the new Agriculture chairman, Thomas S. Foley (D., Wash.), told a reporter in 1975, "but just how much is something we have to wait on. I've tried to urge the farm organizations not to get inflexible on numbers." The fundamental problem, after all, was not of the Committee's making.

WILLIAM M. THOMAS (R., Cal.): The first thing you have to do with [the] administration, especially during a year when the farm bill is up for reconsideration, is to get them to buy the concept of a target price.

CECIL WILLIAMS, JR. (Agricultural Council of Arkansas): Right.

THOMAS: . . . If we can salvage the concept of the target price, doesn't it make more sense that it would be easier to sell a target price concept if it were also based in some way on some market price, if we are so market oriented in terms of our push?

WILLIAMS: I would say that that makes a lot of sense. I don't know that I am ready to agree with you 100 percent, but it sure makes a lot—

THOMAS: Around here you take 51 percent and run.[36]

---

35. *Hearings,* 1973, pp. 262–63; *Hearings,* 1973, pp. 92, 120–22; *Hearings,* 1977, p. 412; *Hearings,* 1981, Part 3, pp. 191–92, 201, 221, Part 5, pp. 84–88, 91–92. Committee members also demonstrated their own good intentions by contrasting them with what would happen if they left the policy decisions up to the secretary of agriculture, who was under pressure from consumers, the president and the budget bureau to pursue a "cheap food" policy. See *Hearings,* 1969, pp. 93–94, 1136; *Hearings,* 1973, pp. 331, 482; *Hearings,* 1977, Part 4, p. 218; *Hearings,* 1981, p. 106.

36. Alan Ehrenhalt, "House Agriculture: New faces, new issues," *Congressional Quarterly Weekly Report* (hereafter *CQWR*), 22 February 1975, p. 384; *Hearings before the House Agriculture Committee, Subcommittee on Cotton, Rice, and Sugar,* "General farm bill of 1981 (Cotton, rice, and sugar programs)," 97th Congress, 1st session, Serial 97-G, Part 3, 1981, pp. 219–20; *Hearings,* 1977, p. 292; *Hearings,* 1981, Part 7, pp. 172–73.

From the late sixties into the early eighties, in sum, the terms of farm lobby access changed dramatically. Sometimes, farm lawmakers could help the farm organizations; sometimes, they could not. When it could, the Committee was ready to cooperate, but it was also ready, if need be, to deny. In the early 1960s, a Kennedy administration official recalled, the endorsement of the farm groups was "very important" to the success of agricultural legislation on the Hill. In the late 1970s, a Carter administration official said, "we didn't spend a lot of time on that."[37] Access to the House Agriculture Committee no longer carried with it carte blanche.

Farm lawmakers, of course, gave much less heed to the views of their farm lobby allies in part out of simple necessity. "In the House of Representatives it is always difficult to get a decent farm bill," Indiana Democrat Floyd J. Fithian reminded the soybean lobby in 1981. "Here about a 100 of us have any sizable number of farmers and about 335 don't have enough farmers to fit in this room. Under those conditions, it is very difficult to convince downtown Chicago or downtown New York or downtown Cleveland that it is in their best interests to come forth with a very generous farm bill." The members of the Agriculture Committee were no longer representative of the whole House, and they refrained from making promises that they knew they could not keep.[38]

Their newfound willingness to stand up to the farm lobby had another source, too, an even more important one. Like their predecessors, members of the House Agriculture Committee represented farm districts. Compared to their forebears, however, they represented substantially fewer farmers. The same migrations that transformed the United States Congress transformed rural constituencies as well (see table 3). Between 1950 and 1970, the countryside emptied with breathtaking rapidity, even in districts represented almost continuously on the House Agriculture Committee. In the Midwest, where farms were traditionally large and owner operated, the farm population fell steadily. Farmers in

37. Interview with Edwin A. Jaenke, December 1986; Interview with Dale E. Hathaway, December 1986. See also *KAL*, 3 January 1975; *KAL*, 31 January 1975; Lyons and Taylor, "Farm politics in transition," pp. 136–37; Robert P. Weber, "Home style and committee behavior: The case of Richard Nolan," pp. 71–94 in Morris P. Fiorina and David W. Rohde, eds., *Home style and Washington work: Studies of congressional politics* (Ann Arbor: University of Michigan Press, 1989), pp. 83–87.

38. *Hearings before the House Agriculture Committee, Subcommittee on Wheat, Soybeans, and Feed Grains,* "General farm bill of 1981 (Wheat, soybeans, and feed grains)," 97th Congress, 1st session, Serial 97-G, Part 5, 1981, p. 91. Compare the Agriculture Committee's anticipation of the floor's reactions to the Interior Committee's in the same period, when they faced similar constraints. See Richard F. Fenno, Jr., *Congressmen in committees* (Boston: Little, Brown and Co., 1973), pp. 57–64, 122–23.

Table 3. Farm population in selected House districts, 1950–1980

State	District	Major city	1950 (%)	1960 (%)	1970 (%)	1980 (%)
			Census/reapportionment year			
Indiana	10-10-10-2	Muncie	20.2	13.6	11.7	5.1
Illinois	20-20-20-20	Quincy	30.3	16.8	10.2	7.5
Iowa	8-6-6-6	Sioux City	32.9	31.7	25.2	18.5
Minnesota	1-1-1-1	Rochester	32.9	22.5	13.6	13.9
North Dakota	AL-1-1-AL	Fargo	41.1	31.0	24.7	15.9
Kansas	5-1-1-1	Dodge City	28.3	23.2	20.2	14.0
North Carolina	4-4-4-4	Raleigh	40.3	19.5	4.4	2.7
Georgia	2-2-2-2	Albany	42.8	22.4	9.5	6.1
Tennessee	6-6-6-7	Clarksville	48.6	28.1	12.0	4.3
Mississippi	3-1-1-1	Tupelo	61.9	31.9	32.8	4.8
Arkansas	1-1-1-1	Jonesboro	56.2	29.7	15.3	7.0
Texas	11-11-11-11	Waco	21.3	10.0	7.7	3.8

Sources. 1950: U.S. Bureau of the Census, *1956 county and city data book;* 1960, 1970: U.S. Bureau of the Census, *Congressional district data book,* 88th Congress and 93d Congress; 1980: U.S. Bureau of the Census, *Congressional districts of the 98th Congress* (except Texas and North Dakota), U.S. Bureau of the Census, *Congressional districts of the 99th Congress* (Texas), U.S. Bureau of the Census, *Statistical abstract of the United States,* 1985 (North Dakota).

Minnesota's First District, where dairy predominated, dropped from 32.9 percent of the population in 1950 to 13.9 percent in 1980. On the other hand, in the South, where farms were traditionally small and tenant operated, the farm population fell precipitously. Farmers in Arkansas's First, where cotton and rice predominated, dropped from 56.2 percent of the population in 1950 to only 7.0 percent in 1980.[39] By the late sixties, farmers were simply a lot less prominent, even in the nation's most agricultural constituencies.

Even in farm districts, therefore, farmers carried a lot less electoral weight than they ever had before. "There is no real farm vote that can be counted on by politicians," Kiplinger argued, with a bit of hyperbole, in 1964. "Rural voting power is now in the hands of the mass of nonfarmers." Because farm districts contained fewer farmers, moreover,

39. The depopulation of the southern farm belt occurred for two primary reasons. First, increasingly attractive employment opportunities in manufacturing and services, especially for blacks, drew tens of thousands of tenants, croppers and smallholders into southern and northern cities. Second, new farming practices displaced agricultural labor. The 1950s saw rapid mechanization of cotton production, especially cotton harvesting. The 1960s, moreover, saw King Cotton deposed, as farmers shifted from labor-intensive cotton and tobacco to soybeans, feed grains and livestock. See Gilbert C. Fite, *Cotton fields no more: Southern agriculture, 1865–1980* (Lexington: University Press of Kentucky, 1984), chaps. 9–10.

price support policy was less salient than ever before. "Fewer farm state congressmen fear for their political lives as to how they vote on farm *price supports than in years gone by—as long as they stand fast against abolishing supports," Darrow observed in 1962. "Many farm district Republicans have voted against Democratic farm bills for 25 years and survived. Their experience hasn't gone unnoticed." Because price support policy was less salient, finally, the electoral impact of the farm lobby was more difficult to discern. "Congressmen seem to be increasingly skeptical of the ability of lobby organizations in general to either deliver or withhold members' votes in most elections," a farm reporter noted. Except in a few isolated instances, the language of "farm revolt" disappeared from the political lexicon.[40]

The consequences of failing to adapt to demographic change were well illustrated by the termination of the career of Harold D. Cooley, the chairman of the House Agriculture Committee from 1949 to 1966. A Yale-trained lawyer, Cooley began his political life in the early 1930s, when he argued the growers' position in negotiations to establish a North Carolina tobacco cooperative. In 1934, he won election to the House from the Fourth Congressional District, and once in Congress, he established himself as a tireless advocate of tobacco growers and a faithful New Dealer. Until 1956, when he refused to sign the segregationist Southern Manifesto, he faced only limited electoral opposition. In 1964, however, Cooley defeated Republican James C. Gardner by only five thousand votes. Gardner attacked the incumbent "for being too oriented to peanuts and tobacco and ignoring the chance to bring new industry into the district." The charges had some merit. When Cooley was first elected, almost half of his constituents were employed in agriculture, and his position on the Agriculture Committee was a substantial boon (see table 4). In 1964, however, only 10 percent of the work force was engaged in farming, and the Fourth's major city, Raleigh, was rapidly developing both industry and finance. In an attempt to preserve him, the state legislature redrew the district's boundaries, but it did him

40. KAL, 22 May 1964; WFL No. 991, 15 September 1962; "What's new in Washington," SF, June 1964, p. 11; WFL No. 961, 17 February 1962; "What's new in Washington," SF, June 1962, p. 17; "What's new in Washington," SF, June 1965, p. 11; WFL No. 1283, 19 April 1968; "Washington report," SF, June/July 1970, p. 7; KAL, 7 August 1970; KAL, 19 February 1971; "Washington report," SF, January 1971, p. 7; WFL No. 1414, 30 October 1970; WFL No. 1415, 6 November 1970; KAL, 14 April 1972; WFL No. 1491, 5 May 1972; KAL, 9 June 1972; WFL No. 1518, 10 November 1972; "What the election did to your ag committees in Congress," Farm Journal, December 1972, p. 19; WFL No. 1622, 8 November 1974; KAL, 31 January 1975; "Washington report," SF, June/July 1975, p. 4; "Washington report," SF, September 1976, p. 4; KAL, 6 October 1978; KAL, 14 November 1980; "Outlook: Washington," Farm Journal, December 1980, p. 7.

Table 4.   Agriculture in the economy of North Carolina's Fourth District, 1930–1965

Reapportionment/ census year	Employed in agriculture[a] (%)	Cropland in tobacco[b] (%)	District income from tobacco[c] (%)
1930	52	47	
1940	40	22	
1950	31	17	23.1
1960	16	15	16.3
1965	10	18	13.6

Sources. U.S. Bureau of the Census, *Census of population (North Carolina)*, 1930, 1940, 1950, 1960; U.S. Bureau of the Census, *Census of agriculture (North Carolina)*, 1930, 1940, 1950, 1959, 1964.
[a] Percentage of the district work force employed in agriculture.
[b] Percentage of crop acreage planted to tobacco.
[c] Receipts from sale of tobacco as a percentage of estimated district income.

no good. In 1966, arguing that the incumbent was too wedded to North Carolina's "agricultural past," Gardner beat Cooley by fourteen thousand votes.[41]

As Cooley's predicament indicated, investments in the welfare of farmers returned smaller and smaller dividends in the sixties and the seventies. Accordingly, lawmakers in districts that had once been incontestably agricultural sought to diversify their coalitions beyond farmers. In the Midwest, the diminishing farm population forced Republican candidates to branch out, while the growing urban population gave Democratic candidates a base on which to build. In the late 1950s, for instance, Iowa Republican Charles B. Hoeven had increasing difficulty holding his seat because of the declining vote in the country and the rising vote in Sioux City. After his retirement in 1964 the district seesawed back and forth between Republicans and Democrats.[42]

41. Like other southern Republicans in 1966, Gardner also tied Cooley to the civil rights policies of the Johnson administration. Cooley was a fairly reliable supporter of the Democratic leadership. "Congress: Running hard to stand still," *Business Week*, 10 October 1964, p. 63; "Biographies of new representatives from the South," *CQWR*, 2 December 1966, p. 2944; *WDWF* No. 656, 7 April 1956; *WFL* 1203, 7 October 1966; *WFL* No. 1208, 11 November 1966; Anthony J. Badger, *Prosperity road: The New Deal, tobacco, and North Carolina* (Chapel Hill: University of North Carolina Press, 1980), pp. 30, 215, 264n. On other Agriculture members with similar difficulties, see *WFL* No. 1490, 28 April 1972; *WFL* No. 1491, 5 May 1972; *WFL* No. 1599, 31 May 1974; and *WFL* No. 1611, 23 August 1974.

42. "What farmers are saying in an election year," *U.S. News and World Report*, 25 April 1958, p. 52; "At the grassroots: Good news for the Democrats," *U.S. News and World Report*, 14 March 1958, pp. 66–67; Dale Kramer, "Pigs and pocketbooks," *Reporter*, 18 October 1956, pp. 25–27. See also F. A. Jimson, "Farm politics," *WF*, 8 Febru-

In the South, in contrast, the shrinking farm vote forced Democratic candidates to branch out, while the advancing suburban population gave Republican candidates a constituency on which to build. In 1968, for instance, the Fifth District of North Carolina elected Republican Wilmer D. (Vinegar Bend) Mizell, once a star southpaw for the Pittsburgh Pirates (14–9 in 1960, the year the Bucs won the World Series). The Fifth's agriculture revolved around tobacco (R. J. Reynolds) and poultry (Holly Farms). Mizell's main interest, however, was rural development. The rapid growth in the Davidson County suburbs of Winston-Salem and High Point fed off of the largest rural water system in the country, providing Mizell with a ready suburban interest in his work on the Agriculture Committee.[43] In short, the collapse of the farm constituency pushed rural lawmakers in the 1960s and 1970s into coalitions less dependent on the good graces of farm producers.

To be sure, farm state representatives still could not ignore farmers, and they devised ingenious new ways of appealing to them. They issued rousing calls for more benefits. The ink was barely dry on the 1973 Agriculture and Consumer Protection Act, for instance, when Minnesota Republican John Zwach introduced legislation to hike its target prices. Likewise, they cast the powers that opposed them—particularly the Department of Agriculture—in the role of the villain. Montana Democrat John Melcher, for example, "tarred [Agriculture Secretary Clifford Hardin] with representing the Budget Bureau and not the farmers" and won election to the House in a 1969 special election. The impossibility of actually raising farm subsidies—and the pleasing effect on farmers of trying—spurred rural lawmakers to ever greater rhetorical heights.[44]

---

ary 1975, p. 6; James C. Larew, *A party reborn: The Democrats of Iowa, 1950–1974* (Iowa City: Iowa State Historical Department, 1980), pp. 21–28; Thomas G. Ryan, "The early years of the Iowa Democratic revival, 1950–1956," *Annals of Iowa*, 46 (Summer 1981), pp. 43–63; Ralph Harvey, *Autobiography of a Hoosier congressman* (Greenfield, Ind.: Mitchell-Fleming Printing, 1975), pp. 60, 64–79. Democrats who attempted to build a coalition of labor and farmers, like Joseph P. Vigorito of Pennsylvania, encountered the same problem. For years, Vigorito recounted, he "had the farmers eating out of my hand" because of his work on the Agriculture Committee. Unfortunately, "every year, there were fewer and fewer farmers." When Vigorito took office, in 1965, the Twenty-fourth District (Erie) included twenty-six thousand farm residents; when Vigorito left office, in 1976, they numbered only fourteen thousand. Interview with Joseph P. Vigorito, July 1990.

43. Interview with Wilmer D. Mizell, December 1986; Jay Richter, "Farm boy congressman," *PF*, February 1970, p. 154.

44. *KAL*, 27 June 1969; *WFL* No. 1575, 14 December 1973; F. R. Jimson, "Farm politics," *WF*, 23 February 1974, p. 12; *KAL*, 8 November 1974; "What's new from Washington," *PF*, January 1975, p. 13; F. R. Jimson, "Farm politics," *WF*, 26 June 1976,

A district in which one-tenth of the population farmed, however, was still very different from a district in which one-half of the population farmed. As the numbers of agricultural producers in congressional constituencies declined, the ability of the farm lobby to serve the information and propaganda needs of rural members of Congress correspondingly shrank. The House Agriculture Committee progressed from militant, even arrogant, promotions of the farm organizations' wishes to candid, pragmatic denials. In the 1960s and 1970s, the farm lobby's forceful and sustained aria faded behind a chorus of urban voices.[45]

The Moment Passes: The Consumer Lobby and Access in Agriculture

By the 1960s, the farm lobby—in one form or another—had monopolized access to farm price support deliberations for an entire generation. Even as rural voting power had waned, and even as the farm bloc's ability to write its own ticket had declined, the farm lobby faced no substantial competition for the loyalties of those in Congress who wrote farm bills. The farm lobby's success in meeting the electoral needs of congressional agrarians guaranteed that the Agriculture Committee would do everything it could to help, even if it could not always do very much.

In the early 1970s, however, the farm lobby's hegemony over access in agriculture faced its first direct challenge since the expulsion of farm processor interests in the late 1920s. It arose from predictable quarters.

In the middle 1960s, American consumerism bloomed for the third time. As in the Progressive Era and in the New Deal, a resurgence of liberal reformism fostered demands for limitations on the prerogatives of producers and expansions of the rights of consumers.[46]

More often leading than following, liberal politicians eased the movement along. In March 1962, President John F. Kennedy sent a consumer message to Congress, the first of its kind and the first of three that

---

p. 8; "The high cost of Herman Talmadge," *New Republic*, 1 April 1978, p. 5; "Outlook: Washington," *Farm Journal*, June/July 1979, p. 8; "Outlook: Washington," *Farm Journal*, September 1979, p. 6; "New faces, new issues," *Congressional Quarterly Weekly Report*, 22 February 1975, p. 383; Weber, "Home style," pp. 71–94; Mayhew, *Congress*, pp. 63–64.

45. For similar conclusions in a different context, see Amihai Glazer and Marc Robbins, "Congressional responsiveness to constituency change," *American Journal of Political Science*, 29 (May 1985), pp. 259–73.

46. Robert N. Mayer, *The consumer movement: Guardians of the marketplace* (Boston: Twayne Publishers, 1989), chap. 2; Mark V. Nadel, *The politics of consumer protection* (Indianapolis: Bobbs-Merrill Company, 1971), chaps. 1–2.

he and Lyndon Johnson would deliver. In January 1964, President Johnson created the President's Council on Consumer Interests, heading it with a half-time special assistant for consumer affairs, Assistant Labor Secretary Esther Peterson. Beginning in 1962, with the Kefauver Amendments to the Food and Drug Act, Congress took up dozens of consumer protection proposals and passed them: the National Traffic and Motor Vehicle Safety Act of 1966, the Fair Packaging and Labeling Act of 1966, the Truth in Lending Act of 1968, the Consumer Product Safety Act of 1972, and others. By the late 1960s, the consumer movement was among the most prominent actors in Washington, with "consumer crusader" Ralph Nader furthest out in front.[47]

In its initial thrust, the consumer movement had little to do with agriculture. Throughout the 1960s, it concentrated on problems of consumer information and product safety rather than on problems of consumer price, even when such issues could potentially be framed.[48] In 1966, for instance, a sudden jump in retail food prices provoked an outcry from consumers and set off local boycotts of supermarket chains, starting in Denver and spreading to other parts of the country. National consumer advocates generally ignored them, however, and local boycott leaders declined to link their problems, even in part, to the government farm program. Despite Republican hopes that the food price issue might be exploited in the 1966 elections, as one more instance of the Democrats' irresponsible management of the economy, the protest faded without the question of federal food policy ever being raised.[49]

47. "A new era in consumer affairs," *Consumer Reports*, March 1964, pp. 143–44; Mayer, *Consumer movement*, chaps. 2–3; Nadel, *Consumer protection*, chaps. 2–5; David E. Price, *Who makes the laws? Creativity and power in Senate committees* (Cambridge: Schenkman Publishing Co., 1972), chap. 2; Jeffrey M. Berry, *Lobbying for the people* (Princeton: Princeton University Press, 1977).

48. When price issues were raised at all, which was seldom, the questioners were typically business interests. See, e.g., "Government keeps food prices high," *Nation's Business,* June 1964, pp. 38ff.

49. Farm state politicians, a little anxious about the food price inflation, used the occasion to attack the monopolistic practices of the food processing industry, an attack that boycott leaders concurred in. "The few and the many," *New Republic,* 26 February 1966, pp. 7–8; "Will food prices rise in coming months?" *Business Week,* 2 April 1966, pp. 31–33; William M. Blair, "Senate requests price rise study," *NYT,* 4 August 1966, p. 67; "Fighting over food bills," *Business Week,* 6 August 1966, pp. 31–32; James J. Nagle, "Food price rises stir resentment," *NYT,* 16 October 1966, p. III 1; "Housewives speak on inflation," *NYT,* 30 October 1966, p. IV 2; "Supermarket price protest spreads to 21 states," *NYT,* 30 October 1966, p. 56; David R. Jones, "G.O.P. fears food boycott weakens its inflation issue," *NYT,* 2 November 1966, p. 1; Ovid Bay, "Who won the food price war?" *Farm Journal,* December 1966, pp. 24ff.; "When middlemen are in the middle," *Business Week,* 26 August 1967, pp. 26–27; Monroe Peter Friedman, "The 1966 con-

Table 5. Food price inflation: Percentage changes in retail consumer prices, 1960–1981

Year	Food (%)	All items (%)	Difference (%)
1960	1.0	1.6	−0.6
1961	1.3	1.0	0.3
1962	0.9	1.1	−0.2
1963	1.4	1.2	0.2
1964	1.3	1.3	0.0
1965	2.2	1.7	0.5
1966	5.0	2.9	2.1
1967	0.9	2.9	−2.0
1968	3.6	4.2	−0.6
1969	5.1	5.4	−0.3
1970	5.5	5.9	−0.4
1971	3.0	4.3	−1.3
1972	4.3	3.3	1.0
1973	14.5	6.2	8.3
1974	14.4	11.0	3.4
1975	8.5	9.1	−0.6
1976	3.1	5.8	−2.7
1977	6.3	6.5	−0.2
1978	10.0	7.7	2.3
1979	10.9	11.3	−0.4
1980	8.6	13.5	−4.9
1981	7.9	10.4	−2.5

Source. Economic report of the president, 1984, p. 284.

In the early 1970s, however, consumer interest in farm policy increased sharply. After several decades of modest increases in food prices—typically smaller than the overall rate of inflation—the retail cost of food leapt skyward. In 1972, food prices rose more quickly than inflation, for the first time since 1966, and in 1973 and 1974 the picture worsened (see table 5). Food prices escalated at a double-digit pace, surpassing 14 percent, or more than twice the overall rate of inflation.

The rapid run-up in food prices was driven by unusually strong demand and unusually short supply, in both of which government had its hand. First, President Nixon's Phase II wage and price controls exempted raw agricultural products and allowed food manufacturers, like other manufacturers, to pass along those increased costs. Second, the administration, and especially Agriculture Secretary Earl L. Butz, eagerly promoted agricultural exports, particularly grains and red meats. In July 1972, in fact, it announced the completion of the first large sale of

sumer protest as seen by its leaders," Journal of Consumer Affairs, 5 (Summer 1971), pp. 1–23.

American wheat to the Soviet Union, beginning a sustained run on the grain exchanges.[50] Finally, the government pursued a policy of artificial scarcity in agricultural markets. With the price support and adjustment programs, it directly regulated the supply of supported commodities (like corn and wheat) and indirectly regulated the supply of downstream commodities (like meat). With the marketing agreement programs, moreover, it tightly controlled the supply and price of milk, nuts, fruits and vegetables.[51]

Consequently, the food price inflation of the early 1970s directed unprecedented public scrutiny onto the role of the federal government in agricultural price making. "A wave of anti-farm-program mail is snowing under a large number of congressmen, senators, and bureaucrats," Kiplinger reported in 1972. "Farm programs in general are in trouble unless [the] public forgets some of the things it has learned from the recent Soviet wheat publicity." Eager to exploit the public discontent, consumer groups mobilized. For a week in April 1973, consumers nationwide boycotted beef, their actions coordinated by labor, women's and consumer groups and encouraged by urban lawmakers. "One welcome consequence of double-digit inflation is that consumers are more curious about who's picking their pockets, and how," the *New Republic*

50. In the last half of 1973, as export demand intensified, wheat and corn broke record prices for every futures contract month on the Chicago Board of Trade, and on single days early in 1974 they broke record prices again, closing at levels 50 to 100 percent above highs established twenty-five (and in some cases sixty-five) years before. Like most speculative runs, the advances were rapid and unstable. For eleven consecutive days in August 1973, wheat closed up the daily trading limit at Chicago, posting over a dollar's rise in two weeks' time. From May to December of 1973, likewise, corn closed up the limit twenty-four times and down the limit twenty-three. The market's volatility forced the Board of Trade to broaden the daily trading limits for wheat, corn, soybeans and feed grains. See Chicago Board of Trade, *Statistical annual* (Chicago: Board of Trade of the City of Chicago, 1973 and 1974).

51. Muriel Allen, "Scapegoats and sacred cows," *New Republic*, 22 July 1972, pp. 13–14; "Critics rail, but supermarkets ask: why us?" *Business Week*, 22 April 1972, pp. 97–98; Julius Duscha, "Up, up, up—Butz makes hay down on the farm," *New York Times Magazine*, 16 April 1972, pp. 34ff.; "A flop and a fraud," *Nation*, 18 June 1973, pp. 772–73; "Selling and buying," *New Republic*, 28 July 1973, p. 10; Roger LeRoy Miller, "The helping hand behind food prices," *Harper's*, February 1974, pp. 16–26; "Those soaring food prices," *New Republic*, 12 October 1974, pp. 5–7; Paul W. MacAvoy, ed., *Federal milk marketing orders and price supports* (Washington: American Enterprise Institute, 1977); Marvin H. Kosters, *Controls and inflation: The Economic Stabilization Program in retrospect* (Washington: American Enterprise Institute, 1975), chaps. 2, 4; Kenneth J. Fedor and Reginald J. Brown, "The design and implementation of food price regulations," pp. 107–43 in John T. Dunlop and Kenneth J. Fedor, eds., *The lessons of wage and price controls: The food sector* (Boston: Harvard University Graduate School of Business Administration, 1977).

noted. "People are asking what portion of recent price hikes represent unavoidably higher costs, what represents high profits, and what reflects noncompetitive market power and politically-secured favors. When they learn that their food bills are bigger because of government mis-regulation or government-sanctioned combinations in restraint of trade, consumers may get mad enough to do more than plant victory gardens."[52]

The consumer uproar over food prices in the early seventies dramatically altered the mix of incentives for urban lawmakers in agriculture. For the first time in decades, food allocation and pricing policy had the earmarks of a big issue. The media's attention to food prices increased tenfold in 1972, and it redoubled in 1973 (see table 6). Rapid food price inflation drew the public's attention to agricultural policy and raised constituents' interest in what their legislators had to say about it. The sharp increase in the cost of food created new opportunities for congressional position taking.

As the spotlight of the consumer movement moved to agricultural policy, then, so did the concerns of congressional consumer advocates. In February 1972, Representative Benjamin S. Rosenthal, a Queens Democrat, and Senator Jacob Javits, a New York Republican, called on President Nixon to bring raw agricultural prices under Phase II wage and price guidelines. In April 1973, the House Banking Committee resolved in favor of a proposal offered by Chicago Democrat Frank Annunzio to roll back prices, including basic agricultural prices. And in March 1973, in front of the Grand Union Supermarket at 86th Street and First Avenue in Manhattan, Congressman Rosenthal issued a call for a national consumer boycott of beef. "Although many local groups had started organizing their own boycotts since meat prices began spiraling upward this year," the *Times* reported, "Mr. Rosenthal said that they were all convinced 'that their protests will be taken seriously and translated into effective Federal action only if their movement has a national focus.'"[53]

52. *KAL*, 13 October 1972; "Those soaring food prices," *New Republic*, 12 October 1974, p. 7; *KAL*, 1 September 1972; "Showdown time for the farm program," *Business Week*, 24 February 1973, pp. 26–27; "The outrage over the food budget," *Business Week*, 3 March 1973, pp. 16–17; Grace Lichtenstein, "Consumer activists urge meat boycott for April 1–7," *NYT*, 17 March 1973, p. 28; Grace Lichtenstein, "Everyone blames U.S. for food prices," *NYT*, 20 March 1973, p. 43; Deirdre Carmody, "Behind the metropolitan boycott, a militant union," *NYT*, 6 April 1973, p. 55; William Robbins, "Boycott leaders plan a protest," *NYT*, 12 April 1973, p. 66; Francis Cerra, "After the meat boycott . . . what?" *Ms.*, August 1974, pp. 112–15.

53. Lichtenstein, "Consumer activists urge meat boycott," p. 28; William M. Blair, "40% rise in retail food prices seen for '72 by farm agency," *NYT*, 11 February 1972, p.

Table 6.   Media coverage of food issues, 1960–1980 (number of stories)

Year	Magazines[a]	Television Consumer movement[b]	Television Food prices[c]
1960	0		
1961	5		
1962	3		
1963	2		
1964	7		
1965	9		
1966	36		
1967	9		
1968	7		
1969	11	0	15
1970	10	0	24
1971	2	1	14
1972	19	1	155
1973	43	8	378
1974	30	6	288
1975	17	6	146
1976	14	1	47
1977	7	0	106
1978	10	0	64
1979	15	0	36
1980	19	1	6

Sources. Popular magazine coverage: Compiled from *Reader's Guide to Periodic Literature*, 1960–1980; Television coverage (all three networks): Compiled from the *Vanderbilt Television News Index and Abstracts*, 1969–1980.
[a]Stories about food prices and food price inflation.
[b]Stories about the consumer movement's views on food issues.
[c]Stories about food prices and food price inflation.

On the basic decisions of agricultural policy, though, consumer advocates in Congress stayed on the sidelines. Precisely at the moment of the most widespread consumer unrest, Congress debated farm policy, but the Agriculture and Consumer Protection Act of 1973 bore little of the imprint of the champions of consumers in Congress, despite its crafty

---

34; "Nixon's problems down on the farm," *Business Week*, 13 January 1973, p. 24; Lichtenstein, "Everybody blames U.S.," p. 43; "House panel backs food price rollback," *NYT*, 4 April 1973, p. 28; Lawrence van Gelder, "Some prices cut by meat boycott," *NYT*, 6 April 1973, p. 1; Judith Cummings, "Rosenthal tours Queens supermarkets," *NYT*, 9 August 1973, p. 31; Philip Shabecoff, "Food processors predict shortages," *NYT*, 25 June 1973, p. 9. On the importance of public salience to the political success of diffuse public interests, see David E. Price, "Policy making in congressional committees: The impact of 'environmental' factors," *American Political Science Review*, 72 (June 1978), pp. 548–74; and James Q. Wilson, "The politics of regulation," pp. 357–94 in James Q. Wilson, ed., *The politics of regulation* (New York: Basic Books, 1980).

title. The congressional agriculture committees, knowing that $1.60 corn and $2.70 wheat tended to undermine the rationale for farm subsidies, first offered a simple extension of the 1970 Agriculture Act. Then, when even that appeared unlikely, they converged on an innovative new farm program, one written by the Senate Agriculture Committee and based on the ideas of a farm state Republican, North Dakota senator Milton R. Young. Under its provisions, the federal government supplemented farm income only when commodity prices fell below legislated "target prices," set well below the levels prevailing in 1973. With an extension of the food stamp program as an additional sweetener, the 1973 farm bill passed by a comfortable margin. Consumer advocates applauded it, but they had nothing directly to do with its writing.[54]

The consumer movement's problem in breaking farm producers' hold on food policy was obvious. Before 1973, the salience of farm policy to urban voters was too low to justify substantial investments of their representatives' time, or even a membership on the House Agriculture Committee. "Not one of the 60 members of the House of Representatives from New York, New Jersey and Connecticut serves on the Agriculture Committee," the *New York Times* observed, "and some, including Rep. Shirley Chisholm, the Brooklyn Democrat, have been vocal in their disdain of the committee while they negotiated transfers to other committees."[55]

In the forties, fifties and sixties, urban representation on Agriculture was a rather hit-or-miss affair (see table 7).[56] Few of the hundreds of city and suburban members joined the Committee of their own free will. In 1969, Shirley Chisholm fought her appointment in the Democratic Caucus and won, but most of her colleagues were neither so bold nor so lucky. In the fifties and sixties, the Democratic organizations of

54. *KAL*, 19 January 1973; *WFL* No. 1529, 26 January 1973; *KAL*, 16 February 1973; F. R. Jimson, "Farm politics," *WF*, 24 March 1973, p. 13; *KAL*, 13 April 1973; "Washington," *Farm Journal*, April 1973, p. 9; "New farm bill faces hard fight," *Farm Journal*, April 1973, p. 32; *KAL*, 11 May 1973; *WFL* No. 1544, 11 May 1973; *KAL*, 6 July 1973; *WFL* No. 1552, 6 July 1973; *KAL*, 3 August 1973; "Washington report," *SF*, August 1973, p. 7; Barton, "Coalition-building," pp. 141–61. For most farm program purposes, the 1973 act also abandoned the use of the parity index in favor of legislated subsidy prices tied to cost of production formulae.

55. Martin Tolchin, "Metropolitan areas found lagging in food-stamp use," *NYT*, 9 September 1973, p. 56.

56. Before the war, urban representation was more common, owing to the perennial presence of the delegate from the Fourth District of Illinois. The Fourth, on Chicago's South Side, was the site of the Union Stockyards and Packingtown, the home of the nation's large meat packers. Its congressmen served on Agriculture from 1909, shortly after Congress passed the Meat Inspection Act (1906), until 1942, with only two years' exception.

Table 7.   Urban and suburban representation on the House Agriculture Committee, 1947–1982

Congress (Years)	Committee size	Urban members[a]	Suburban members[b]
80th (1947–48)	27		
81st (1949–50)	27		
82d (1951–52)	30	1	
83d (1953–54)	30		
84th (1955–56)	34	1	
85th (1957–58)	34	1	
86th (1959–60)	34		
87th (1961–62)	35		
88th (1963–64)	36	1	
89th (1965–66)	35	1	
90th (1967–68)	35	2	
91st (1969–70)	36	1	1
92d (1971–72)	35	1	
93d (1973–74)	36	1	2
94th (1975–76)	42	2	3
95th (1977–78)	46	1	2
96th (1979–80)	42	1	2
97th (1981–82)	43	1	1

Source. Compiled from the *Congressional directory,* 80th–96th Congresses.

[a]Eugene J. McCarthy (D., St. Paul, 82), Victor Anfuso (D., Brooklyn, 84–85), Benjamin Rosenthal (D., Queens, 88), Joseph P. Vigorito (D., Erie, Pa., 89–94), Frank J. Brasco (D., Brooklyn, 90), Frederick W. Richmond (D., Brooklyn, 94–97).

[b]Allard K. Lowenstein (D., Nassau County, N.Y., 91), George E. Brown, Jr. (D., Riverside, Cal., 93–97), Peter A. Peyser (R., Yonkers/Westchester/Bronx, 93–94), Margaret Heckler (R., Wellesley/Fall River, Mass., 94–96).

Brooklyn and Queens sentenced a trio of New York City freshmen to the panel, probably as a favor to the House leadership, which needed a few dependable farm bill votes at the time. During his only term, likewise, the peripatetic Allard K. Lowenstein, a maverick antiwar Democrat from Nassau County, New York, was stuck onto Agriculture, "it is generally assumed, as a kind of banishment."[57]

Once detained, Agriculture's urban members rarely pressed consumer viewpoints very aggressively. They tended, rather, to "go native." "We had a city member from New York on this committee for a while," Mississippi Democrat Thomas Abernethy remembered, speaking of

57. Robert G. Sherrill, "Reaping the subsidies," *Nation,* 24 November 1969, p. 565; Carroll Kilpatrick, "What happened to the farm bloc?" *Harper's,* November 1957, p. 59; "Last minute news straight from Washington," *Farm Journal,* March 1969, p. 11; Kenneth A. Shepsle, *The giant jigsaw puzzle: Democratic committee assignments in the modern House* (Chicago: University of Chicago Press, 1978), pp. 223, 286, 305; Mayhew, *Congress,* p. 42; Arthur Maass, *Congress and the common good* (New York: Basic Books, 1983), pp. 100–101.

Brooklyn Democrat Victor Anfuso. "I thought he was a very valuable member in that he got a better understanding of the farmers' problems and was very helpful in handling farm legislation on the floor." The Committee had its gadflies, but they were never from city constituencies.[58]

Once on the Agriculture Committee, finally, urban members turned their attention to getting off. With one exception, every urban member transferred, typically after a single term. "No city person wants to stay there," explained Queens Democrat Benjamin S. Rosenthal, the leading consumer advocate in the House and himself a transfer off the Committee. "Back in your district, it's not considered an attractive committee."[59]

In January 1974, however, New York representative Peter A. Peyser broke the precedent.[60] He gave up his position on Education and Labor to take over a vacancy on Agriculture. From there, he "proclaimed himself its only consumer advocate and began talking about what he saw as waste in federal farm subsidies." Vocal, but typically on the short end of lopsided Committee votes, Peyser carried his objections to government livestock and sugar programs to the floor of the House of Representatives.[61]

Peyser's transfer was part of a remarkable metamorphosis of a congressional career. In 1970, he won his first election to Congress from the Twenty-fifth District, comprising Yonkers and the Hudson Valley towns

58. *Hearings before the House Agriculture Committee,* "Agricultural Act of 1961," 87th Congress, 1st session, Serial E, 1961, p. 219. See also Fenno's description of "the socialization of Fred Santangelo" on the House Appropriations Committee's agriculture subcommittee. Richard F. Fenno, Jr., *The power of the purse* (Boston: Little, Brown and Co., 1966), pp. 215–19.

59. Tolchin, "Metropolitan areas found lagging," p. 56. The only urban lawmaker to last beyond two terms on Agriculture was Pennsylvania Democrat Joseph P. Vigorito, who represented Erie and surrounding areas. A self-proclaimed liberal Democrat, he was best known for his unswerving devotion to organized labor. His district, however, was normally GOP territory, and Vigorito reasoned that he could pick up some Republican support from dairy farmers with his work on Agriculture. Vigorito interview; Ehrenhalt, "House Agriculture," p. 383; "Governor, Senate standoff, GOP gain in House seen," *CQWR,* 30 September 1966, p. 2284; "Washington," *Farm Journal,* December 1976, p. 8.

60. California Democrat George E. Brown, Jr., who joined the Committee a year before Peyser, represented a suburban district (centered on Riverside) that also included large citrus groves.

61. Ehrenhalt, "House Agriculture," p. 381; "Livestock loan guarantee," *CQWR,* 13 July 1974, p. 1827; "Price controls, the wheat deal, inflation, monopoly . . . all are blamed as reasons for meat price dilemma," *CQWR,* 20 July 1974, pp. 1908–9, 1916; "Congress probes soaring sugar prices," *CQWR,* 14 December 1974, pp. 3316–18.

in Westchester and Rockland Counties. A Republican, his platform stressed social and fiscal conservatism and support of President Nixon's policy in Indochina. In 1972, however, events conspired against him. The state legislature redistricted him unfavorably, removing Rockland and adding the northern Bronx, and the district's former incumbent, Democrat Richard L. Ottinger, decided to contest his seat. Exploiting his position on Education and Labor, Peyser campaigned against school busing and wrapped himself in Nixon's coattails, but he squeezed by Ottinger with only 1,400 votes to spare.[62]

Since he was already marginal, the Watergate scandal sent Peyser casting for new issues, and after an unsuccessful bid for a seat on Interior (the venue of environmentalism), he landed on Agriculture. The results, in 1974, were encouraging. "The most dramatic example of a Republican candidate emerging unscathed from the debris of Watergate was the [substantial] victory by Representative Peter Peyser in the 23d Congressional District," the *Times* observed. In the campaign, Peyser rode his consumer record hard, to the frustration of his luckless opponent. " 'Take his assignment to the Agriculture Committee,' where Mr. Peyser has attracted considerable attention this year in opposing farm subsidy programs. 'It was a grandstand move,' " Democrat William Greenawalt complained. " 'His record on subsidies and agricultural matters was virtually non-existent until this year.' " With his seat on Agriculture, and with his increasingly liberal voting record, Peyser recreated himself and weathered a GOP disaster.[63]

On his return to Congress, therefore, Peyser related "some advice for the class of '75." "One of the first tasks facing the new Congress will be to take a critical look at the entire food sector of the economy," he wrote, in urging city and suburban lawmakers to request positions on

62. "Biographies and photos of new members of the House," *CQWR*, 25 December 1970, p. 3085; Richard L. Madden, "Peyser sees challenge by Ottinger in November," *NYT*, 12 February 1972, pp. 14; "Peyser blames foe for Dirty-Dozen list," *NYT*, 13 June 1972, p. 36; Thomas P. Ronan, "Ottinger expects to defeat Peyser," *NYT*, 17 September 1972, p. 41; Linda Greenhouse, "Ottinger attempting a comeback against Representative Peyser," *NYT*, 13 October 1972, p. 21.

63. James Feron, "In Westchester, trend resisted," *NYT*, 7 November 1974, p. 37; James Feron, "Peyser record is big issue in Westchester campaign," *NYT*, 2 November 1974, p. 14; Richard L. Madden, "Miss Holtzman given Judiciary post made vacant by her defeat of Celler," *NYT*, 13 January 1973, p. 13; James Feron, "Light vote seen in Westchester," *NYT*, 8 September 1974, p. 47; "Vulnerable Republicans: Trying harder to win," *CQWR*, 22 June 1974, p. 1623. Peyser immediately set his sights higher. In 1976, he mounted an unsuccessful primary challenge to conservative GOP senator James L. Buckley. "Candidates '76," *CQWR*, 6 December 1975, p. 2656; "New York: Bella, Moynihan chase Buckley," *CQWR*, 4 September 1976, p. 2392.

Judiciary, Commerce and Agriculture. "A new member to [Agriculture] could add weight to the movement to abolish these farm programs which inflate the price of our food."[64]

In 1975, two activists took up Peyser's challenge. First, Massachusetts Republican Margaret M. Heckler, of suburban Wellesley, gave up eight years of seniority on Banking, Currency and Housing to move over to Agriculture. Second, New York Democrat Frederick W. Richmond, of Brooklyn, swapped his initial assignment on Education and Labor for his preferred appointment to Agriculture. "The eagerness of Mr. Richmond and Mr. Peyser to get on Agriculture . . . underlined its new importance as a forum for consumer advocates in the wake of skyrocketing food prices and the rapid development of the consumer movement," the *Times* reported. In 1975, for the first time in memory, "with Peyser, Heckler and Richmond on the committee, there is potential for serious farmer-consumer conflict."[65]

Contrary to these expectations, however, the placement of congressional consumer advocates on the House Agriculture Committee signaled no appreciable change in the way that agricultural policy was made. For one thing, it occasioned no concerted urban attack on the farm program. In Committee, Peyser, Heckler and Richmond each opposed the 1975 emergency farm bill, which raised target prices for grains, cotton and dairy products. On the floor, however, while the Republican, Peyser, led the opposition, the Democrat, Richmond, rallied urban Democratic support. Seeking to put President Gerald R. Ford on the spot in the farm belt, urban and rural Democrats conspired in a Christmas-tree farm bill, which the House passed by a wide margin, which Ford predictably vetoed and which the House then failed to revive. City legislators registered their preferences in committee, to no effect, but partisanship overshadowed interest in coalition building on the floor.[66]

For another thing, the inclusion of urban representatives on Agricul-

---

64. Peter Peyser, "Some advice for the class of '75," *NYT,* 1 December 1974, p. IV 15.

65. Thomas P. Ronan, "Urban congressman takes on farm post," *NYT,* 10 May 1975, p. 19; Ehrenhalt, "House Agriculture," p. 381; "Will ag committee work for farmers?" *WF,* 8 February 1975, p. 18; Lyons and Taylor, "Farm politics in transition," p. 133. See also Fenno's account of the consequences of eastern representatives opting onto Interior. Fenno, *Congressmen in committees,* pp. 285–87.

66. "House passes farm bill despite veto threats," *CQWR,* 22 March 1975, pp. 624–26; William Robbins, "Bill would raise crop-price level," *NYT,* 6 March 1975, p. 29; William Robbins, "Butz opposes bill raising farm supports that Democrats back," *NYT,* 12 March 1975, p. 19; *KAL,* 14 March 1975; *KAL,* 9 May 1975; "What's new from Washington," *PF,* June 1975, p. 13; "Washington report," *SF,* June/July 1975, p. 4; Barton, "Coalition-building," pp. 141-61.

ture bought no substantial measure of access for the consumer lobby. In 1977, the consumer organizations came hopefully before the Committee. "This is the first time that the national consumer organizations of this country have taken a unified position on the food and agriculture bill that will be before you," Consumer Coalition representative Ellen Haas announced in 1977. The Committee, however, responded as usual with ostentatious indifference. It immersed itself in discussion with some farmers from Kansas, and it wholly ignored the consumer lobby's historic testimony. Texas Democrat Bob Poage's offhand barb at the ideas of "the ladies from New York" was the closest it came to a serious consideration of the lobby's viewpoints. In the formulation of farm policy, in short, the consumer movement remained on the outside. "For those programs providing direct financial assistance to farmers," Berry concluded in 1982, "public interest groups have been a negligible force."[67]

In agricultural policy-making, then, the reformist promise of the consumer movement was never quite fulfilled, for reasons that are theoretically apparent. As Peyser's experience demonstrated, attacks on the farm program as a part of a broad strategy of appeals to consumers had definite electoral power, tapping into voters' resentments against rising costs at the supermarket. The concerns of the consumer movement enjoyed competitive advantage, that is, because food prices had escalated out of control.

Those conditions, however, were fleeting. In 1975, farm surpluses mounted, farm prices plunged and food price inflation abated, running well behind the overall rate of inflation in six out of the next seven years (see table 5). As food prices stabilized, public attention wandered away from federal food policy and toward other things. Media coverage of food and agriculture issues dropped to a third or less of the 1973 peak (see table 6). In the late 1970s, in short, food policy reached the down side of its "issue-attention cycle." Conditions failed to keep the issue on

67. *Hearings*, 1977, Part 2, pp. 222, 245; Jeffrey M. Berry, "Consumers and the hunger lobby," pp. 68–78 in Don F. Hadwiger and Ross B. Talbot, eds., *Food policy and farm programs* (New York: Academy of Political Science, 1982), p. 74; *Hearings*, 1981, pp. 206–7; James L. Guth, "Consumer organizations and federal dairy policy," *Policy Studies Journal*, 6 (Summer 1978), p. 499–503. The Consumer Coalition included the Consumer Federation of America, the Community Nutrition Institute, the Center for Science in the Public Interest, the National Consumer Congress, the Consumer Committee of Americans for Democratic Action and Ralph Nader's Public Citizen. For a survey of these organizations, see Robert O. Herrmann, Edward J. Walsh and Rex H. Warland, "The organizations of the consumer movement: A comparative perspective," pp. 470–94 in E. Scott Maynes, ed., *The frontier of research in the consumer interest* (Columbia, Mo.: American Council on Consumer Interests, 1988).

constituent agendas. The consumer lobby failed to achieve access because its issue was not recurrent.

Without a dependable consumer audience for the farm program, city Democrats and suburban Republicans faced disparate incentives. Urban Democrats played an inside game, brokering urban votes for the farm program and rural votes for urban projects, most prominently food stamps. As Democrats, they enjoyed membership in the majority party, easing the arrangement of enforceable agreements. As city legislators, moreover, they represented constituencies that benefited from food stamps, an interest more easily accommodated by the farm bloc than the suburban consumer interest in unsubsidized farm markets. As the representative of a district in which 17 percent of the families earned less than three thousand dollars in 1970, for example, Brooklyn Democrat Fred Richmond played the inside game and was rewarded for it. In 1977, after just two years of experience, he became the chairman of the Subcommittee on Domestic Marketing, Consumer Relations and Nutrition, from which he more or less ran the House end of the food stamp program. As we shall see in a moment, urban Democrats occupied a key position in farm policy coalitions, and the farm bloc was keen to satisfy them.[68]

Suburban Republicans, on the other hand, played an outside game, using amendments on the floor to pry particularly vincible commodity programs out of their protective coalitions. With rare exceptions, they steered clear of the politically important commodities produced in larger numbers of congressional districts, like cotton, corn, wheat and milk, and zeroed in on the politically vulnerable crops grown in smaller numbers of constituencies, like tobacco, sugar and peanuts.[69] In 1979 and 1981, for example, Peter Peyser and Margaret Heckler marshaled

68. "House passes farm bill despite veto threats," *CQWR*, 22 March 1975, p. 624; Martin Tolchin, "House backs Carter's plan on free food stamps," *NYT*, 28 July 1977, p. 1; Martin Tolchin, "Urban-rural coalition successful on farm and food stamp measure," *NYT*, 29 July 1977, p. 19; Martin Tolchin, "Urban and rural lawmakers join to support each bloc's interests," *NYT*, 30 July 1977, p. 1; Steven V. Roberts, "Congressional battle on food stamps is joined and is already half over," *NYT*, 8 April 1981, p. 25; Ehrenhalt, "House Agriculture," p. 381; Barton, "Coalition-building," pp. 141–61; Berry, "Consumers and the hunger lobby," p. 76; John G. Peters, "The 1977 farm bill: Coalitions in Congress," pp. 23–35 in Don F. Hadwiger and William P. Browne, eds., *The new politics of food* (Lexington, Mass.: Lexington Books, 1978), pp. 31–32.

69. In 1978, seven congressional districts grew about half of the tobacco, seven produced almost three-quarters of the peanuts, six grew about half of the sugar beets and four produced nine-tenths of the sugarcane. (See also David G. Abler, "Vote trading on farm legislation in the U.S. House," *American Journal of Agricultural Economics*, 71 [August 1989], p. 584.) The only politically important commodity to draw more than passing attention from congressional consumer advocates was milk, partly because of the direct im-

consumer and food industry opposition to sugar price support proposals, causing their defeat on the House floor.[70]

Excluded from any meaningful role in the initial formulation of farm policy, and forced to fight rearguard actions on the House floor, suburban lawmakers soon departed Agriculture. When Peyser returned to the House in 1979, this time as a Democrat, he went back to Education and Labor. When Heckler began her eighth term in 1981, she switched to Science and Technology.

For want of an audience, then, the consumer lobby's challenge to the hegemony of the farm lobby over agricultural policy expired barely five years after it began. In the early 1970s, rapid food price inflation roused urban consumers out of their apathy, and attacks on the farm program served the electoral interests of city and suburban representatives rather well. As was soon readily apparent, however, the cause of constituent unrest was passing. By the late 1970s, farm policy was once again far from consumers' minds, and congressional attacks on the federal agricultural program yielded no better results than efforts on any one of dozens of other fronts. In the mid-1970s, in short, the consumer lobby succeeded in proving its competitive advantage, but it failed to prove its recurrence. The representatives of consumers remained outside the gates.[71]

---

pact of the dairy program on retail prices, partly because of the industry's shady dealings in the 1972 presidential campaign and partly because of scrutiny by the Justice Department in the Ford administration. See Guth, "Consumer organizations," pp. 499–503; Herbert E. Alexander, *Financing the 1972 election* (Lexington, Mass.: Lexington Books, 1976), pp. 486–500; and MacAvoy, *Federal milk marketing orders.*

70. "Defeat of rice bill," *CQWR,* 11 January 1975, p. 98; "House approves $11.7-billion for agriculture," *CQWR,* 19 June 1976, p. 1600–1602; Bob Livernash, "Power of sugar lobby wanes, but it helps write the bill," *CQWR,* 5 May 1979, p. 835; Bob Livernash, "Consumer-labor votes kill House sugar bill," *CQWR,* 27 October 1979, p. 2396; Elizabeth Wehr, "House repudiates peanut, sugar programs," *CQWR,* 17 October 1981, p. 2031; Elizabeth Wehr, "Former Rep. Heckler named to head HHS," *CQWR,* 15 January 1983, p. 86; Guth, "Consumer organizations," pp. 502–3; David Vogel and Mark Nadel, "The consumer coalition: Dimensions of political conflict," pp. 7–28 in Robert N. Katz, ed., *Protecting the consumer interest* (Cambridge: Ballinger Publishing Co., 1976), pp. 16–19.

71. The episode underscores the well-known difficulties of maintaining an "entrepreneurial politics" that relies on mobilization of ordinarily "inattentive publics." In consumers' perceptions, at least, only in unusual times like the early seventies did they bear "large and direct costs" of farm price support policies. See Wilson, *Regulation,* pp. 370–71; and R. Douglas Arnold, *The logic of congressional action* (New Haven: Yale University Press, 1990), pp. 68–71, esp. p. 70. See also Jayachandran N. Variyam, Jeffrey L. Jordan and James E. Epperson, "Preferences of citizens for agricultural policies: Evidence from a national survey," *American Journal of Agricultural Economics,* 72 (May 1990), pp. 259, 264–65.

Agricultural Adjustment: Rolling Logs in an Urban House

In the 1960s and 1970s, the widening gulf between the wishes of the farm bloc and the preferences of the full House of Representatives confronted the agriculture committees with a repeated Hobson's choice. Every few years, commonly four, the committees had to reconsider the farm program. If on the one hand they chose to report a new farm law proposal, they exposed the price support program to the danger of debilitating amendments imposed by the metropolitan representatives who ruled the House floor. If on the other hand they chose not to report, the authorizations for the current policies expired, and the agricultural price support programs reverted to the terms of the nation's "permanent" farm legislation, the 1938 Agricultural Adjustment Act as amended by the 1949 Agriculture Act, legislation too far out of date to meet the modern needs of the industry.[72]

In the 1960s and 1970s, accordingly, the House Agriculture Committee turned its attention to the problem of passing a farm bill in an increasingly inhospitable House. At a symbolic level, it camouflaged its farm bills in a new rhetoric of food. Throughout the fifties and into the sixties, congressional sponsors straightforwardly titled their legislation the "Agricultural Act" of whatever year (see table 8). Starting in 1962, however, the "Food and Agriculture Act" became a more and more popular designation, whether or not the bills actually contained anything relevant to consumption. After a brief experiment with "Consumer Protection" in 1973, in deference to the public concern over food prices, "Food and Agriculture" reigned as the preferred expression. As metropolitan numbers mounted in the House, the new language of consumption took its place with the traditional language of production.

At a more pragmatic level, the House agrarians rolled logs. Into the early 1960s, the House Agriculture Committee continued to report legislation for single commodities as needs arose, but after the Agricultural Act of 1964, the wheat and cotton bill, it did so less and less. Beginning in 1965, it bundled all the price-supported commodities (except sugar) into single, omnibus bills. The strategy was plain. "I would assume the

72. Formal analyses of congressional committees stress powers of origination as the keystone of committee influence on legislative outcomes, but the difficulties committees experience in exercising their powers are probably not unique to agriculture. Most policies require periodic reauthorizations, forcing committees to act unless they prefer *no policy*—*not* current policy—to the outcomes they expect on the floor. If committees comprise high-demand lawmakers (as researchers usually allege), such preferences are likely to be quite rare. See Kenneth A. Shepsle, "Institutional arrangements and equilibrium in multidimensional voting models," *American Journal of Political Science*, 23 (February 1979), pp. 27–59; and the studies reviewed by Keith Krehbiel, "Spatial models of legislative choice," *Legislative Studies Quarterly*, 13 (August 1988), pp. 259–319.

Table 8.   Major agricultural acts, 1948–1981

Year	Title
1948	Agricultural Act of 1948
1949	Agricultural Act of 1949
1954	Agricultural Act of 1954
1956	Agricultural Act of 1956
1958	Agricultural Act of 1958
1961	Agricultural Act of 1961
1962	Food and Agriculture Act of 1962
1964	Agricultural Act of 1964
1965	Food and Agriculture Act of 1965
1970	Agricultural Act of 1970
1973	Agriculture and Consumer Protection Act of 1973
1977	Food and Agriculture Act of 1977
1981	Agriculture and Food Act of 1981

wisest course of action . . . would then be to include the dairy program within the parameters of the entire farm bill," Iowa Democrat Tom Harkin advised Patrick B. Healy of the National Milk Producers Federation in 1981.

HEALY: Yes, sir. It is my understanding that the leadership of the Congress, both in the Senate and here, have a really well-founded desire to keep all of agriculture together. The plain fact is there are too few of us even when we are all together.

HARKIN: That is right.

With its all-encompassing commodity logrolls, the farm bloc sought to invoke the interests of the largest possible number of rural representatives, to present a "united front" of farm lawmakers on the House floor and to minimize dependence on the good will of city and suburban legislators.[73]

By the 1960s, however, the farm bloc, even united, could hardly go it alone. It reached out, therefore, to legislators from the city. As opportunities arose, the farm organizations and the labor unions cooperated to their mutual advantage, arranging vote swaps between rural and urban Democrats. In 1965, city Democrats gave their support to the farm bill in exchange for the assistance of farm Democrats in attempting re-

73. *Hearings before the House Agriculture Committee, Subcommittee on Livestock, Dairy and Poultry,* "General farm bill of 1981 (Dairy, beekeeper and wool programs)," 97th Congress, 1st session, Serial 97-G, Part 7, 1981, p. 102; Peters, "The 1977 farm bill," pp. 24, 27–28; Peters, "The 1981 farm bill"; Browne, *Private interests,* pp. 171–90; Abler, "Vote trading," pp. 583–91. The farm bloc's dependence on broad-gauged commodity logrolls underscored the subversive dangers of floor attacks on even minor crops, like peanuts and rice.

peal of Section 14(b), the "right-to-work" provisions, of the Taft-Hartley Act. In 1973, city Democrats lent their help to the farm bill in exchange for the aid of farm Democrats in passing a minimum wage bill.[74]

From the late sixties on, though, the primary vehicle for the farm bloc's defense of the farm program was the food stamp program. The modern version began in the late 1950s, primarily at the instigation of an urban Democrat, Representative Leonor Sullivan of St. Louis. In 1959, after repeated failures, Sullivan induced the House Agriculture Committee to authorize a pilot food stamp program, which it did on a party-line vote. The lopsidedly Democratic Eighty-sixth Congress passed the food stamp bill, and President Eisenhower approved it. Agriculture Secretary Ezra Taft Benson, a doctrinaire conservative, refused to implement the program, but in 1961, upon the inauguration of John F. Kennedy, pilot food stamp projects began in eight different states, mostly in depressed mining areas. Encouraged by their success, Kennedy requested authorization for a larger, nationwide food stamp program in 1963.[75]

Almost a year later, in March 1964, the Agriculture Committee approved the expansion of the food stamp program, but only after Committee chairman Harold D. Cooley and President Lyndon B. Johnson dragged it kicking and screaming into a quid pro quo. Fearing defeat for the 1964 wheat-cotton bill, the Committee reversed an earlier decision and sent the food stamp bill to the floor, entirely as a sweetener. The stratagem worked; the House approved both bills.[76]

74. With its long-standing ties to organized labor, the National Farmers Union was especially instrumental in arranging the trades. The most consistent farm and labor exchange maintained the "cargo-preference" provisions in agricultural export programs—requirements that a certain percentage of subsidized farm exports be shipped in American bottoms. Johnson interview; *WFL* No. 1140, 23 July 1965; *WFL* No. 1141, 30 July 1965; Martin Tolchin, "Urban and rural lawmakers join to support each bloc's interests," *NYT,* 30 July 1977, p. 1; Barton, "Coalition-building"; Karen Orren, "Union politics and post-war liberalism in the United States, 1946–1979," *Studies in American Political Development,* 1 (1986), pp. 219–28.

75. For the political history of the food stamp program, see John Ferejohn, "Logrolling in an institutional context: A case study of food stamp legislation," pp. 223–53 in Gerald C. Wright, Jr., Leroy N. Rieselbach and Lawrence C. Dodd, eds., *Congress and policy change* (New York: Agathon Press, 1986); and Jeffrey M. Berry, *Feeding hungry people: Rule making in the food stamp program* (New Brunswick: Rutgers University Press, 1984). See also Julius Duscha, "Is the food stamp plan working?" *Reporter,* 1 March 1962, pp. 38–41; and "First food stamp families remember 1961," *NYT,* 20 October 1979, p. 10.

76. *WFL* No. 1068, 6 March 1964; *WFL* No. 1069, 13 March 1964; *WFL* No. 1070, 20 March 1964; "2 Johnson bills passed by House," *NYT,* 9 April 1964, p. 1; "Johnson

As Ferejohn pointed out, however, the construction of a coalition of urban and rural members around food stamps and farm supports did not directly follow from 1964's experience. Despite the political utility of the food aid program, the Committee's hostility toward food stamps in the late 1960s was implacable.[77]

The most obvious reason was ideological. The Agriculture Committee was the bailiwick of southern Democrats and midwestern Republicans, neither of whom had adjusted very well to the new urban liberalism.[78]

A second, more direct reason, however, was contextual. In 1965 and 1966, the food stamp program grew quietly and steadily. "The big change came," an Agriculture Department official recalled, "when Bobby Kennedy got into the act." In April 1967, the Subcommittee on Employment, Manpower and Poverty of the Senate Labor Committee, led by Pennsylvania senator Joseph S. Clark and New York senator Robert F. Kennedy, traveled to Mississippi. Touring the byways of the Delta, ducking into the shacks of poor black tenants, Clark and Kennedy discovered alarming evidence of widespread hunger and malnutrition.[79]

Within the year, Clark's and Kennedy's spotlight on hunger had activated the civil rights movement and galvanized liberal opinion. In June 1967, four physicians, led by Harvard psychiatrist Robert Coles, reported the grim findings of their own tour of the South to the Clark subcommittee. In April 1968, the Citizens Board of Inquiry into Hunger and Malnutrition issued its report, *Hunger U.S.A.*, which identified 256 "hunger counties" (mostly rural and southern) in need of immediate food assistance. In May 1968, CBS aired its documentary "Hunger in America," a dramatic exposé of malnutrition and want in the forgotten

---

phone effort credited with House victory on farm bill," *NYT*, 10 April 1964, p. 15; "Food subsidy for city folk," *Business Week*, 11 April 1964, p. 164; Ripley, "Legislative bargaining"; Rowland Evans and Robert Novak, *Lyndon B. Johnson: The exercise of power* (New York: New American Library, 1966), pp. 380–81.

77. Ferejohn, "Logrolling," pp. 231–38.

78. William G. Carleton noted the situation of 1940s reaction in the hotbeds of 1890s populism. He wrote, "Why are these old Populist areas [the South and the Midwest] least liberal today? Largely because the new liberalism is more and more urban, and the old agrarian liberalism is having a hard time adjusting itself to the new industrial liberalism, in spite of farm programs, farm subsidies, and agricultural price supports." William G. Carleton, "The southern politician—1900 and 1950," *Journal of Politics*, 13 (May 1951), pp. 215–31, quoted at p. 225.

79. Berry, *Feeding hungry people*, p. 43; Robert Sherrill, "It isn't true that nobody starves in America," *New York Times Magazine*, 4 June 1967, pp. 22ff.; Nick Kotz, *Let them eat promises: The politics of hunger in America* (Englewood Cliffs, N.J.: Prentice-Hall, 1969), chap. 1.

corners of the country. Finally, in June 1968, the Poor People's Campaign, led by the Reverend Ralph David Abernathy, moved its protest to the Department of Agriculture, demanding that President Johnson and Secretary Freeman order an immediate expansion of the federal food aid program.[80]

The newly framed hunger issue was a distinct threat to rural lawmakers, especially southerners. First, the sight of northern liberals poking their heads into southern sharecroppers' shacks quickened the animosities that still lingered from the battles over civil rights. "The House Agriculture Committee . . . is, to state it gently, disinterested in the poor," Elizabeth Drew commented. "The members of most committees see to it that the benefits of programs they preside over reach their constituents in full measure, but it is no accident that the home districts of the Agriculture Committee members do not have food stamp programs. 'These programs are not desired by the power structures back home,' says one close observer, 'and that's what elects them. The recipients of these programs don't vote.' "[81]

Second, and more generally important, the clamor over hunger and malnutrition threatened the safety of the price support program itself. Urban liberals contrasted the magnificence of federal farm aid with the squalor of federal food aid. In Lyndon B. Johnson's home state of Texas, they pointed out, farmers received $448 million in farm support payments, but over half of the counties participated in neither of the major federal food programs. In the Texas congressional district of Agriculture chairman W. R. (Bob) Poage, they showed, the federal government spent $5.3 million to idle the land of 400 farmers, but it spent only $224,000 to feed 144,000 poor people. In Mississippi, they discovered, Senator James O. Eastland, a cotton planter, accepted nearly $212,000 in agricultural subsidy payments, but in Washington he steadfastly opposed more generous food assistance. The hunger issue, in short, provided the occasion for a new assault on the farm program, inspiring retributive

80. Nan Robertson, "Severe hunger found in Mississippi," *NYT*, 17 June 1967, p. 14; Joseph A. Loftus, "Hunger of millions laid to farm policy," *NYT*, 23 April 1968, p. 22; Jack Gould, "TV: Hunger amid plenty," *NYT*, 22 May 1968, p. 95; William M. Blair, "Mandatory food plans for poor to void state option are urged," *NYT*, 24 May 1968, p. 30; "Poor put food first in a protest rally," *NYT*, 13 June 1968, p. 10; Rudy Johnson, "Poverty protest may draw 40,000," *NYT*, 18 June 1968, p. 28; Jack Gould, "Hunger is not for quibbling," *NYT*, 23 June 1968, p. II 19; Elizabeth B. Drew, "Going hungry in America," *Atlantic*, December 1968, pp. 53-61; Berry, *Feeding hungry people*, chap. 2; Kotz, *Promises*, chaps. 1, 7; and Norwood Allen Kerr, "Drafted into the War on Poverty: USDA food and nutrition programs, 1961–1969," *Agricultural History*, 64 (Spring 1990), pp. 154–66.

81. Drew, "Going hungry," p. 56.

proposals ranging from outright suspension to limitations on subsidy payments. "What is significant about the Findley-Conte effort [to cap farm program payments] is that they have hooked up hunger . . . with the farm subsidy program," the *Nation* observed in 1969. "So here is another conflict in which the heretofore accepted priorities are being challenged. . . . If the amendment is adopted, Congress might decide to scrutinize farm policy, a thing it has not done for years."[82]

In 1969, under liberal pressure in the Congress and under budget pressure from the White House, the House Agriculture Committee took the food stamp program hostage. Concerned that the expansion of food stamps might come out of the hide of farm payments, as President Nixon initially intended, Committee chairman Bob Poage wrote a food stamp title into the 1969 farm bill. The motives were transparent. "The truth is that the close relationship between the food stamp program and the farm program and I guess I am saying now what has been the undercut [*sic*] in all these hearings, is dictated not by logic but by politics," the director of the National Council on Hunger and Malnutrition, John Kramer, charged. "From your point of view, food stamps is still a program to benefit the farmer—by permitting renewed passage of the farm welfare system." Making sure that the House agrarians understood the stakes, Senator Jacob Javits (R., N.Y.) appeared before the Committee to warn it of the consequences should it fail to do well by food stamp recipients. At first only out of necessity, farm state legislators tied the fate of farm policy to the appeal of federal food assistance.[83]

82. "The sweet smell of subsidy," *Nation*, 16 June 1969, p. 249; "Hunger," *Reporter*, 2 November 1967, p. 16; Joseph A. Loftus, "Hunger of millions laid to farm policy," *NYT*, 23 April 1968, p. 22; "Let 'em eat cake," *New Republic*, 4 May 1968, p. 9; Earl Caldwell, "Abernathy seeks poverty explanation," *NYT*, 22 June 1968, p. 23; Drew, "Going hungry," p. 56; William M. Blair, "Senate unit votes a broadened plan for food stamps," *NYT*, 2 July 1969, p. 1; T.R.B., "NIT-ing for a living," *New Republic*, 5 July 1969, p. 2. The joint efforts of liberal Democrats and conservative Republicans to limit farm program payments culminated in the inclusion of a fifty-five-thousand-dollar limit per crop in the 1970 farm bill. Congress lowered the price support limit for most crops to twenty thousand dollars in 1973, raised it to forty thousand dollars escalating to fifty thousand dollars in 1977, and left it at fifty thousand dollars in 1981. See "New drive to cut subsidies for giant farms," *U.S. News and World Report*, 27 July 1970, pp. 54–55; *KAL*, 7 August 1970; "Farm bill makes superficial cuts," *Business Week*, 15 August 1970, p. 22.

83. *Hearings, 1969*, p. 738, pp. 790–801; *KAL*, 27 June 1969; William M. Blair, "Senate unit bars free food stamps," *NYT*, 1 July 1969, p. 1; William M. Blair, "Hardin rules out an abrupt cut in farm supports," *NYT*, 16 July 1969, p. 19; Claude W. Gifford, "The fight behind a new farm plan for '71," *Farm Journal*, September 1969, p. 66; *KAL*, 3 October 1969; "House panel bars food stamp gains," *NYT*, 11 December 1969, p. 1; *KAL*, 3 October 1969; "Farm bill likely to pass Congress," *WF*, 11 July 1970, p. 12; "Washington report," *SF*, November 1970, p. 7; Kotz, *Promises*, pp. 210, 218. Poage was

In the 1970s, however, the political context of the food stamp program changed markedly. Federal food aid expanded rapidly, mollifying urban liberals. Federal farm aid continued, calming rural conservatives.

In addition, though, the value of the food stamp program to the agrarians increased markedly, both on the floor and at home. Between 1969 and 1972, Congress and the president steadily liberalized food stamp requirements, and the number of food stamp recipients more than tripled, from a scant 2.9 million in 1969 to 11.1 million in 1972. Moreover, between 1972 and 1981, with the onset of stagflation, the number of beneficiaries redoubled. By 1981, at participation's peak, 22.4 million Americans—nearly one in every ten—received food stamps, and nearly as many were reckoned to be eligible. In the seventies, in short, food stamps became a major source of economic benefit to hundreds of congressional districts, and their value on the floor in barter increased correspondingly.[84]

At the same time, genuine agrarian sympathy for the needy deepened. In part, the newfound tolerance mirrored the pattern of distribution: rural lawmakers toted up the costs and the benefits and discovered that food stamps were a pretty good deal. Because eligibility for food stamps was assessed on a national basis, underweighting local variations in the cost of living, the program was particularly generous to small towns and rural areas, where incomes (and expenses) were generally lower. In 1973, for example, states in the rural South and Southwest received as many dollars for food stamps as much larger states in the urban Northeast.[85]

On the other hand, however, the newfound tolerance mirrored changes in rural constituencies and the people who represented them. The generational composition of the House Agriculture Committee changed markedly in the early 1970s (see table 9). Up through the Ninety-second Congress (1971–1972), lawmakers first elected in the thirties, forties and fifties monopolized Committee leadership. After a

---

frank about his intentions. The interest of the Agriculture Committee in social programs, he recalled, "doesn't derive from the effect these programs have on the needy people. The role—the power derives from the effect that those programs have upon agricultural products, farm prices, and producers." Poage memoirs, p. 1285.

84. In dollar terms, in fact, the size of the food stamp program surpassed the size of the farm support program in 1975. Moreover, by the late 1970s, food stamps accounted for about 8 percent of retail grocery sales.

85. Martin Tolchin, "Metropolitan area found lagging in food-stamp use," *NYT,* 9 September 1973, p. 56; "Southern states' tally," *NYT,* 9 September 1973, p. V 5. On "deductions" and the determination of eligibility, see Berry, *Feeding hungry people,* pp. 68–99.

Table 9.   First election of House Agriculture Committee members, 1951–1980
(number first elected in decade)

Congress (Years)	1920s	1930s	1940s	1950s	1960s[a]	1970s
82d (1951–52)	2	5	22	1		
83d (1953–54)	2	4	18	6		
84th (1955–56)	2	4	14	14		
85th (1957–58)	1	4	14	15		
86th (1959–60)		4	11	19		
87th (1961–62)		4	9	16	6	
88th (1963–64)		4	7	8	16	
89th (1965–66)		3	7	6	17	
90th (1967–68)		2	5	3	25	
91st (1969–70)		1	4	3	28	
92d (1971–72)		1	4	2	22	6
93d (1973–74)		1		2	20	13
94th (1975–76)		1			12	29
95th (1977–78)		1			10	35
96th (1979–80)					10	32

Sources. Compiled from the Congressional directory, 82d–96th Congresses.
[a]William C. Wampler (R., Va.) served one term in the 1950s (83d Congress) but did not return until 1967. His first election is dated as 1966.

spate of retirements in 1972, however, younger, more moderate members moved into positions of authority.

The generational contrast between the old and the new guard was personified by the contrast between Committee chairman W. R. Poage and his successor, Thomas S. Foley. When Bob Poage was first elected, in 1936, from the Eleventh District of Texas, twice as many of his constituents lived on farms (44.6 percent) as in the District's metropolis, Waco (22.2 percent). In the Blackland region of central Texas, the business was cotton. On the other hand, when Tom Foley was first elected, in 1964, from the Fifth District of Washington, five times as many of his constituents lived in the District's metropolis, Spokane (45.5 percent), as lived on farms (8.6 percent). In the "Inland Empire" of eastern Washington, the business was services: transportation, wholesale supply, retail trade and agricultural trade.[86]

86. On Foley, see John Newhouse, "Profiles: The navigator," New Yorker, 10 April 1989, pp. 48–84. On Foley's efforts on behalf of food stamps, see "Rise in food stamps opposed in House," NYT, 26 June 1968, p. 30; "House panel bars food stamp gains," NYT, 11 December 1969, p. 1; "House panel votes food stamp curbs," NYT, 24 July 1970, p. 38; Marjorie Hunter, "House approves food stamp bill with work plan," NYT, 31 December 1970, p. 1. In the Senate, the corresponding contrast was between Louisiana senator Allen J. Ellender and South Dakota senator George S. McGovern, both Democrats. Ellender, the chairman of Senate Agriculture, was an old-line southern conservative

Like Foley and Poage, the new agrarians contrasted with the old agrarians on three important dimensions.[87] First, residentially, the younger representatives were northern, and particularly western. Unlike their predecessors, they were not bound to the defense of white supremacy in the rural South. Second, ideologically, the new agrarians were products of the New Frontier and the Great Society. Compared to their predecessors, southerners were more attentive to the needs of newly enfranchised, poor black voters, and northerners were more pragmatic toward social welfare policies. Finally, representationally, the young agrarians were envoys of districts that were economically diverse, not wholly dominated by farmers and agriculture. They had attained office in circumstances that were strikingly different from their predecessors'. Appeals to farmers were only one part of their electoral stocks in trade.[88]

Accordingly, the antipathy of congressional agrarians to the food stamp program gradually faded in the 1970s, allowing the construction of their "committee-based logroll" with city lawmakers. In 1974 and 1975, rural representatives helped to defend the government food program against the conservative backlash of the Ford administration. In 1977, they helped to rid the program of the provision most offensive to urban liberals, the purchase requirement. Finally, in 1973 and in every farm bill renewal year subsequent, the House and Senate Agriculture Committees incorporated the farm program and the food stamp pro-

---

opponent of social welfare programs, including food stamps. Owing to the hostility of Ellender and the other southerners on his committee, McGovern carved out the Senate Select Committee on Nutrition and Human Needs in 1968 and ran it as a rump food policy committee for the entirety of its legislative life (until 1977). See George S. McGovern, *Grassroots: The autobiography of George McGovern* (New York: Random House, 1977), pp. 168–69; Robert Sam Anson, *McGovern: A biography* (New York: Holt, Rinehart and Winston, 1972), chap. 10; McGovern's introduction to Kotz, *Promises*, pp. vii–x; Nancy Hicks, "Ford's food stamp plan seeks $1.2-billion savings," *NYT,* 21 October 1975, p. 1; "Senate panel stalls on plan to provide free food stamps," *NYT,* 24 February 1977, p. 27.

87. Foley became the chairman of Agriculture in 1975, when the Democratic Caucus purged Poage and two others from their chairmanships. The Caucus, with its huge influx of liberal "Watergate babies," took the actions for reasons of both policy and style. All three deposed chairmen were autocratic southerners; all three new chairmen were more accommodating northerners.

88. Marjorie Hunter, "Hollings fight on hunger is stirring the South," *NYT,* 8 March 1969, p. 14; *KAL,* 31 January 1975; *KAL,* 14 February 1975; F. R. Jimson, "Farm politics," *WF,* 8 February 1975, p. 6; "Washington report," *SF,* May 1975, p. 4; "House committee votes for free food stamps as proposed by Carter," *NYT,* 16 June 1977, p. 21; Steven V. Roberts, "As it grows, food stamp program sprouts debate," *NYT,* 29 July 1979, p. IV 2.

gram into the same omnibus authorization bill. Rural lawmakers like Foley served as legislative arbiters between the congressional representatives of farmers and the congressional representatives of the poor.[89]

The accommodation of food stamps created no difficult political problems inside the House Agriculture Committee. The leadership created a subcommittee, staffed it with members sympathetic to food stamps, let them work out the program, and then bundled their proposals together with all the rest. With the occasional intervention of a rural colleague, for example, Brooklyn Democrat Frederick W. Richmond, the chairman of the Subcommittee on Domestic Marketing, Consumer Relations and Nutrition, pretty much ran the House end of the food stamp program, openly offering his support for a more generous farm program in trade for the commodity chairmen's support for a more generous food stamp program. "Inner-city districts and farm districts are both outnumbered by suburbanites in Congress," Richmond explained. "Without the urban-rural coalition, you wouldn't have farm programs and we wouldn't have food stamp programs." Politically, food stamps were just another commodity.[90]

As the 1980s demonstrated, however, the farm bloc's strategy of

89. Ferejohn, "Logrolling," pp. 239–45; Ehrenhalt, "House Agriculture," pp. 379–84; Nancy Hicks, "Food stamps plan opposed in House," NYT, 31 January 1975, p. 27; Richard D. Lyons, "Bill will fight food stamp rise," NYT, 30 January 1975, p. 24; Martin Tolchin, "House backs Carter's plan for free food stamps," NYT, 28 July 1977, p. 1; Martin Tolchin, "Urban-rural coalition successful on farm and food stamp measure," NYT, 29 July 1977, p. 19; Martin Tolchin, "Urban and rural lawmakers join to support each bloc's interests," NYT, 30 July 1977, p. 1. In 1976, in fact, Foley hired John R. Kramer as a special counsel—the same John R. Kramer who in 1969 had so bitterly attacked the Agriculture Committee for its indifference to the poor.

90. Marcia Zarley, "Farm gains linked to food stamps," SF, March 1979, p. 34; Fred Richmond, "Farmers and consumers CAN work together," Farm Journal, January 1977, p. 14; Hearings, 1977, p. 1; Hearings before the House Agriculture Committee, Subcommittee on Domestic Marketing, Consumer Relations and Nutrition, "General farm bill of 1981 (Food stamp program)," 97th Congress, 1st session, Serial 97-G, Part 2, 1981; Nancy Hicks, "Food stamp price freeze voted by House," NYT, 5 February 1975, p. 1; "Washington report," SF, May 1975, p. 4; Tolchin, "House backs Carter's plan," p. 1; Tolchin, "Urban-rural coalition," p. 19; Tolchin, "Urban and rural lawmakers join," p. 1; "Washington report," WF, September 1977, p. 4; Steven V. Roberts, "Supporters and critics of food stamps prepare to battle on scope of program," NYT, 14 February 1981, p. 9; Steven V. Roberts, "Congressional battles over food stamps is joined and is already half over," NYT, 8 April 1981, p. 25; Fred Powledge, "Brooklyn supports its congressman," Nation, 29 April 1978, pp. 507–8; Pete Hamill and Denis Hamill, "The rise and fall of Fred Richmond," New York, 22 November 1982, pp. 36–44; Lyons and Taylor, "Farm politics in transition," p. 133; Peters, "The 1977 farm bill," pp. 31–32. In the Senate, the guardians of food stamps were more diverse: South Dakota Democrat George S. McGovern, Kansas Republican Robert Dole and Vermont Democrat Patrick Leahy.

logrolls—commodities with commodities, farm subsidies with food stamps—had a significant shortcoming. As Peters put it, whenever "there is not enough to go around, for every farm interest the tendency to 'go it alone' and 'protect one's own interest' is heightened." In 1981, the Reagan administration launched an offensive on federal spending, particularly federal social spending. Moreover, through creative use of the new federal budget process, it forced Congress to consider more drastic cuts than it had ever recently made. In the Agriculture Committee, rural conservatives defected in droves from food stamps, forcing Committee liberals to accept the Reagan proposals as a compromise. On the floor, likewise, the commodity programs suffered several damaging amendments (although they at least emerged with their integrity intact).[91]

Both programs, though, survived the most difficult challenges of their lifetimes. "By the end of the first session of the Ninety-seventh Congress [1981]," Ferejohn summarized, "it was clear that the Reagan administration had made a serious and partly successful assault on the farm-city alliance." But, he continued, "as the events in the two [agriculture] committees illustrated, President Reagan had not succeeded in breaking up the agricultural 'political economy.'" Within the limits set by the new budgetary environment, the committee-based logroll was robust.[92]

In the 1970s, then, the remnants of the farm bloc settled onto an agreeable defensive strategy. Their complex web of logrolls helped to preserve the farm programs with a minimum of concession, sugarcoating farm subsidies with food stamps. Where the farm bloc had once had all the votes it needed, it now had all the goods.

Conclusion

This chapter has chronicled decline and rise, failure and success, but the connection was not the obvious one. The decline was of farmers: the epic migrations from the country to the city moved congressional power

---

91. Peters, "The 1981 farm bill," p. 163; Roberts, "Supporters and critics," p. 9; Steven V. Roberts, "Coalition forms to defend food stamps," *NYT*, 24 February 1981, p. B 11; Steven V. Roberts, "'Anti-hunger' lobbyists start their rounds," *NYT*, 11 March 1981, p. B 5; Steven V. Roberts, "Food stamp program: How it grew and how Reagan wants to cut it back," *NYT*, 4 April 1981, p. 11; Roberts, "Congressional battle," p. 25; Steven V. Roberts, "Committees settling on Reagan cuts in food stamps," *NYT*, 7 May 1981, p. B 10; Steven V. Roberts, "House unit voids 2 votes in clash on food stamps," *NYT*, 12 May 1981, p. D 22; Steven V. Roberts, "Congressional panels adopt Reagan's plan to slash food stamp program," *NYT*, 13 May 1981, p. 28.

92. Ferejohn, "Logrolling," p. 248, pp. 245–50.

from the country to the city. The failure, however, was of consumers: their numerical predominance was insufficient to entrench them in congressional deliberations over agricultural policy.

In the late 1960s, the farm lobby saw the terms of its access shift very drastically. Congressional agrarians accommodated the farm lobby to the degree that they could, but they denied the farm lobby when necessary. Their more substantial independence in part was practical—the farm bloc simply could not get what it once had gotten on the floor—but it was also more directly pragmatic. The migration from countryside to town and to city undercut the electoral value of what it had to offer as representative of farmers.

Still, the farm lobby maintained its access, successfully negotiating a change in its structure. As the general farm organizations, particularly the Farm Bureau, gradually forfeited their access to congressional deliberations, the commodity organizations rose to take their place. The commodity groups provided the specialized electoral information and propaganda that lawmakers needed, services that were not likely to lose their value, given farmers' continued preference for farm subsidy legislation. The farm lobby maintained its access because it maintained its competitive advantage and it enjoyed its issue's recurrence.

The consumer lobby, in contrast, failed to secure even a foothold. In the early 1970s, spectacular food price inflation installed its issues on the agricultural agenda, and a handful of urban and suburban lawmakers picked up its call. In the late 1970s, however, the inflation subsided, and with it the issue, and congressional attention turned elsewhere. The competitive advantage of the consumer lobby, so promising in the early 1970s, failed for want of recurrence.

As the events of the mideighties demonstrated, this state of affairs could still be quite profitable for farmers. In the mideighties, under the most conservative presidential administration in a generation, the amount of federal money devoted to the price support programs actually increased for a time, rising to almost 3 percent of federal spending, its largest share since the mid-1960s. On average, even discounting for inflation, farm program beneficiaries received record sums of money; at the 1986 peak, the federal government spent over thirteen thousand dollars per farm on agricultural stabilization activities.

Two main factors lay behind the increased government investment in agriculture. First, economically, agriculture became mired in its deepest depression since the thirties.[93] As always, farm program expenses varied inversely with the state of the farm economy; more farmers participated

---

93. For a picture of the depression's effect in the quintessential farm state, see Mark Friedberger, *Shake-out: Iowa farm families in the 1980s* (Lexington: University Press of Kentucky, 1989).

when prices were low. The programs were designed to shore up farm income, and they did. Second, politically, the farm depression was potentially a catastrophe for the Reagan administration and the Republican Party. Its hold on the Senate was tenuous and its alliance with southern "Boll Weevil" Democrats was delicate. Consequently, as Budget Director David Stockman complained, the administration put aside its principles to avert disaster. In 1981 and 1985, it accepted farm bills that violated its free-market precepts. Moreover, in 1983, it implemented the fabulously expensive Payment-in-Kind (PIK) program, acting on its own authority after Congress failed to give it an explicit authorization.[94]

The pattern of access in agriculture, however, remained unchanged. First, the consumer lobby, the potential counterweight to more generous farm programs, remained outside Congress's farm policy deliberations. Second, the farm lobby, its hand strengthened by lawmakers' panic over farmers' desperate financial straits, fended off the administration's repeated attempts to pare down farm spending. Farm state Republicans joined Democrats, especially in the GOP-controlled Senate. Third, the House farm bloc, afraid that a too-generous farm bill might run aground on the House floor, accepted a draft of the 1985 farm bill that froze target prices for five years. As usual, the Senate's more liberal proposal was the fulcrum that moved subsidies upward.[95] Finally, at this writing, agriculture has begun to pull out of its long depression, and the constraints of the sixties, seventies and eighties are fully in evidence: the 1990 farm bill reflected the preferences of the farm lobby, not the consumer lobby; the farm bloc had to compromise its desires severely to pass the bill in the House; and the farm bloc accepted even deeper cuts in conference, as part of the 1990 budget accord, rather than throw the bill open on the floor.

In short, the agricultural politics of the 1980s was politics as usual. The farm lobby remained fragmented, but it maintained its place in congressional deliberations. The consumer lobby remained excluded. The farm bloc remained dependent on the good will of urban liberals.

In the 1960s, the 1970s *and* the 1980s, that is, farm organizations dominated access in agriculture and consumer organizations looked on. Farmers and consumers had equal measures of interest in agricultural policy, but farmers were in it for the long haul.

94. David A. Stockman, *The triumph of politics: Why the Reagan revolution failed* (New York: Harper and Row, 1986), pp. 165–68, 286, 416–19. The Payment-in-Kind program compensated farmers who participated in crop reduction with certificates redeemable for government-held surplus commodities. Because payment was in kind rather than in cash, the PIK program allowed the USDA to skirt program payments limits.

95. See Browne, *Private interests*.

Commentary and Conclusions

Uncertainty dominates the electoral life of representatives in Congress. Despite their past successes, they need information about the preferences of their constituents, about the salience of issues to their constituents and about the ability of various policy options to satisfy the desires of their constituents. Any number of policy advocates—political parties, interest groups or local elites—provide such information as they guide legislative decisions. The reliability of their counsel, however, is not known to representatives without cost. The lawmakers' problem lies not in obtaining advice but in discerning whose advice is worth obtaining.

After all, the quantity of advice that legislators can heed is limited by their time, by their resources and, most of all, by the indivisibility of their votes. Accordingly, they must choose among those that would consult with them. Two considerations structure their decision.

First, lawmakers judge the usefulness of informants' advice and assistance in congressional elections. Drawing from the experiences of themselves and of others situated similarly, they evaluate the competitive advantage of interest groups relative to other informants. Second, lawmakers assess whether their informants' performance is sustainable. Drawing from their workaday theories of popular agitation, they evaluate the likelihood that the conditions that established competitive advantage will in fact recur.

When events fulfill both conditions, when legislators judge that interest groups enjoy competitive advantage over rival informants, and when they expect the conditions that maintain competitive advantage to recur, they build close consultative relationships with political advocacy groups. Lawmakers give their views privileged consideration. Representatives grant them access.

215

In the preceding pages, the argument has held up well. Interpretations of competitive advantage and forecasts of recurrence, this study has shown, account for the variations in the relationship between the Congress and the farm lobby since World War I. They account for the initial incorporation of the farm lobby, particularly the American Farm Bureau Federation, into congressional farm policy consultations with midwestern representatives in the late twenties and with southern representatives in the early thirties. They account for the maintenance of farm organization access throughout the thirties and forties. They account for the diminution of consultation with the Farm Bureau from the late fifties forward. Finally, they account for subsequent patterns of access in agriculture: for the incorporation of the commodity lobbies in the sixties, for the exclusion of the consumer lobby in the seventies and for the confinement of the farm lobby in the sixties and beyond.

Three observations about the performance of the theoretical argument in its empirical setting deserve special emphasis. First, the theory of access correctly identified the turning points of congressional interactions with the farm organizations. Interpretations of competitive advantage and predictions of recurrence, for example, situated the genesis of farm lobby access in the latter half of the 1920s rather than in the early half. In the early part of the decade, despite the formation of the American Farm Bureau Federation, despite its location in Washington, and despite its prominence in the farm relief movement, the conditions for farm lobby access fell short of fulfillment. Elections revealed only ambiguous evidence of the farm lobby's competitive advantage, and assays of economic trends portended its nonrecurrence. In the later part of the decade, however, the conditions were met. Evidence of the electoral potency of the farm relief issue mounted, and expectations of its sustained salience grew. Representatives from the Middle West, who had earlier remained guarded in the presence of the farm groups, eagerly incorporated them into their advisory circle. The theory of access, in sum, specified the timing of access in agriculture. Its ability to do so, in fact, is crucial to demonstrations of its explanatory efficacy.

Second, the theory of access accounted for losses of access as well as it accounted for gains. In the late fifties, for instance, the widely held interpretation that farm voters had rejected the program of the Eisenhower administration, and with it the program of the American Farm Bureau, undermined the Federation's access in Congress. A decade of disagreement between agrarian representatives and the Farm Bureau leadership was not enough. Loss of Farm Bureau access awaited indications from elections that the Farm Bureau's competitive advantage had eroded. The theory of access, in sum, identified conditions under which interest groups might forfeit their access as well as conditions under which they might advance it. Its ability to do so is crucial to demonstrations of its explanatory robustness.

Finally, the theory of access explained denials as well as grants of interest group access. In the early seventies, for example, rapid food price inflation put consumer concerns on the farm policy agenda and drew a handful of urban and suburban members to the Agriculture Committee. The national consumer lobbies, however, remained outside the deliberations. Although there were indications of their competitive advantage in meeting the electoral needs of metropolitan members, their advantage was not sustainable. The efficacy of appeals to consumer interests in farm policy depended upon a set of circumstances that were not recurrent. The theory of access, in sum, identified conditions that, if fulfilled, led to grants of access and conditions that, if not fulfilled, led to denials. Its ability to do so is crucial to demonstrations of its explanatory generality.

The theoretical apparatus developed here solves a wide range of puzzles posed by agricultural price politics since the First World War. Now comes time to consider whether it clarifies anything else. What does the theory of access say about policy relationships in other issue arenas? What does it reveal about the connection between pressure politics and party politics? What are its implications for our understanding of the nature and extent of interest group influence?

Access Across Time and Space

The theory of access lodges the close consultative relationships between representatives and interest groups in the fulfillment of two separate conditions: (1) that interest groups enjoy competitive advantage over other informants, and (2) that the circumstances that underlie the advantage seem likely to recur. It generates insights into variations of policy relationships along two separate dimensions: across time and across space.

First, the theory helps to account for variations in access in policy arenas examined across time. According to the argument, lobbies gain access when events allow them to meet the conditions, but they lose access when events prevent it. The rise and decline of the American Farm Bureau Federation offered a compelling instance, and in many of its particulars, the rise and decline of the Anti-Saloon League suggests a striking parallel.

In the early twentieth century, the Anti-Saloon League was the leading proponent of prohibition on the local, state and national levels.

Founded in Ohio in 1893, it drew its program and its sustenance from the evangelical Protestant churches, particularly in the rural areas of the Middle West.

In the first two decades of the twentieth century, the League rode a surge of dry sentiment to policy success. Between 1903 and 1917, twenty-four states adopted prohibition laws, sometimes at the League's behest and sometimes not. Prodded by Anti-Saloon agitation, Congress submitted the Eighteenth Amendment to the states in 1917, and all but two states ratified national prohibition within a year and a half.

At both the state and national levels, the League's successes clearly built upon perceptions of its competitive advantage. First in local, then in state and then in federal elections, the Anti-Saloon League benefited from the popular appeal of prohibition. As Kerr phrased it, "the decision for [national] prohibition was not made in Washington; it was made on election days in the precincts and townships across America." "Had the Anti-Saloon League not demonstrated its ability to elect and defeat candidates for public office," Odegard commented, likewise,

[had] the League been confined to moral appeals, it would have accomplished no more in the realm of practical legislation than Christian missionaries could accomplish in a well-fed heathen land. But with the appeal of bread to starving heathens, and with the appeal of re-election to aspiring politicians, converts are readily made. . . .The League boasted of its power, but . . . without a substantial foundation in the hearts of the electorate, its influence in the lobby and committee room would have been negligible.[1]

Similarly, the League's policy successes evidently built upon a sense that the social conditions underlying the agitation for prohibition would not soon abate (if I might extrapolate from extant histories, all written for other purposes). In the predominantly rural states of the West, the Midwest and the South, the social base of prohibition sentiment was middle-class white Protestants, their values and political status threatened by a tide of Roman Catholic immigrants from southern and eastern Europe. From the turn of the century and into the twenties, until the Great Depression mooted it, political leaders foresaw continuing moral conflict, pitting their native-stock Protestant constituents against the rising hordes of urban Catholics. The motivating power of the prohibition issue was a sure bet for the future.[2]

1. K. Austin Kerr, *Organized for prohibition: A new history of the Anti-Saloon League* (New Haven: Yale University Press, 1985), p. 183 and chaps. 3–8; and Peter H. Odegard, *Pressure politics: The story of the Anti-Saloon League* (New York: Columbia University Press, 1928), p. 105 and chaps. 1–6.

2. See Joseph R. Gusfield, *Symbolic crusade: Status politics and the American temperance movement* (Urbana: University of Illinois Press, 1963); James H. Timberlake,

In the 1920s, electoral victories of dry candidates maintained the Anti-Saloon League's access, even as the organization itself secretly crumbled. In the early 1930s, however, it lost its competitive advantage. The proportions of dry voters fell dramatically as the candidacies of Al Smith mobilized urban Catholic immigrants. Moreover, despite their intentions to remain nonpartisan, the ascent and nomination of Smith pushed prohibition forces into the arms of Herbert Hoover and the Republican Party, staking their success to the performance of the GOP administration. Accordingly, the elections of 1930 and 1932 demonstrated conclusively that, relative to other advocates, the League had nothing special to offer. It rapidly lost the attention of public officials. "When Congress adjourned in the summer of 1932 there were large dry majorities in both Houses, and they included all the heaviest boozers of each," remarked the bilious, wet critic, H. L. Mencken. "But when the election returns came in November those majorities vanished, and by Christmas Prohibition was done for. All the driest drys were converted overnight. The day before election day they were still bowing their necks to the Anti-Saloon League, but two days later they were howling for beer."[3]

In sum, the Anti-Saloon League, like the Farm Bureau, secured its access to public officials with evident successes in elections and with expectations that the social conditions underlying its successes would continue. The Anti-Saloon League, like the Farm Bureau, maintained its access with evident continuations of its victories. Finally, the Anti-Saloon League, like the Farm Bureau, lost its access with dramatic electoral reversals. Like the Farm Bureau, demographic and political changes mobbed its constituency. And like the Farm Bureau, its ties with an incumbent president linked its reputation, unhappily, to the administration's. Its access rose and fell with demonstrations of competitive advantage and anticipations of recurrence.

In this particular instance, then, the theory of access provides a framework for explanation that does no great violence to existing historical studies. Across time, competitive advantage and recurrence account for variations in the access of the prohibition lobby.[4]

Prohibition and the progressive movement, 1900–1920 (Cambridge: Harvard University Press, 1963); and David Burner, *The politics of provincialism: The Democratic Party in transition, 1918–1932* (New York: Alfred A. Knopf, 1968).

3. H. L. Mencken, *A carnival of buncombe: Writings on politics* (Chicago: University of Chicago Press, 1984), pp. 315–16, also p. 285; Kerr, *Organized for prohibition,* chaps. 9–10.

4. Other studies that follow particular policy arenas over time provide only sketchy information relevant to this argument, although at points they are suggestive. See, for ex-

Second, the theory helps to account for variations in access in policy arenas across space. As a model of development and change, the theory implies that interest groups should gain access in some policy arenas but fail to gain access in others. On the one hand, lobbying organizations should be prominent in policy arenas where they enjoy competitive advantage over their rivals and where the circumstances that established their competitive advantage recur. On the other hand, lobbying organizations should not be prominent in situations that prevent them from meeting the conditions. Where interest groups do not enjoy competitive advantage relative to their rivals or where circumstances that maintain competitive advantage do not recur, interest group access will not exist.

Across the range of policy arenas, interest group access is not uniformly in evidence. Many absences reflect failures of competitive advantage. In the late thirties, for example, several organizations purporting to represent small business owners set themselves up in Washington. None, however, had the membership, commitment or money to draw much attention; in fact, they all were little more than fanatics with P.O. boxes. Consequently, Zeigler observed, employing the parallel language of policy subsystems, "nothing approximating a subsystem of activity is possible" in the interactions of the small business lobby with Congress. "Instead of a subsystem, a pattern of interaction between the small business groups and the [congressional] committees has developed which might best be described as a 'struggle for legitimacy.'" The Small Business Committees of the House and the Senate, locked into a battle over turf with their respective Banking Committees, finally abandoned the small business lobby altogether. "Finding no advantage in using [the National Small Business Men's Association], the Senate Committee turned to trade associations" like the National Association of Retail Druggists. Small business lobbies lacked the constituency connections essential to demonstrations of competitive advantage.[5]

Other absences, probably fewer, reflect forestalled recurrence. Through the mid-1970s, for instance, members of Congress shied from establishing close consultative ties with the environmental lobbies, despite their willingness to enact environmental legislation. "The normal

---

ample, William Pencak, *For God and country: The American Legion, 1919-1941* (Boston: Northeastern University Press, 1989); Henry J. Pratt, *The gray lobby* (Chicago: University of Chicago Press, 1976); and Jo Freeman, *The politics of women's liberation* (New York: Longman, 1975).

5. L. Harmon Zeigler, *The politics of small business* (Washington: Public Affairs Press, 1961), pp. 84, 85, 79. See also Joseph C. Palamountain, *The politics of distribution* (Cambridge: Harvard University Press, 1955), pp. 82–100, 108–41, 163, 175–82, 242, 258.

congressional response," Price reported, "has been a certain wariness of becoming identified as a pro-environmentalist 'extremist.'" Among the reasons why, one is especially pertinent here: the enthusiasm for ecology was distinctly transitory. Environmentalism swept into Congress on a wave of public enthusiasm that crested in 1970 with Earth Day, but its momentum proved difficult to sustain. In 1970, 53 percent of Gallup's respondents identified "pollution" as the nation's most important problem. Within a few years, however, worries over inflation and energy eclipsed ecological concerns, and opponents of environmental regulation enjoyed a resurgence. Thus, once the initial wave of public enthusiasm was spent, the environmental lobbies were hard-pressed to demonstrate a privileged claim on the attention of legislators. As Hays observed, "the national [environmental] organizations were most successful in mobilizing people in periods of environmental crisis. But they were well aware that effectiveness required sustained, not intermittent, influence. This alone would enable them to cope successfully with the much more continuous political presence of the development advocates."[6] Like other organizations that depended upon high public salience to motivate their diffuse memberships, the ecology groups suffered from congressional fears that public apathy would once more leave them vulnerable when the political fad had passed.[7]

6. David E. Price, "Policy making in congressional committees: The impact of 'environmental' factors," *American Political Science Review*, 72 (June 1978), p. 564; Samuel P. Hays, *Beauty, health, and permanence: Environmental politics in the United States, 1955–1985* (New York: Cambridge University Press, 1987), p. 64; Anthony Downs, "Up and down with ecology: The 'issue-attention cycle,'" *Public Interest*, 28 (Summer 1972), pp. 38–50; Mary Etta Cook and Roger H. Davidson, "Deferral politics: Congressional decision making on environmental issues in the 1980s," pp. 47–76 in Helen M. Ingram and R. Kenneth Godwin, eds., *Public policy and the natural environment* (Greenwich, Conn.: JAI Press, 1985); Charles O. Jones, *Clean air* (Pittsburgh: University of Pittsburgh Press, 1975), p. 56; Daniel R. Grant, "Carrots, sticks, and consensus," pp. 99–115 in Leslie L. Roos, Jr., ed., *The politics of ecosuicide* (New York: Holt, Rinehart and Winston, 1971), p. 101; J. Clarence Davies III and Barbara S. Davies, *The politics of pollution*, 2d ed. (Indianapolis: Bobbs-Merrill Co., 1975); Randall B. Ripley and Grace A. Franklin, *Congress, the bureaucracy, and public policy*, rev. ed. (Homewood, Ill.: Dorsey Press, 1980), pp. 125–31. In recent years, environmental issues seem to have achieved a better hold on their salience, especially in the more affluent constituencies on the West and Northeast coasts, to the environmental lobbies' benefit. See Hays, *Beauty*, pp. 44–52, 459–69, 505–6.

7. The lack of recurrence has been a consistent problem for the whole array of public interest groups. As one "knowledgeable" member of Congress put it, "A cardinal rule of politics is not so much to make friends as to avoid making enemies. Voting for a consumer protection bill will win you the temporary approval of large groups of consumers but, perhaps, the undying enmity of smaller but more powerful groups—the major money contributors to a political campaign, the molders of public opinion. The housewife forgets;

In these two particular instances, then, the theory of access offers a framework for understanding the absence of close working relationships between lobbies and Congress, an understanding consistent with the facts of the cases. Across space, competitive advantage and recurrence account for important variations in interest group access.[8]

An exhaustive survey of interest group access in Congress across time and across space awaits investigation and report (and probably will for decades to come). Still, this brief survey, coupled with the detailed exploration of chapters 1–6, suggests that the argument is helpful in a variety of settings. Across time and across space, it identifies the sources of interest group access in Congress.

The Party System and the Pressure System

Representatives need political counsel, but they can get it from any number of sources. In concept and in fact, however, they must choose from among those that would advise them those they will heed and those they will ignore. Representatives need to reach decisions, and their decisions are indivisible. They cannot accommodate every recommendation.

Accordingly, interest groups contend with other informants to get their ideas across to Congress. Typically, they compete with each other, and they compete with political parties. Their competition has important implications, both for understanding policy interactions in other policy arenas and for understanding the nature of the relationship between pressure groups and political parties.

Under some circumstances, for example, interest groups and political parties do not contend, and where they do not, political parties dominate the congressional environment. "The subjects of labor, education,

---

big business never forgets." That is, issues of regulation seldom lose their salience for business to the same extent that they lose their salience for more diffuse publics. "Uncle Sam: Consumers' champion," *Business Week*, 2 April 1966, p. 77. On the point, see also David Vogel, *Fluctuating fortunes: The political power of business in America* (New York: Basic Books, 1989).

8. Ripley and Franklin trace cross-sectional variations in interest group access to the types of policy that are produced by different arenas, drawing upon Lowi's famous typology. Because of their rather mechanical model of governmental responsiveness, however, they seem unable to account for instances like small business, where lawmakers denied access despite organized interests, and instances like agriculture, where lawmakers accommodated some groups but excluded others. Likewise, because of their reliance upon policy types, which mutate slowly (if at all) over time, they appear unlikely to explain longitudinal variations in interest group access. See Ripley and Franklin, *Congress;* and Theodore J. Lowi, "American business, public policy, case studies, and political theory," *World Politics*, 16 (July 1964), pp. 677–715.

and poverty pose issues over which Democrats and Republicans have tended to divide and which have often been the major points of domestic disagreement in Presidential and congressional campaigns," Fenno observed. "Put conversely, the executive branch, clientele groups, and House members have been especially quick to use party resources to fight their battles in nationally controversial policy arenas." In such circumstances, interest group consultations with Congress are not very important. "The policy coalitions facing Education and Labor," Fenno reported, "[were] distinctively *party-led.*"[9] Where party cleavages reproduce interest group cleavages, competitive advantage is not at issue. Parties and lobbies send exactly the same signals. Party politics subsumes interest group politics; access is partisan.

Where party cleavages reproduce interest group cleavages, then, lobbies march in lockstep with political parties. In the New Deal party system, business and labor were the leading cases. They, as Schattschneider pointed out, had nowhere else to go.[10] Where parties fail or refuse to reproduce interest group cleavages, however, lobbies compete with political parties for the allegiances of political leaders. In the New Deal party system, agriculture is a prime example among many, as indeed we have seen. It, as Schattschneider neglected to point out, did have elsewhere to go.

The points of difference between history's two most important veterans' lobbies make a good illustration. Both the Grand Army of the Republic (GAR) and the American Legion represented American war veterans, but they differed in the alignment of their memberships relative to the party system. In the aftermath of secession and the Civil War, the political parties divided along sectional lines, the Republicans dominating the North and the Democrats the South. As the representative of Union Army veterans of the Civil War, mustered primarily from the North, the GAR therefore had nowhere else to go. The Democratic Party was quite unlikely to accommodate its demands, and its members were quite unlikely to vote Democratic. In contrast, as the representative

9. Richard F. Fenno, Jr., *Congressmen in committees* (Boston: Little, Brown and Co., 1973), pp. 31–32 (emphasis Fenno's). See also Harold L. Wolman and Norman C. Thomas, "Black interests, black groups, and black influence in the federal policy process: The cases of housing and education," *Journal of Politics*, 32 (November 1970), pp. 875–97; and Martha Derthick, *Policymaking for Social Security* (Washington: Brookings Institution, 1979).

10. E. E. Schattschneider, *The semisovereign people: A realist's view of democracy in America* (Hinsdale, Ill.: Dryden Press, 1975), chap. 3; J. David Greenstone, *Labor in American politics* (Chicago: University of Chicago Press, 1977), chap. 2. See also Fay Calkins, *The CIO and the Democratic Party* (Chicago: University of Chicago Press, 1952).

of American Expeditionary Force veterans of World War I, mustered from all over the country, the Legion did have elsewhere to go. The Legion's membership straddled the partisan cleavage while the Grand Army's membership lined up along one side of it. The Legion remained a conscientious nonpartisan while the GAR became a committed partisan, an adjunct of the Republican Party.[11]

Contra McConnell, then, policy advocates have not the luxury to opt in or opt out of the party system.[12] The party game, to use Schattschneider's phrase, is played at a different, higher level. Political parties choose which interests they will promote and which interests they will neglect, and policy advocates—organized or not—respond accordingly. In the 1920s, the two major parties opposed initiatives for farm relief and forced the farm lobby to compete with them for the loyalties of their partisans. In the 1950s, the Republican Party adopted the policy of the American Farm Bureau and (for all practical purposes) forced its partisans to adopt it as well. In sum, policy advocates work inside or outside of the party system depending not upon their own choices but upon the choices of political parties.

Pressure politics, then, reflects the failure of party politics, a failure that is necessary and inherent. Social conflicts are numerous, and parties cannot fight battles on all the possible fronts. They must choose their conflicts carefully, closely constrained by the realities of majoritarianism. Because they need to win elections, parties align along a particular cleavage only if the matchup is beneficial to themselves, only if they think they can gain support by it. Because their opponents need equally to win elections, parties align along a particular cleavage only if the matchup is beneficial to their opposition as well, only if the opposition can gain countervailing support from the other side.

The contrasting styles of mobilization among American ethnic groups provide an important example. On the one hand, the political parties mobilized the Irish and Germans into partisan activity and out of sectarian activity. First, the very size of the Irish and German com-

11. Pencak, For God and country, chaps. 1–7; Marcus Duffield, King Legion (New York: Jonathan Cape and Harrison Smith, 1931); Mary R. Dearing, Veterans in politics: The story of the G.A.R. (Baton Rouge: Louisiana State University Press, 1952). Incidently, the GAR apparently fared better within the party system than the Legion did outside it. At their brief peak after the early payout of soldiers' bonuses in 1932, expenditures on behalf of 4.7 million World War I veterans amounted to a little under 1 percent of gross national product (GNP), a little over 14 percent of federal spending. At their extended peak in the 1890s, in contrast, expenditures on behalf of 2.2 million Union Army veterans amounted to more than 1 percent of GNP, more than 40 percent of federal spending.

12. Grant McConnell, The decline of agrarian democracy (Berkeley and Los Angeles: University of California Press, 1953), chaps. 1, 3, 5.

munities made them attractive to party leaders. Irish Catholics were the mainstays of the Democratic Party in the North; German Protestants were the mainstays of the Republican Party in the Midwest. Second, the very size of the domestic opposition to the foreign policy interests of American Irish and American Germans made the opposition equally attractive to the opposite party. In the Northeast, Yankee business elites with economic and sentimental ties to England contested the Irish. In the nation, Yankee business elites in the North and Anglo-Saxon agricultural elites in the South, both with long-standing affection for England, contested the Germans. Because of their numbers, the Irish and Germans did not need to develop the apparatus for exerting pressure on Congress. The parties mobilized Irish and Germans because the conflict was attractive to both parties.[13]

On the other hand, the political parties failed to mobilize American Jews into partisan activity and away from sectarian activity. First, the smallness of the Jewish community in all but a few cities made its co-optation into party activities less than urgent. Second, and more important, the even greater smallness of the domestic opposition to pro-Israeli foreign policy made it unattractive to politicians of either party to take the other side. "I'm sorry, gentlemen," Harry Truman reportedly told a delegation of State Department experts pressing for a softer policy toward Middle Eastern Arabs, "but I have to answer to hundreds of thousands who are anxious for the success of Zionism; I do not have hundreds of thousands of Arabs among my constituents." Because of their small numbers, Jewish supporters of Israel had to develop an apparatus for exerting pressure on Congress. Disputes over American policy toward Israel were not an attractive venue for party competition.[14]

As a consequence, conflicts over American foreign policy in Europe were fought within the party system, whereas conflicts over American foreign policy in the Middle East were fought within the pressure system. In the early twentieth century, isolationism was the policy of Republicans representing the German parts of the Middle West (like Robert M. La Follette in Wisconsin and Gerald P. Nye in North Dakota), sometimes supported by Democrats representing the Irish constituencies in the East and Midwest. Interest groups advancing support for Germany, for Ireland or for England were not much in evidence. In the late twentieth century, in contrast, support for Israel was the

13. Louis L. Gerson, "The influence of hyphenated Americans on U.S. diplomacy," pp. 19–32 in Abdul Aziz Said, ed., *Ethnicity and U.S. foreign policy,* rev. ed. (New York: Praeger Publishers, 1981).

14. William A. Eddy, *F.D.R. meets Ibn Saud* (New York: American Friends of the Middle East, 1954), p. 36.

policy of both parties, and the disputes over its exact contours were attended by robust pro-Israel advocacy organizations. "The leading pro-Israel lobby in Washington, the American Israel Public Affairs Committee," a recent article asserted, "has become a major force in shaping United States policy in the Middle East." Despite Americans' ties of kinship and sentiment to the nations of the Old World, interest group access was largely absent from the politics of foreign policy, with the singular exception of Israel, the exception that proved the rule.[15]

Where numbers of proponents and numbers of opponents were large enough to entice parties onto opposite sides, policy advocates fought their battles inside the party system. Where the numbers of proponents and opponents were insufficient to draw parties to opposite sides, policy advocates took their battles outside.

Throughout this study, in sum, I have imagined that interest groups and political parties were fundamentally at odds, fundamentally in competition for the attention of elected officials. As this section has acknowledged, that assertion is not always true. On occasion, interest groups line up with political parties, and on such occasions, interest groups lag behind political parties in their claims on lawmakers' allegiances. On such occasions, that is, the party system dominates the pressure system, as Schattschneider indeed averred.

As this section has also argued, however, party dominance is necessarily rare. Parties seek to win elections. Together, political parties choose the issues that they will contest in ways that maximize their probability of winning, subject to the constraint that the opposition party does the same. By the nature of majoritarian politics, then, political parties structure a few important social conflicts, but they fail to structure many more. Where they fail to structure social conflicts, the pressure system does.

Consequently, strengthening political parties will not overcome the biases and inefficiencies of pressure politics. Inherently, party cleavages can reflect only a few important cleavages, and those conflicts that parties fail to channel will be pursued elsewhere. The fashion of our time

15. David K. Shipler, "On Middle East policy, a major influence," *New York Times*, 6 July 1987, p. 1; John Milton Cooper, Jr., *The vanity of power: American isolationism and the First World War, 1914–1917* (Westport, Conn.: Greenwood Publishing, 1969); Wayne S. Cole, *Roosevelt and the isolationists, 1932–1945* (Lincoln: University of Nebraska Press, 1983); Robert Pear with Richard L. Berke, "Pro-Israel group exerts quiet might as it rallies supporters in Congress," *New York Times*, 7 July 1987, p. 7; Edward Tivnan, *The lobby: Jewish political power and American foreign policy* (New York: Simon and Schuster, 1987). These observations are equally true of Greeks, the other foreign policy lobby success story.

has been to identify close relationships between representatives and interest groups as the illness and stronger political parties as the cure. The experience of the farmers in the twenties should give us pause. Strong political parties cannot absorb the social conflicts that otherwise find their outlets in the pressure system; they can only suppress them.[16]

Toward a More Subtle Understanding of Interest Group Influence

The basic lesson of this book is that Schattschneider was right, but, ironically, for reasons that Bauer, Pool and Dexter identified.[17] That is, interest groups *are* influential, but not because of their ability to bring "pressures" to bear on members of Congress. Rather, interest groups are influential because they direct lawmakers' attention to some pressures rather than to others.[18]

Throughout the study, we have observed interest group influence, but we have observed "pressure" only in scattered instances, at most. Typically, interest groups, so far as we can see, did next to nothing in political campaigns. There is little evidence that they bought off political candidates; there is little evidence that they canvassed the countryside and knocked on all the doors; there is little evidence that whole legions of their loyalists marched off as directed to the polls. In fact, lobbies sel-

16. For similar skeptical soundings, see Jack L. Walker, "Interests, political parties, and policy formation in American democracy," pp. 141–70 in Donald T. Critchlow and Ellis W. Hawley, eds., *Federal social policy: The historical dimension* (University Park: Pennsylvania State University Press, 1988), pp. 143–45, 163–67.

17. E. E. Schattschneider, *Politics, pressures and the tariff* (New York: Prentice-Hall, 1935), esp. part 5; Raymond A. Bauer, Ithiel de Sola Pool and Lewis Anthony Dexter, *American business and public policy: The politics of foreign trade,* 2d ed. (Chicago: Aldine-Atherton, 1972), esp. parts 4 and 5.

18. Strikingly, recent work on the influence of campaign money on congressional deliberations comes to a similar conclusion: money directs attention and effort rather than switches votes. See Richard L. Hall and Frank W. Wayman, "Buying time: Moneyed interests and the mobilization of bias in congressional committees," *American Political Science Review,* 84 (September 1990), pp. 797–820. Are campaign contributions, then, another path to interest group access? At his point, my answer would be "yes," with two qualifications. First, and less important, expensive congressional campaigns are a fairly recent occurrence historically. Second, and more important, campaign money is probably more influential when it has a link to constituency. Incumbent members of Congress have little difficulty raising campaign funds, and even the largest contributions are small relative to total spending. Consequently, lawmakers can find contributors who want them to do more or less what their constituents also want them to do, and lawmakers know what their constituents want them to do in part because of the information activities of interest groups. The upshot, then, is that money supplements rather than supplants information as a medium of exchange for access.

dom, if ever, went after the hides of politicians whose policy views were contrary. They were loath to antagonize their adversaries into crusaders. They were loath to submit their reputations to absolutely decisive tests.[19]

Instead, lobbying organizations made sure that constituents knew exactly what their representatives were up to in Washington. They saw to it that their supporters had easy access to their memberships. They lionized their allies but spoke loud silences about their adversaries. They let it be known that they would not appreciate challengers to their friends, but they also let it be known that they might countenance competitors for their foes.[20]

But so does everybody else, every interest group, every political party and every local influential. Lobbies, therefore, lay special claims to the attentions of members of Congress *only* because legislators suppose that they represent constituents' preferences accurately, more accurately, in fact, than other informants. In their everyday dealings with Congress, interest groups contend that they represent constituents and will continue to represent them. Legislators evaluate whether or not their contentions are true. (In fact, the theory of access propounded in this book describes the process by which lawmakers decide whether contentions are true.) They may be, or they may not. Lobbies, then, are not always influential, but when they are, they are influential because—in the judgment of their congressional partisans—they represent congressional constituents.

But, one might object, this argument implies that interest groups are *not* in fact influential. By this telling, they actually add nothing to the mix. They simply report the preferences of voters that would exist even in their absence. Interest groups themselves are not influential, one might argue; instead, *constituents* are influential.

The argument sustains the objection, as far as it goes. Interest groups do reproduce the demands of constituents.[21] The demands they reproduce, however, are different from the demands that exist in their absence. Put another way, representatives listen closely to constituents'

19. Undoubtedly, such episodes occur, but they are much less common than one might suppose. Moreover, most often, offensive mobilization in elections is undertaken by interest groups with clear partisan leanings, like organized labor and ideological organizations.

20. For example, see, among others, Pencak, *For God and country,* pp. 110, 123; Pratt, *Gray lobby,* pp. 151, 161–67; Duffield, *King Legion,* pp. 52–53.

21. See especially John W. Kingdon, *Congressmen's voting decisions,* 2d ed. (New York: Harper and Row, 1981), chap. 5.

opinions, but the opinions they hear are reengineered in the presence of interest groups.

First, and most obviously, interest groups represent some voters but not others. They monitor and transmit the complaints and desires of one set of constituents, their members, but they neglect to monitor or neglect to transmit the complaints and desires of others. Lobbying organizations enable some voters to speak more loudly than others. Indeed, they enable some voters to speak who otherwise would not speak at all.[22]

Second, and more subtly, interest groups turn complaints into demands with appropriate policy responses. Typically, public opinion is inchoate, conveying more a reproof of the present than a blueprint for the future. Interest groups bring demands into focus. They formulate complaints into problems, and they develop (or adopt) policy options to solve them. In short, they frame issues. They insure that legislators receive articulate demands rather than inarticulate grievances.

Third, related, and also subtly, lobbies aid the detection of voter demands that would otherwise go unnoticed. Voters can only respond to the issues that candidates articulate, and interest groups raise the probability that candidates articulate the right ones. Lobbies identify issues—problems and solutions—that will resonate with constituents. They encourage sympathetic candidates to run when the issues are salient. They encourage candidates to try the issues out when they are salient. Thus, by increasing the chance that candidates raise the issues, interest groups increase the chance that voters respond to them. By increasing the chance that voters respond to them, interest groups increase the chance that elected officials conclude that the problems are real and important and that the solutions are tested and popular.

Finally, and easily overlooked, interest groups homogenize and generalize demands. As representatives of constituents in a number of states and congressional districts, they assemble cognate complaints from all over the nation into single, common demands. They identify common problems and put forth common solutions. Thereby, lobbies insure that representatives from different constituencies receive the same messages. They insure that representatives perceive common interests. They insure that representatives perceive national problems with appropriate national responses.

In sum, interest groups are influential because they determine the kinds of information that are available to legislators and the kinds of information that are not. They amplify voices; they articulate demands;

22. See especially Schattschneider, *Semisovereign people*, chap. 2.

they promote issues; they identify common interests. Their stock in trade is information—political intelligence—not pressure. Thus, Schattschneider *was* right for reasons that Bauer, Pool and Dexter identified. Interest groups are influential because they direct lawmakers' attention to some problems and pressures rather than to others.

Therein lies our ambivalence. On the one hand, we sympathize with interest groups because they *represent* popular demands, in many cases more effectively than parties or unassisted public officials (as we have seen in this book). On the other hand, we distrust interest groups because they represent only *some* demands, and by no means the most popular (as we have also seen in this book). Interest groups are both democratic and elitist institutions. It is a measure of our commitment to the ideals of popular government that this confuses and troubles us.

Select Bibliography

Books and Articles

Abler, David G. "Vote trading on farm legislation in the U.S. House." *American Journal of Agricultural Economics,* 71 (August 1989), pp. 583–91.

Albert, Carl (with Danney Goble). *Little giant: The life and times of Speaker Carl Albert.* Norman: University of Oklahoma Press, 1990.

Albertson, Dean. *Roosevelt's farmer: Claude R. Wickard in the New Deal.* New York: Columbia University Press, 1955.

Albjerg, Victor L. "Allan Blair Kline: The Farm Bureau, 1955." *Current History,* 28 (June 1955), pp. 362–68.

Alchian, Armen A. "Uncertainty, evolution, and economic theory." *Journal of Political Economy,* 58 (June 1950), pp. 211–21.

Alexander, Charles C. *The Ku Klux Klan in the Southwest.* Lexington: University of Kentucky Press, 1965.

Alexander, Herbert E. *Financing the 1972 election.* Lexington, Mass.: Lexington Books, 1976.

Anderson, William. *The wild man from Sugar Creek: The political career of Eugene Talmadge.* Baton Rouge: Louisiana State University Press, 1975.

Anson, Robert Sam. *McGovern: A biography.* New York: Holt, Rinehart and Winston, 1972.

Arnold, R. Douglas. *The logic of congressional action.* New Haven: Yale University Press, 1990.

Axelrod, Robert. *The evolution of cooperation.* New York: Basic Books, 1984.

Babcock, Bruce A., Colin A. Carter and Andrew Schmitz. "The political economy of U.S. wheat legislation." *Economic Inquiry,* 28 (April 1990), pp. 335–53.

Badger, Anthony J. *Prosperity road: The New Deal, tobacco, and North Carolina.* Chapel Hill: University of North Carolina Press, 1980.

Baker, Gladys. *The county agent.* Chicago: University of Chicago Press, 1939.

Baldwin, Sidney. *Poverty and politics: The rise and decline of the Farm Security Administration.* Chapel Hill: University of North Carolina Press, 1968.

Barton, Weldon V. "Coalition-building in the United States House of Representatives: Agricultural legislation in 1973." Pp. 141–61 in James E. Anderson, ed., *Cases in public policy-making*. New York: Praeger, 1976.

Bauer, Raymond A., Ithiel de Sola Pool and Lewis Anthony Dexter. *American business and public policy: The politics of foreign trade*. 2d ed. Chicago: Aldine-Atherton, 1972.

Becker, Gary S. "A theory of competition among pressure groups for political influence." *Quarterly Journal of Economics*, 98 (August 1983), pp. 371–400.

Behr, Roy L., and Shanto Iyengar. "Television news, real-world cues, and changes in the public agenda." *Public Opinion Quarterly*, 49 (Spring 1985), pp. 38–57.

Bendor, Jonathan, and Terry M. Moe. "Agenda control, committee capture, and the dynamics of institutional politics." *American Political Science Review*, 80 (December 1986), pp. 1187–1207.

Benedict, Murray R. *Farm policies of the United States, 1790–1950*. New York: Twentieth Century Fund, 1953.

Benson, Ezra Taft. *Freedom to farm*. Garden City, N.Y.: Doubleday and Co., 1960.

———. *Cross fire: The eight years with Eisenhower*. Garden City, N.Y.: Doubleday and Co., 1962.

Berdahl, Clarence A. "Some notes on party membership in Congress, I." *American Political Science Review*, 43 (April 1949), pp. 309–21.

———. "Some notes on party membership in Congress, II." *American Political Science Review*, 43 (June 1949), pp. 492–508.

Berger, Samuel. *Dollar harvest: The story of the Farm Bureau*. Lexington, Mass.: D. C. Heath and Co., 1971.

Bernstein, Robert A. *Elections, representation, and congressional voting behavior: The myth of constituency control*. Englewood Cliffs, N.J.: Prentice-Hall, 1989.

Berry, Jeffrey M. *Lobbying for the people*. Princeton: Princeton University Press, 1977.

———. "Consumers and the hunger lobby." Pp. 68–78 in Don F. Hadwiger and Ross B. Talbot, eds., *Food policy and farm programs*. New York: Academy of Political Science, 1982.

———. *Feeding hungry people: Rule making in the food stamp program*. New Brunswick: Rutgers University Press, 1984.

———. "Subgovernments, issue networks, and political conflict." Pp. 239–60 in Richard Harris and Sidney Milkis, eds., *Remaking American politics* (Boulder: Westview Press, 1989).

Billington, Monroe Lee. *Thomas P. Gore: The blind senator from Oklahoma*. Lawrence: University of Kansas Press, 1967.

Black, John D. "The McNary-Haugen movement." *American Economic Review*, 18 (September 1928), pp. 405–27.

Blackorby, Eugene C. *Prairie rebel*. Lincoln: University of Nebraska Press, 1963.

Blaisdell, Donald C. *Government and agriculture.* New York: Farrar and Rinehart, 1940.

Blakey, George T. "Ham that never was: The 1933 emergency hog slaughter." *Historian,* 30 (November 1967), pp. 41–57.

Bogue, Donald J., and Calvin L. Beale. *Economic areas of the United States.* New York: The Free Press of Glencoe, 1961.

Bolling, Richard. *House out of order.* New York: Dutton, 1965.

Bonnen, James T. "Observations on the nature of national agricultural policy decision processes, 1946–76." Pp. 309–27 in Trudy Huskamp Peterson, ed., *Farmers, bureaucrats, and middlemen.* Washington: Howard University Press, 1980.

Brown, Norman D. *Hood, bonnet, and little brown jug.* College Station: Texas A&M University Press, 1984.

Browne, William P. "Farm organizations and agribusiness." Pp. 198–211 in Don F. Hadwiger and Ross B. Talbot, eds., *Food policy and farm programs.* New York: Academy of Political Science, 1982.

———. "Policy and interests: Instability and change in a classic issue subsystem." Pp. 182–201 in Allan J. Cigler and Burdett A. Loomis, eds., *Interest group politics.* 2d ed. Washington: Congressional Quarterly Press, 1986.

———. *Private interests, public policy, and American agriculture.* Lawrence: University Press of Kansas, 1988.

Browne, William P., and Charles W. Wiggins. "Interest group strength and organizational characteristics: The general farm organizations and the 1977 farm bill." Pp. 109–21 in Don F. Hadwiger and William P. Browne, eds., *The new politics of food.* Lexington, Mass.: Lexington Books, 1978.

Burner, David. *The politics of provincialism: The Democratic Party in transition, 1918–1932.* New York: Alfred A. Knopf, 1968.

Calkins, Fay. *The CIO and the Democratic Party.* Chicago: University of Chicago Press, 1952.

Calvert, Randall L. "The value of biased information: A rational choice model of political advice." *Journal of Politics,* 47 (May 1985), pp. 530–55.

Campbell, Angus, Philip E. Converse, Warren E. Miller and Donald E. Stokes, *The American voter.* New York: John Wiley and Sons, 1960.

Campbell, Christiana McFadyen. *The Farm Bureau and the New Deal.* Urbana: University of Illinois Press, 1962.

Capper, Arthur. *The agricultural bloc.* New York: Harcourt, Brace and Co., 1922.

Carleton, William G. "The southern politician—1900 and 1950." *Journal of Politics,* 13 (May 1951), pp. 215–31.

———. "Gray Silver and the rise of the Farm Bureau." *Current History,* 28 (June 1955), pp. 343–50.

Cavanaugh, Thomas E., ed. *The JCPS congressional district fact book.* Washington: Joint Center for Political Studies, 1984.

Chalmers, David. "The Ku Klux Klan in the politics of the 1920s." *Mississippi Quarterly,* 18 (Fall 1965), pp. 234–47.

Chase, Stuart. *Democracy under pressure*. New York: Twentieth Century Fund, 1945.

Chicago Board of Trade. *Statistical annual*. Chicago: Board of Trade of the City of Chicago, 1973, 1974.

Christensen, Alice M. "Agricultural pressure and government response in the United States, 1919–1929." Ph.D. dissertation, University of California at Berkeley, 1936.

Christenson, Reo M. *The Brannan Plan: Farm politics and policy*. Ann Arbor: University of Michigan Press, 1959.

Chubb, John E. *Interest groups and the bureaucracy: The politics of energy*. Stanford: Stanford University Press, 1983.

Clapp, Charles L. *The congressman: His work as he sees it*. Washington: Brookings Institution, 1963.

Cochrane, Willard W., and Mary E. Ryan. *American farm policy, 1948–1973*. Minneapolis: University of Minnesota Press, 1976.

Cole, Wayne S. *Roosevelt and the isolationists, 1932–1945*. Lincoln: University of Nebraska Press, 1983.

Congressional Quarterly. *Farm policy: The politics of soil, surpluses and subsidies*. Washington: Congressional Quarterly Press, 1984.

Congressional Quarterly Service. *U.S. agricultural policy in the postwar years, 1945–1963*. Washington: Congressional Quarterly Press, 1963.

Connally, Tom. *My name is Tom Connally*. New York: Thomas Y. Crowell Co., 1954.

Conrad, David E. *The forgotten farmers: The story of sharecroppers in the New Deal*. Urbana: University of Illinois Press, 1965.

Coode, Thomas H. "Tennessee congressmen and the New Deal, 1933–1938." *West Tennessee Historical Society Papers*, 31 (October 1977), pp. 132–58.

Cook, Mary Etta, and Roger H. Davidson. "Deferral politics: Congressional decision making on environmental issues in the 1980s." Pp. 47–76 in Helen M. Ingram and R. Kenneth Godwin, eds., *Public policy and the natural environment*. Greenwich, Conn.: JAI Press, 1985.

Cook, Thomas D., and Donald T. Campbell. *Quasi-experimentation: Design and analysis issues for field settings*. Boston: Houghton Mifflin Co., 1979.

Cooper, John Milton, Jr. *The vanity of power: American isolationism and the First World War, 1914–1917*. Westport, Conn.: Greenwood Publishing, 1969.

Cooper, Joseph, and David W. Brady. "Toward a diachronic analysis of Congress." *American Political Science Review*, 75 (December 1981), pp. 988–1006.

Council on Consumer Information. *Consumers look at farm price policies*. Oxford, Ohio: Council on Consumer Information, 1954.

Crampton, John A. *The National Farmers Union: Ideology of a pressure group*. Lincoln: University of Nebraska Press, 1965.

Crawford, Kenneth. *The pressure boys*. New York: Julian Messner, 1939.

Dalstrom, Harl A. "The defeat of George W. Norris in 1942." *Nebraska History,* 59 (Summer 1978), pp. 231–58.

Dangerfield, Royden J., and Richard H. Flynn. "Voter motivation in the 1936 Oklahoma Democratic primary." *Southwestern Social Science Quarterly,* 17 (September 1936), pp. 97–105.

Davidson, Roger H. "Breaking up those 'cozy triangles.'" Pp. 30–53 in Susan Welch and John G. Peters, eds., *Legislative reform and public policy.* New York: Praeger, 1977.

————. "Subcommittee government: New channels for policy making." Pp. 99–133 in Thomas E. Mann and Norman J. Ornstein, eds., *The new Congress.* Washington: American Enterprise Institute, 1981.

Davies, J. Clarence, III, and Barbara S. Davies. *The politics of pollution.* 2d ed. Indianapolis: Bobbs-Merrill Co., 1975.

Davis, Joseph Stancliffe. *The farm export debenture plan.* Stanford: Food Research Institute, 1929.

Davis, P. O. *One man: Edward Asbury O'Neal III of Alabama.* Auburn: Alabama Polytechnic Institute, 1945.

Dearing, Mary R. *Veterans in politics: The story of the G.A.R.* Baton Rouge: Louisiana State University Press, 1952.

Derthick, Martha. *Policymaking for Social Security.* Washington: Brookings Institution, 1979.

Dexter, Lewis Anthony. *How organizations are represented in Washington.* Indianapolis: Bobbs-Merrill Co., 1969.

————. *The sociology and politics of Congress.* Chicago: Rand McNally and Co., 1969.

Douglas, Paul H. *In the fullness of time.* New York: Harcourt Brace Jovanovich, 1972.

Downs, Anthony. *An economic theory of democracy.* New York: Harper and Row, 1957.

————. "Up and down with ecology: The 'issue-attention cycle.'" *Public Interest,* 28 (Summer 1972), pp. 38–50.

Duffield, Marcus. *King Legion.* New York: Jonathan Cape and Harrison Smith, 1931.

Duke, Escal Franklin. "The political career of Morris Sheppard, 1875–1941." Ph.D. dissertation, University of Texas, 1958.

Duncan, Marvin, and C. Edward Harshbarger. "A primer on agricultural policy." *Federal Reserve Bank of Kansas City Monthly Review* (September–October 1977), pp. 3–10.

Duscha, Julius. *Taxpayer's hayride: The farm problem from the New Deal to the Billie Sol Estes case.* Boston: Little, Brown and Co., 1964.

Eddy, William A. *F.D.R. meets Ibn Saud.* New York: American Friends of the Middle East, 1954.

Ellis, William E. "Robert Worth Bingham and the crisis of cooperative marketing in the twenties." *Agricultural History,* 56 (January 1982), pp. 99–116.

Erbring, Lutz, Edie N. Goldenberg and Arthur H. Miller. "Front-page news and real world cues: A new look at agenda setting by the media." *American Journal of Political Science,* 24 (February 1980), pp. 16–49.

Erwin, Carl C. "The Dark Tobacco Growers Cooperative Association, 1922–1926." *Business History Review,* 40 (Winter 1966), pp. 403–31.

Evans, Rowland, and Robert Novak. *Lyndon B. Johnson: The exercise of power.* New York: New American Library, 1966.

Fedor, Kenneth J., and Reginald J. Brown. "The design and implementation of food price regulations." Pp. 107–43 in John T. Dunlop and Kenneth J. Fedor, eds., *The lessons of wage and price controls: The food sector.* Boston: Harvard University Graduate School of Business Administration, 1977.

Fenno, Richard, F., Jr. *The power of the purse.* Boston: Little, Brown and Co., 1966.

———. *Congressmen in committees.* Boston: Little, Brown and Co., 1973.

———. *Home style: House members in their districts.* Boston: Little, Brown and Co., 1978.

Fenton, John H. *Politics in the border states.* New Orleans: Hauser Press, 1957.

Ferejohn, John A. "Logrolling in an institutional context: A case study of food stamp legislation." Pp. 223–53 in Gerald C. Wright, Jr., Leroy N. Rieselbach and Lawrence C. Dodd, eds., *Congress and policy change.* New York: Agathon Press, 1986.

Fiorina, Morris P. *Congress: Keystone of the Washington establishment.* New Haven: Yale University Press, 1977.

Fisher, Commodore B. *The Farmers' Union.* Lexington: University of Kentucky Press, 1920.

Fite, Gilbert C. *Peter Norbeck: Prairie statesman.* Columbia: University of Missouri Press, 1948.

———. "John A. Simpson: The Southwest's militant farm leader." *Mississippi Valley Historical Review,* 35 (March 1949), pp. 563–84.

———. *George N. Peek and the fight for farm parity.* Norman: University of Oklahoma Press, 1954.

———. "Farmer opinion and the Agricultural Adjustment Act, 1933." *Mississippi Valley Historical Review,* 48 (March 1962), pp. 656–73.

———. "Gilbert N. Haugen: Pragmatic progressive." Pp. 1–14 in John N. Schacht, ed., *Three progressives from Iowa.* Iowa City: Center for the Study of the Recent History of the United States, 1980.

———. *Cotton fields no more: Southern agriculture, 1865–1980.* Lexington: University Press of Kentucky, 1984.

Fleming, Roger. "Political history of the farm price support issue." Pamphlet, American Farm Bureau Federation, 1955.

Fornari, Harry D. "The big change: Cotton to soybeans." *Agricultural History,* 53 (January 1979), pp. 245–53.

Forsythe, James L. "Postmortem on the election of 1948: An evaluation of Congressman Clifford R. Hope's views." *Kansas Historical Quarterly,* 38 (Autumn 1972), pp. 338–59.

————. "Clifford Hope of Kansas: Practical congressman and agrarian idealist." *Agricultural History*, 51 (April 1977), pp. 406–20.

Fossett, Roy E. "The impact of the New Deal on Georgia politics, 1933–1941." Ph.D. dissertation, University of Florida, 1960.

Freeman, Jo. *The politics of women's liberation*. New York: Longman, 1975.

Freidel, Frank. *F.D.R. and the South*. Baton Rouge: Louisiana State University Press, 1965.

Friedberger, Mark. *Shake-out: Iowa farm families in the 1980s*. Lexington: University Press of Kentucky, 1989.

Friedman, Milton. "The methodology of positive economics." Pp. 3–43 in Milton Friedman, *Essays in positive economics*. Chicago: University of Chicago Press, 1953.

Friedman, Monroe Peter. "The 1966 consumer protest as seen by its leaders." *Journal of Consumer Affairs*, 5 (Summer 1971), pp. 1–23.

Fuller, Varden. "Wheat, cotton and political arithmetic." *California Monthly*, July/August 1964, pp. 12ff.

Gais, Thomas L., Mark A. Peterson and Jack L. Walker. "Interest groups, iron triangles and representative institutions in American national government." *British Journal of Political Science*, 14 (April 1984), pp. 161–85.

Galambos, Louis. "The emerging organizational synthesis in modern American history." *Business History Review*, 44 (Autumn 1970), pp. 279–90.

————. "'Choosing sides': Comment." *Studies in American Political Development*, 2 (1987), pp. 230–34.

Gardner, Bruce L. "Efficient redistribution through commodity markets." *American Journal of Agricultural Economics*, 65 (May 1983), pp. 225–34.

————. "Causes of U.S. farm commodity programs." *Journal of Political Economy*, 95 (April 1987), pp. 290–310.

Gardner, Charles M. *The Grange: Friend of the farmer*. Washington: National Grange, 1949.

Gee, Wilson, and Edward Allison Terry. *The cotton cooperatives in the Southeast*. New York: D. Appleton-Century Co., 1933.

Genung, A. B. *The agricultural depression following World War I and its political consequences*. Ithaca, N.Y.: Northeast Farm Foundation, 1954.

Gerson, Louis L. "The influence of hyphenated Americans on U.S. diplomacy." Pp. 19–32 in Abdul Aziz Said, ed., *Ethnicity and U.S. foreign policy*. Rev. ed. New York: Praeger Publishers, 1981.

Gilpatrick, Thomas V. "Price support policy and the Midwest farm vote." *Midwest Journal of Political Science*, 3 (November 1959), pp. 319–35.

Glazer, Amihai, and Marc Robbins. "Congressional responsiveness to constituency change." *American Journal of Political Science*, 29 (May 1985), pp. 259–73.

Grant, Daniel R. "Carrots, sticks, and consensus." Pp. 99–115 in Leslie L. Roos, Jr., ed., *The politics of ecosuicide*. New York: Holt, Rinehart and Winston, 1971.

Grant, Philip A., Jr. "Southern congressmen and agriculture, 1921–1932." *Agricultural History*, 53 (January 1979), pp. 338–51.

———. " 'Save the farmer': Oklahoma congressmen and farm relief legislation, 1924–1928." *Chronicles of Oklahoma*, 64 (Summer 1986), pp. 75–87.

Greenstone, J. David. *Labor in American politics*. Chicago: University of Chicago Press, 1977.

Groves, D. B., and Kenneth Thatcher. *The first fifty: History of Farm Bureau in Iowa*. Lake Mills, Ia.: Graphic Publishing Co., 1968.

Guither, Harold D. *The food lobbyists*. Lexington, Mass.: Lexington Books, 1980.

Gusfield, Joseph R. *Symbolic crusade: Status politics and the American temperance movement*. Urbana: University of Illinois Press, 1963.

Guth, James L. "The National Board of Farm Organizations." *Agricultural History*, 48 (July 1974), pp. 418–40.

———. "The National Cooperative Council and farm relief, 1929–1942." *Agricultural History*, 51 (April 1977), pp. 441–58.

———. "Consumer organizations and federal dairy policy." *Policy Studies Journal*, 6 (Summer 1978), pp. 499–503.

Hadwiger, Don F., and Ross B. Talbot. *Pressures and protests: The Kennedy farm program and the wheat referendum of 1963*. San Francisco: Chandler Publishing Co., 1965.

Hall, Richard L., and Frank W. Wayman. "Buying time: Moneyed interests and the mobilization of bias in congressional committees." *American Political Science Review*, 84 (September 1990), pp. 797–820.

Hall, Tom G. "The Aiken bill, price supports, and the wheat farmer in 1948." *North Dakota History*, 39 (Winter 1972), pp. 13–22, 47.

Hamilton, Virginia Van der Veer. *Hugo Black: The Alabama years*. Baton Rouge: Louisiana State University Press, 1972.

———. *Lister Hill: Statesman from the South*. Chapel Hill: University of North Carolina Press, 1987.

Hamm, Keith E. "Patterns of influence among committees, agencies, and interest groups." *Legislative Studies Quarterly*, 8 (August 1983), pp. 379–426.

Hansen, John Mark. "The political economy of group membership." *American Political Science Review*, 79 (March 1985), pp. 79–96.

———. "Choosing sides: The creation of an agricultural policy network in Congress, 1919–1932." *Studies in American Political Development*, 2 (1987), pp. 183–229.

Hardin, Charles M. "The Republican Department of Agriculture: A political interpretation." *Journal of Farm Economics*, 36 (May 1954), pp. 210–27.

———. "Farm price policy and the farm vote." *Journal of Farm Economics*, 37 (November 1955), pp. 601–24.

Harrington, Jerry. "Senator Guy Gillette foils the execution committee." *Palimpsest*, 62 (November/December 1981), pp. 170–80.

Harvey, Ralph. *Autobiography of a Hoosier congressman*. Greenfield, Ind.: Mitchell-Fleming Printing, 1975.

Haynes, John Earl. "Farm coops and the election of Hubert Humphrey to the Senate." *Agricultural History,* 57 (April 1983), pp. 201–11.

Hays, Samuel P. *The response to industrialism.* Chicago: University of Chicago Press, 1957.

———. *Beauty, health, and permanence: Environmental politics in the United States, 1955–1985.* New York: Cambridge University Press, 1987.

Haystead, Ladd, and Gilbert C. Fite. *The agricultural regions of the United States.* Norman: University of Oklahoma Press, 1955.

Heclo, Hugh. "Issue networks and the executive establishment." Pp. 87–124 in Anthony King, ed., *The new American political system.* Washington: American Enterprise Institute, 1978.

Heinz, John. "The political impasse in farm support legislation." *Yale Law Journal,* 71 (1962), pp. 952–78.

Herring, E. Pendleton. *Group representation before Congress.* Baltimore: Johns Hopkins University Press, 1929.

Herrmann, Robert O., Edward J. Walsh and Rex H. Warland. "The organizations of the consumer movement: A comparative perspective." Pp. 470–94 in E. Scott Maynes, ed., *The frontier of research in the consumer interest.* Columbia, Mo.: American Council on Consumer Interests, 1988.

Hershey, Marjorie Randon. *Running for office: The political education of campaigners.* Chatham, N.J.: Chatham House Publishers, 1984.

Hicks, John D. *The populist revolt.* Minneapolis: University of Minnesota Press, 1931.

Hixson, Walter L. "The 1938 Kentucky Senate election." *Register of the Kentucky Historical Society,* 80 (Summer 1982), pp. 309–29.

Hobson, Asher. "The evolution of farm relief." *American Scholar,* 11 (Autumn 1942), pp. 495–501.

Hoffman, George. "Executive-legislative relations in the first AAA." Ph.D. dissertation, University of Chicago, 1961.

Hollis, Daniel W. "'Cotton Ed Smith'—Showman or statesman?" *South Carolina Historical Magazine,* 71 (October 1970), pp. 235–56.

———. "Cole L. Blease and the senatorial campaign of 1924." *Proceedings of the South Carolina Historical Association,* 1978, pp. 53–68.

Howard, Robert P. *James R. Howard and the Farm Bureau.* Ames: Iowa State University Press, 1983.

Hubbard, Preston J. *Origins of the TVA.* New York: W. W. Norton and Co., 1961.

Huitt, Ralph K. "The congressional committee: A case study." *American Political Science Review,* 48 (June 1954), pp. 340–65.

Hunter, Robert F. "The AAA between neighbors: Virginia, North Carolina, and the New Deal farm program." *Journal of Southern History,* 44 (November 1978), pp. 537–70.

Huntington, Samuel P. "The election tactics of the Nonpartisan League." *Mississippi Valley Historical Review,* 36 (March 1950), pp. 613–32.

Iyengar, Shanto, and Donald R. Kinder. *News that matters: Television and*

American opinion. Chicago: University of Chicago Press, 1987.

Jacobson, Gary C. *The politics of congressional elections.* 2d ed. Boston: Little, Brown and Co., 1987.

Jacobson, Gary C., and Samuel Kernell. *Strategy and choice in congressional elections.* 2d ed. New Haven: Yale University Press, 1983.

Johnson, Charles S., Edwin R. Embree and W. W. Alexander. *The collapse of cotton tenancy.* Chapel Hill: University of North Carolina Press, 1935.

Johnson, Keach. "The Corn Belt Meat Producers' Association of Iowa: Origins of a progressive pressure group." *Annals of Iowa,* 43 (Spring 1976), pp. 242–60.

Johnson, Roger T. "Part-time leader: Senator Charles L. McNary and the McNary-Haugen bill." *Agricultural History,* 54 (October 1980), pp. 527–41.

Jones, Charles O. "Representation in Congress: The case of the House Agriculture Committee." *American Political Science Review,* 55 (June 1961), pp. 358–67.

———. *Clean air.* Pittsburgh: University of Pittsburgh Press, 1975.

Jones, Marvin (Joseph M. Ray, ed.). *Marvin Jones memoirs.* El Paso: Texas Western Press, 1973.

Kalt, Joseph P., and Mark A. Zupan. "Capture and ideology in the economic theory of politics." *American Economic Review,* 74 (June 1984), pp. 279–300.

Kau, James B., and Paul H. Rubin. *Congressmen, constituents, and contributors.* Boston: Martinus Nijhoff, 1982.

Kelly, Karen Kalmar. "Richard B. Russell: Democrat from Georgia." Ph.D. dissertation, University of North Carolina, 1979.

Kerr, K. Austin. *Organized for prohibition: A new history of the Anti-Saloon League.* New Haven: Yale University Press, 1985.

Kerr, Norwood Allen. "Drafted into the War on Poverty: USDA food and nutrition programs, 1961–1969." *Agricultural History,* 64 (Spring 1990), pp. 154–66.

Key, V. O., Jr. *Politics, parties and pressure groups.* New York: Thomas Y. Crowell, 1942.

———. *Southern politics in state and nation.* New York: Alfred A. Knopf, 1949.

———. *American state politics.* New York: Alfred A. Knopf, 1956.

Kidder, Louise H. "Qualitative research and quasi-experimental frameworks." Pp. 226–56 in Marilynn B. Brewer and Barry E. Collins, eds., *Scientific inquiry and the social sciences.* San Francisco: Jossey-Bass Publishers, 1981.

Kile, Orville M. *The Farm Bureau through three decades.* Baltimore: Waverly Press, 1948.

Kingdon, John W. "A House Appropriations subcommittee." *Southwestern Social Science Quarterly,* 47 (June 1966), pp. 68–78.

———. *Congressmen's voting decisions.* 2d ed. New York: Harper and Row, 1981.

————. *Agendas, alternatives, and public policies.* Boston: Little, Brown and Co., 1984.

Kiplinger, Willard M. *Washington is like that.* New York: Harper and Brothers Publishers, 1942.

Kirkendall, Richard S. *Social scientists and farm politics in the age of Roosevelt.* Ames: Iowa State University Press, 1982.

Kirwan, Albert D. *Revolt of the rednecks: Mississippi politics, 1876–1925.* New York: Harper and Row, 1965.

Kosters, Marvin H. *Controls and inflation: The Economic Stabilization Program in retrospect.* Washington: American Enterprise Institute, 1975.

Kotz, Nick. *Let them eat promises: The politics of hunger in America.* Englewood Cliffs, N.J.: Prentice-Hall, 1969.

Kousser, J. Morgan. "Toward 'total political history': A rational-choice program." *Journal of Interdisciplinary History,* 20 (Spring 1990), pp. 521–60.

Krehbiel, Keith. "Spatial models of legislative choice." *Legislative Studies Quarterly,* 13 (August 1988), pp. 259–319.

Lacey, John J. *Farm Bureau in Illinois: History of Illinois Farm Bureau.* Bloomington, Ill.: Illinois Agricultural Association, 1965.

Larew, James C. *A party reborn: The Democrats of Iowa, 1950–1974.* Iowa City: Iowa State Historical Department, 1980.

Larsen, Grace H., and Henry E. Erdman. "Aaron Sapiro: Genius of farm cooperative promotion." *Mississippi Valley Historical Review,* 49 (September 1962), pp. 242–68.

Latham, Earl. *The group basis of politics.* Ithaca: Cornell University Press, 1952.

Lincoln, Murray D. *Vice president in charge of revolution.* New York: McGraw Hill Book Co., 1960.

Lord, Russell. *The Wallaces of Iowa.* Boston: Houghton Mifflin Co., 1947.

Lowi, Theodore J. "How the farmers get what they want." *Reporter,* 21 May 1964, pp. 34–37.

————. "American business, public policy, case studies, and political theory." *World Politics,* 16 (July 1964), pp. 677–715.

————. *The end of liberalism.* 2d ed. New York: W. W. Norton and Co., 1979.

Lowitt, Richard. *George W. Norris: The persistence of a progressive.* Urbana: University of Illinois Press, 1971.

————. *George W. Norris: The triumph of a progressive.* Urbana: University of Illinois Press, 1978.

Luebke, Frederick C. "Political response to agricultural depression in Nebraska, 1922." *Nebraska History,* 47 (March 1966), pp. 15–55.

Luthin, Reinhard H. "Smith Wildman Brookhart of Iowa." *Agricultural History,* 25 (October 1951), pp. 187–97.

Lyons, Michael S., and Marcia Whicker Taylor. "Farm politics in transition: The House Agriculture Committee." *Agricultural History,* 55 (April 1981), pp. 128–46.

Maass, Arthur. *Muddy waters.* Cambridge: Harvard University Press, 1951.

————. *Congress and the common good.* New York: Basic Books, 1983.

MacAvoy, Paul W., ed. *Federal milk marketing orders and price supports.* Washington: American Enterprise Institute, 1977.

McCarty, Jeanne Bozzell. *The struggle for sobriety.* El Paso: Texas Western Press, 1980.

McConnell, Grant. *The decline of agrarian democracy.* Berkeley and Los Angeles: University of California Press, 1953.

————. *Private power and American democracy.* New York: Alfred A. Knopf, 1966.

McCormick, Richard L. "The party period and public policy." *Journal of American History,* 66 (September 1979), pp. 279–98.

McCoy, Donald R. "George S. McGill of Kansas and the Agricultural Adjustment Act of 1938." *Historian,* 45 (February 1983), pp. 186–205.

McCubbins, Mathew D., and Thomas Schwartz. "Congress, the courts, and public policy: Consequences of the one man, one vote rule." *American Journal of Political Science,* 32 (May 1988), pp. 388–415.

McCune, Wesley. *The farm bloc.* Garden City, N.Y.: Doubleday, Doran and Co., 1943.

————. *Who's behind our farm policy?* New York: Frederick A. Praeger, 1956.

————. *Ezra Taft Benson: Man with a mission.* Washington: Public Affairs Press, 1958.

————. "Farmers in politics." Pp. 41–51 in Donald C. Blaisdell, ed., "Unofficial government: Pressure groups and lobbies." *Annals of the American Academy of Political and Social Science,* 319 (September 1958).

McDonald, Rita, and Robert G. Dunbar. "The initiation of the McNary-Haugen movement in Montana and the Pacific Northwest." *Pacific Northwest Quarterly,* 71 (April 1980), pp. 63–71.

McGovern, George S. *Grassroots: The autobiography of George McGovern.* New York: Random House, 1977.

McKean, Dayton David. *Party and pressure politics.* Boston: Houghton Mifflin Co., 1949.

Manheimer, Eric. "The public career of Elmer Thomas." Ph.D. dissertation, University of Oklahoma, 1952.

Mann, Thomas E. *Unsafe at any margin: Interpreting congressional elections.* Washington: American Enterprise Institute, 1978.

Marsh, Benjamin C. *Lobbyist for the people.* Washington: Public Affairs Press, 1953.

Martin, Robert E. "The referendum process in the agricultural adjustment programs of the United States." *Agricultural History,* 25 (January 1951), pp. 34–47.

Matthews, Donald R. *U.S. senators and their world.* Chapel Hill: University of North Carolina Press, 1960.

Matusow, Allen J. *Farm policies and politics in the Truman years.* Cambridge: Harvard University Press, 1967.

May, Irvin M., Jr. *Marvin Jones: The public life of an agrarian advocate.* College Station: Texas A&M University Press, 1980.

Mayer, Robert N. *The consumer movement: Guardians of the marketplace.* Boston: Twayne Publishers, 1989.

Mayhew, David R. *Party loyalty among congressmen: The difference between Democrats and Republicans, 1947–1962.* Cambridge: Harvard University Press, 1966.

———. *Congress: The electoral connection.* New Haven: Yale University Press, 1974.

———. *Placing parties in American politics.* Princeton: Princeton University Press, 1986.

Mead, Howard N. "Russell vs. Talmadge: Southern politics and the New Deal." *Georgia Historical Quarterly,* 65 (Spring 1981), pp. 28–45.

"Membership paid to the American Farm Bureau Federation." Mimeo, American Farm Bureau Federation, 1982.

Mencken, H. L. *A carnival of buncombe: Writings on politics.* Chicago: University of Chicago Press, 1984.

Milbrath, Lester W. *The Washington lobbyists.* Chicago: Rand McNally and Co., 1963.

Mill, John Stuart. *A system of logic.* London: Longmans, Green, Reader and Dyer, 1872.

Moe, Terry M. "The new economics of organization." *American Journal of Political Science,* 28 (November 1984), pp. 739–77.

Montgomery, Robert Hargrove. *The cooperative pattern in cotton.* New York: Macmillan Co., 1929.

Moore, John Robert. *Senator Josiah William Bailey of North Carolina.* Durham: Duke University Press, 1968.

Morgan, Chester M. *Redneck liberal: Theodore G. Bilbo and the New Deal.* Baton Rouge: Louisiana State University Press, 1985.

Morgan, Iwan. "Factional conflict in Indiana politics during the later New Deal years, 1936–1940." *Indiana Magazine of History,* 79 (March 1983), pp. 29–60.

———. "The 1942 mid-term elections in Illinois." *Journal of the Illinois State Historical Society,* 76 (Summer 1983), pp. 115–30.

Nadel, Mark V. *The politics of consumer protection.* Indianapolis: Bobbs-Merrill Co., 1971.

Neal, Steve. *McNary of Oregon: A political biography.* Portland: Western Imprints, 1985.

Neprash, Jerry A. *The Brookhart campaigns in Iowa.* New York: Columbia University Press, 1932.

Nisbett, Richard, and Lee Ross. *Human inference: Strategies and shortcomings of social judgment.* Englewood Cliffs, N.J.: Prentice-Hall, 1980.

Nourse, Edwin G., Joseph S. Davis and John D. Black. *Three years of the Agricultural Adjustment Administration.* Washington: Brookings Institution, 1937.

O'Brien, Patrick G. "Senator Robert B. Howell: A midwestern progressive and insurgent during 'normalcy.' " *Emporia State Research Studies,* 19 (December 1970), pp. 5–28.

———. "William H. McMaster: An agrarian dissenter during 'normalcy.' " *Emporia State Research Studies,* 20 (June 1972), pp. 24–39.

Odegard, Peter H. *Pressure politics: The story of the Anti-Saloon League.* New York: Columbia University Press, 1928.

Olson, Mancur, Jr. *The logic of collective action: Public goods and the theory of groups.* Cambridge: Harvard University Press, 1971.

Olssen, Erik. "The progressive group in Congress, 1922–1929." *Historian,* 42 (February 1980), pp. 244–63.

Orren, Karen. "Union politics and postwar liberalism in the United States, 1946–1979." *Studies in American Political Development,* 1 (1986), pp. 215–52.

Palamountain, Joseph C. *The politics of distribution.* Cambridge: Harvard University Press, 1955.

Palmby, Clarence D. *Made in Washington: Food policy and the political expedient.* Danville, Ill.: The Interstate Printers and Publishers, 1985.

Patterson, James T. *Congressional conservatism and the New Deal: The growth of the conservative coalition in Congress, 1933–1939.* Lexington: University of Kentucky Press, 1967.

Patton, James G. *The case for farmers.* Washington: Public Affairs Press, 1959.

Peek, George N. (with Samuel Crowther). *Why quit our own.* New York: D. Van Nostrand Co., 1936.

Peltzman, Sam. "Constituent interest and congressional voting." *Journal of Law and Economics,* 27 (April 1984), pp. 181–210.

Pencak, William. *For God and country: The American Legion, 1919–1941.* Boston: Northeastern University Press, 1989.

Pennock, J. Roland. "Party and constituency in postwar agricultural price-support legislation." *Journal of Politics,* 18 (May 1956), pp. 167–210.

Perkins, Van L. *Crisis in agriculture: The Agricultural Adjustment Administration and the New Deal, 1933.* Berkeley and Los Angeles: University of California Press, 1969.

Peters, John G. "The 1977 farm bill: Coalitions in Congress." Pp. 23–35 in Don F. Hadwiger and William P. Browne, eds., *The new politics of food.* Lexington, Mass.: Lexington Books, 1978.

———. "The 1981 farm bill." Pp. 157–73 in Don F. Hadwiger and Ross B. Talbot, eds., *Food policy and farm programs.* New York: Academy of Political Science, 1982.

Plesur, Milton. "The Republican congressional comeback of 1938." *Review of Politics,* 24 (October 1962), pp. 525–62.

Plummer, Leonard Neil. "Ellison Durant Smith: 'A politician from the Old South.' " Pp. 344–54 in J. T. Salter, ed., *Public men in and out of office.* Chapel Hill: University of North Carolina Press, 1946.

Polsby, Nelson W. "The institutionalization of the U.S. House of Representatives." *American Political Science Review,* 62 (March 1968), pp. 144–68.

Pope, Robert Dean. "Senatorial baron: The long political career of Kenneth D. McKellar." Ph.D. dissertation, Yale University, 1976.

Pratt, Henry J. *The gray lobby.* Chicago: University of Chicago Press, 1976.

Pratt, William C. "Glenn J. Talbott, the Farmers Union, and American liberalism after World War II." *North Dakota History,* 55 (Winter 1988), pp. 3–13.

Price, David E. *Who makes the laws? Creativity and power in Senate committees.* Cambridge: Schenkman Publishing Co., 1972.

———. "Policy making in congressional committees: The impact of 'environmental' factors." *American Political Science Review,* 72 (June 1978), pp. 548–74.

Ranney, Austin, and Willmoore Kendall. *Democracy and the American party system.* New York: Harcourt, Brace and Co., 1956.

Richards, Henry I. *Cotton and the AAA.* Washington: Brookings Institution, 1936.

Ripley, Randall B. "Legislative bargaining and the Food Stamp Act, 1964." Pp. 279–310 in Frederic N. Cleaveland, ed., *Congress and urban problems.* Washington: Brookings Institution, 1969.

Ripley, Randall B., and Grace A. Franklin. *Congress, the bureaucracy and public policy.* Rev. ed. Homewood, Ill.: Dorsey Press, 1980.

Ross, Irwin. *The loneliest campaign: The Truman victory of 1948.* New York: New American Library, 1968.

Rowley, William D. *M. L. Wilson and the campaign for the domestic allotment.* Lincoln: University of Nebraska Press, 1970.

Ryan, Thomas G. "Farm prices and the farm vote in 1948." *Agricultural History,* 54 (July 1980), pp. 387–401.

———. "The early years of the Iowa Democratic revival, 1950–1956." *Annals of Iowa,* 46 (Summer 1981), pp. 43–63.

Salisbury, Robert H. "An exchange theory of interest groups." *Midwest Journal of Political Science,* 13 (February 1969), pp. 1–32.

———. "Interest representation: The dominance of institutions." *American Political Science Review,* 78 (March 1984), pp. 64–76.

Saloutos, Theodore. "Edward A. O'Neal: The Farm Bureau and the New Deal." *Current History,* 28 (June 1955), pp. 356–61.

———. "The Alabama Farm Bureau Federation." *Alabama Review,* 13 (July 1960), pp. 185–98.

———. *Farmer movements in the South, 1865–1933.* Berkeley and Los Angeles: University of California Press, 1960.

———. "Agricultural organizations and farm policy in the South after World War II." *Agricultural History,* 53 (January 1979), pp. 377–404.

———. *The American farmer and the New Deal.* Ames: Iowa State University Press, 1982.

Saloutos, Theodore, and John D. Hicks. *Agricultural discontent in the Middle West, 1900–1939.* Madison: University of Wisconsin Press, 1951.

Sayre, J. L. "Gerald P. Nye: 'Essentially negative.'" Pp. 127–46 in J. T. Salter, ed., *Public men in and out of office*. Chapel Hill: University of North Carolina Press, 1946.

Schapsmeier, Edward L., and Frederick H. Schapsmeier. "Paul H. Douglas: From pacifist to soldier-statesman." *Journal of the Illinois State Historical Society,* 67 (June 1974), pp. 307–23.

———. *Ezra Taft Benson and the politics of agriculture: The Eisenhower years, 1953–1961.* Danville, Ill.: The Interstate Printers and Publishers, 1975.

———. "Scott W. Lucas of Havana: His rise and fall as Majority Leader in the United States Senate." *Journal of the Illinois State Historical Society,* 70 (November 1977), pp. 302–20.

———. *Dirksen of Illinois: Senatorial statesman.* Urbana: University of Illinois Press, 1985.

Schattschneider, E. E. *Politics, pressures and the tariff.* New York: Prentice-Hall, 1935.

———. *The semisovereign people: A realist's view of democracy in America.* Hinsdale, Ill.: Dryden Press, 1975.

Schatz, Arthur W. "The Reciprocal Trade Agreements Program and the 'farm vote,' 1934–1940." *Agricultural History,* 46 (October 1972), pp. 498–514.

Schlesinger, Arthur M., Jr. *The coming of the New Deal.* Boston: Houghton Mifflin Co., 1958.

Schruben, Francis W. *Kansas in turmoil, 1930–1936.* Columbia: University of Missouri Press, 1969.

Schuyler, Michael W. "The politics of change: The battle for the Agricultural Adjustment Act of 1938." *Prologue,* 15 (Fall 1983), pp. 165–78.

Sellers, James Benson. *The prohibition movement in Alabama.* Chapel Hill: University of North Carolina Press, 1943.

Shannon, J. B. "Alben W. Barkley: 'Reservoir of energy.' " Pp. 240–56 in J. T. Salter, ed., *Public men in and out of office.* Chapel Hill: University of North Carolina Press, 1946.

Shepsle, Kenneth A. *The giant jigsaw puzzle: Democratic committee assignments in the modern House.* Chicago: University of Chicago Press, 1978.

———. "Institutional arrangements and equilibrium in multi-dimensional voting models." *American Journal of Political Science,* 23 (February 1979), pp. 27–59.

Shideler, James H. *Farm crisis, 1919–1923.* Berkeley and Los Angeles: University of California Press, 1957.

Shover, John L. "Populism in the nineteen-thirties: The battle for the AAA." *Agricultural History,* 39 (January 1965), pp. 17–24.

Smith, Richard A. "Advocacy, interpretation, and influence in the U.S. Congress." *American Political Science Review,* 78 (March 1984), pp. 44–63.

Smith, Steven S., and Christopher J. Deering. *Committees in Congress.* Washington: Congressional Quarterly Press, 1984.

Snyder, Ralph. *We Kansas farmers.* Topeka: F. M. Steves and Sons, 1953(?).

Snyder, Robert E. *Cotton crisis.* Chapel Hill: University of North Carolina Press, 1984.

Socolofsky, Homer E. *Arthur Capper: Publisher, politician, and philanthropist.* Lawrence: University of Kansas Press, 1962.

Solberg, Carl. *Hubert Humphrey: A biography.* New York: W. W. Norton and Co., 1984.

Soth, Lauren. *Farm trouble.* Princeton: Princeton University Press, 1957.

Stigler, George J. "The theory of economic regulation." *Bell Journal of Economics and Management Science,* 2 (Spring 1971), pp. 3–21.

Stockman, David A. *The triumph of politics: Why the Reagan revolution failed.* New York: Harper and Row, 1986.

Storm, William Bruce. "An analysis of the Illinois Agricultural Association as a pressure group for farmers." Ph.D. dissertation, University of Chicago, 1950.

Sundquist, James L. *Dynamics of the party system.* Rev. ed. Washington: Brookings Institution, 1983.

Swain, Martha H. *Pat Harrison: The New Deal years.* Jackson: University Press of Mississippi, 1978.

Talbot, Ross B. "The North Dakota Farmers Union and North Dakota politics." *Western Political Quarterly,* 10 (December 1957), pp. 875–901.

Tierney, John T. "Subgovernments and issue networks." Paper presented at the annual meeting of the American Political Science Association, New Orleans, 1985.

Tiffany, David Miller. "Agricultural policy-making in the Eisenhower Administration." Ph.D. dissertation, State University of New York at Binghamton, 1974.

Timberlake, James H. *Prohibition and the progressive movement, 1900–1920.* Cambridge: Harvard University Press, 1963.

Tivnan, Edward. *The lobby: Jewish political power and American foreign policy.* New York: Simon and Schuster, 1987.

Tontz, Robert L. "Origin of the base period concept of parity: A significant value judgment in agricultural history." *Agricultural History,* 32 (January 1958), pp. 3–13.

———. "Memberships of general farmers' organizations, United States, 1874–1960." *Agricultural History,* 38 (July 1964), pp. 143–57.

Truman, David B. *The governmental process.* 2d ed. New York: Alfred A. Knopf, 1971.

Tufte, Edward R. *Political control of the economy.* Princeton: Princeton University Press, 1978.

Turner, Julius. "Primary elections as the alternative to party competition in 'safe' districts." *Journal of Politics,* 15 (May 1953), pp. 197–210.

Variyam, Jayachandran N., Jeffrey L. Jordan and James E. Epperson. "Preferences of citizens for agricultural policies: Evidence from a national survey." *American Journal of Agricultural Economics,* 72 (May 1990), pp. 257–67.

Vogel, David. *Fluctuating fortunes: The political power of business in America.* New York: Basic Books, 1989.

Vogel, David, and Mark Nadel. "The consumer coalition: Dimensions of political conflict." Pp. 7–28 in Robert N. Katz, ed., *Protecting the consumer interest*. Cambridge: Ballinger Publishing Co., 1976.

Walker, Jack L. "Setting the agenda in the U.S. Senate." *British Journal of Political Science*, 7 (August 1977), pp. 423–45.

———. "The origins and maintenance of interest groups in America." *American Political Science Review*, 77 (June 1983), pp. 390–406.

———. "Interests, political parties, and policy formation in American democracy." Pp. 141–70 in Donald T. Critchlow and Ellis W. Hawley, eds., *Federal social policy: The historical dimension*. University Park: Pennsylvania State University Press, 1988.

Weber, Robert P. "Home style and committee behavior: The case of Richard Nolan." Pp. 71–94 in Morris P. Fiorina and David W. Rohde, eds., *Home style and Washington work*. Ann Arbor: University of Michigan Press, 1989.

Wefald, Jon M. "Congressman Knud Wefald: A Minnesota voice for farm parity." *Minnesota History*, 38 (December 1962), pp. 177–85.

Wiebe, Robert H. *The search for order*. New York: Hill and Wang, 1967.

Wiest, Edward. *Agricultural organization in the United States*. Lexington: University of Kentucky Press, 1923.

Wilcox, Walter W. *The farmer in the Second World War*. Ames: Iowa State College Press, 1947.

Williams, Charles Frederick. "William M. Jardine and the development of Republican farm policy." Ph.D. dissertation, University of Oklahoma, 1970.

Williams, T. Harry. *Huey Long*. Alfred A. Knopf, 1969.

Williamson, Oliver E. *Markets and hierarchies*. New York: The Free Press, 1975.

———. *The economic institutions of capitalism*. New York: The Free Press, 1985.

Wilson, Graham K. *Special interests and policymaking: Agricultural policies and politics in Britain and the United States of America, 1956–1970*. London: John Wiley and Sons, 1977.

Wilson, James Q. *Political organizations*. New York: Basic Books, 1973.

———. "The politics of regulation." Pp. 357–94 in James Q. Wilson, ed., *The politics of regulation*. New York: Basic Books, 1980.

Wilson, Joan Hoff. "Herbert Hoover's agricultural policies, 1921–1928." Pp. 115–42 in Ellis W. Hawley, ed., *Herbert Hoover as Secretary of Commerce*. Iowa City: University of Iowa Press, 1981.

Winters, Donald L. *Henry Cantwell Wallace as Secretary of Agriculture, 1921–1924*. Urbana: University of Illinois Press, 1970.

Wolman, Harold L., and Norman C. Thomas. "Black interests, black groups, and black influence in the federal policy process: The cases of housing and education." *Journal of Politics*, 32 (November 1970), pp. 875–97.

Yost, Nellie Snyder. *Medicine Lodge*. Chicago: Swallow Press, 1970.

Young, Roland. *Congressional politics in the Second World War*. New York: Columbia University Press, 1956.

Zeigler, L. Harmon. *The politics of small business.* Washington: Public Affairs Press, 1961.

Zeigler, Luther Harmon, Jr. "Senator Walter George's 1938 campaign." *Georgia Historical Quarterly,* 43 (December 1959), pp. 333–52.

Government Documents

Bowers, Douglas E., Wayne D. Rasmussen and Gladys L. Baker. *History of agricultural price support and adjustment programs, 1933–84.* Agriculture Information Bulletin No. 485, Economic Research Service, U.S. Department of Agriculture, 1984.

Bureau of Agricultural Economics. *An analysis of the effects of the processing taxes levied under the Agricultural Adjustment Act.* U.S. Department of Agriculture, 1937.

Committee on Agriculture, House of Representatives. *Hearings before the House Agriculture Committee.* "Stabilizing prices of farm products," 67th Congress, 2d session, Serial O, 1922.

———. "McNary-Haugen export bill." 68th Congress, 1st session, Serial E, 1924.

———. "Agricultural relief." 68th Congress, 2d session, Serial CC, 1925.

———. "Agricultural relief." 69th Congress, 1st session, Serial C, 1926.

———. "Agricultural relief." 70th Congress, 1st session, Serial E, 1928.

———. "Program of the national farm organizations." 72d Congress, 1st session, Serial A, 1932.

———. "Farm marketing program." 72d Congress, 1st session, Serial E, 1932.

———. "Agricultural adjustment program." 72d Congress, 2d session, Serial M, 1932.

———. "Amendments to the Agricultural Adjustment Act." 74th Congress, 1st session, Serial E, 1935.

———. "General farm legislation." 75th Congress, 1st session, Serial C, 1937.

———. "Farm program of the American Farm Bureau Federation." 80th Congress, 1st session, 1947.

———. "Long range agricultural policy." 80th Congress, 1st session, 1947.

———. "Farm program of the American Farm Bureau Federation." 80th Congress, 2d session, 1948.

———. "Long range farm program." 83rd Congress, 1st session, Serial R, 1953.

———. "Long range farm program." 83rd Congress, 2d session, Serial R, 1954.

———. "Price supports for basic commodities." 84th Congress, 1st session, Serial E, 1955.

———. "General farm legislation." 84th Congress, 2d session, Serial MM, 1956.

———. "Soil bank program." 85th Congress, 1st session, Serial A, 1957.

———. "General farm legislation." 86th Congress, 1st session, Serial GG, 1959.

———. "Agricultural Act of 1961." 87th Congress, 1st session, Serial E, 1961.

———. "Extend the Food and Agriculture Act of 1965." 90th Congress, 2d session, Serial SS, 1968.

———. "General farm program and food stamp program." 91st Congress, 1st session, Serial Q, 1969.

———. "General farm program." 93rd Congress, 1st session, Serial 93-K, 1973.

———. "General farm bill." 95th Congress, 1st session, Serial 95-H, 1977.

———. "General farm bill of 1981." 97th Congress, 1st session, Serial 97-G, 1981.

Committee on Agriculture, House of Representatives. *Hearings before the Subcommittee on Food Shortages of the House Agriculture Committee,* "Potato surpluses and the prevention of wastage." 80th Congress, 1st session, 1947.

Committee on Agriculture, House of Representatives. *Hearings before the Special Subcommittee of the House Agriculture Committee.* "Agricultural Act of 1948 (Aiken bill)." 81st Congress, 1st session, Serial D, 1949.

———. "General farm program." 81st Congress, 1st session, Serials O, P, R and U, 1949.

Committee on Agriculture, House of Representatives. *Hearings before the House Agriculture Committee, Subcommittee on Livestock and Feed Grains and Subcommittee on Wheat.* "Wheat and feed grains." 89th Congress, 1st session, Serial J, 1965.

Committee on Banking and Currency, House of Representatives. *Hearings before the House Banking and Currency Committee.* "Farm organizations." 66th Congress, 3d session, 1921.

Special Subcommittee to Investigate Political Activities, Lobbying and Campaign Contributions, Senate. *Hearings before the Special Senate Subcommittee to Investigate Political Activities, Lobbying and Campaign Contributions.* "Campaign contributions, political activities and lobbying." 84th Congress, 2d session, 1956.

Truman, Harry S. "Address at Dexter, Iowa, on the occasion of the National Plowing Match, September 18, 1948." *Public papers of the Presidents of the United States: Harry S Truman, 1948.* Washington: Government Printing Office, 1964.

Interviews

Author's interviews:
   Bob Bergland, December 1986.
   Roger Fleming, December 1986.
   Dale E. Hathaway, December 1986.
   Edwin A. Jaenke, December 1986.

Reuben L. Johnson, July 1990.

Thomas Kleppe, November 1986.

Wesley McCune, November 1986.

George S. McGovern, November 1986.

Wilmer D. Mizell, December 1986.

Hyde Murray, December 1986.

Graham B. Purcell, December 1986.

John A. Schnittker, November 1986.

Lynn E. Stalbaum, December 1986.

Joseph P. Vigorito, July 1990.

William C. Wampler, December 1986.

Abernethy, Thomas G. Interview with the Honorable Thomas G. Abernethy. Mississippi Oral History Program, vol. 23. McCain Library, University of Southern Mississippi, 1973.

Bedell, Catherine May. Oral History Interview with Catherine May Bedell. Association of Former Members of Congress Oral History Project, Library of Congress, 1979.

Davis, Chester C. Reminiscences of Chester C. Davis. Columbia Oral History Collection, 1953.

Laird, Melvin R. Interview with Melvin R. Laird. Association of Former Members of Congress Oral History Project, Library of Congress, 1979.

McGee, Gale W. Oral History Interview with Gale W. McGee. Association of Former Members of Congress Oral History Project, Library of Congress, 1979.

Poage, William Robert. Oral memoirs of William Robert "Bob" Poage. Baylor University Institute for Oral History, 1985.

Thye, Edward J. Interview with Edward J. Thye. Minnesota Historical Association, 1963.

Voorhis, Horace Jerome. Interview with Horace Jerome Voorhis. Oral History Program, Claremont Graduate School, 1971.

Wilson, Milburn L. Reminiscences of Milburn L. Wilson. Columbia Oral History Collection, 1956.

Periodicals

Agricultural Review

American Farm Bureau Federation Weekly Newsletter

American Farmer

American Review of Reviews

Atlantic

Better Farming

Bureau Farmer

Business Week

Changing Times

Collier's

Congressional Digest

Congressional Quarterly Log for Editors

Congressional Quarterly Weekly Report

Consumer Reports

Country Gentleman

Current History

Farm Journal

Fortune
Harper's
Hoard's Dairyman
Independent
Kiplinger Agricultural Letter
Kiplinger Washington Letter
Literary Digest
Ms.
Nation
Nation's Agriculture
National Butter and Cheese Journal
National Grange Monthly
New Republic
New York Times
North American Review

Prairie Farmer
Progressive Farmer
Reporter
Rural America
Saturday Evening Post
Successful Farming
Time
U.S. News and World Report
Wallaces' Farmer
Washington Farmletter
Washington Post
*Wayne Darrow's Washington Farm-
letter*
World's Work

Index